CHRONICLES OF THE CURSED SWORD

Volume 17

Story by
YEO BEOP-RYONG
Art by
PARK HUI-JIN

HAMBURG // LONDON // LOS ANGELES // TOKYO

3 3210 2287882

Chronicles of the Cursed Sword Vol. 17
Written by Yeo Beop-Ryong
Illustrated by Park Hui-Jin

Translation - Ellen Choi
English Adaptation - Matt Varosky
Retouch and Lettering - Starprint Brokers
Production Artist - Jennifer Carbajal
Cover Design - Fawn Lau

Editor - Hope Donovan
Digital Imaging Manager - Chris Buford
Pre-Production Supervisor - Erika Terriquez
Art Director - Anne Marie Horne
Production Manager - Elisabeth Brizzi
VP of Production - Ron Klamert
Managing Editor - Vy Nguyen
Editor-in-Chief - Rob Tokar
Publisher - Mike Kiley
President and C.O.O. - John Parker
C.E.O. and Chief Creative Officer - Stuart Levy

A  Manga

TOKYOPOP Inc.
5900 Wilshire Blvd. Suite 2000
Los Angeles, CA 90036

E-mail: info@TOKYOPOP.com
Come visit us online at www.TOKYOPOP.com

ISBN: 978-1-59816-204-2

First TOKYOPOP printing: January 2007
10 9 8 7 6 5 4 3 2 1
Printed in the USA

Chronicles

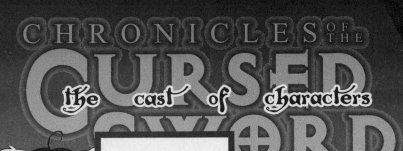

CHRONICLES OF THE CURSED SWORD

the cast of characters

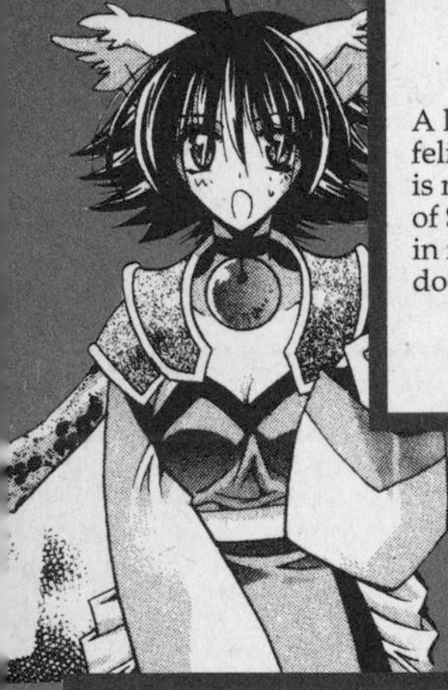

MINGLING

A lesser demon with feline qualities, Mingling is now the loyal follower of Shyao Lin. She lives in fear of Rey, who still doesn't trust her.

THE PASA SWORD

A living sword that hungers for demon blood. It grants its user incredible power, but at a great cost—it can take over the user's body and, in time, his soul.

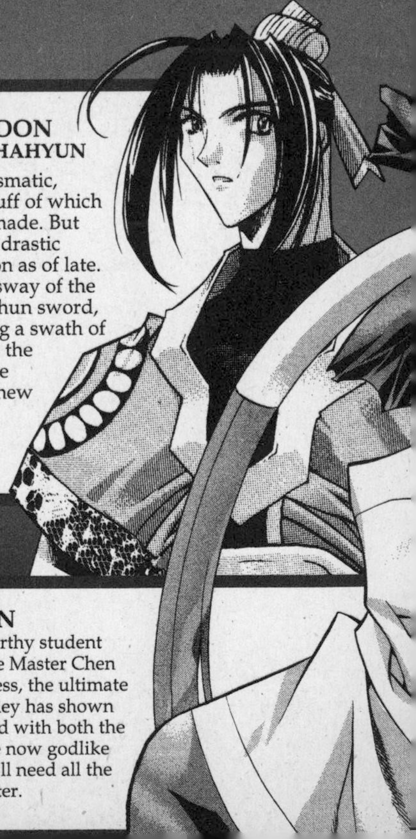

JARYOON
KING OF HAHYUN

Noble and charismatic, Jaryoon is the stuff of which great kings are made. But there has been a drastic change in Jaryoon as of late. Now under the sway of the spirit of the PaChun sword, Jaryoon is cutting a swath of humanity across the countryside as he searches for his new prey: Rey.

SHYAO LIN

A sorceress, previously Rey's traveling companion and greatest ally. Shyao has recently discovered that she is, in fact, one of the Eight Sages of the Azure Pavilion, sent to gather information in the Human Realm. Much to her dismay, her first duty as Rana, the Lady Sohwa, is to kill Rey Yan.

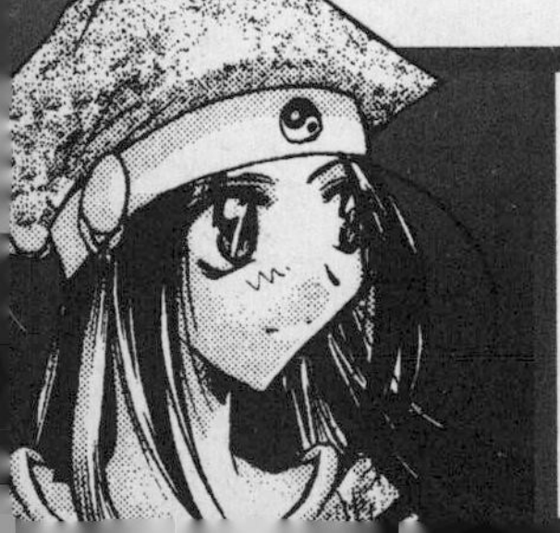

REY YAN

Rey has proven to be a worthy student of the wise and diminutive Master Chen Kaihu. At the Mujin Fortress, the ultimate warrior testing grounds, Rey has shown his martial arts mettle. And with both the possessed Jaryoon and the now godlike Shyao after his blood—he'll need all the survival skills he can muster.

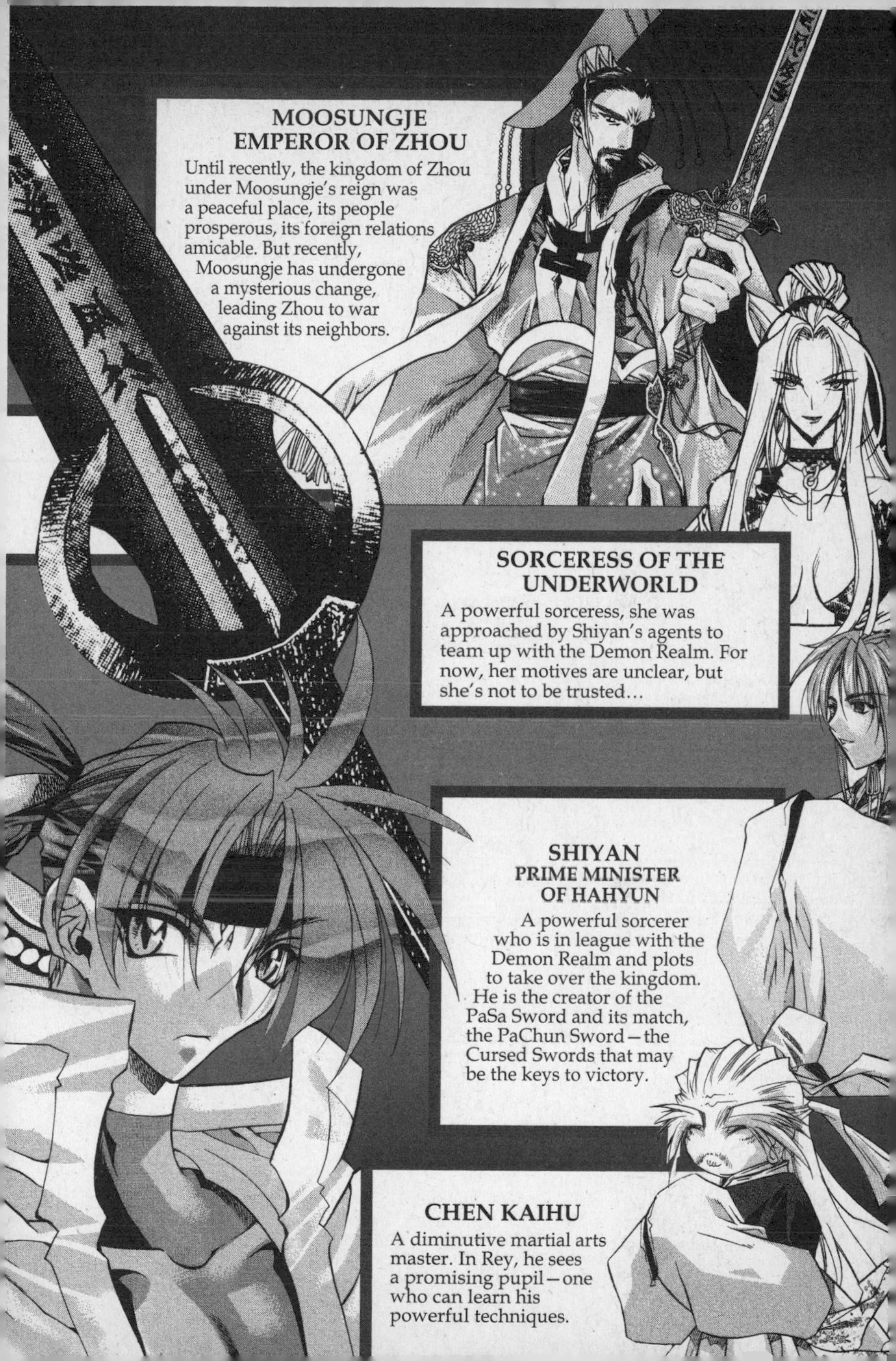
MOOSUNGJE
EMPEROR OF ZHOU
Until recently, the kingdom of Zhou under Moosungje's reign was a peaceful place, its people prosperous, its foreign relations amicable. But recently, Moosungje has undergone a mysterious change, leading Zhou to war against its neighbors.
SORCERESS OF THE UNDERWORLD
A powerful sorceress, she was approached by Shiyan's agents to team up with the Demon Realm. For now, her motives are unclear, but she's not to be trusted...
SHIYAN
PRIME MINISTER OF HAHYUN
A powerful sorcerer who is in league with the Demon Realm and plots to take over the kingdom. He is the creator of the PaSa Sword and its match, the PaChun Sword—the Cursed Swords that may be the keys to victory.
CHEN KAIHU
A diminutive martial arts master. In Rey, he sees a promising pupil—one who can learn his powerful techniques.

Thus Far In...

CHRONICLES OF THE CURSED SWORD

In an era of warring states, warlords become kings, dynasties crumble, and heroes can rise from the most unlikely places. Rey Yan was an orphan with no home, no skills and no purpose. But when he comes upon the PaSa sword, a cursed blade made from the bones of the Demon Emperor, he suddenly finds himself with the power to be a great hero…

Rey and an unlikely company of demons, sages and warriors have made their way to the Great Azure Pavilion, the home of the Eight Great Sages. However, King Jaryoon, under the possession of the evil PaChun sword, has beaten them there, cutting a swath of blood across the countryside in his single-minded quest to obliterate the sages and absorb their souls. Sage Heian and Sage Kochun have already fallen before Jaryoon and his three powerful generals. As sage and demon-born powers collide, it is no longer a clash of men, but of Titans, and the gods themselves have taken note…

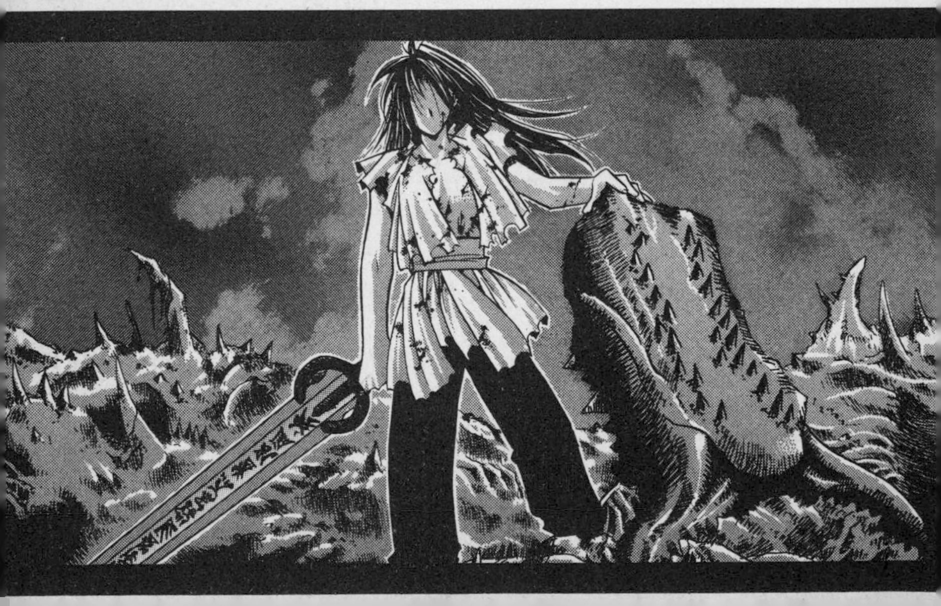

Chapter 67: Destruction of the Great Azure Pavilion

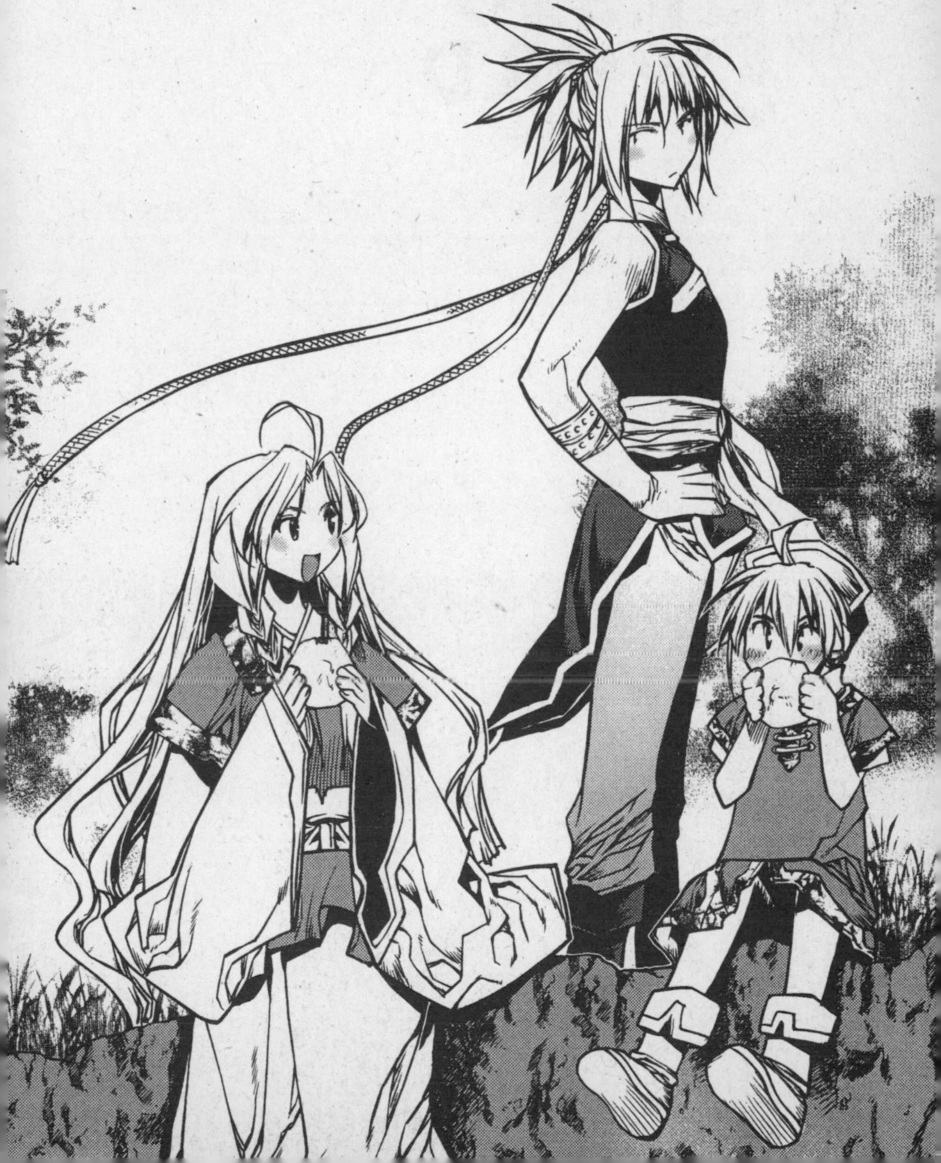

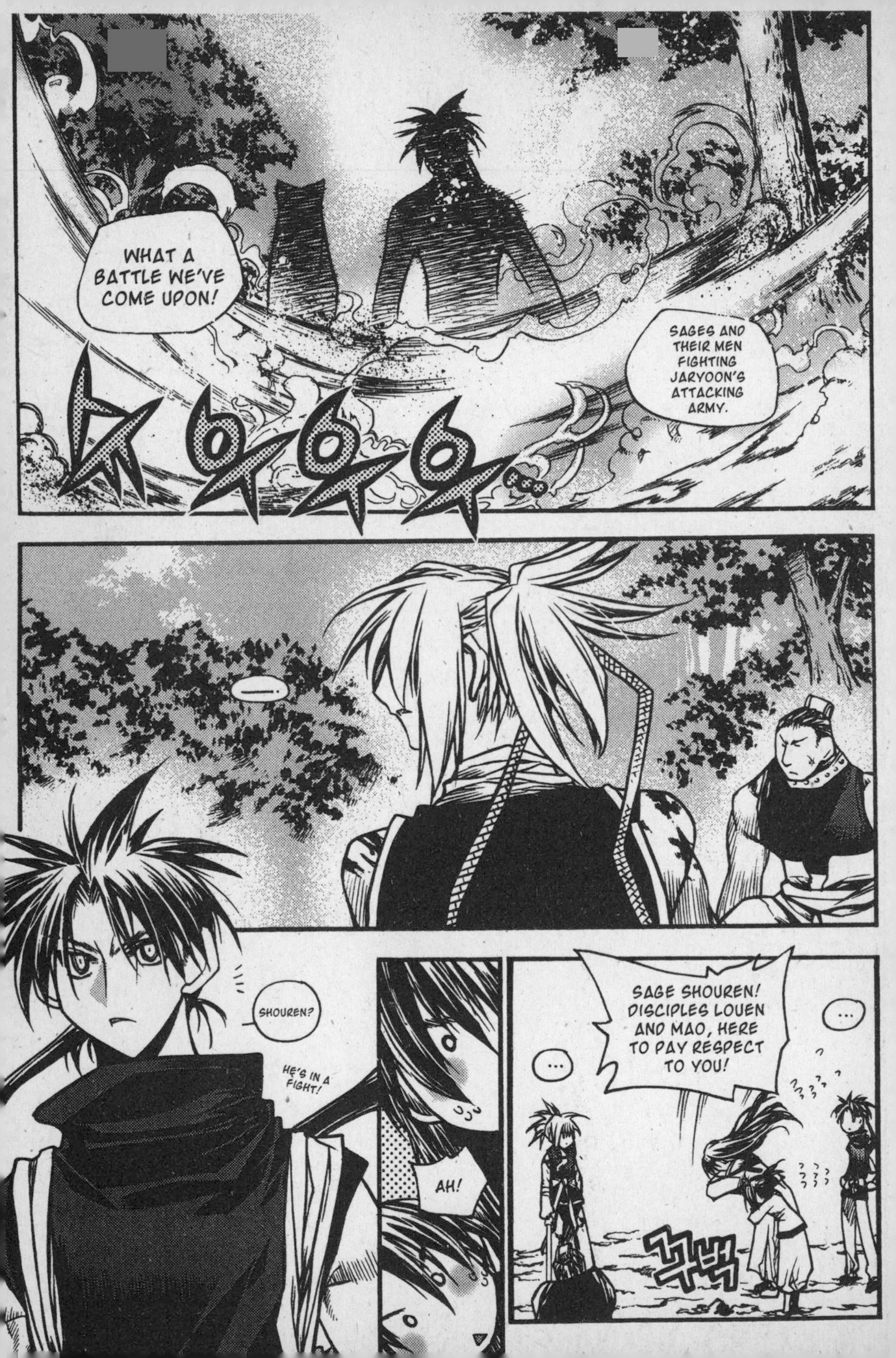
WHAT A BATTLE WE'VE COME UPON!
SAGES AND THEIR MEN FIGHTING JARYOON'S ATTACKING ARMY.
—.
SHOUREN?
HE'S IN A FIGHT!
AH!
...
SAGE SHOUREN! DISCIPLES LOUEN AND MAO, HERE TO PAY RESPECT TO YOU!
...

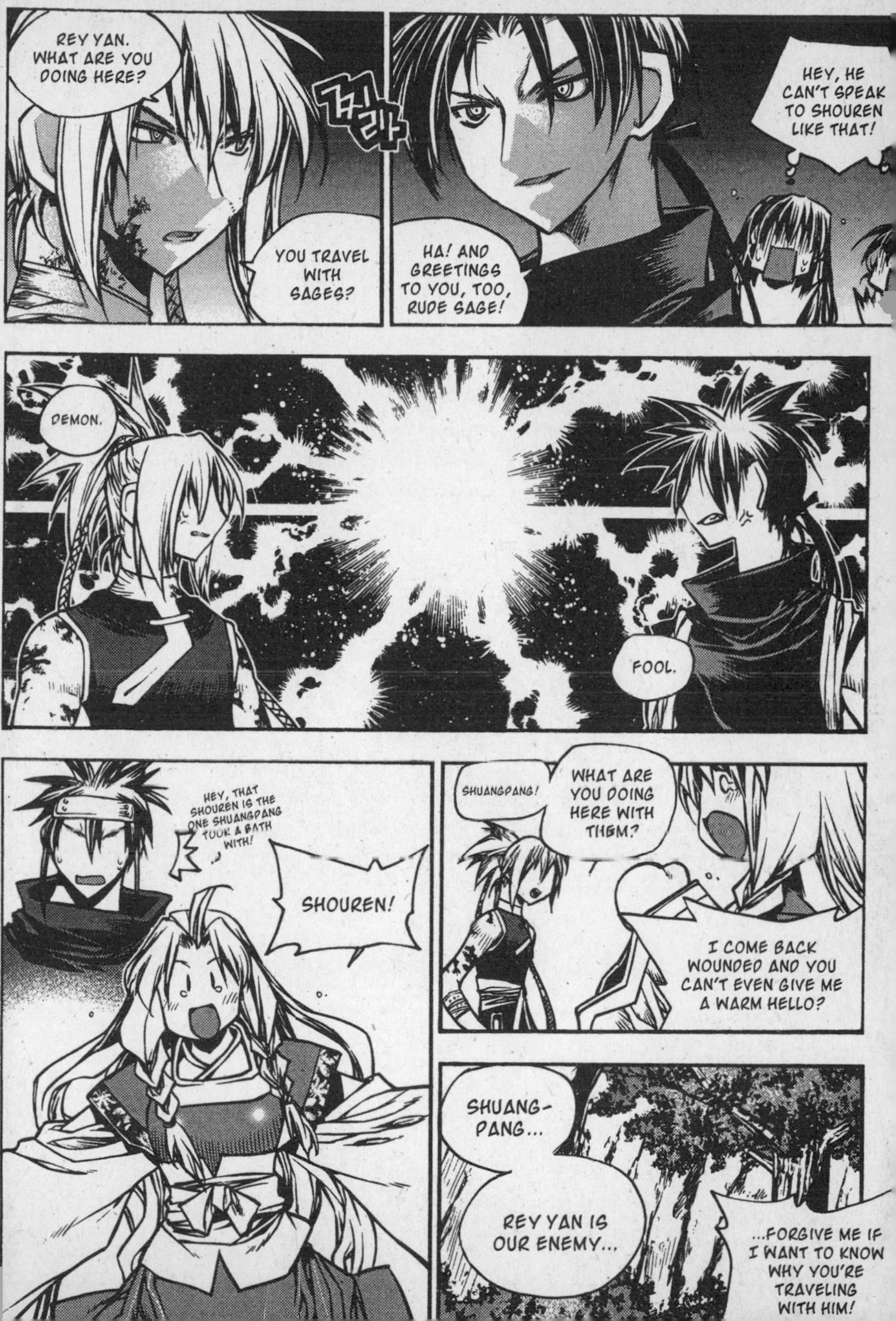
REY YAN. WHAT ARE YOU DOING HERE?
YOU TRAVEL WITH SAGES?
HA! AND GREETINGS TO YOU, TOO, RUDE SAGE!
HEY, HE CAN'T SPEAK TO SHOUREN LIKE THAT!
DEMON.
FOOL.
HEY, THAT SHOUREN IS THE ONE SHUANGPANG TOOK A BATH WITH!
SHOUREN!
SHUANGPANG!
WHAT ARE YOU DOING HERE WITH THEM?
I COME BACK WOUNDED AND YOU CAN'T EVEN GIVE ME A WARM HELLO?
SHUANG-PANG...
REY YAN IS OUR ENEMY...
...FORGIVE ME IF I WANT TO KNOW WHY YOU'RE TRAVELING WITH HIM!

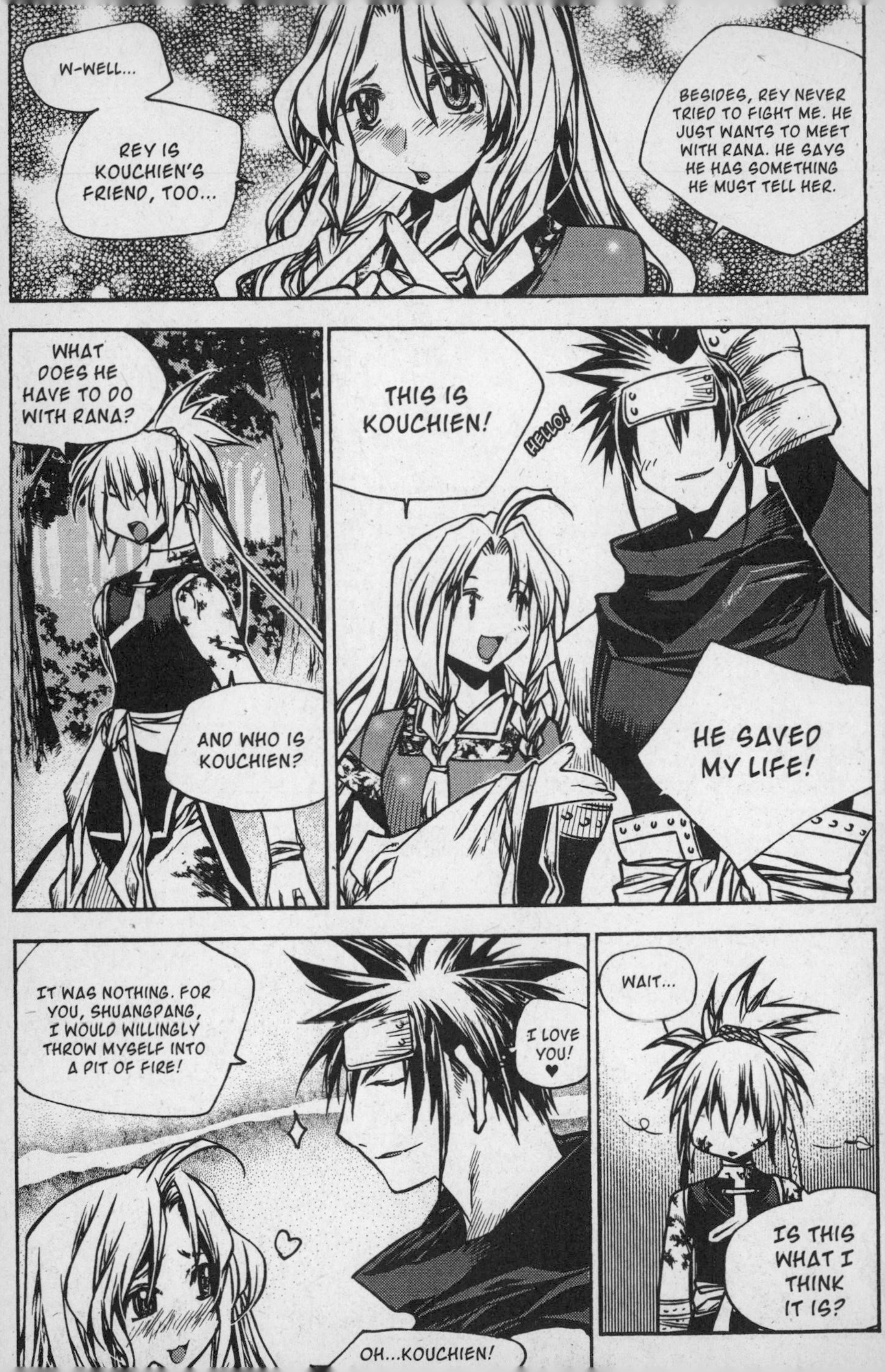
W-WELL...
REY IS KOUCHIEN'S FRIEND, TOO...
BESIDES, REY NEVER TRIED TO FIGHT ME. HE JUST WANTS TO MEET WITH RANA. HE SAYS HE HAS SOMETHING HE MUST TELL HER.
WHAT DOES HE HAVE TO DO WITH RANA?
AND WHO IS KOUCHIEN?
THIS IS KOUCHIEN!
HELLO!
HE SAVED MY LIFE!
IT WAS NOTHING. FOR YOU, SHUANGPANG, I WOULD WILLINGLY THROW MYSELF INTO A PIT OF FIRE!
I LOVE YOU! ♥
OH...KOUCHIEN!
WAIT...
IS THIS WHAT I THINK IT IS?

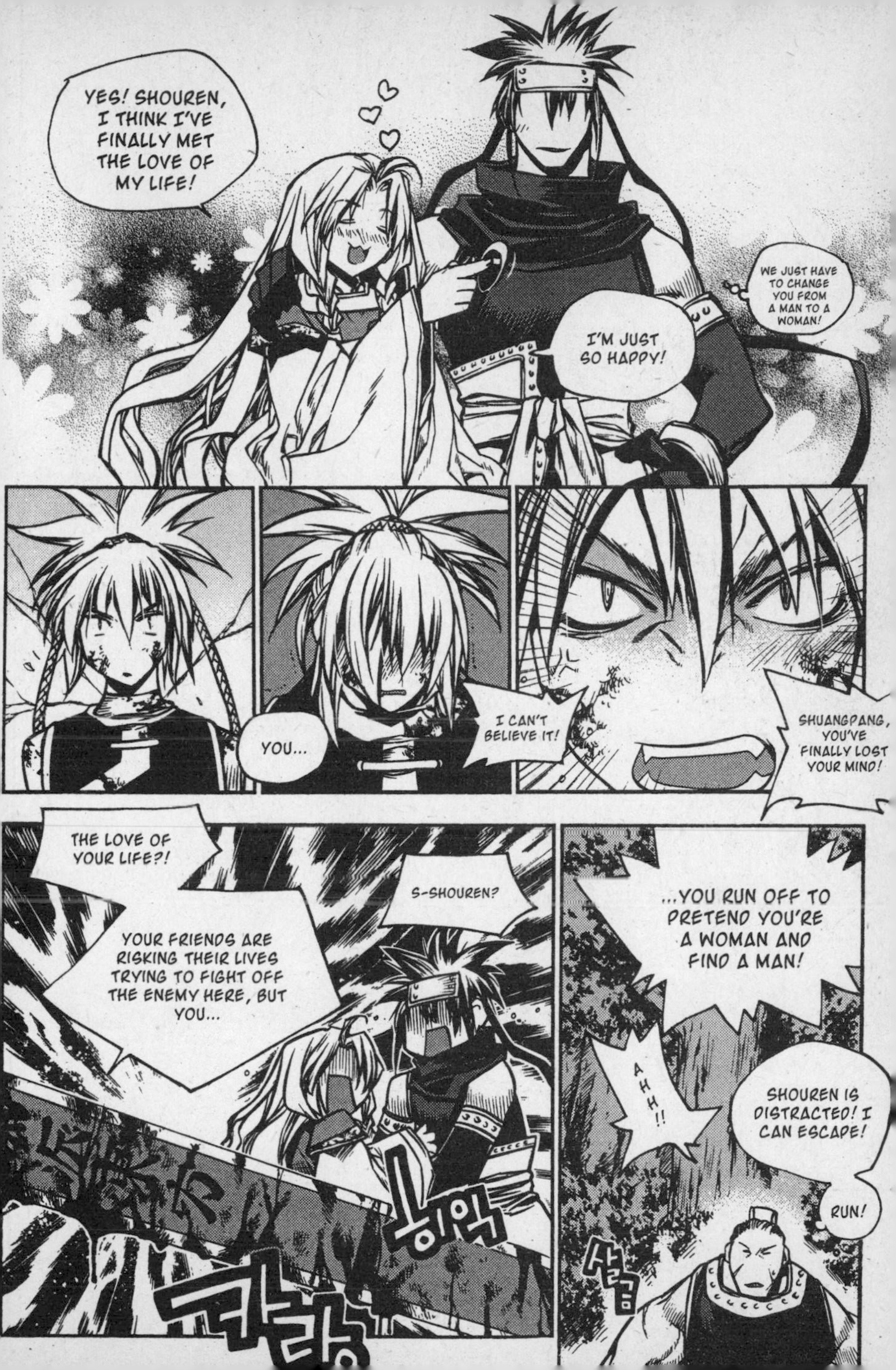
YES! SHOUREN, I THINK I'VE FINALLY MET THE LOVE OF MY LIFE!
I'M JUST SO HAPPY!
WE JUST HAVE TO CHANGE YOU FROM A MAN TO A WOMAN!
YOU...
I CAN'T BELIEVE IT!
SHUANGPANG, YOU'VE FINALLY LOST YOUR MIND!
THE LOVE OF YOUR LIFE?!
S-SHOUREN?
YOUR FRIENDS ARE RISKING THEIR LIVES TRYING TO FIGHT OFF THE ENEMY HERE, BUT YOU...
...YOU RUN OFF TO PRETEND YOU'RE A WOMAN AND FIND A MAN!
AHH!!
SHOUREN IS DISTRACTED! I CAN ESCAPE!
RUN!

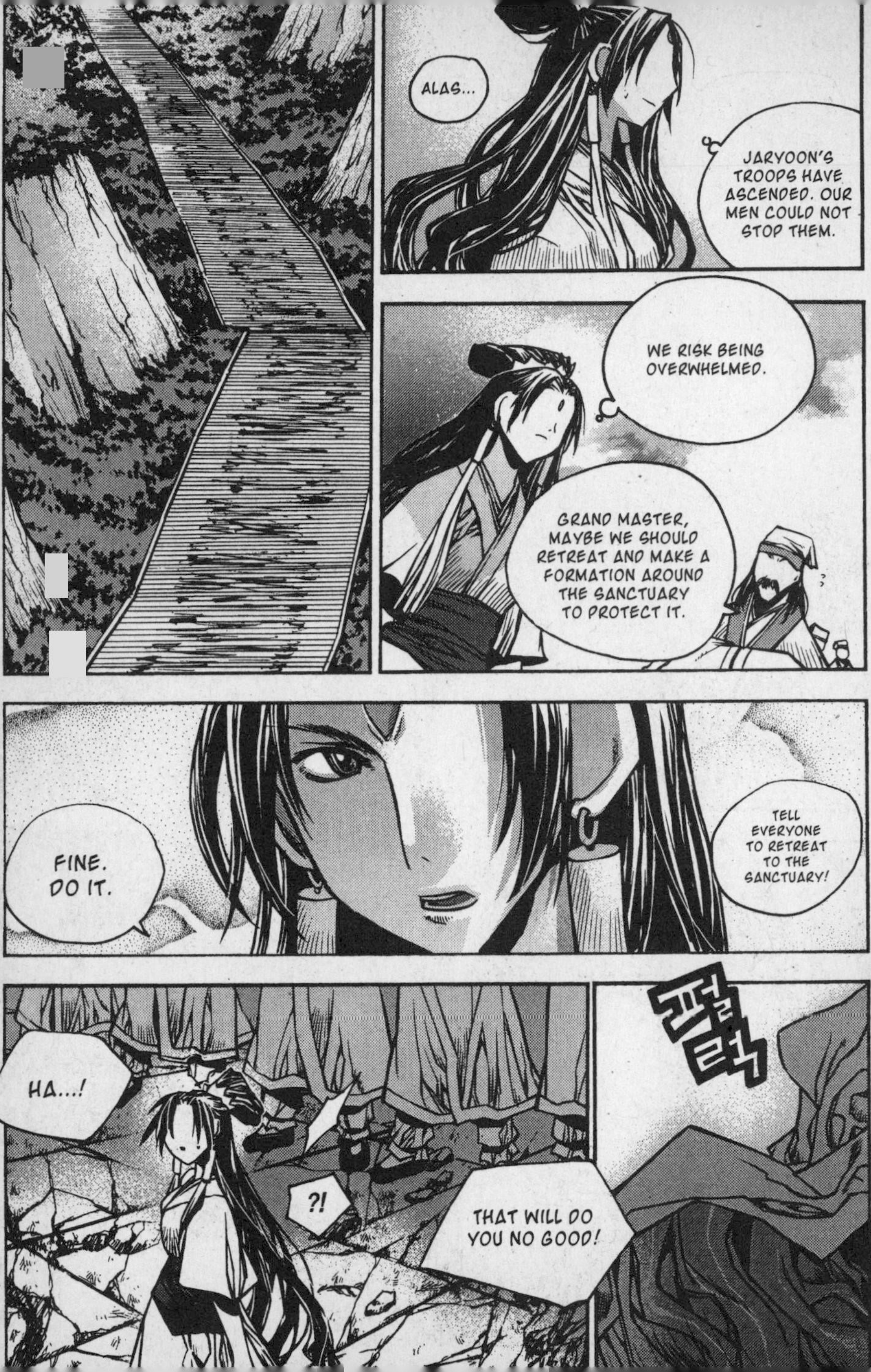
ALAS...
JARYOON'S TROOPS HAVE ASCENDED. OUR MEN COULD NOT STOP THEM.
WE RISK BEING OVERWHELMED.
GRAND MASTER, MAYBE WE SHOULD RETREAT AND MAKE A FORMATION AROUND THE SANCTUARY TO PROTECT IT.
FINE. DO IT.
TELL EVERYONE TO RETREAT TO THE SANCTUARY!
HA...!
?!
THAT WILL DO YOU NO GOOD!
펄럭

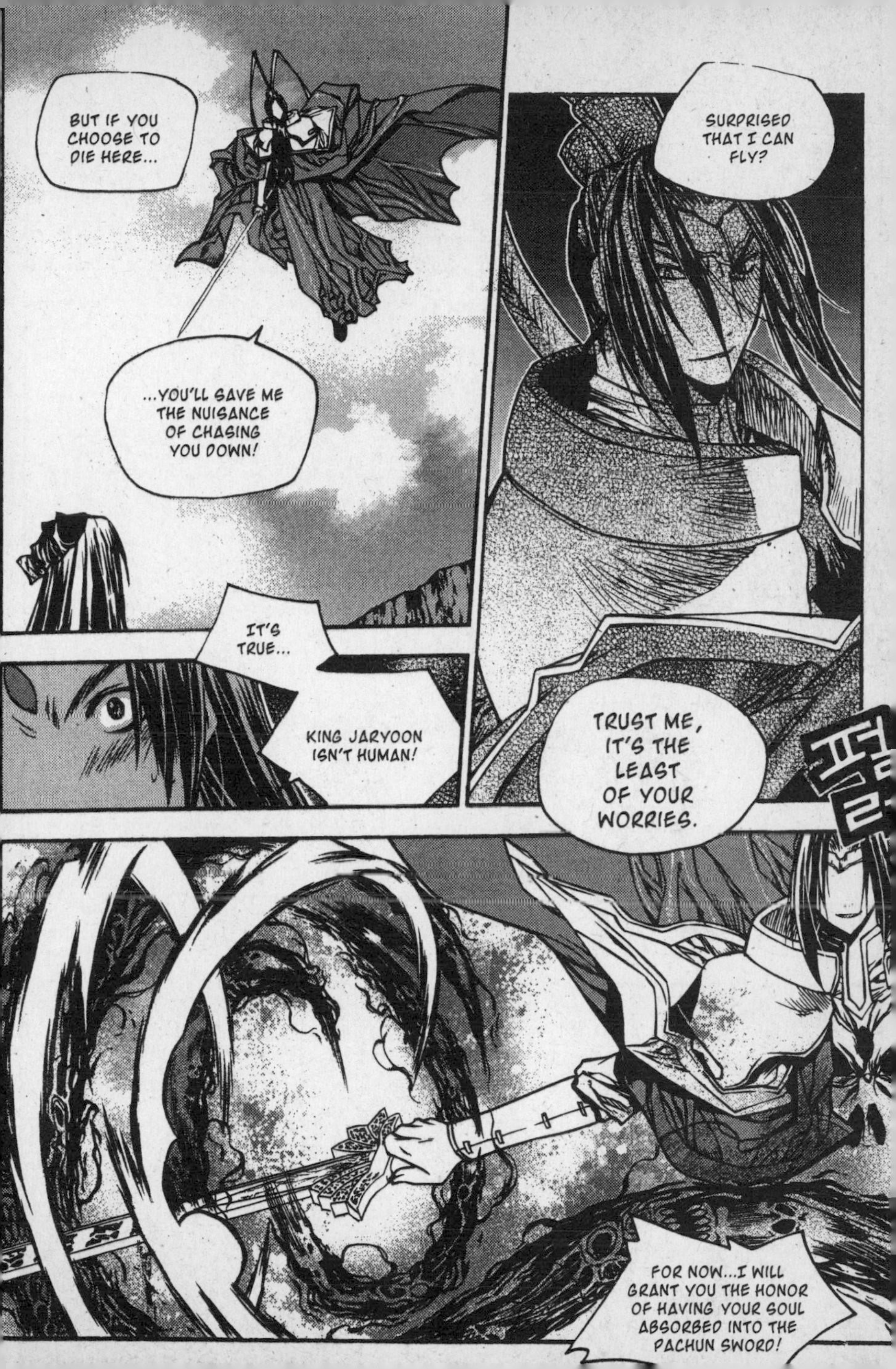
BUT IF YOU CHOOSE TO DIE HERE...
...YOU'LL SAVE ME THE NUISANCE OF CHASING YOU DOWN!
IT'S TRUE...
KING JARYOON ISN'T HUMAN!
SURPRISED THAT I CAN FLY?
TRUST ME, IT'S THE LEAST OF YOUR WORRIES.
FOR NOW...I WILL GRANT YOU THE HONOR OF HAVING YOUR SOUL ABSORBED INTO THE PACHUN SWORD!

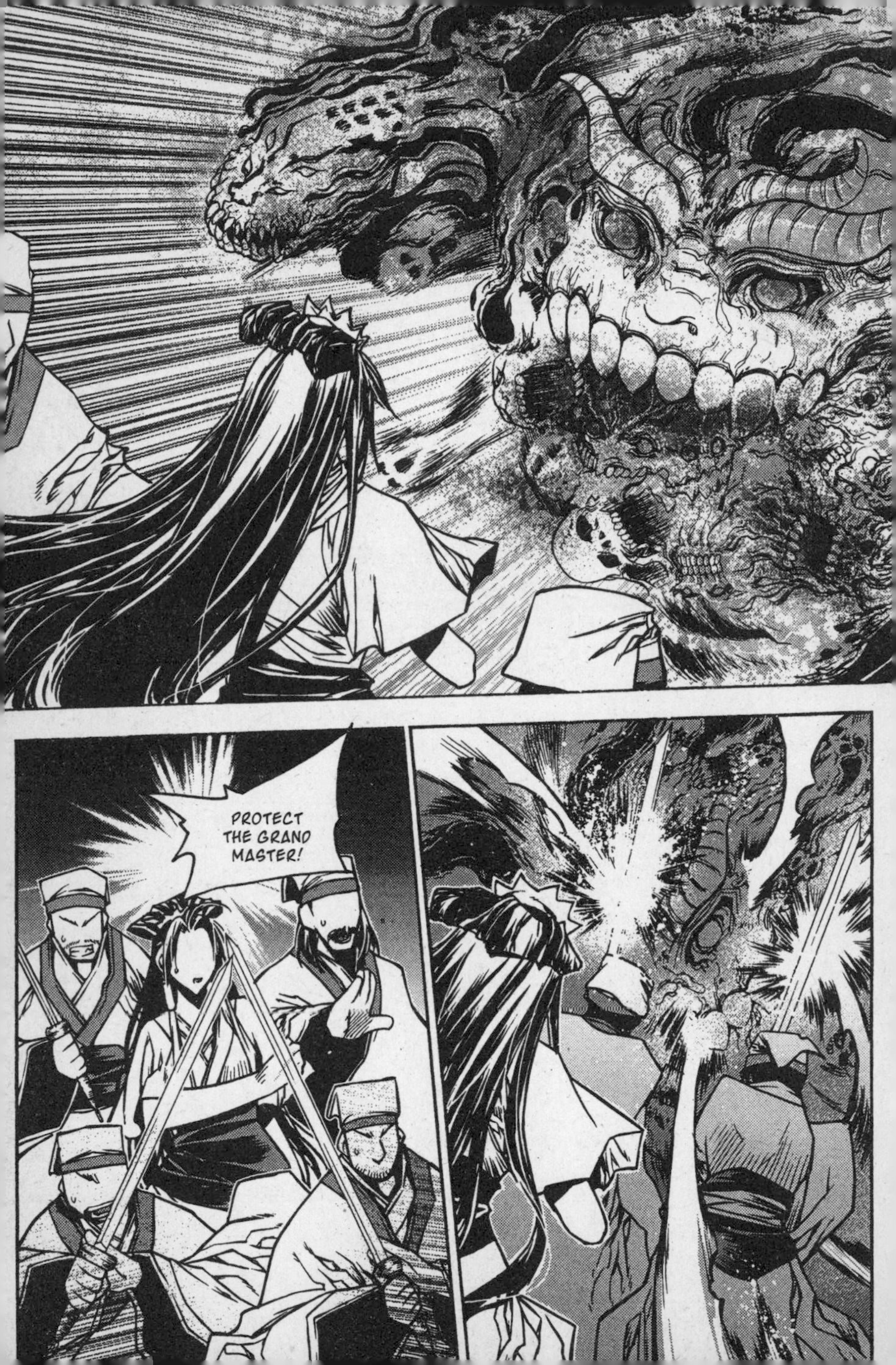
PROTECT THE GRAND MASTER!

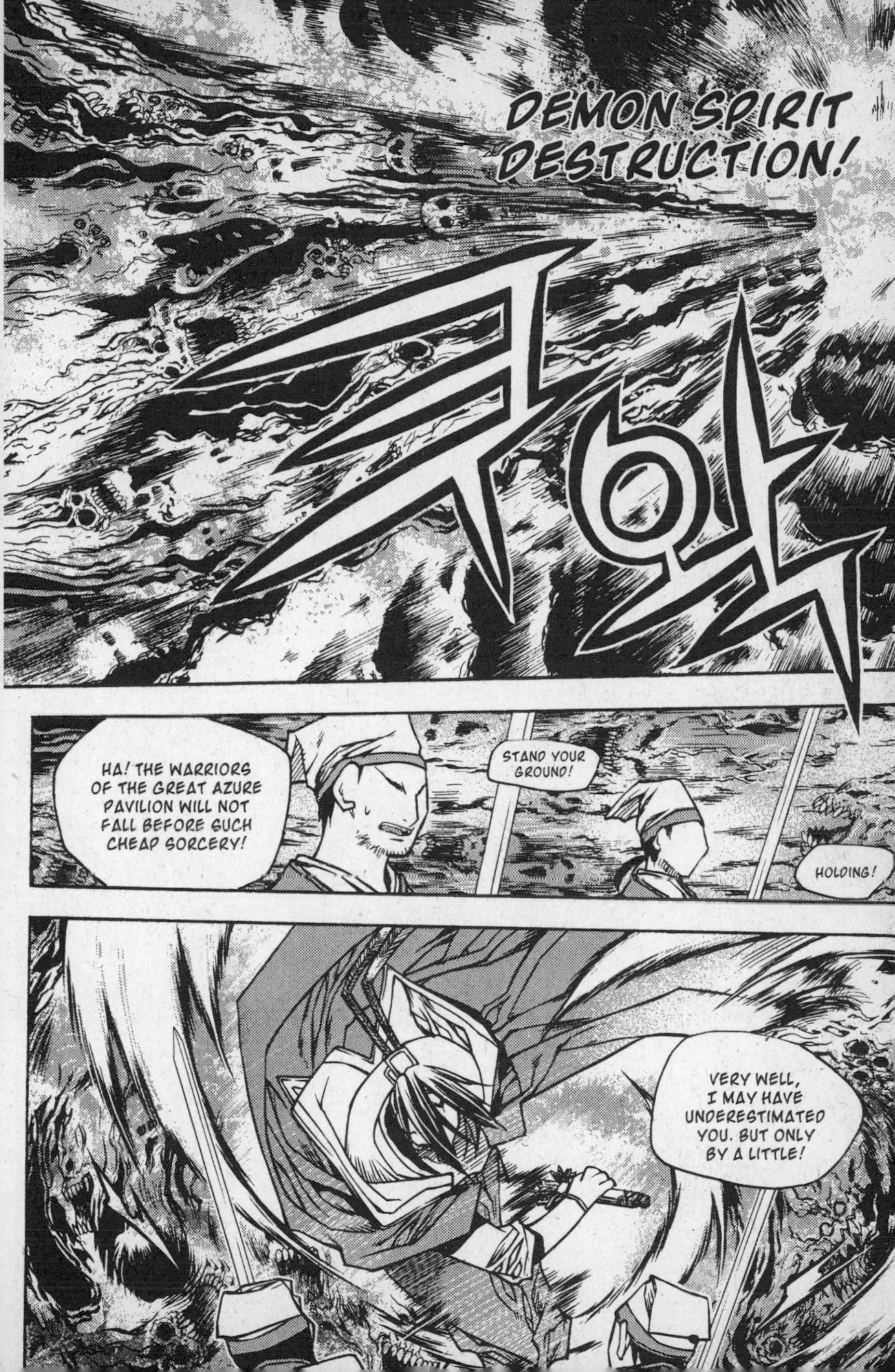
DEMON SPIRIT DESTRUCTION!
HA! THE WARRIORS OF THE GREAT AZURE PAVILION WILL NOT FALL BEFORE SUCH CHEAP SORCERY!
STAND YOUR GROUND!
HOLDING!
VERY WELL, I MAY HAVE UNDERESTIMATED YOU. BUT ONLY BY A LITTLE!

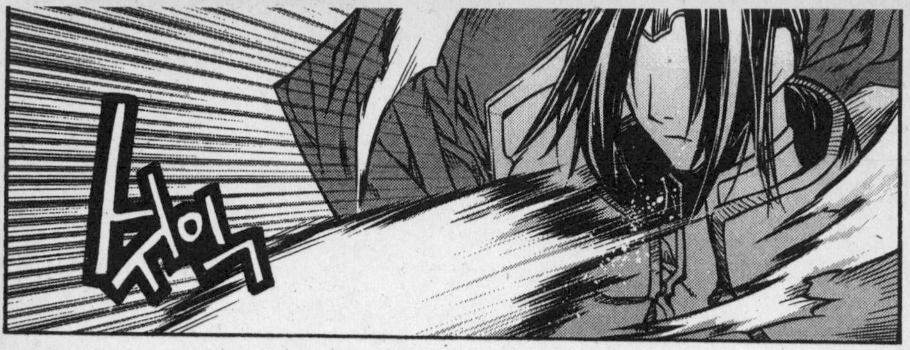
쉬익
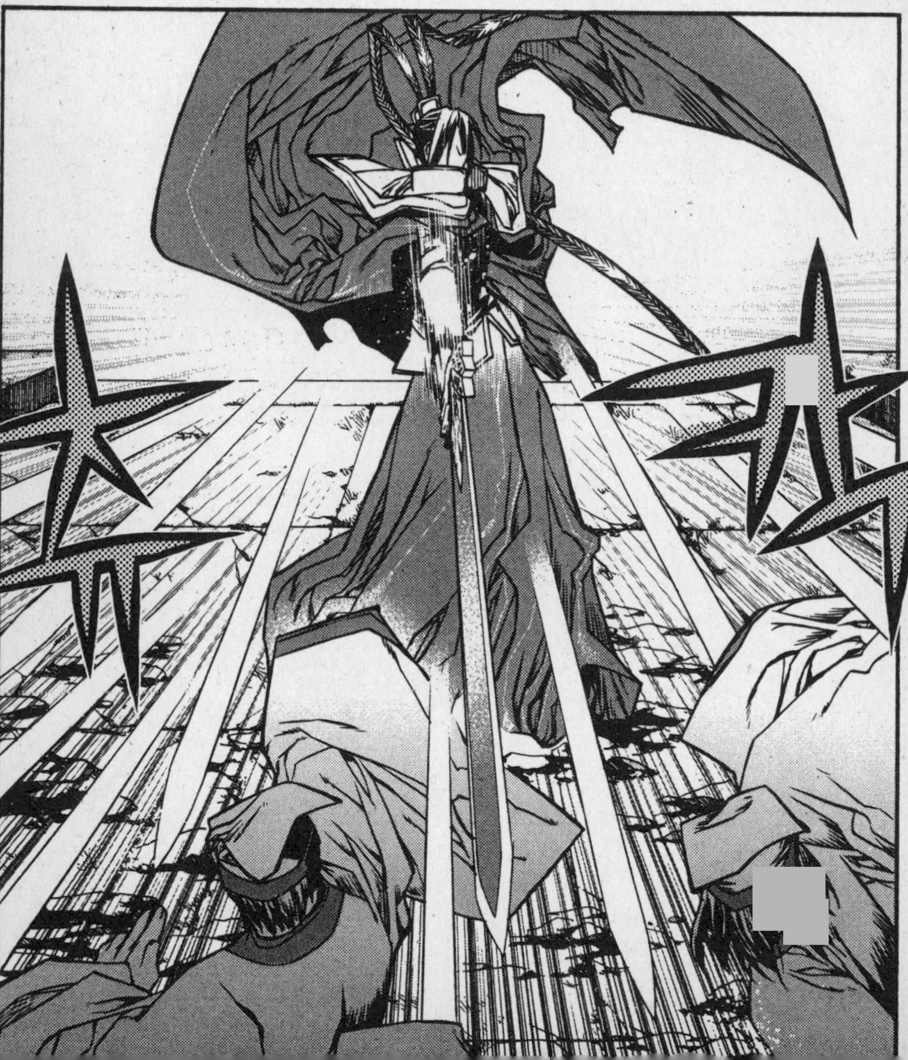

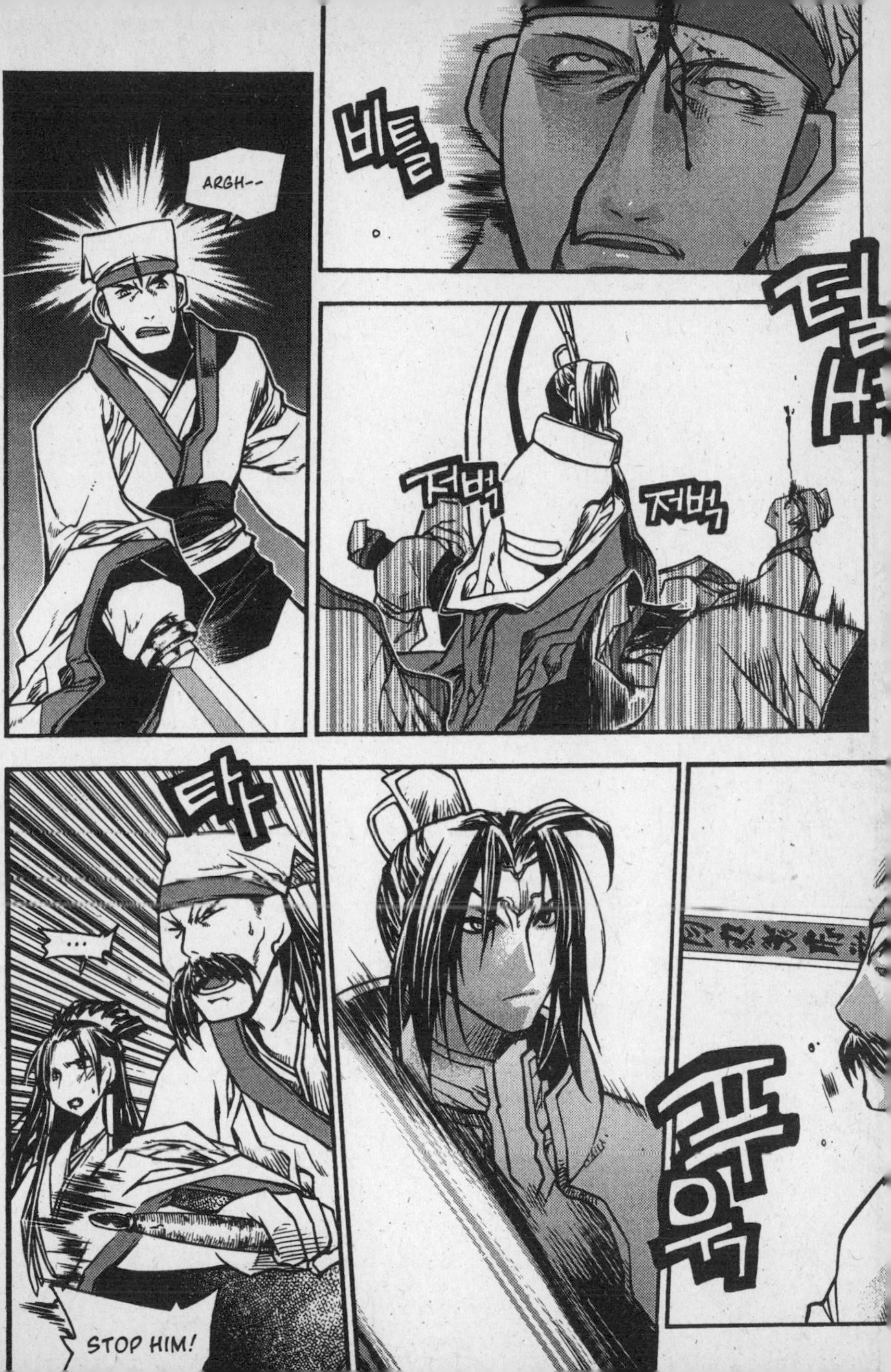
ARGH--
비틀
저벅
저벅
...
탁
STOP HIM!

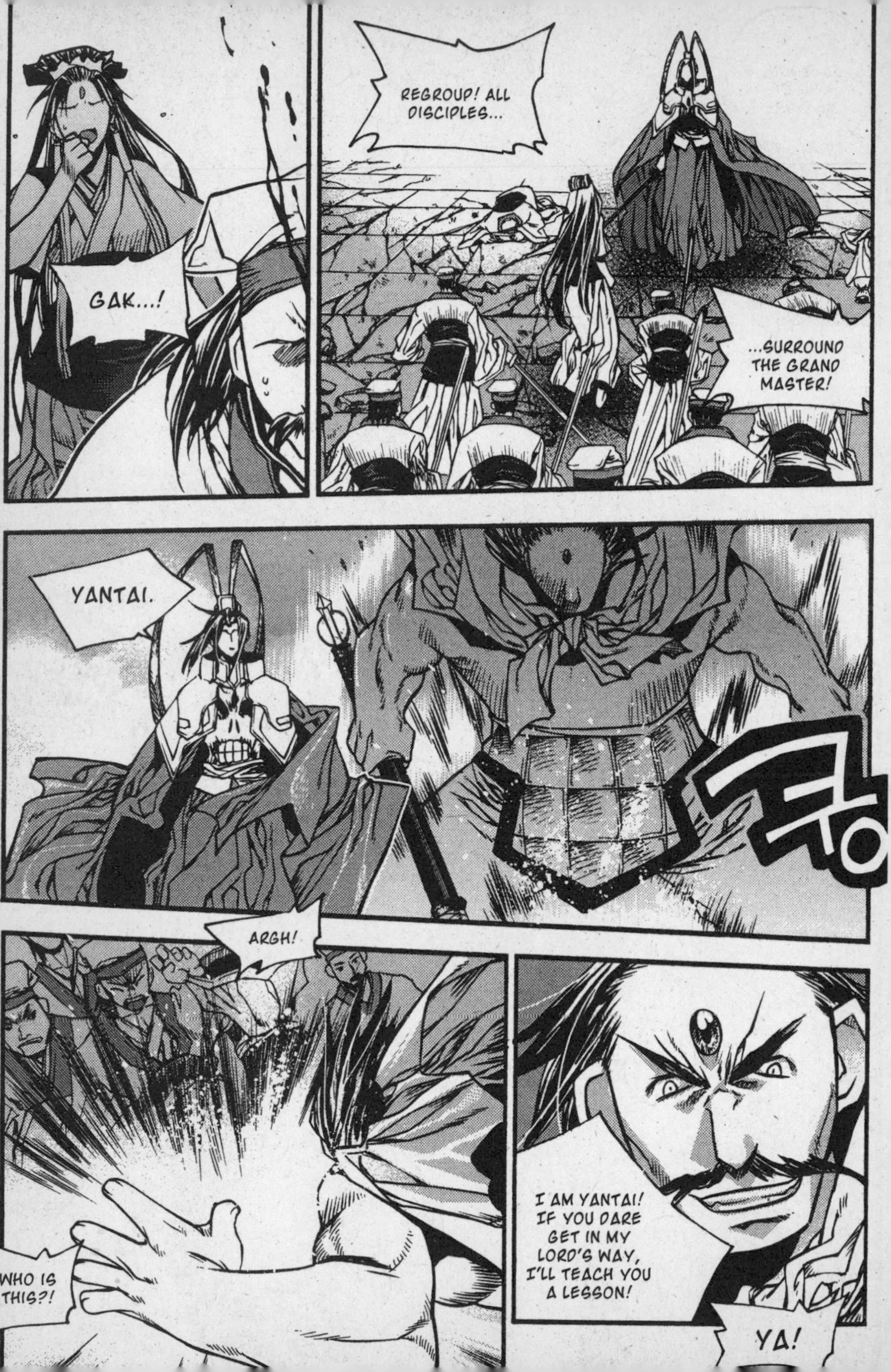
GAK...!
REGROUP! ALL DISCIPLES...
...SURROUND THE GRAND MASTER!
YANTAI.
ARGH!
WHO IS THIS?!
I AM YANTAI! IF YOU DARE GET IN MY LORD'S WAY, I'LL TEACH YOU A LESSON!
YA!

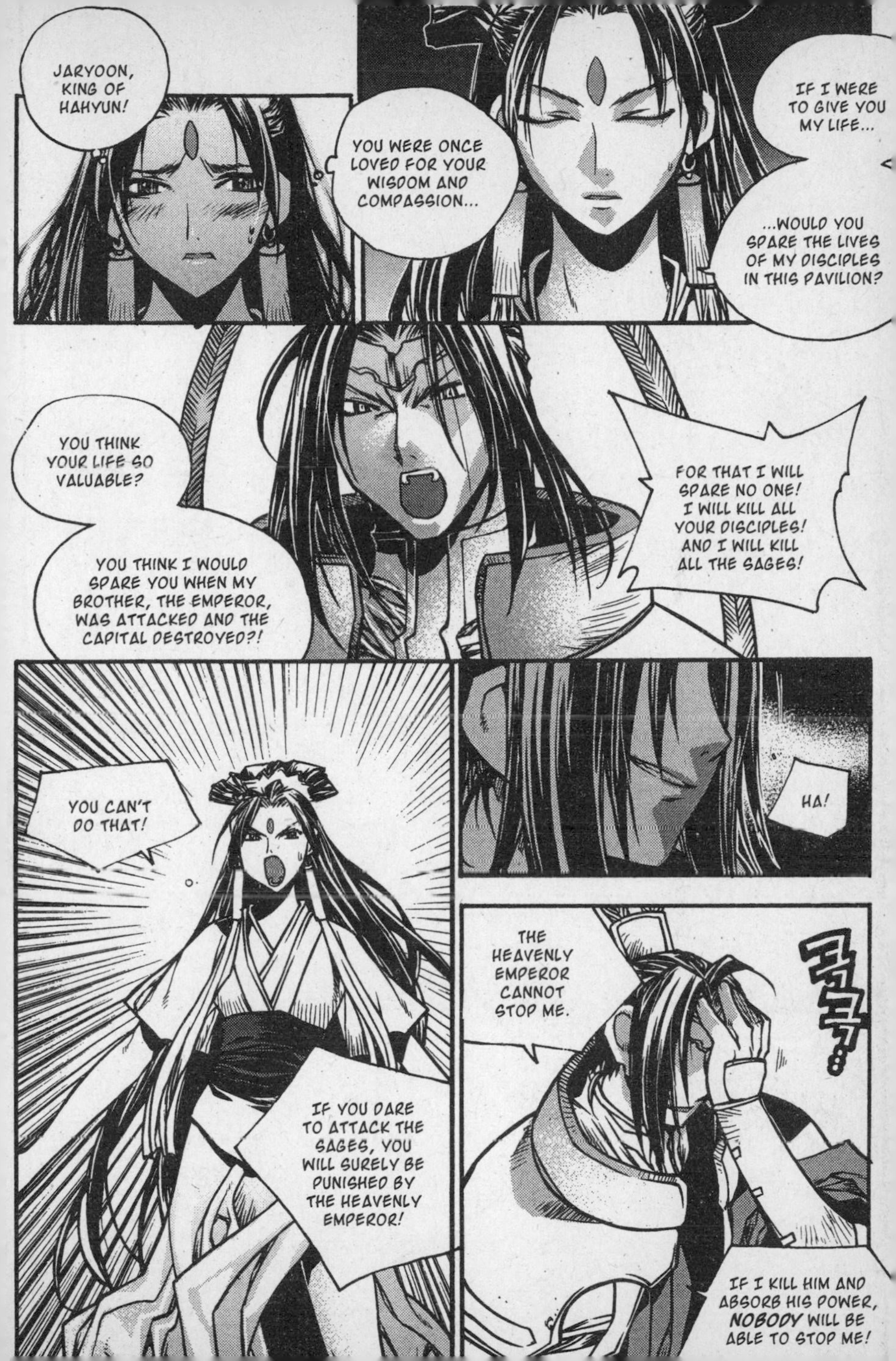
JARYOON, KING OF HAHYUN!
YOU WERE ONCE LOVED FOR YOUR WISDOM AND COMPASSION...
IF I WERE TO GIVE YOU MY LIFE...
...WOULD YOU SPARE THE LIVES OF MY DISCIPLES IN THIS PAVILION?
YOU THINK YOUR LIFE SO VALUABLE?
YOU THINK I WOULD SPARE YOU WHEN MY BROTHER, THE EMPEROR, WAS ATTACKED AND THE CAPITAL DESTROYED?!
FOR THAT I WILL SPARE NO ONE! I WILL KILL ALL YOUR DISCIPLES! AND I WILL KILL ALL THE SAGES!
YOU CAN'T DO THAT!
IF YOU DARE TO ATTACK THE SAGES, YOU WILL SURELY BE PUNISHED BY THE HEAVENLY EMPEROR!
HA!
THE HEAVENLY EMPEROR CANNOT STOP ME.
IF I KILL HIM AND ABSORB HIS POWER, **NOBODY** WILL BE ABLE TO STOP ME!

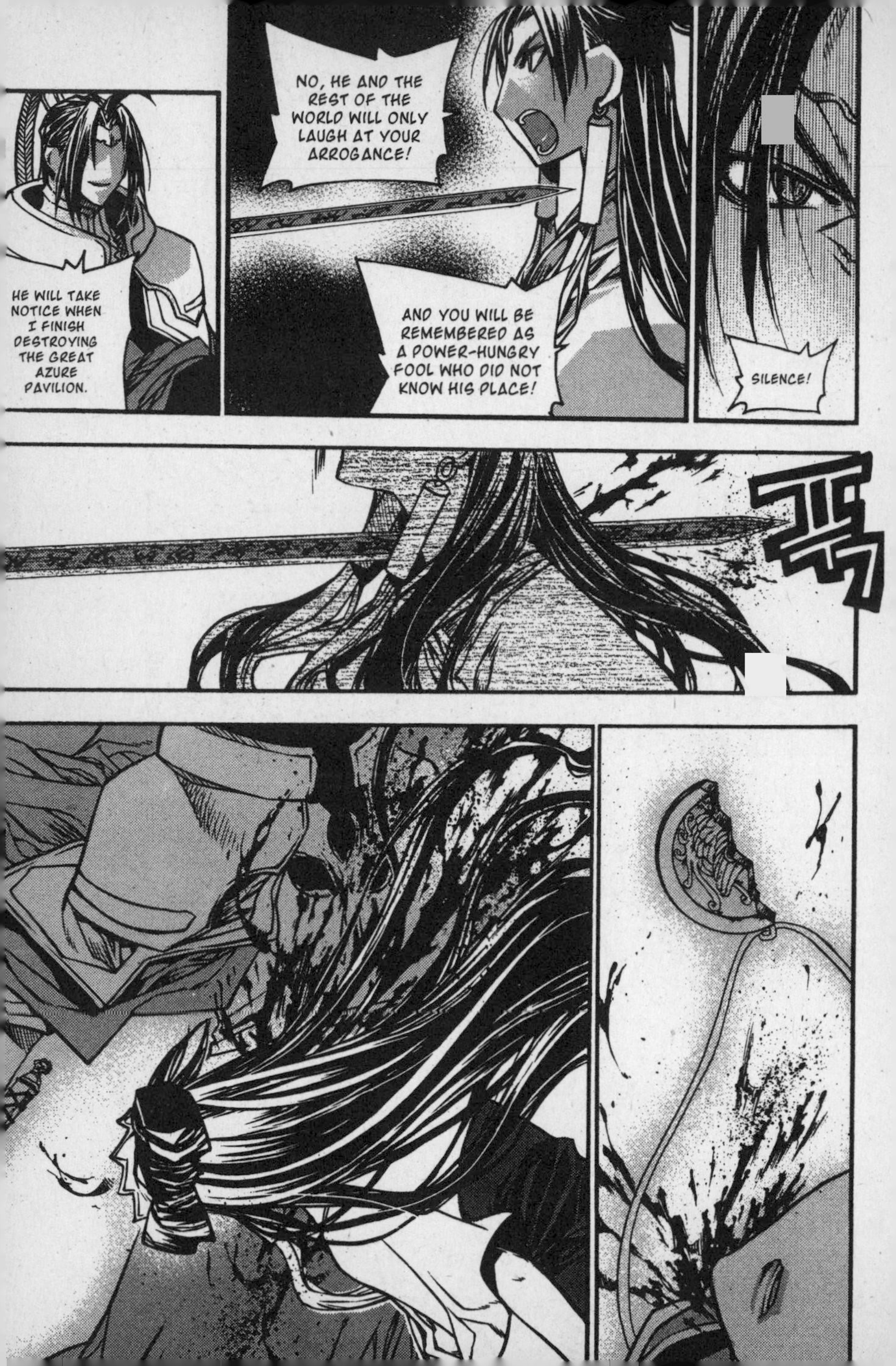

HE WILL TAKE NOTICE WHEN I FINISH DESTROYING THE GREAT AZURE PAVILION.
NO, HE AND THE REST OF THE WORLD WILL ONLY LAUGH AT YOUR ARROGANCE!
AND YOU WILL BE REMEMBERED AS A POWER-HUNGRY FOOL WHO DID NOT KNOW HIS PLACE!
SILENCE!

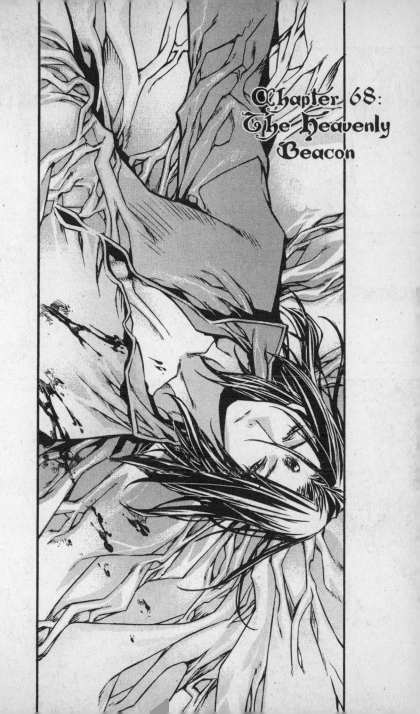

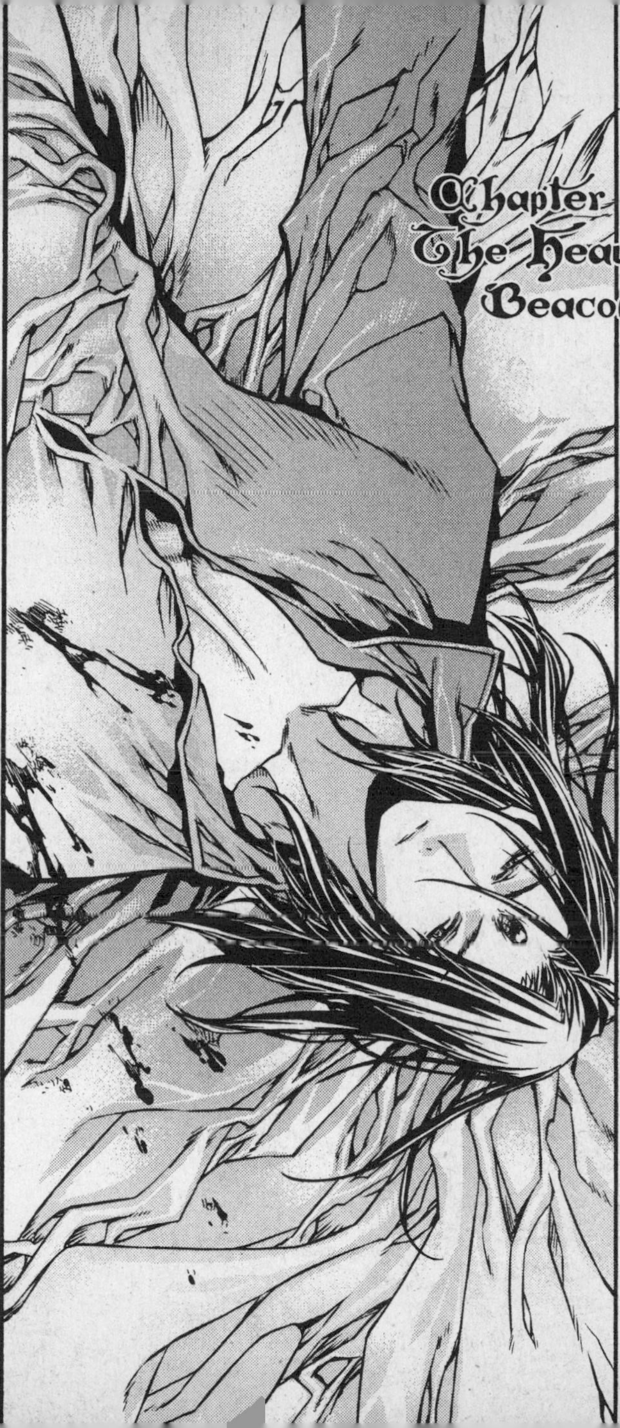
Chapter 68:
The Heavenly
Beacon

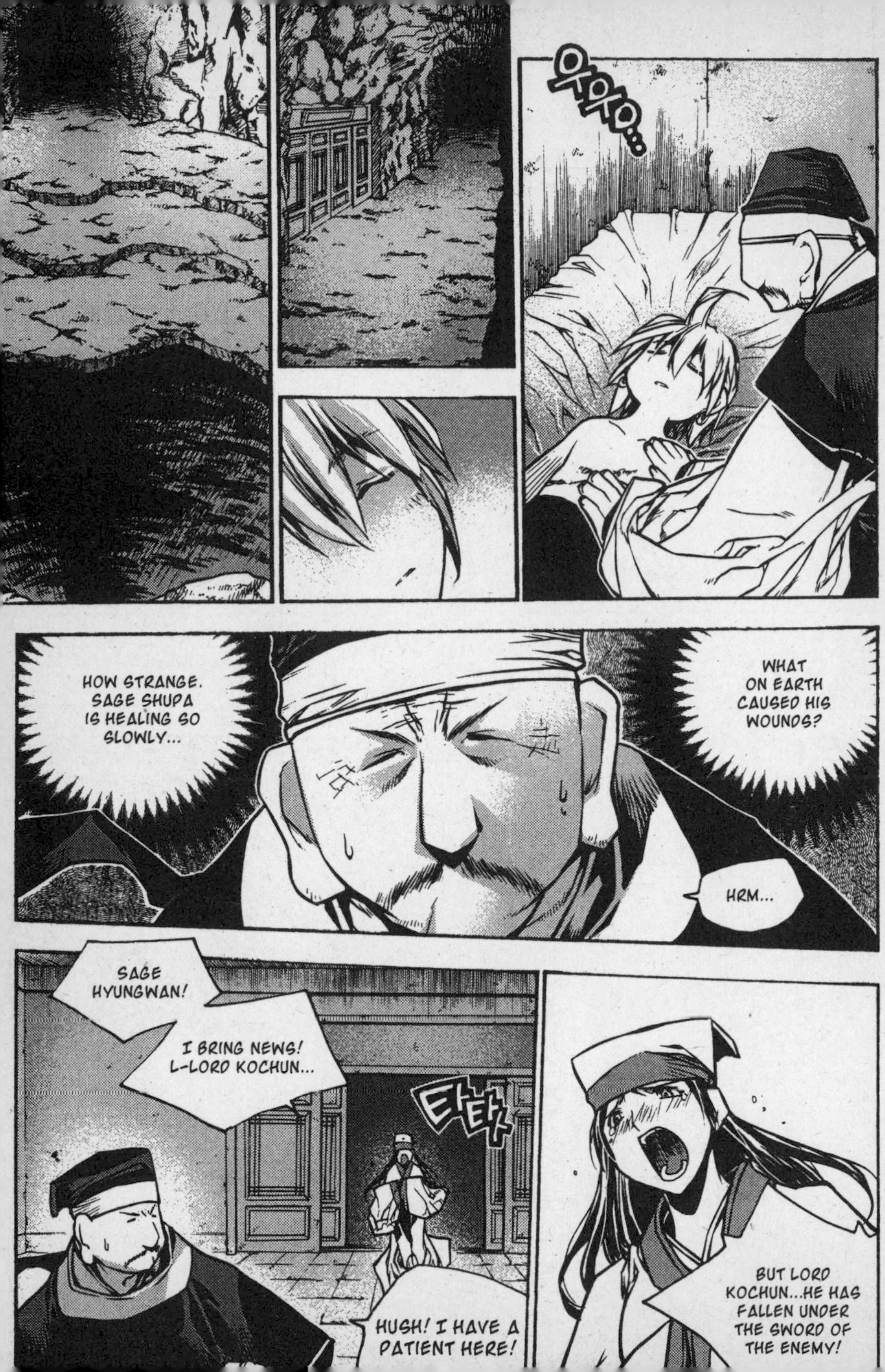
우우우...
HOW STRANGE. SAGE SHUPA IS HEALING SO SLOWLY...
WHAT ON EARTH CAUSED HIS WOUNDS?
HRM...
SAGE HYUNGWAN!
I BRING NEWS! L-LORD KOCHUN...
타타탁
HUSH! I HAVE A PATIENT HERE!
BUT LORD KOCHUN...HE HAS FALLEN UNDER THE SWORD OF THE ENEMY!

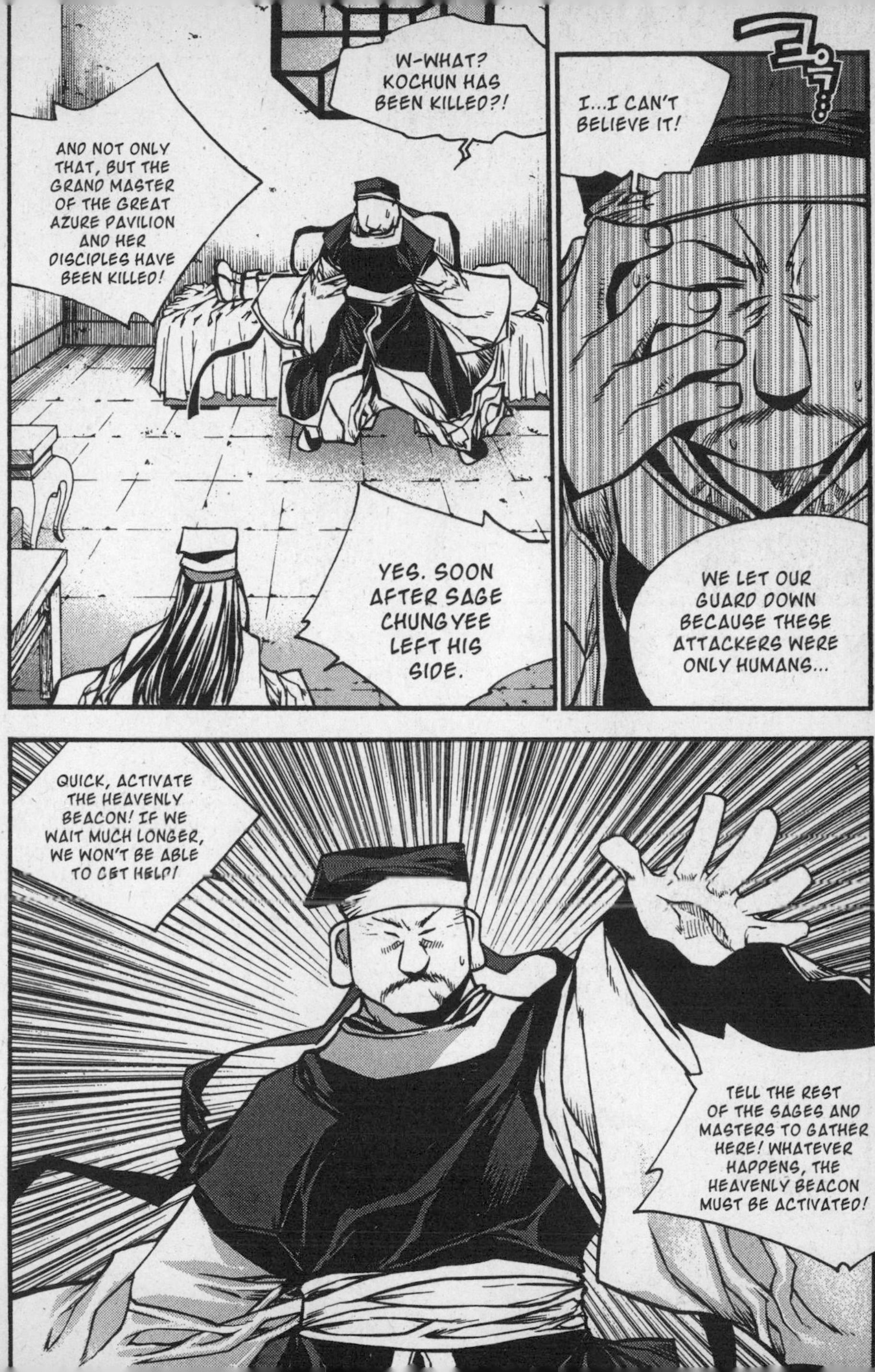
W-WHAT? KOCHUN HAS BEEN KILLED?!
AND NOT ONLY THAT, BUT THE GRAND MASTER OF THE GREAT AZURE PAVILION AND HER DISCIPLES HAVE BEEN KILLED!
YES. SOON AFTER SAGE CHUNGYEE LEFT HIS SIDE.
I...I CAN'T BELIEVE IT!
WE LET OUR GUARD DOWN BECAUSE THESE ATTACKERS WERE ONLY HUMANS...
QUICK, ACTIVATE THE HEAVENLY BEACON! IF WE WAIT MUCH LONGER, WE WON'T BE ABLE TO GET HELP!
TELL THE REST OF THE SAGES AND MASTERS TO GATHER HERE! WHATEVER HAPPENS, THE HEAVENLY BEACON MUST BE ACTIVATED!

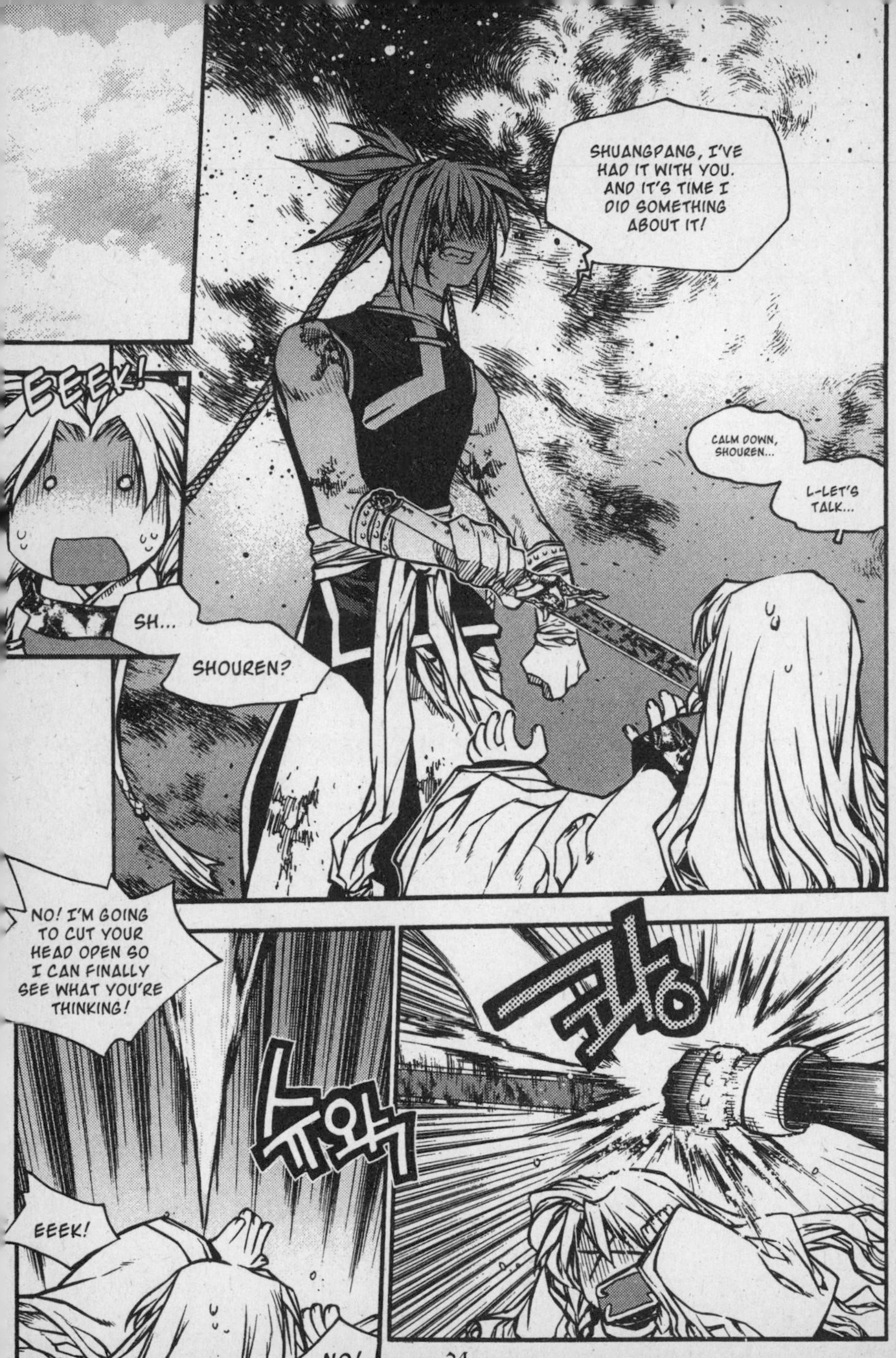
EEEK!
SH...
SHOUREN?
SHUANGPANG, I'VE HAD IT WITH YOU. AND IT'S TIME I DID SOMETHING ABOUT IT!
CALM DOWN, SHOUREN...
L-LET'S TALK...
NO! I'M GOING TO CUT YOUR HEAD OPEN SO I CAN FINALLY SEE WHAT YOU'RE THINKING!
EEEK!
NO!

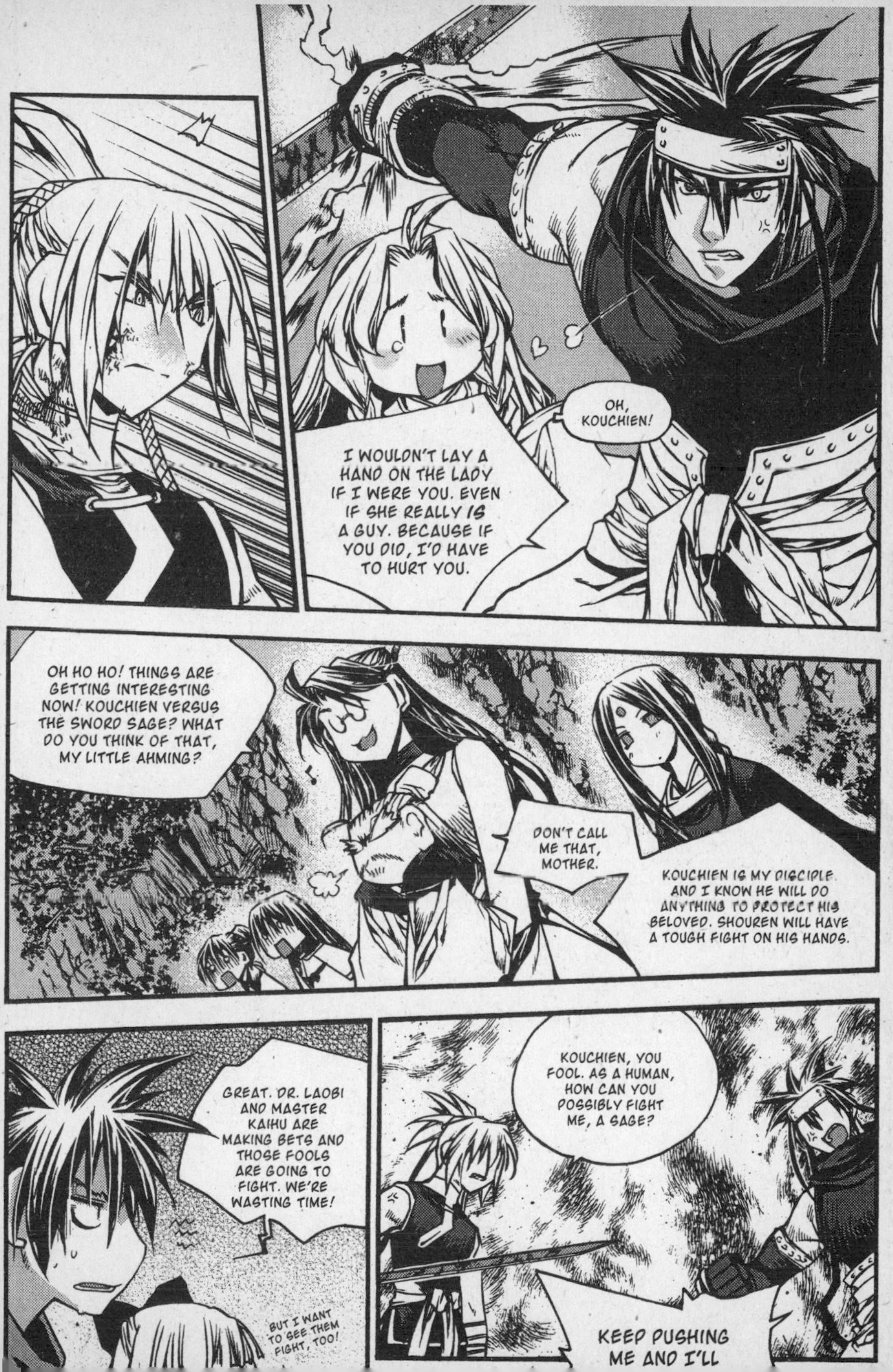
OH, KOUCHIEN!
I WOULDN'T LAY A HAND ON THE LADY IF I WERE YOU. EVEN IF SHE REALLY IS A GUY. BECAUSE IF YOU DID, I'D HAVE TO HURT YOU.
OH HO HO! THINGS ARE GETTING INTERESTING NOW! KOUCHIEN VERSUS THE SWORD SAGE? WHAT DO YOU THINK OF THAT, MY LITTLE AHMING?
DON'T CALL ME THAT, MOTHER.
KOUCHIEN IS MY DISCIPLE AND I KNOW HE WILL DO ANYTHING TO PROTECT HIS BELOVED. SHOUREN WILL HAVE A TOUGH FIGHT ON HIS HANDS.
GREAT. DR. LAOBI AND MASTER KAIHU ARE MAKING BETS AND THOSE FOOLS ARE GOING TO FIGHT. WE'RE WASTING TIME!
BUT I WANT TO SEE THEM FIGHT, TOO!
KOUCHIEN, YOU FOOL. AS A HUMAN, HOW CAN YOU POSSIBLY FIGHT ME, A SAGE?
KEEP PUSHING ME AND I'LL

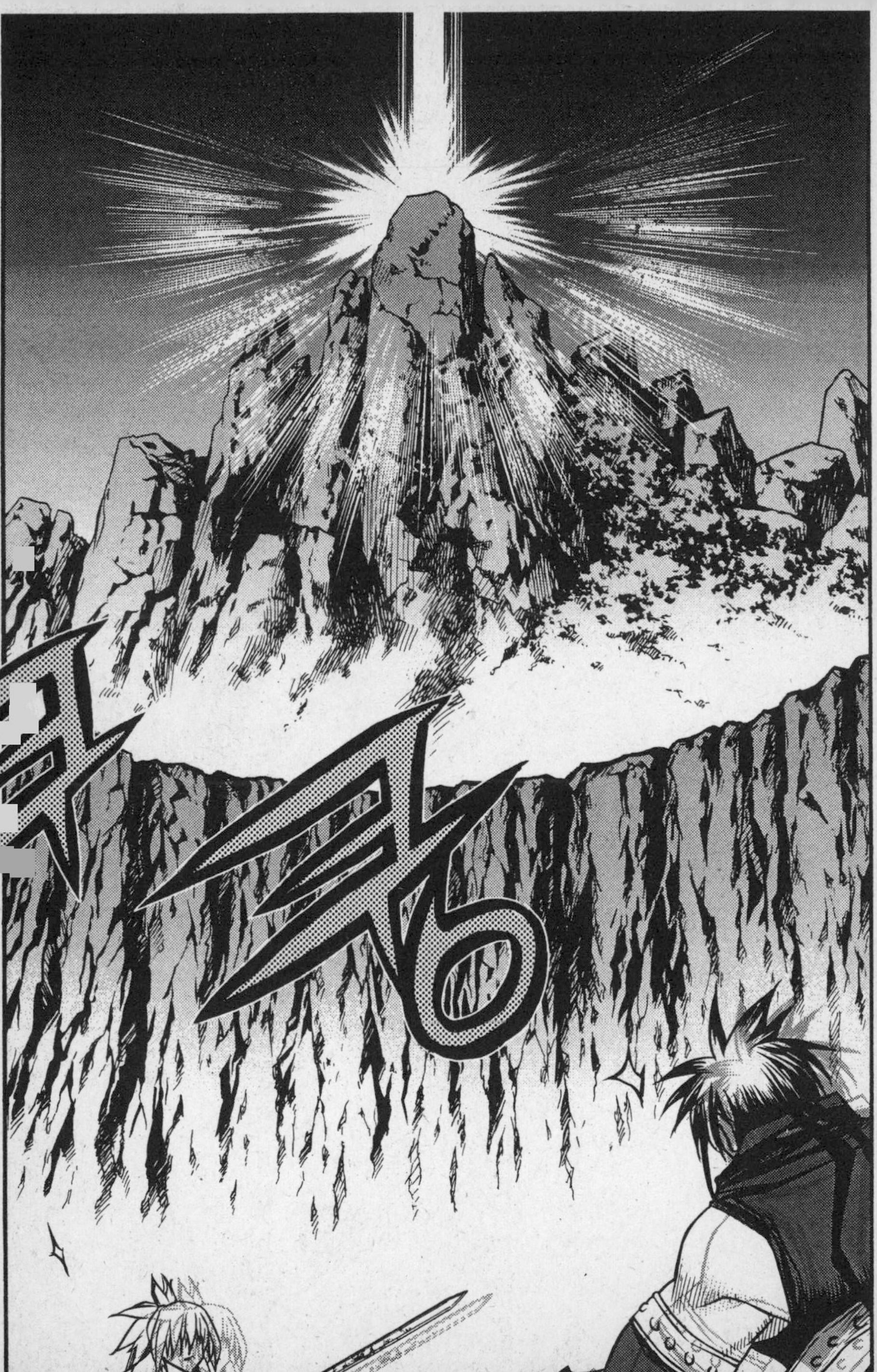

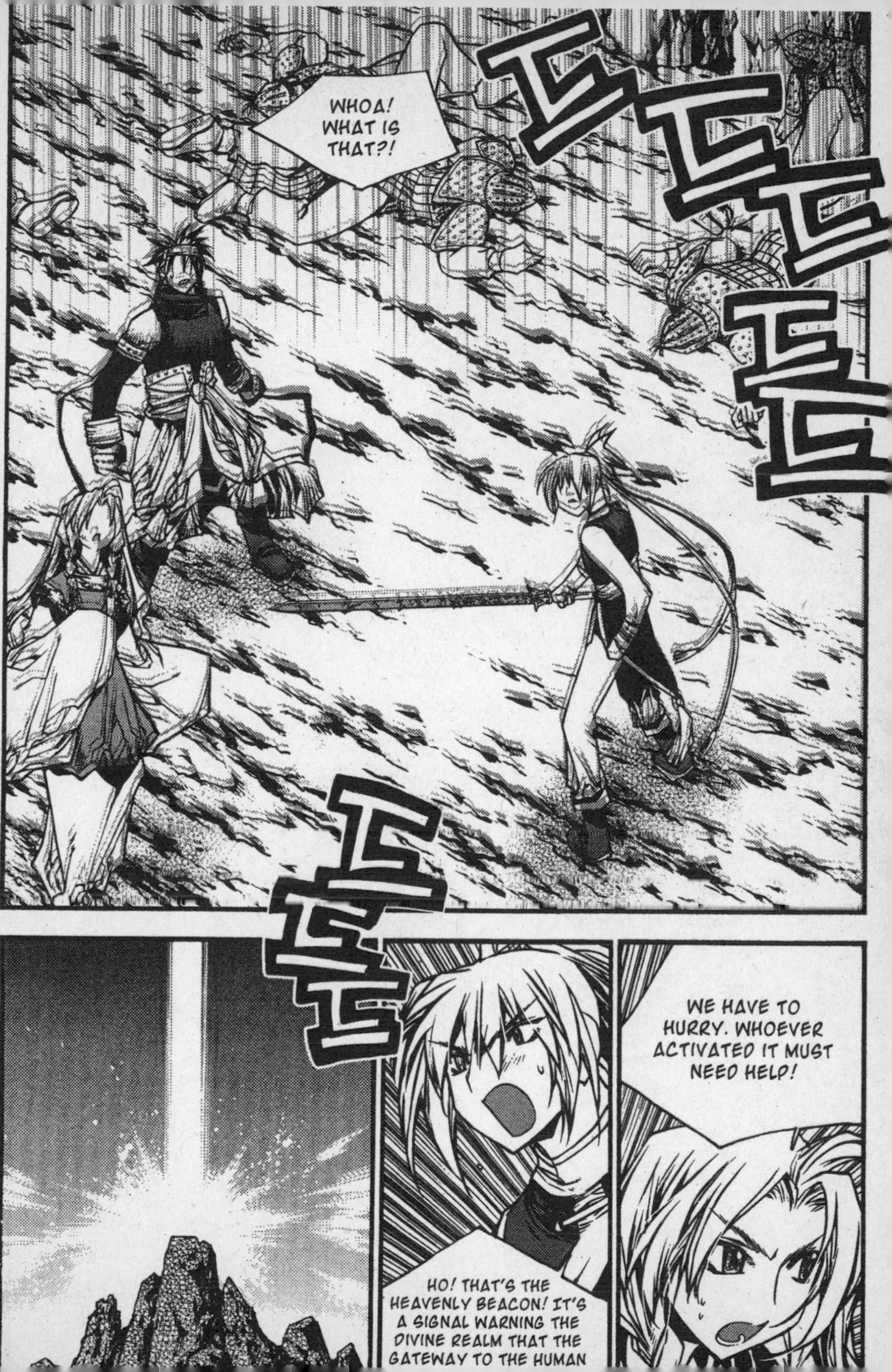
WHOA! WHAT IS THAT?!
HO! THAT'S THE HEAVENLY BEACON! IT'S A SIGNAL WARNING THE DIVINE REALM THAT THE GATEWAY TO THE HUMAN
WE HAVE TO HURRY. WHOEVER ACTIVATED IT MUST NEED HELP!

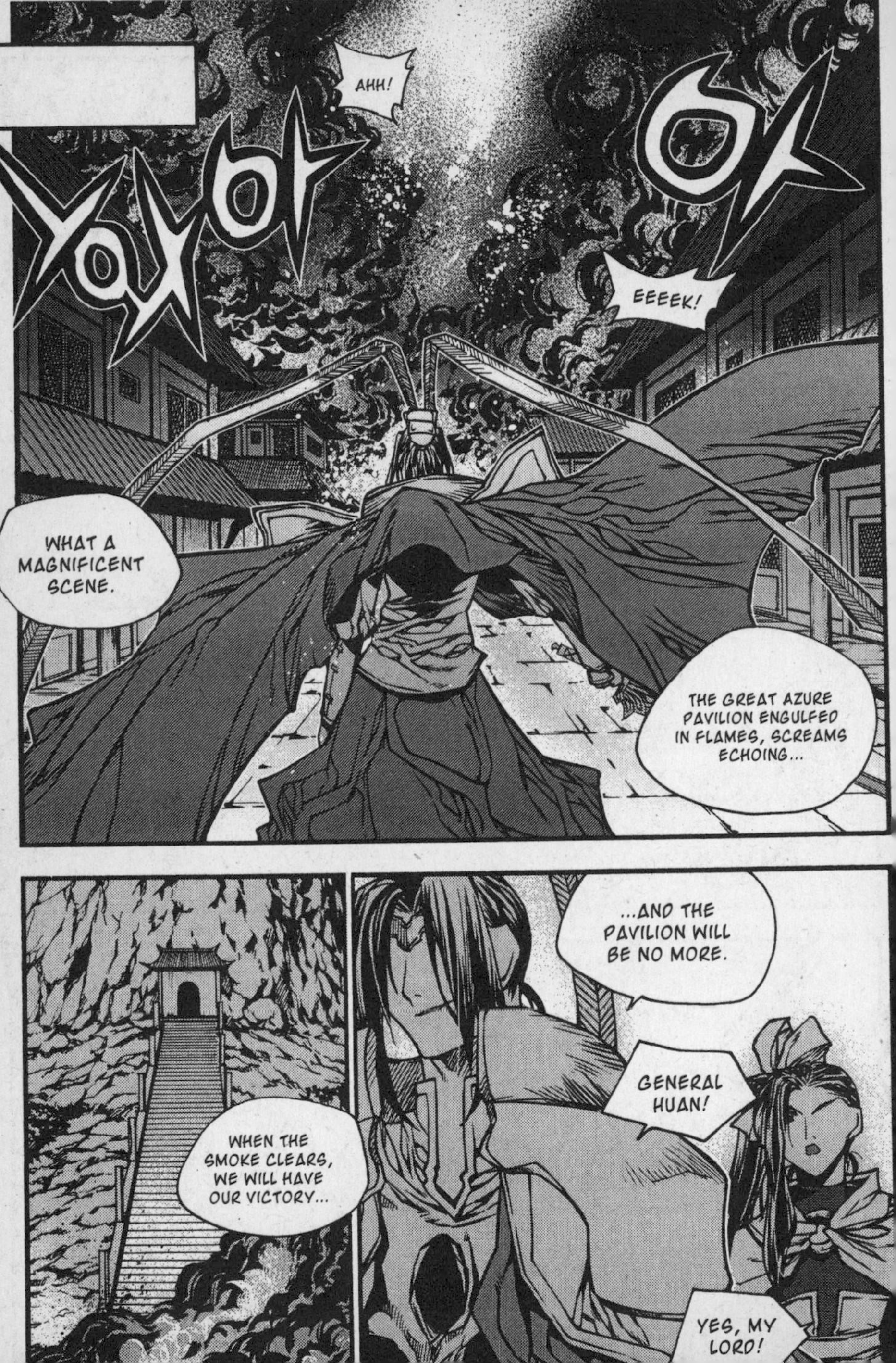
AHH!
EEEEK!
WHAT A MAGNIFICENT SCENE.
THE GREAT AZURE PAVILION ENGULFED IN FLAMES, SCREAMS ECHOING...
WHEN THE SMOKE CLEARS, WE WILL HAVE OUR VICTORY...
...AND THE PAVILION WILL BE NO MORE.
GENERAL HUAN!
YES, MY LORD!

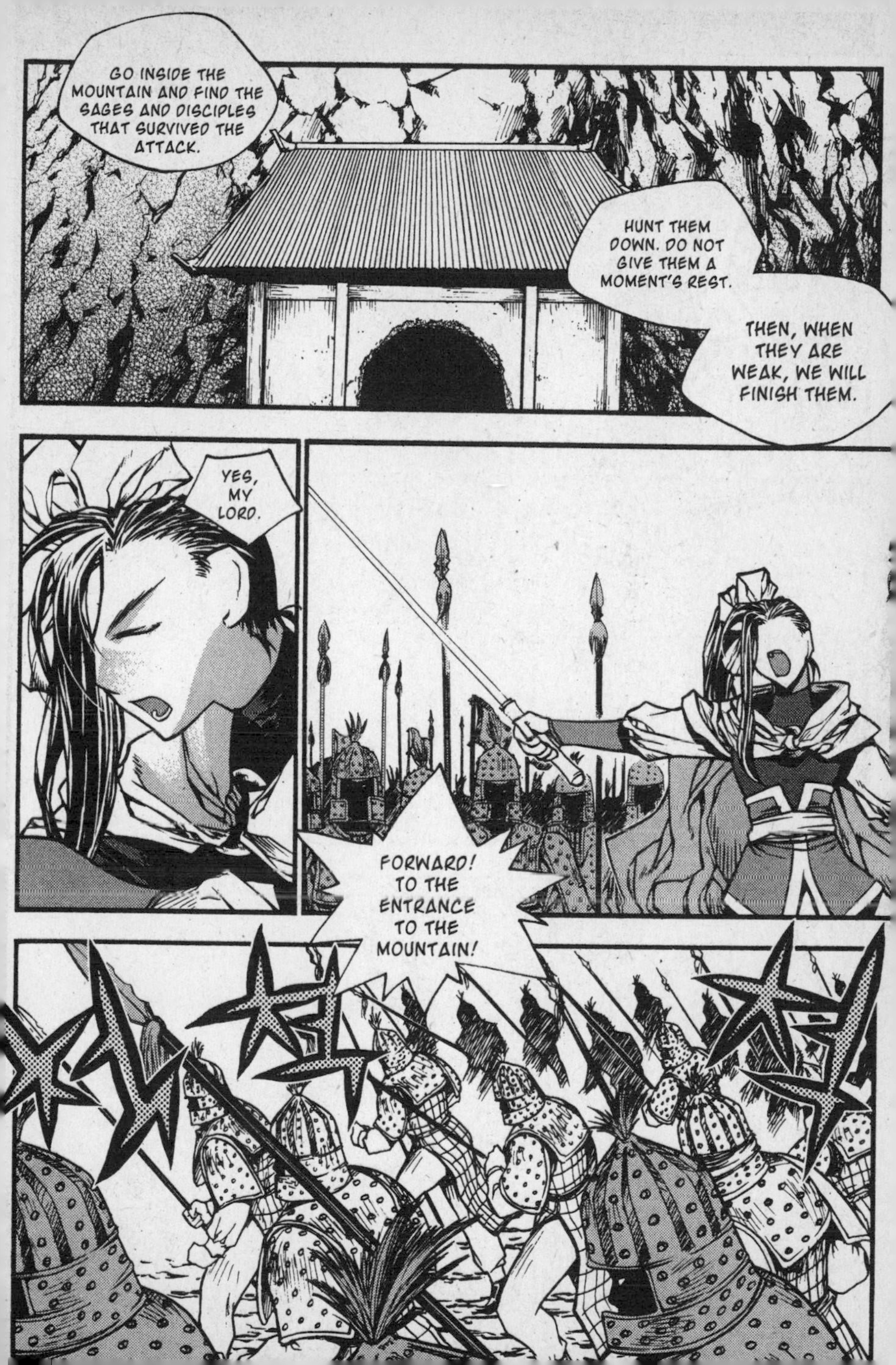
GO INSIDE THE MOUNTAIN AND FIND THE SAGES AND DISCIPLES THAT SURVIVED THE ATTACK.
HUNT THEM DOWN. DO NOT GIVE THEM A MOMENT'S REST.
THEN, WHEN THEY ARE WEAK, WE WILL FINISH THEM.
YES, MY LORD.
FORWARD! TO THE ENTRANCE TO THE MOUNTAIN!

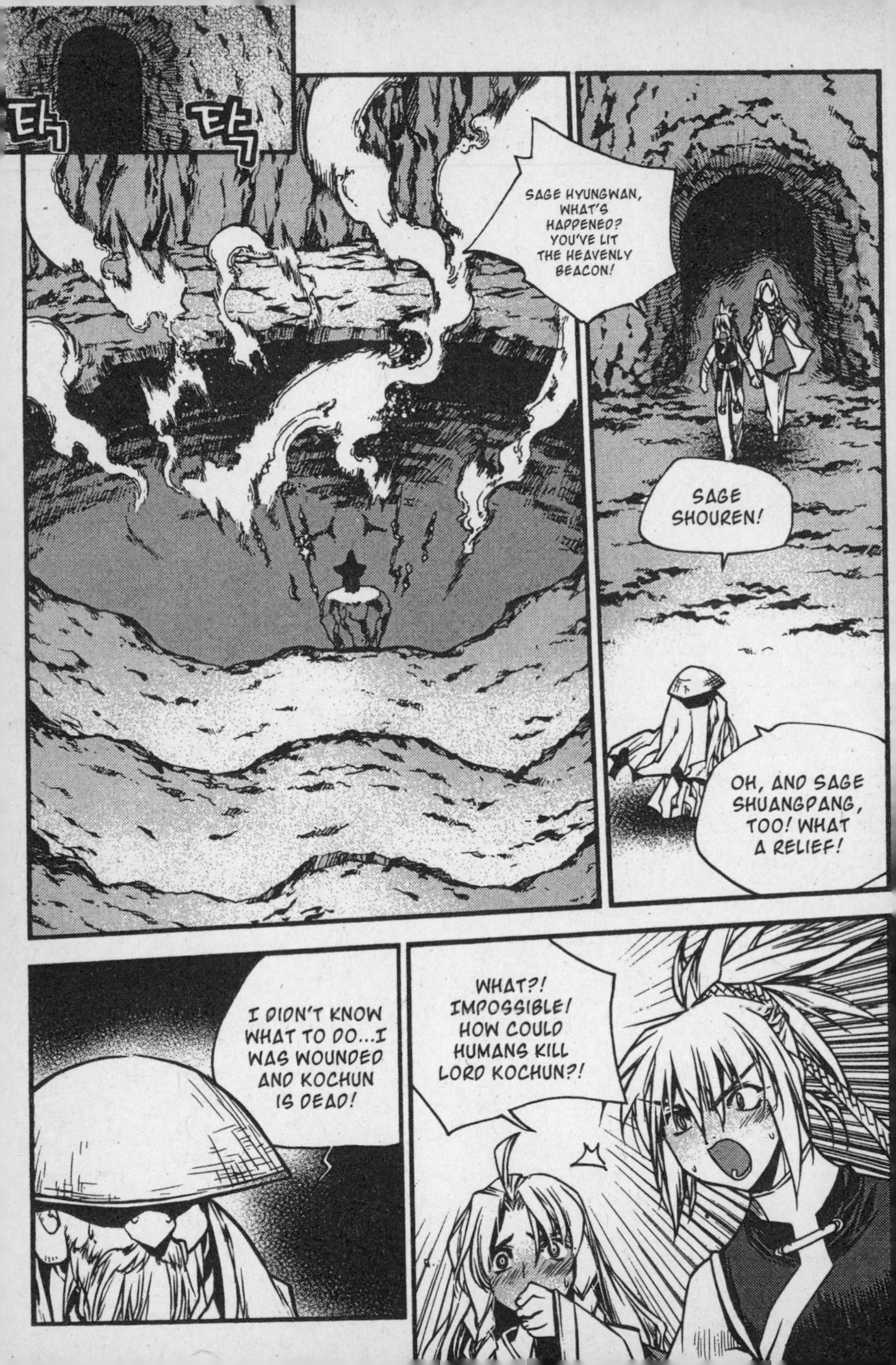

탁
탁
SAGE HYUNGWAN, WHAT'S HAPPENED? YOU'VE LIT THE HEAVENLY BEACON!
SAGE SHOUREN!
OH, AND SAGE SHUANGPANG, TOO! WHAT A RELIEF!
I DIDN'T KNOW WHAT TO DO...I WAS WOUNDED AND KOCHUN IS DEAD!
WHAT?! IMPOSSIBLE! HOW COULD HUMANS KILL LORD KOCHUN?!

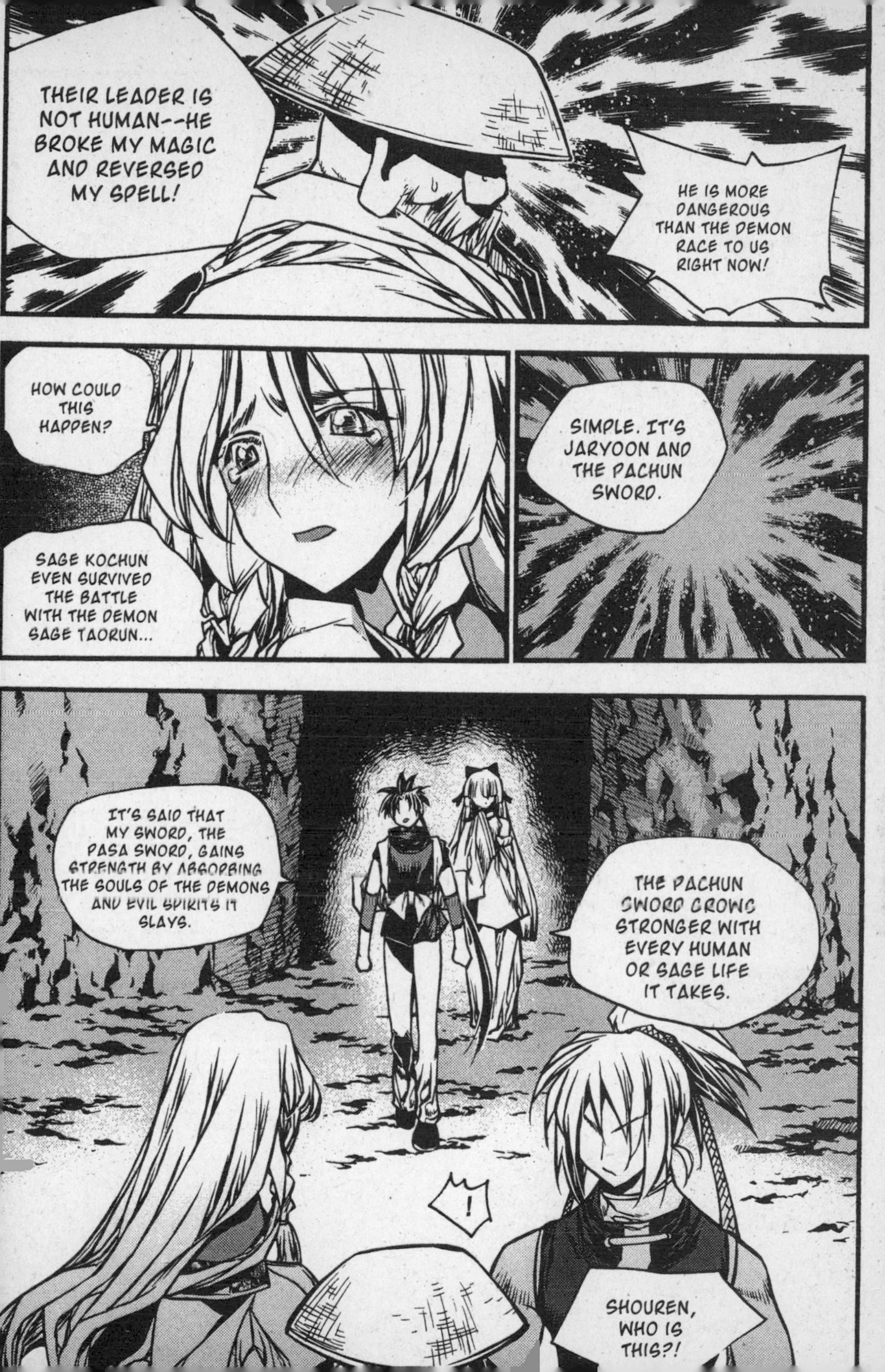
THEIR LEADER IS NOT HUMAN--HE BROKE MY MAGIC AND REVERSED MY SPELL!
HE IS MORE DANGEROUS THAN THE DEMON RACE TO US RIGHT NOW!
HOW COULD THIS HAPPEN?
SAGE KOCHUN EVEN SURVIVED THE BATTLE WITH THE DEMON SAGE TAORUN...
SIMPLE. IT'S JARYOON AND THE PACHUN SWORD.
IT'S SAID THAT MY SWORD, THE PASA SWORD, GAINS STRENGTH BY ABSORBING THE SOULS OF THE DEMONS AND EVIL SPIRITS IT SLAYS.
THE PACHUN SWORD GROWS STRONGER WITH EVERY HUMAN OR SAGE LIFE IT TAKES.
!
SHOUREN, WHO IS THIS?!

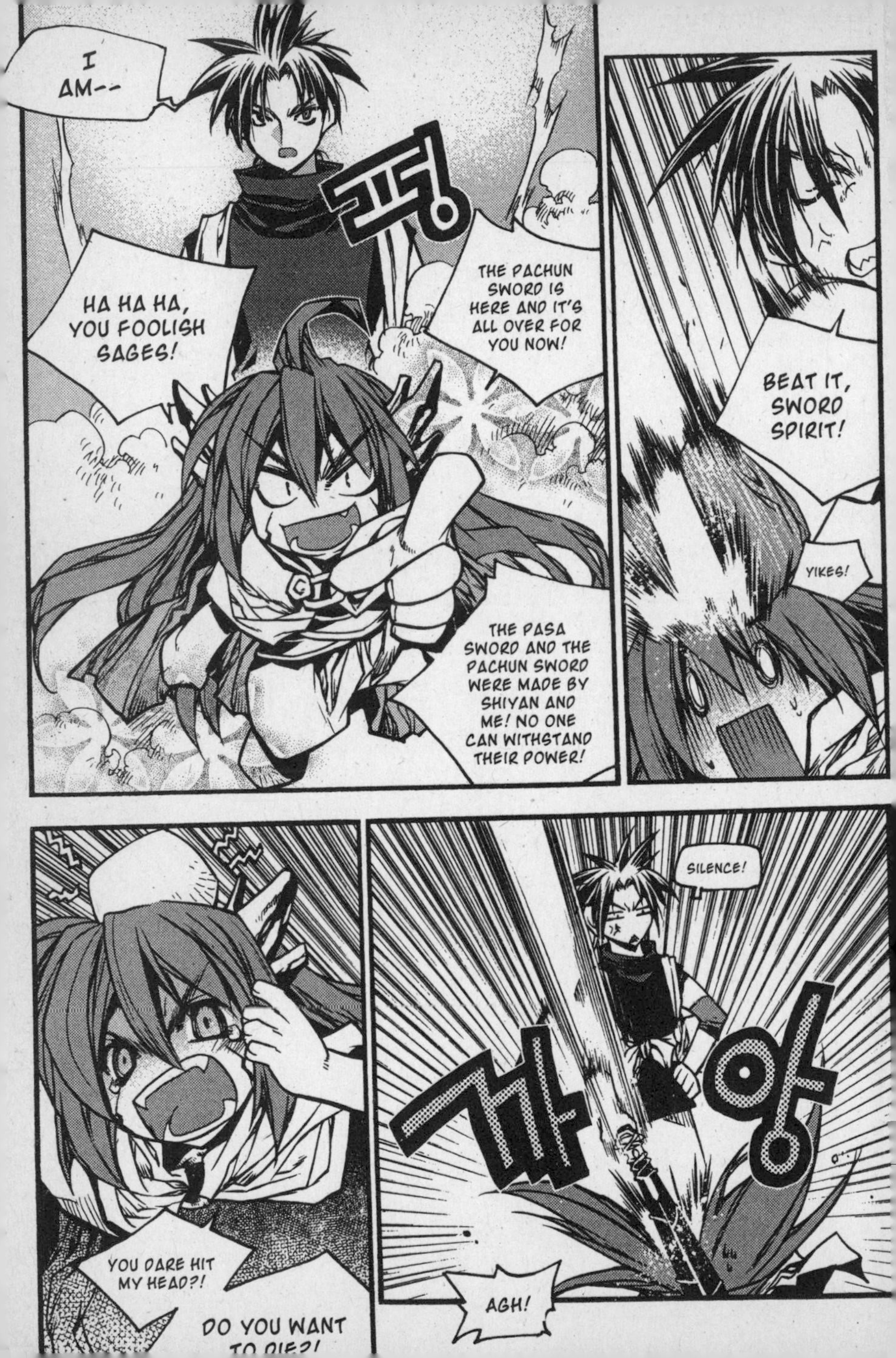
I AM--
HA HA HA, YOU FOOLISH SAGES!
THE PACHUN SWORD IS HERE AND IT'S ALL OVER FOR YOU NOW!
THE PASA SWORD AND THE PACHUN SWORD WERE MADE BY SHIYAN AND ME! NO ONE CAN WITHSTAND THEIR POWER!
BEAT IT, SWORD SPIRIT!
YIKES!
YOU DARE HIT MY HEAD?!
DO YOU WANT TO DIE?!
SILENCE!
AGH!

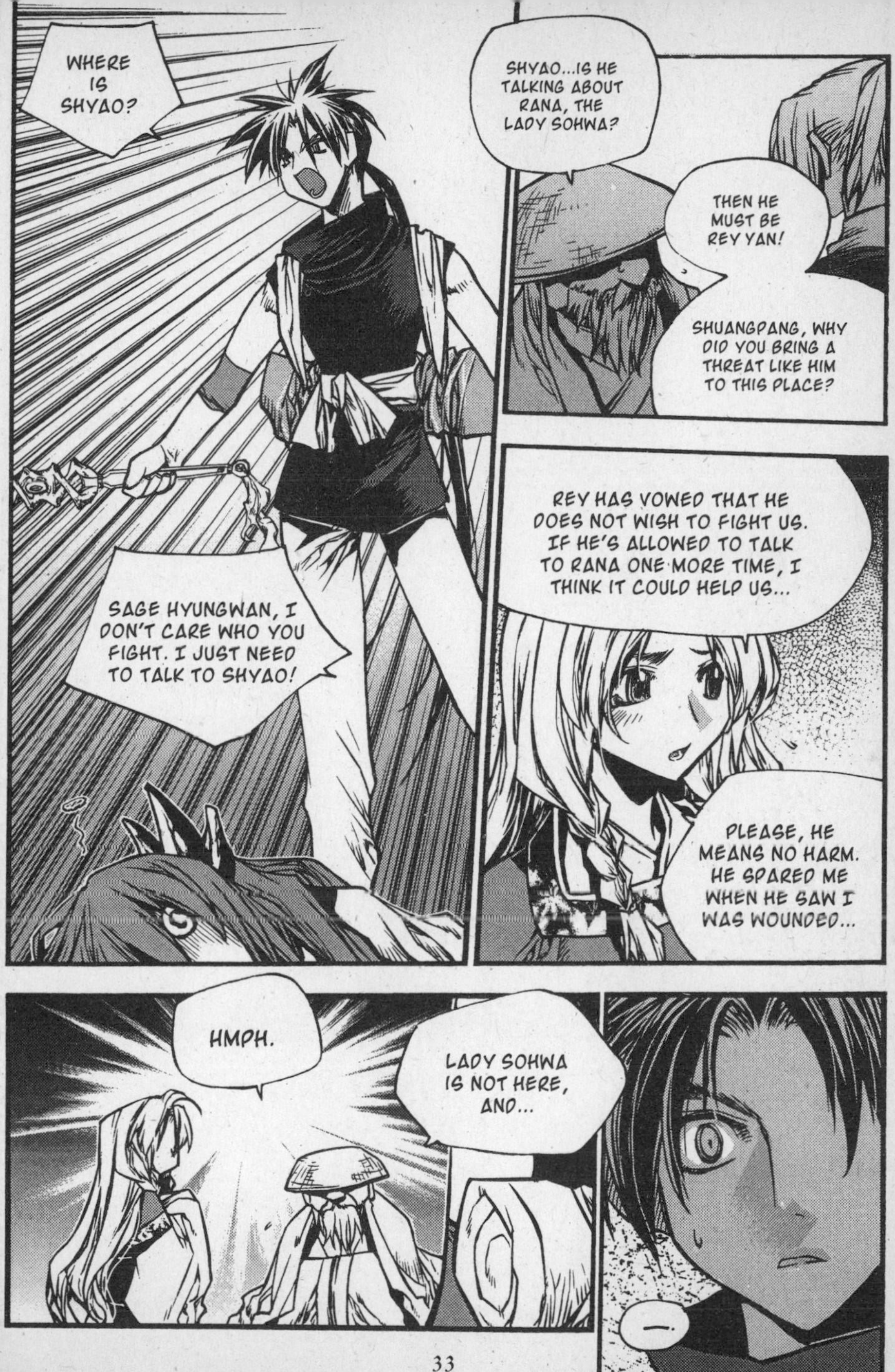
WHERE IS SHYAO?
SAGE HYUNGWAN, I DON'T CARE WHO YOU FIGHT. I JUST NEED TO TALK TO SHYAO!
SHYAO...IS HE TALKING ABOUT RANA, THE LADY SOHWA?
THEN HE MUST BE REY YAN!
SHUANGPANG, WHY DID YOU BRING A THREAT LIKE HIM TO THIS PLACE?
REY HAS VOWED THAT HE DOES NOT WISH TO FIGHT US. IF HE'S ALLOWED TO TALK TO RANA ONE MORE TIME, I THINK IT COULD HELP US...
PLEASE, HE MEANS NO HARM. HE SPARED ME WHEN HE SAW I WAS WOUNDED...
HMPH.
LADY SOHWA IS NOT HERE, AND...
—.

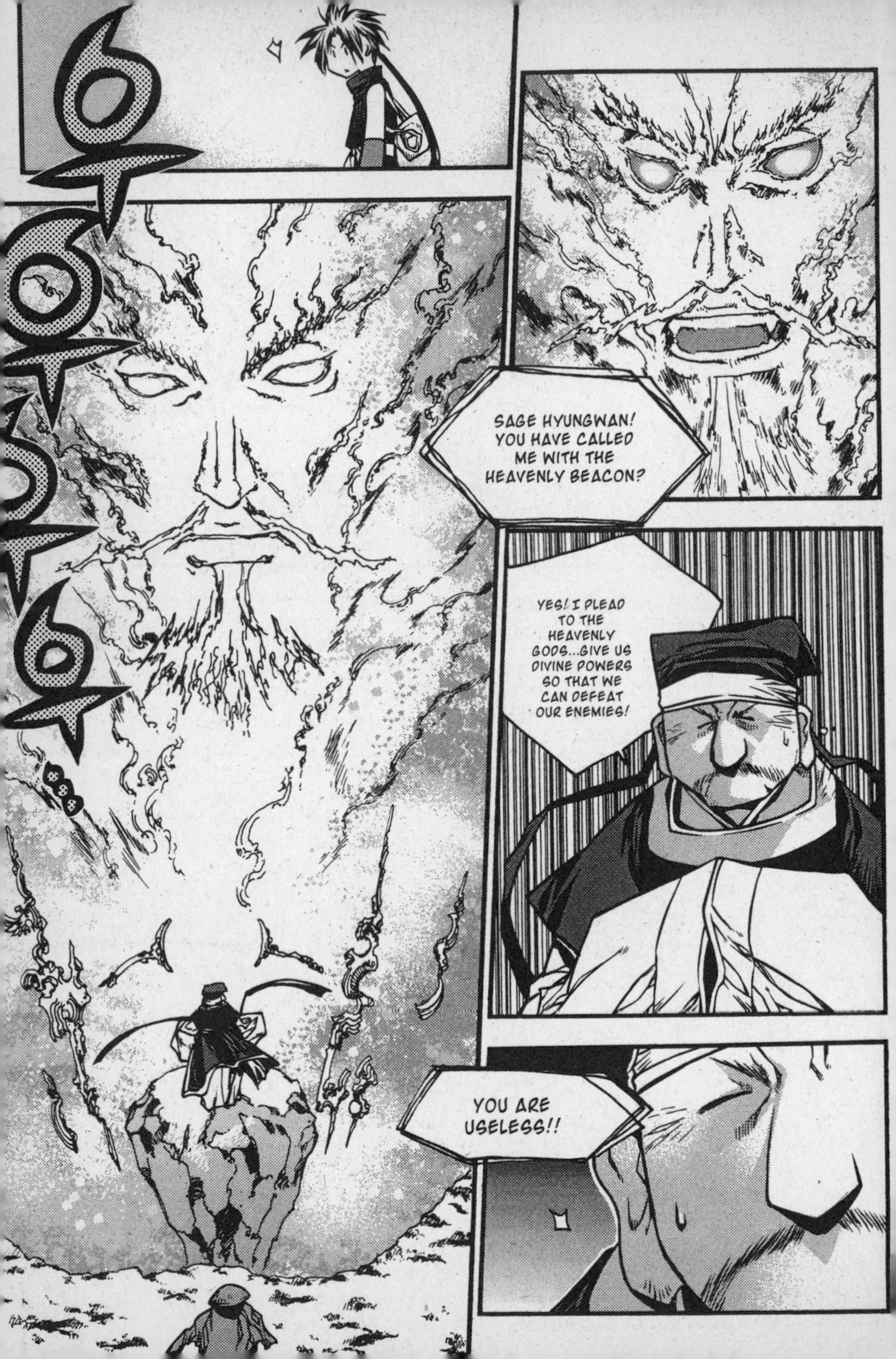
SAGE HYUNGWAN! YOU HAVE CALLED ME WITH THE HEAVENLY BEACON?
YES! I PLEAD TO THE HEAVENLY GODS...GIVE US DIVINE POWERS SO THAT WE CAN DEFEAT OUR ENEMIES!
YOU ARE USELESS!!

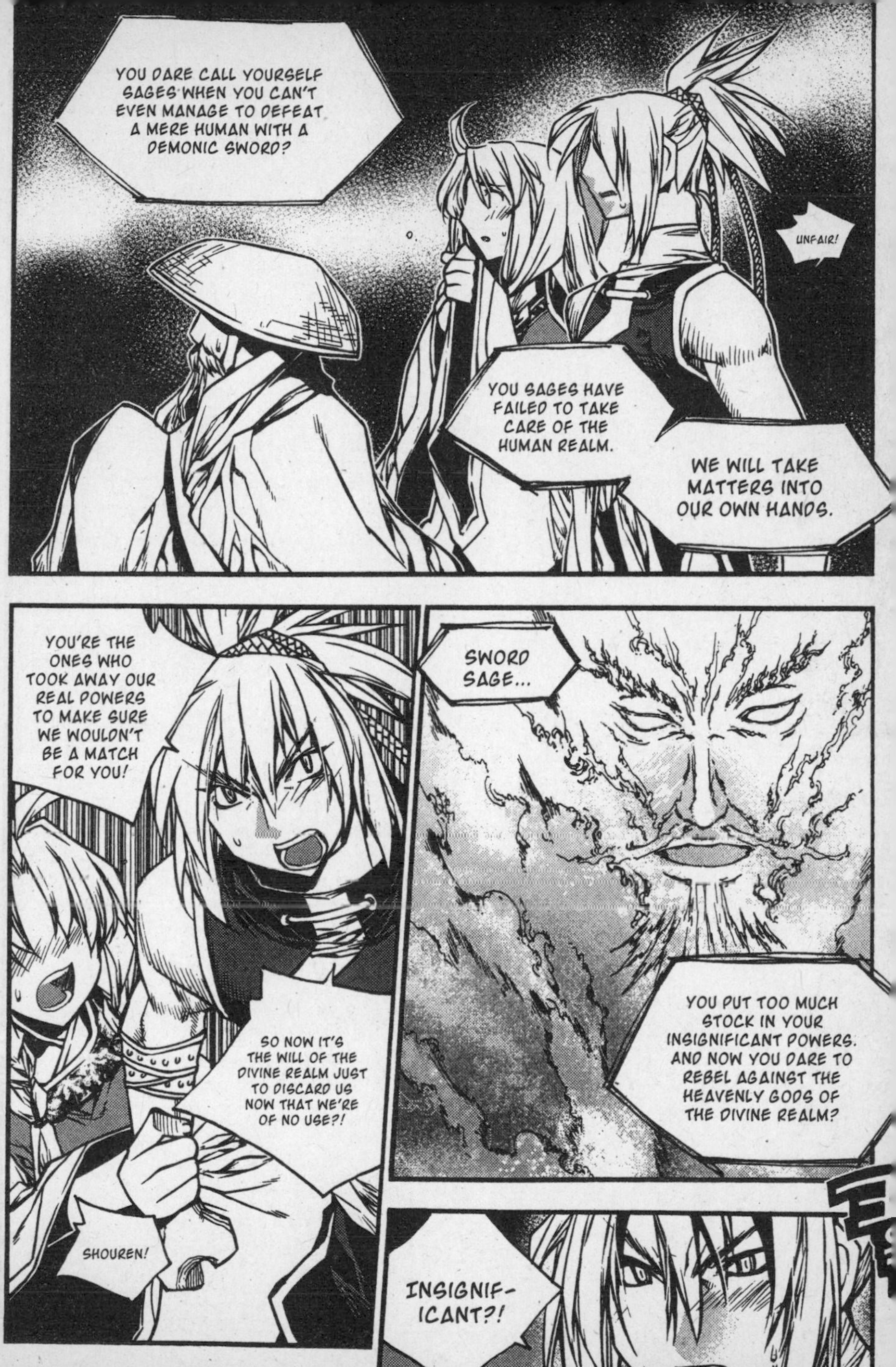
YOU DARE CALL YOURSELF SAGES WHEN YOU CAN'T EVEN MANAGE TO DEFEAT A MERE HUMAN WITH A DEMONIC SWORD?
UNFAIR!
YOU SAGES HAVE FAILED TO TAKE CARE OF THE HUMAN REALM.
WE WILL TAKE MATTERS INTO OUR OWN HANDS.
YOU'RE THE ONES WHO TOOK AWAY OUR REAL POWERS TO MAKE SURE WE WOULDN'T BE A MATCH FOR YOU!
SO NOW IT'S THE WILL OF THE DIVINE REALM JUST TO DISCARD US NOW THAT WE'RE OF NO USE?!
SHOUREN!
SWORD SAGE...
YOU PUT TOO MUCH STOCK IN YOUR INSIGNIFICANT POWERS. AND NOW YOU DARE TO REBEL AGAINST THE HEAVENLY GODS OF THE DIVINE REALM?
INSIGNIF-ICANT?!

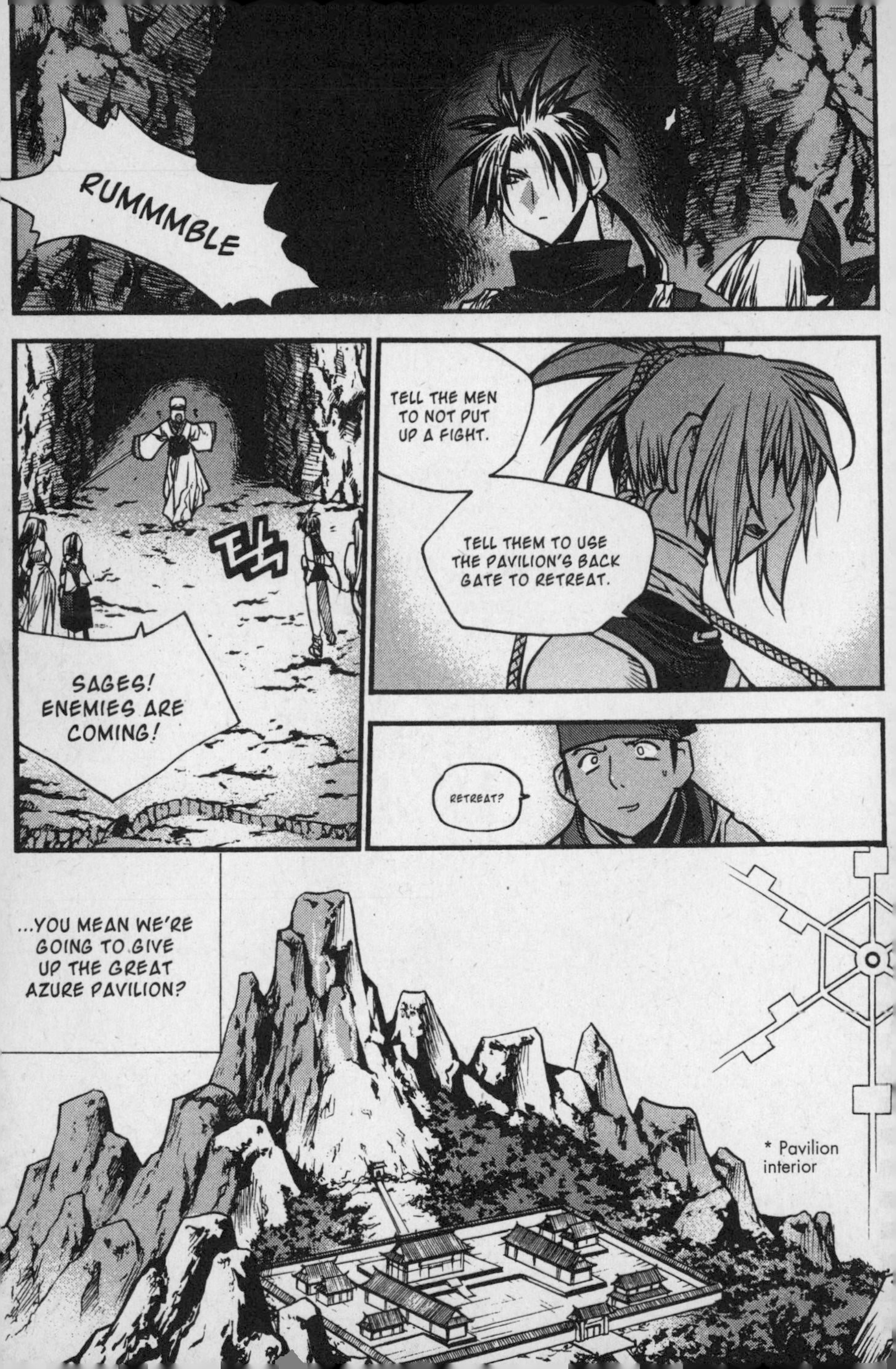
RUMMMBLE
SAGES! ENEMIES ARE COMING!
TELL THE MEN TO NOT PUT UP A FIGHT.
TELL THEM TO USE THE PAVILION'S BACK GATE TO RETREAT.
RETREAT?
...YOU MEAN WE'RE GOING TO GIVE UP THE GREAT AZURE PAVILION?
* Pavilion interior

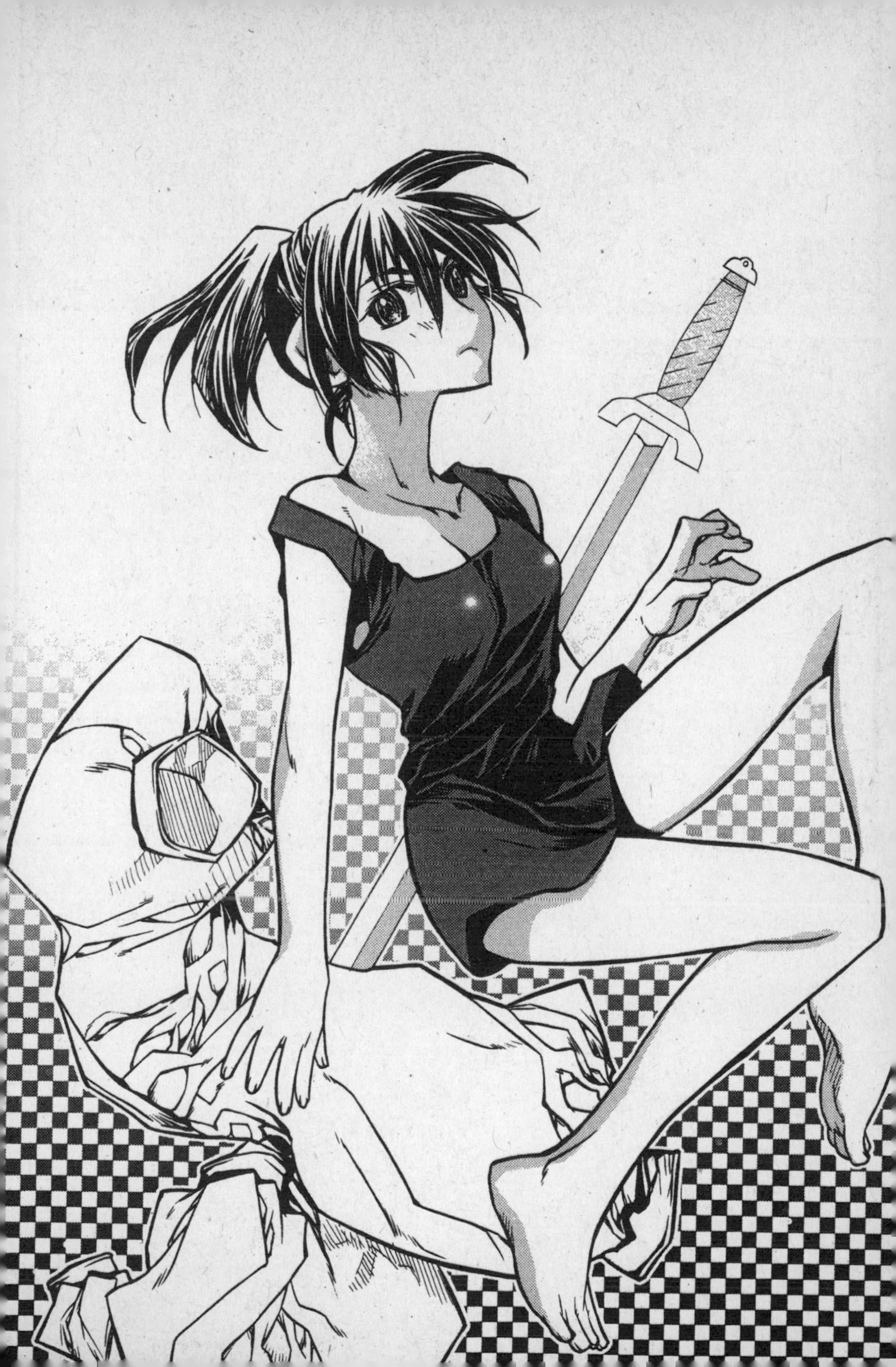

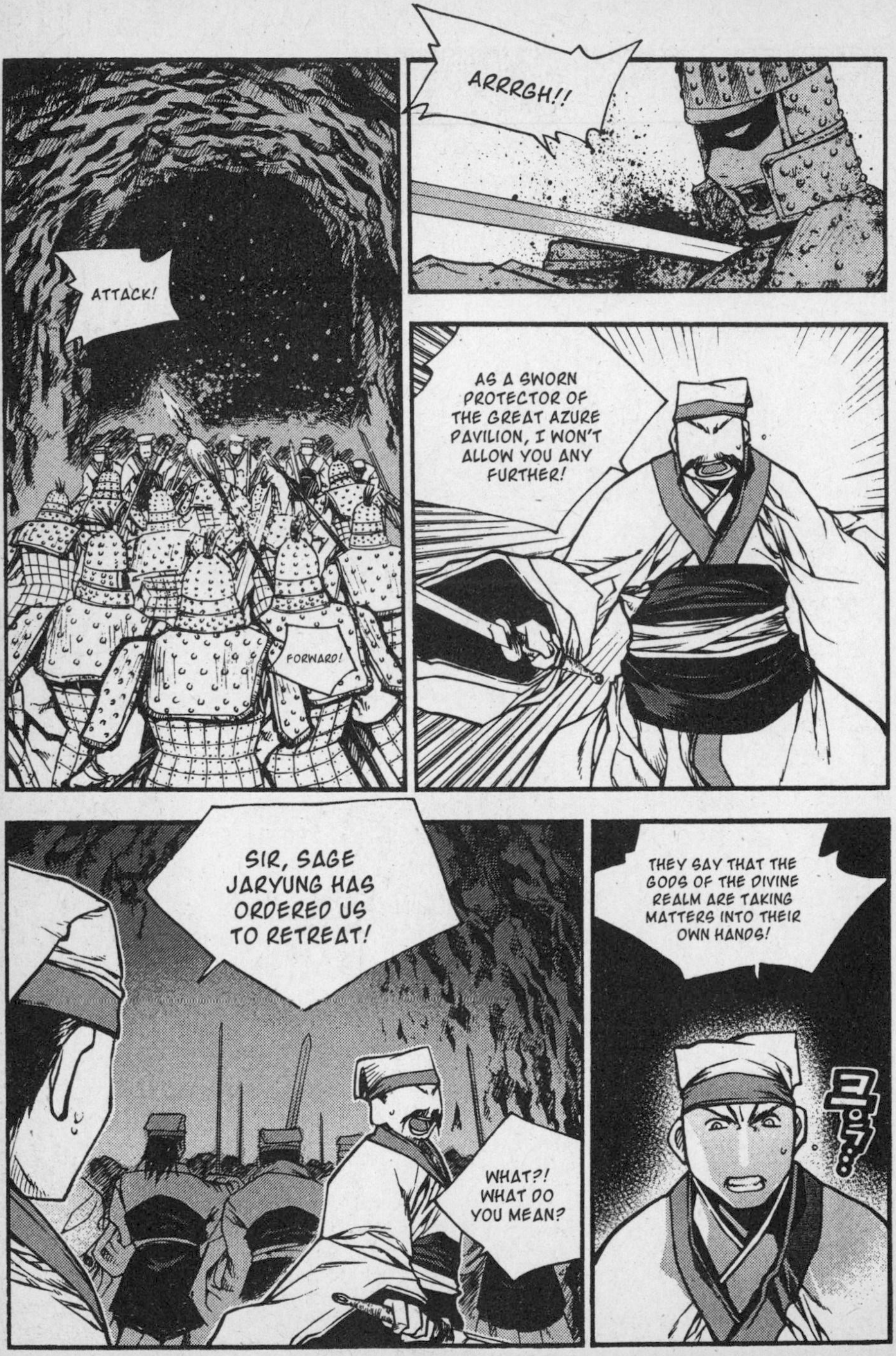
ATTACK!
FORWARD!
ARRRGH!!
AS A SWORN PROTECTOR OF THE GREAT AZURE PAVILION, I WON'T ALLOW YOU ANY FURTHER!
SIR, SAGE JARYUNG HAS ORDERED US TO RETREAT!
WHAT?! WHAT DO YOU MEAN?
THEY SAY THAT THE GODS OF THE DIVINE REALM ARE TAKING MATTERS INTO THEIR OWN HANDS!

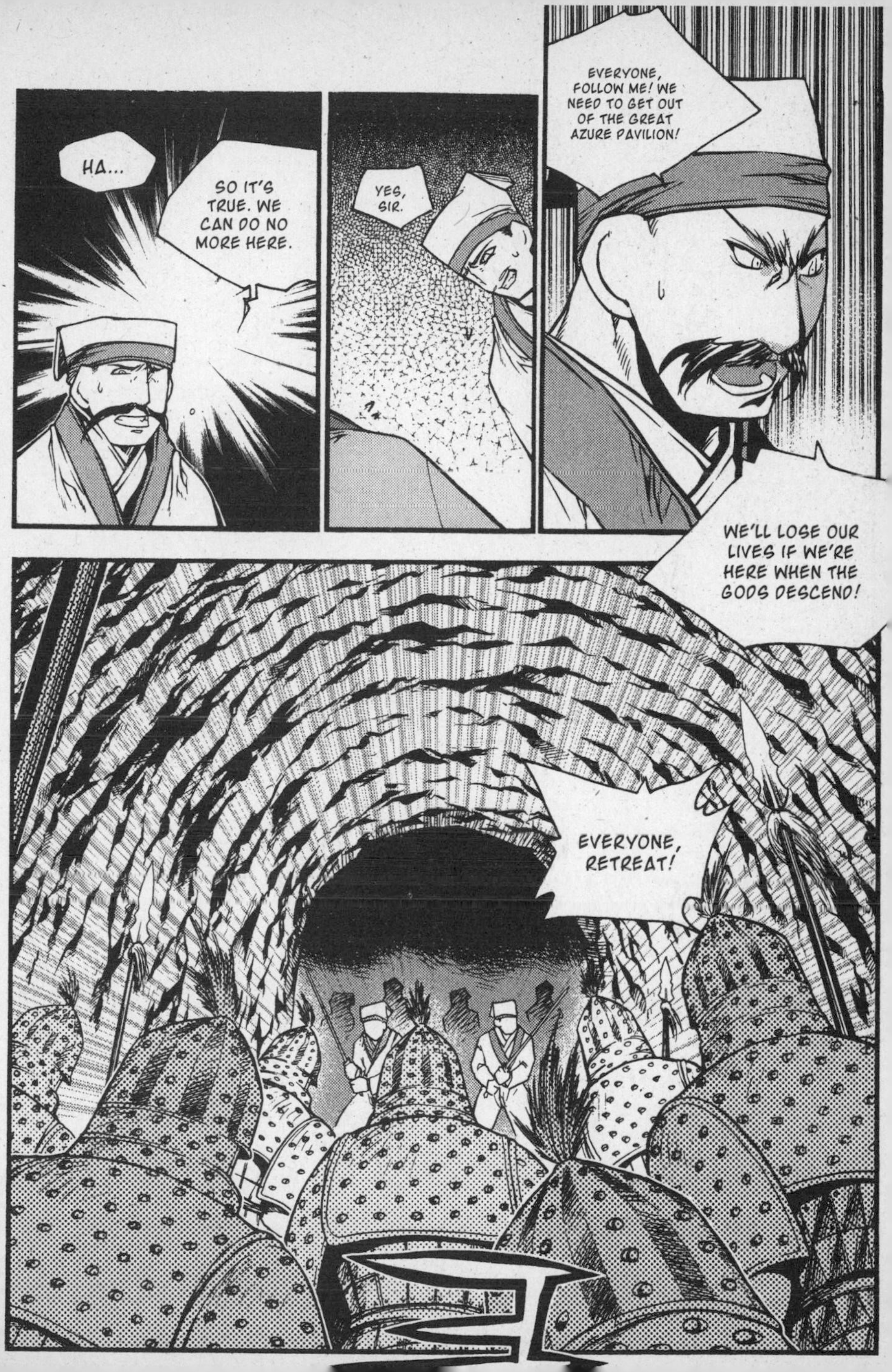
HA...
SO IT'S TRUE. WE CAN DO NO MORE HERE.
YES, SIR.
EVERYONE, FOLLOW ME! WE NEED TO GET OUT OF THE GREAT AZURE PAVILION!
WE'LL LOSE OUR LIVES IF WE'RE HERE WHEN THE GODS DESCEND!
EVERYONE, RETREAT!

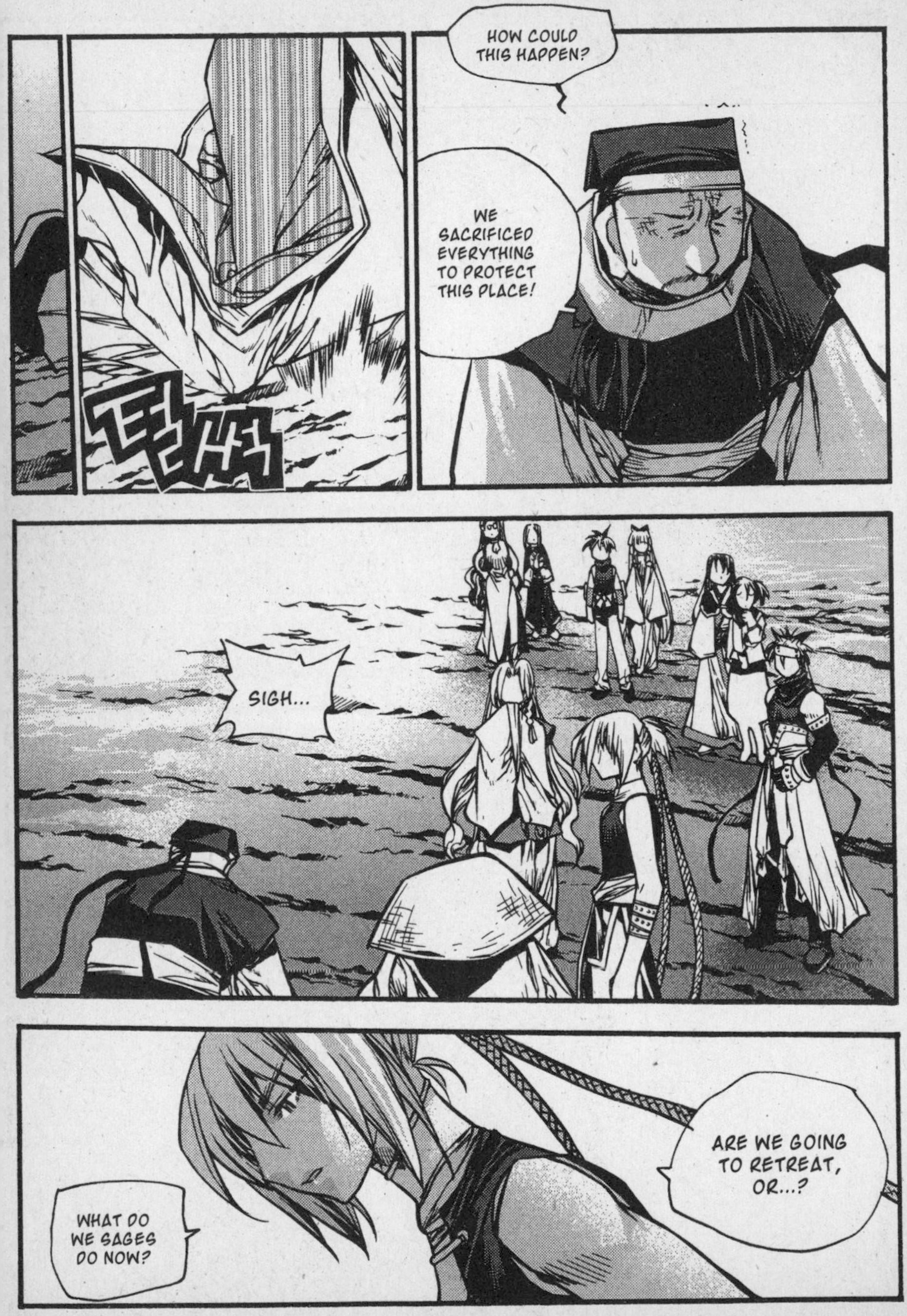
HOW COULD THIS HAPPEN?
WE SACRIFICED EVERYTHING TO PROTECT THIS PLACE!
SIGH...
ARE WE GOING TO RETREAT, OR...?
WHAT DO WE SAGES DO NOW?

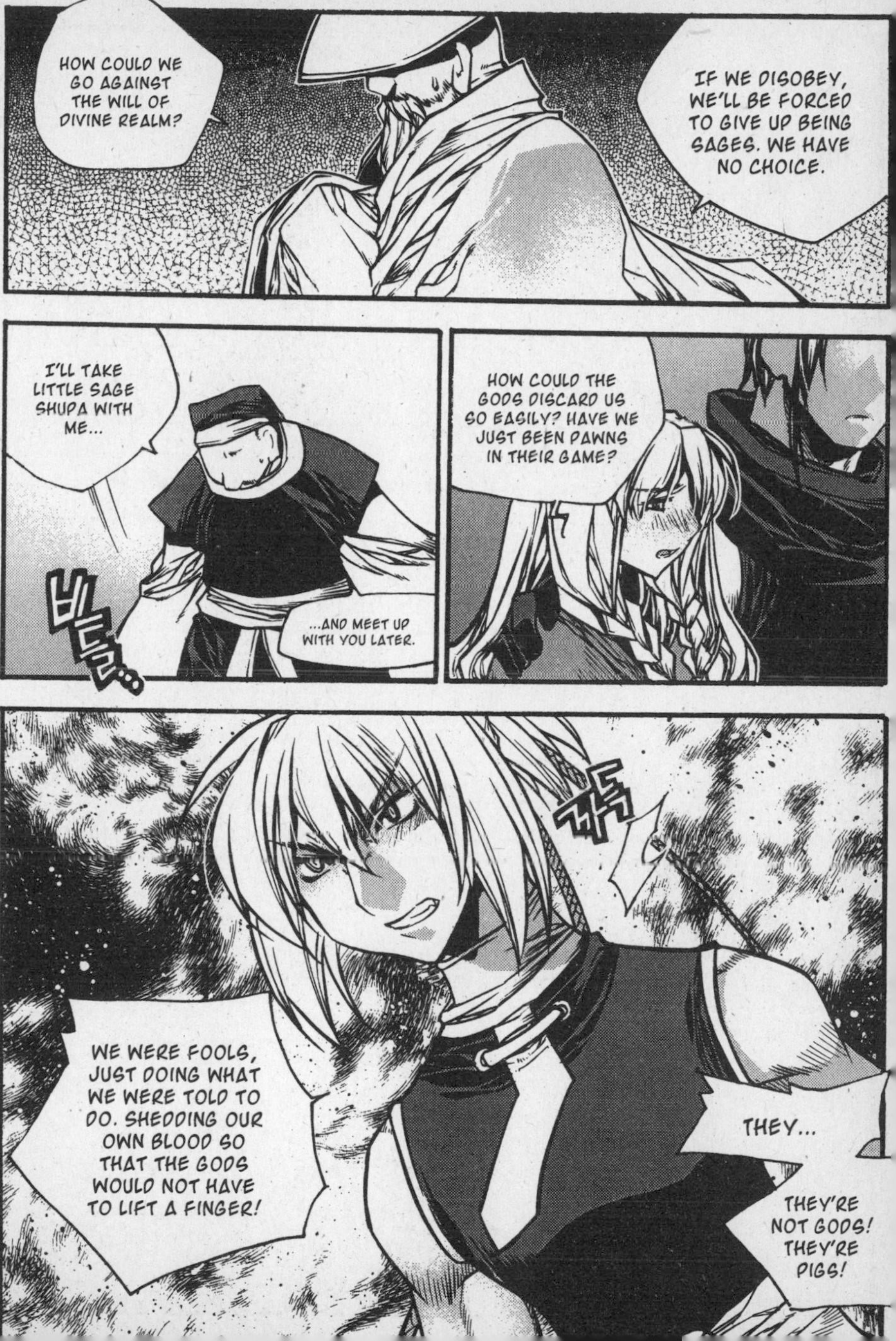
HOW COULD WE GO AGAINST THE WILL OF DIVINE REALM?
IF WE DISOBEY, WE'LL BE FORCED TO GIVE UP BEING SAGES. WE HAVE NO CHOICE.
I'LL TAKE LITTLE SAGE SHUPA WITH ME...
...AND MEET UP WITH YOU LATER.
HOW COULD THE GODS DISCARD US SO EASILY? HAVE WE JUST BEEN PAWNS IN THEIR GAME?
WE WERE FOOLS, JUST DOING WHAT WE WERE TOLD TO DO. SHEDDING OUR OWN BLOOD SO THAT THE GODS WOULD NOT HAVE TO LIFT A FINGER!
THEY...
THEY'RE NOT GODS! THEY'RE PIGS!

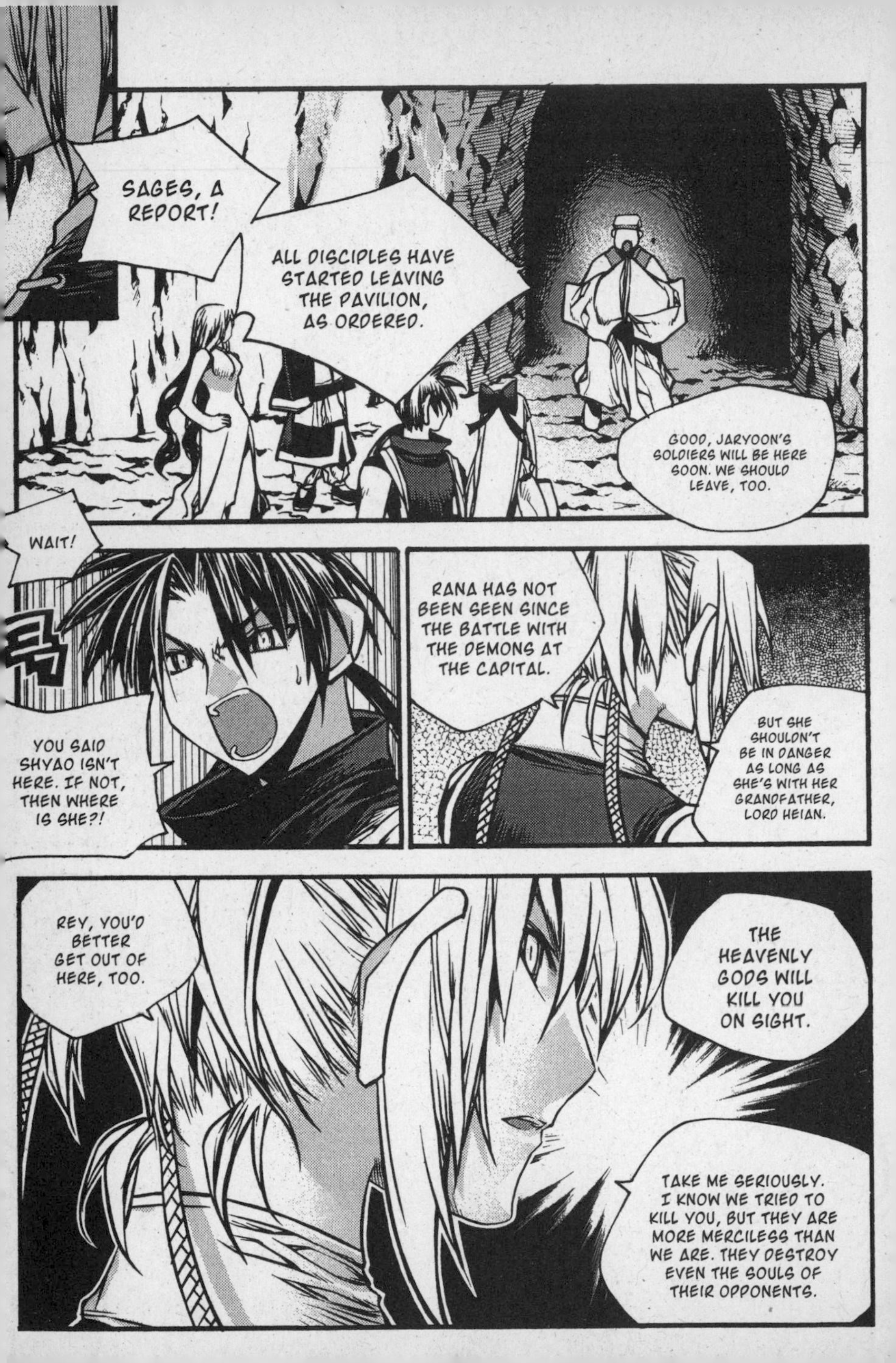
SAGES, A REPORT!
ALL DISCIPLES HAVE STARTED LEAVING THE PAVILION, AS ORDERED.
GOOD, JARYOON'S SOLDIERS WILL BE HERE SOON. WE SHOULD LEAVE, TOO.
WAIT!
YOU SAID SHYAO ISN'T HERE. IF NOT, THEN WHERE IS SHE?!
RANA HAS NOT BEEN SEEN SINCE THE BATTLE WITH THE DEMONS AT THE CAPITAL.
BUT SHE SHOULDN'T BE IN DANGER AS LONG AS SHE'S WITH HER GRANDFATHER, LORD HEIAN.
REY, YOU'D BETTER GET OUT OF HERE, TOO.
THE HEAVENLY GODS WILL KILL YOU ON SIGHT.
TAKE ME SERIOUSLY. I KNOW WE TRIED TO KILL YOU, BUT THEY ARE MORE MERCILESS THAN WE ARE. THEY DESTROY EVEN THE SOULS OF THEIR OPPONENTS.

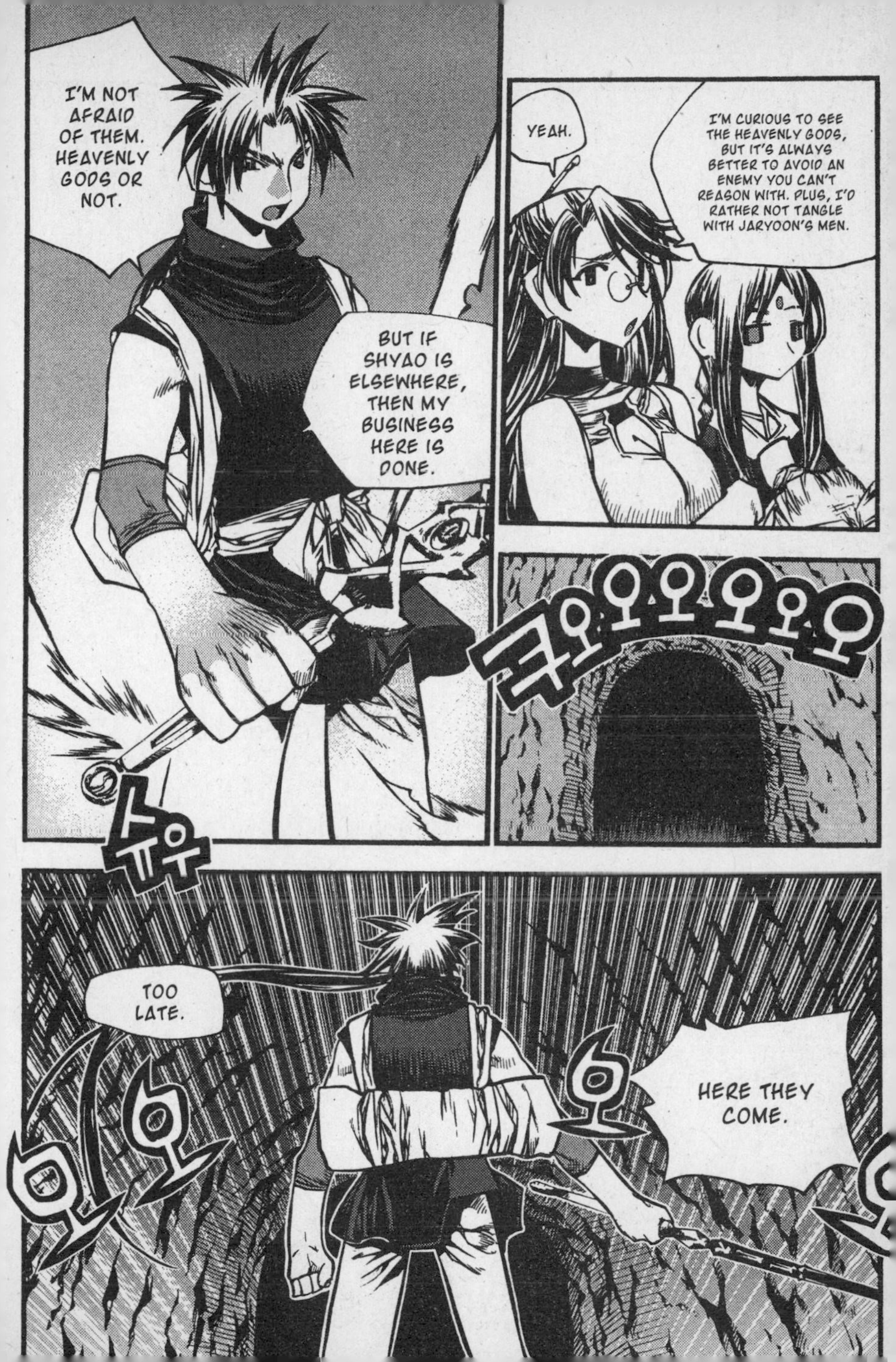
I'M NOT AFRAID OF THEM. HEAVENLY GODS OR NOT.
BUT IF SHYAO IS ELSEWHERE, THEN MY BUSINESS HERE IS DONE.
YEAH.
I'M CURIOUS TO SEE THE HEAVENLY GODS, BUT IT'S ALWAYS BETTER TO AVOID AN ENEMY YOU CAN'T REASON WITH. PLUS, I'D RATHER NOT TANGLE WITH JARYOON'S MEN.
TOO LATE.
HERE THEY COME.

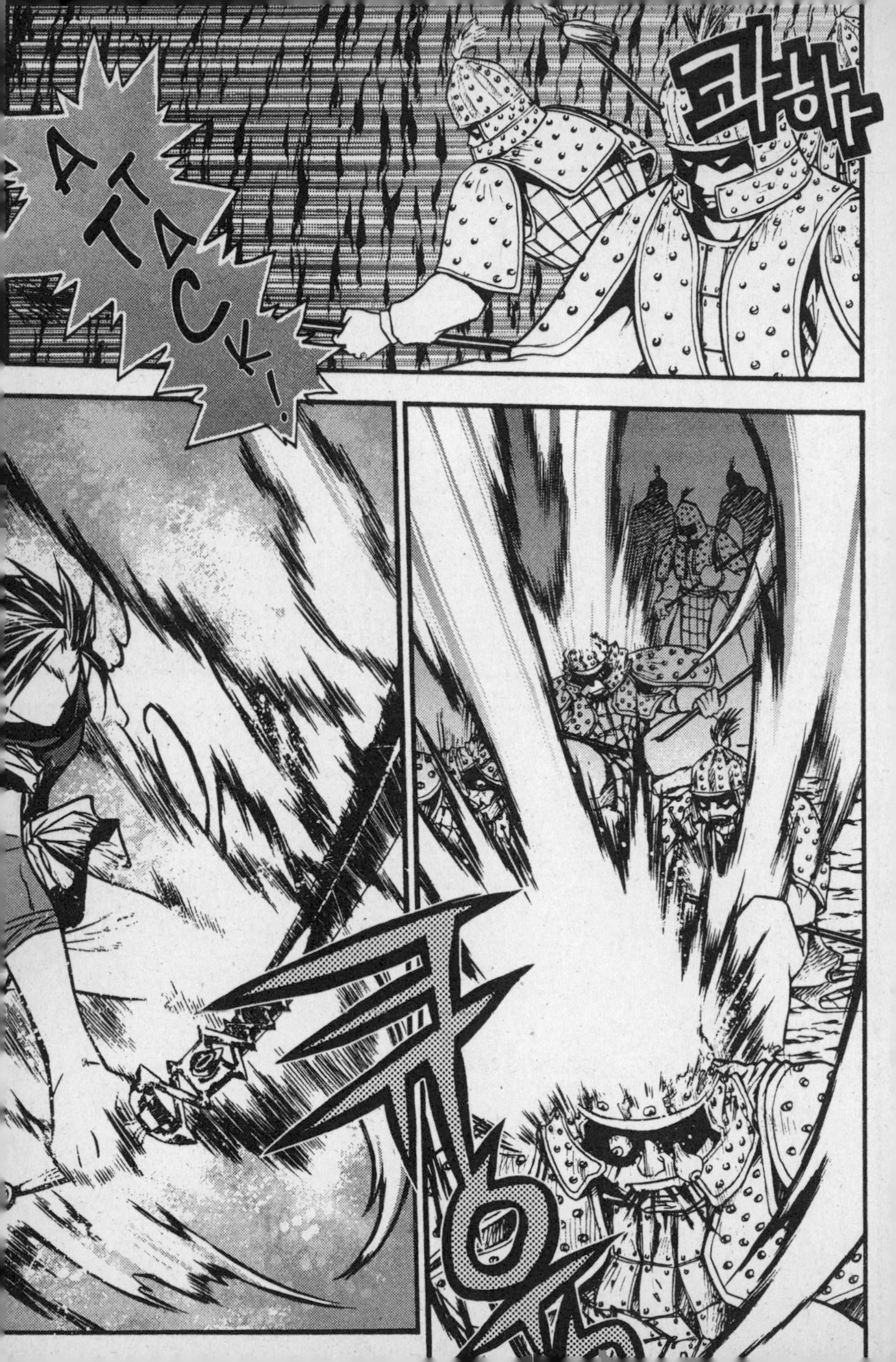
ATTACK!
콰아
쿵

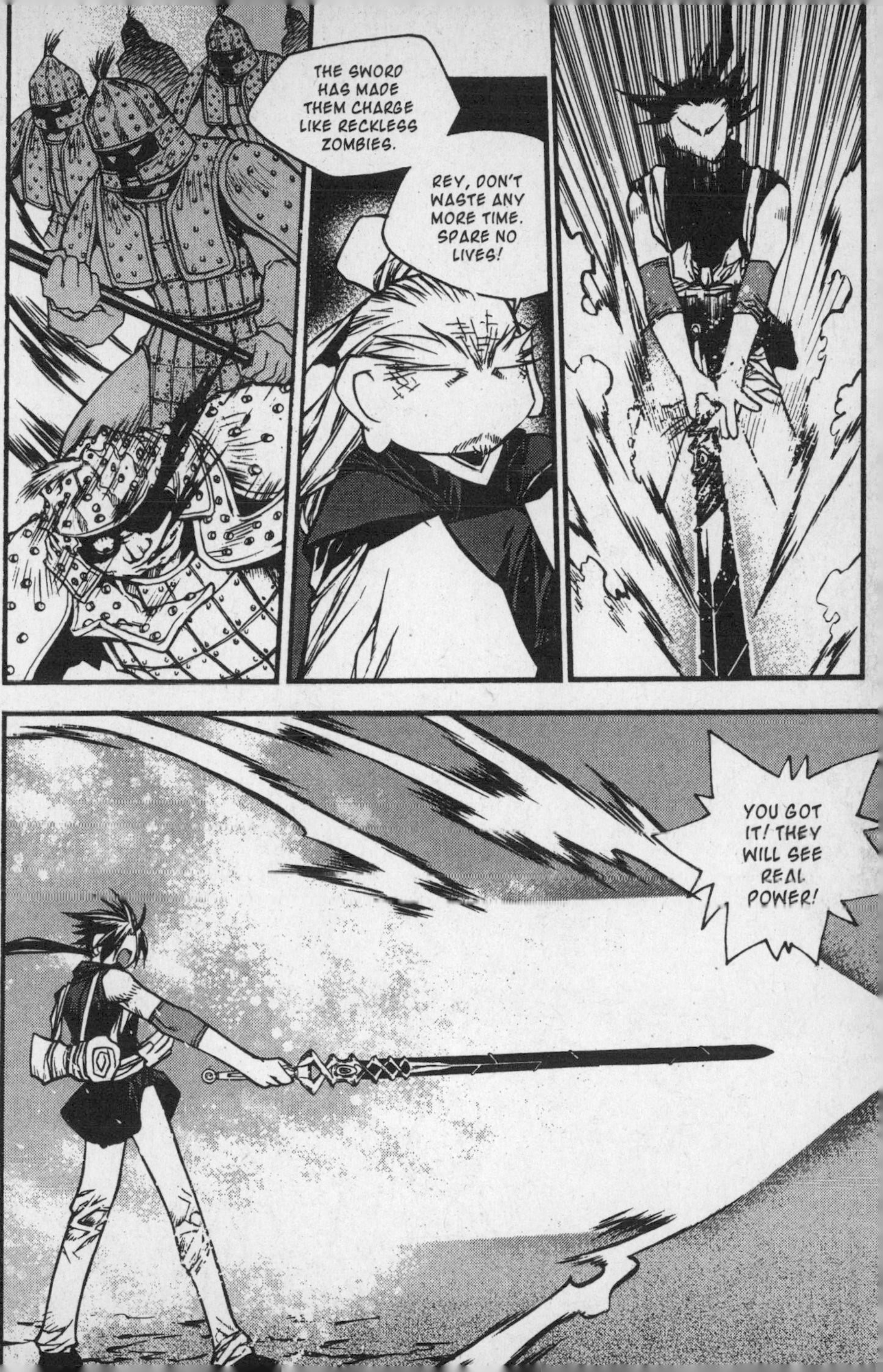
THE SWORD HAS MADE THEM CHARGE LIKE RECKLESS ZOMBIES.
REY, DON'T WASTE ANY MORE TIME. SPARE NO LIVES!
YOU GOT IT! THEY WILL SEE REAL POWER!

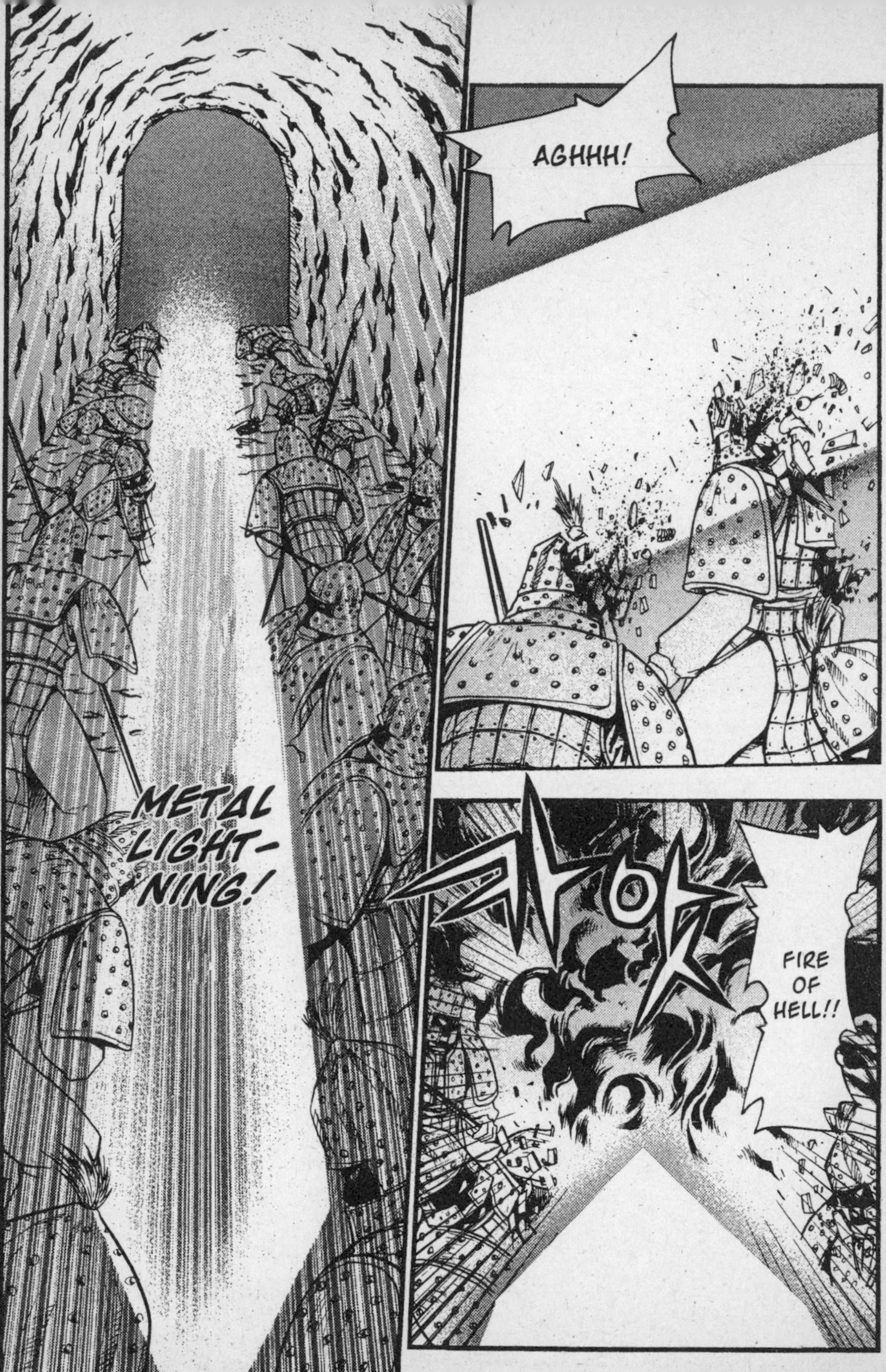
METAL LIGHT-NING!
AGHHH!
FIRE OF HELL!!

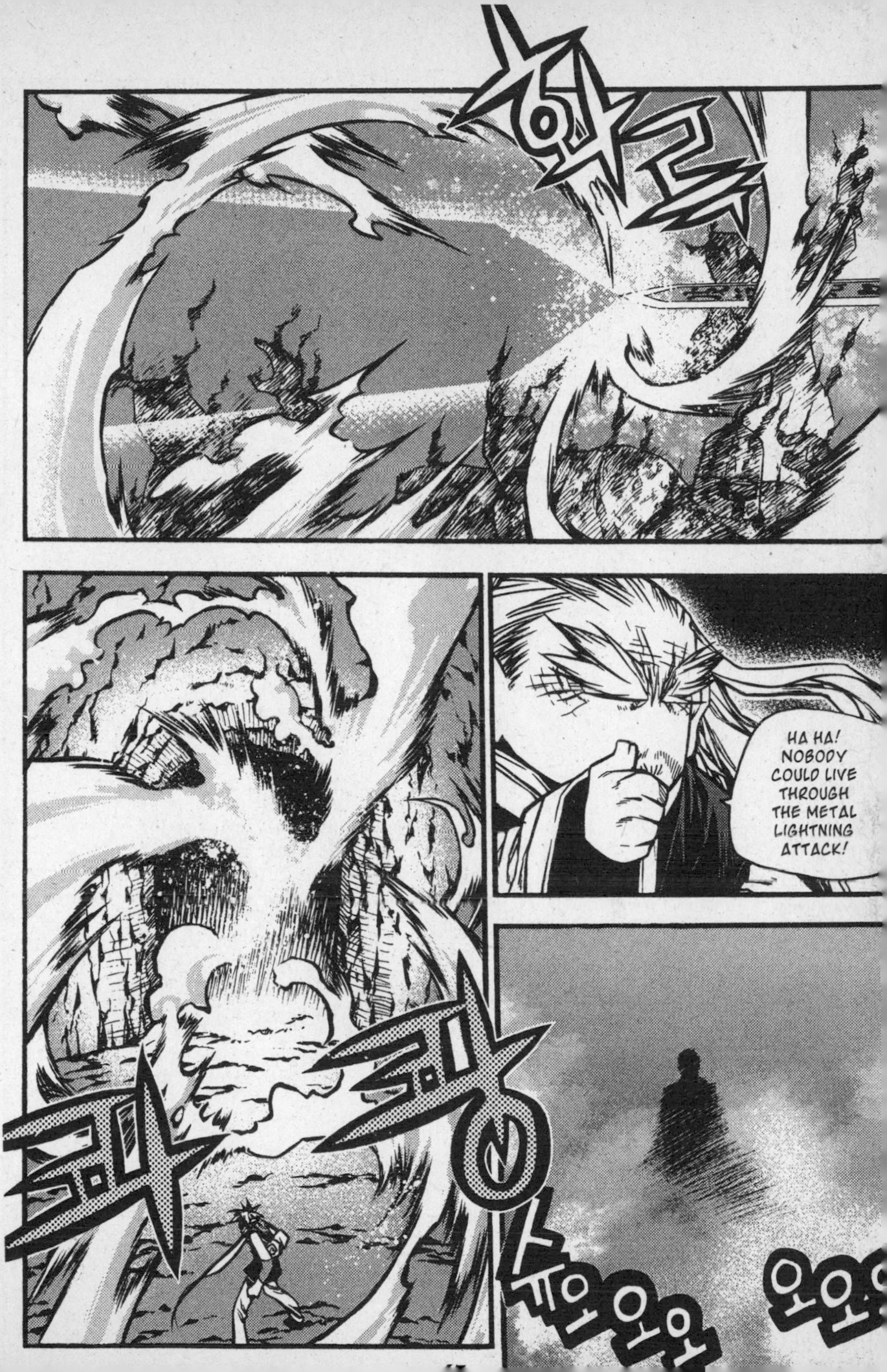
HA HA! NOBODY COULD LIVE THROUGH THE METAL LIGHTNING ATTACK!

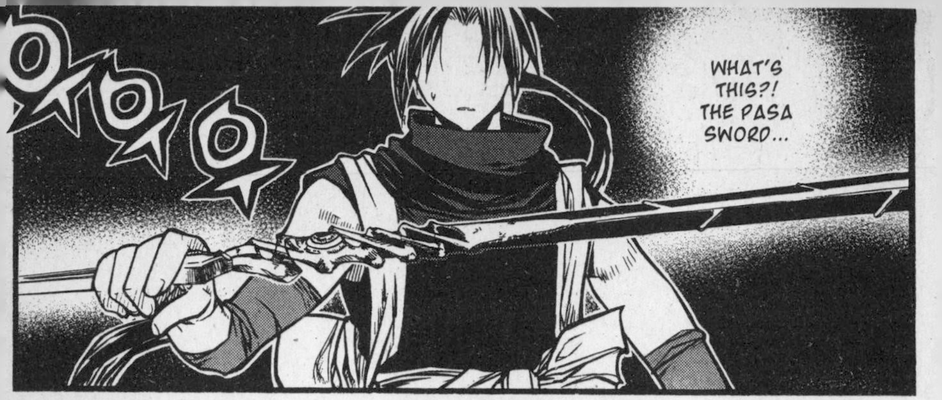
WHAT'S THIS?! THE PASA SWORD...

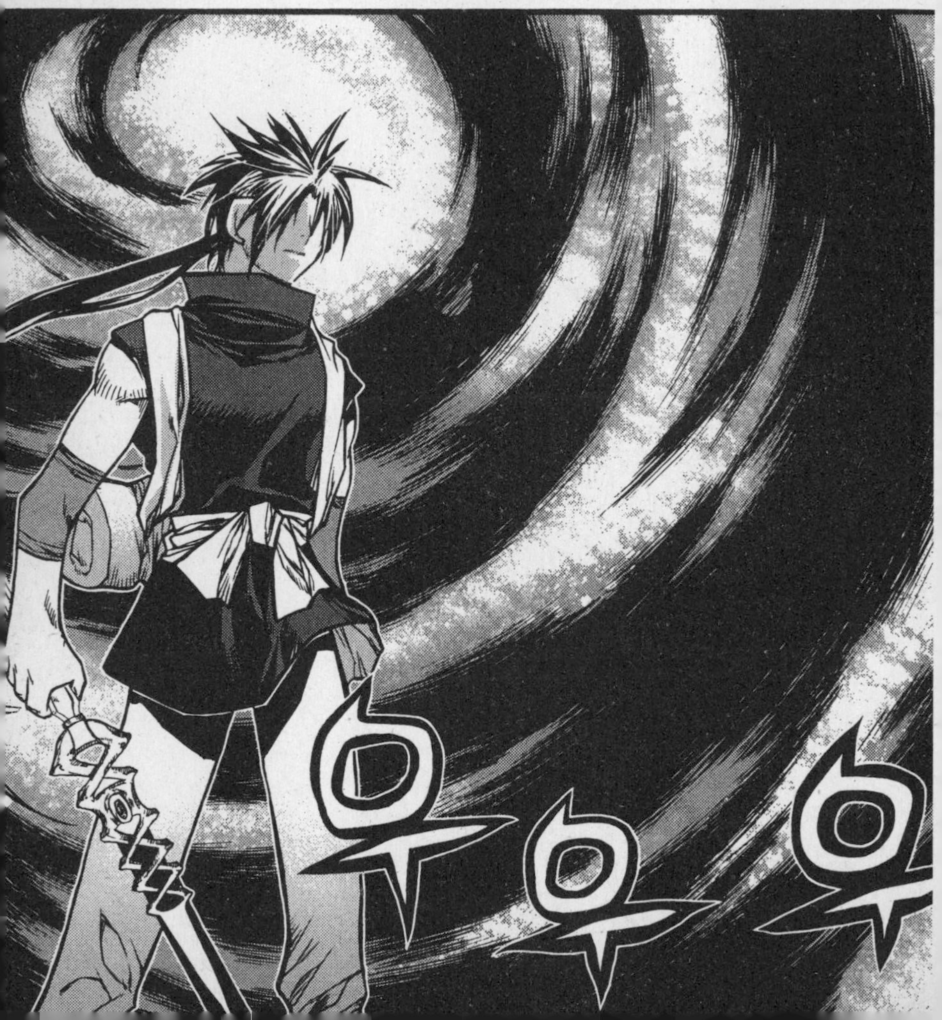

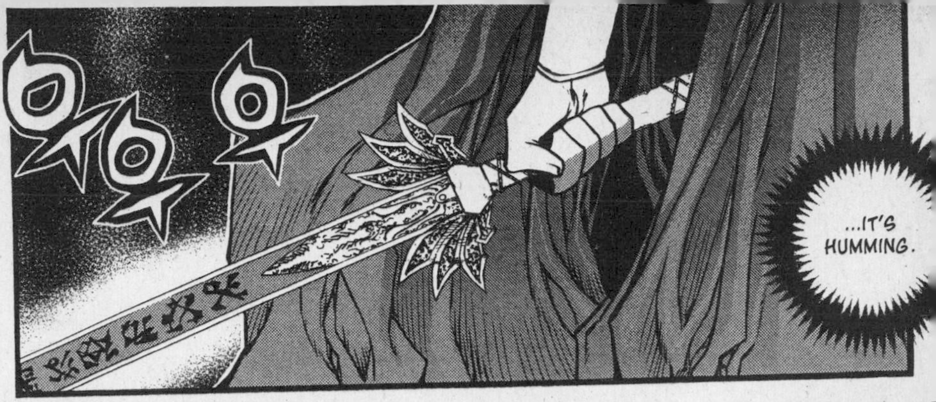
...IT'S HUMMING.

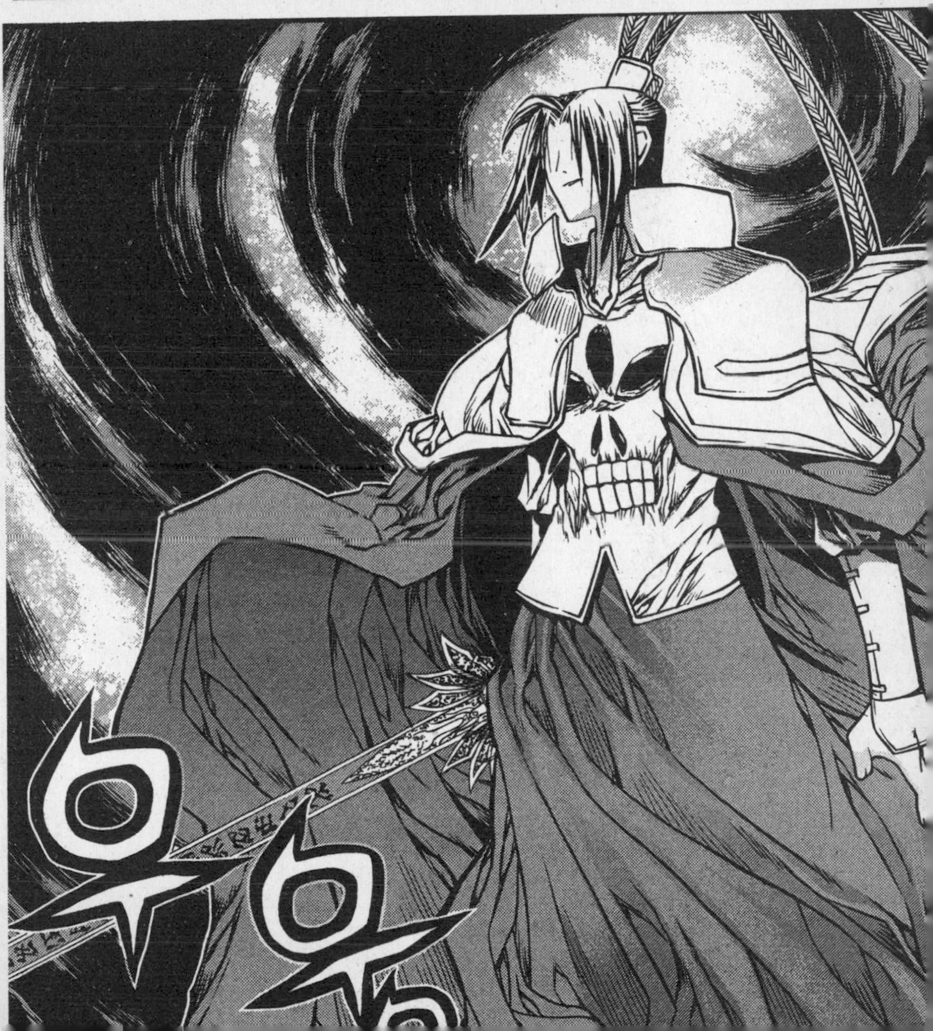

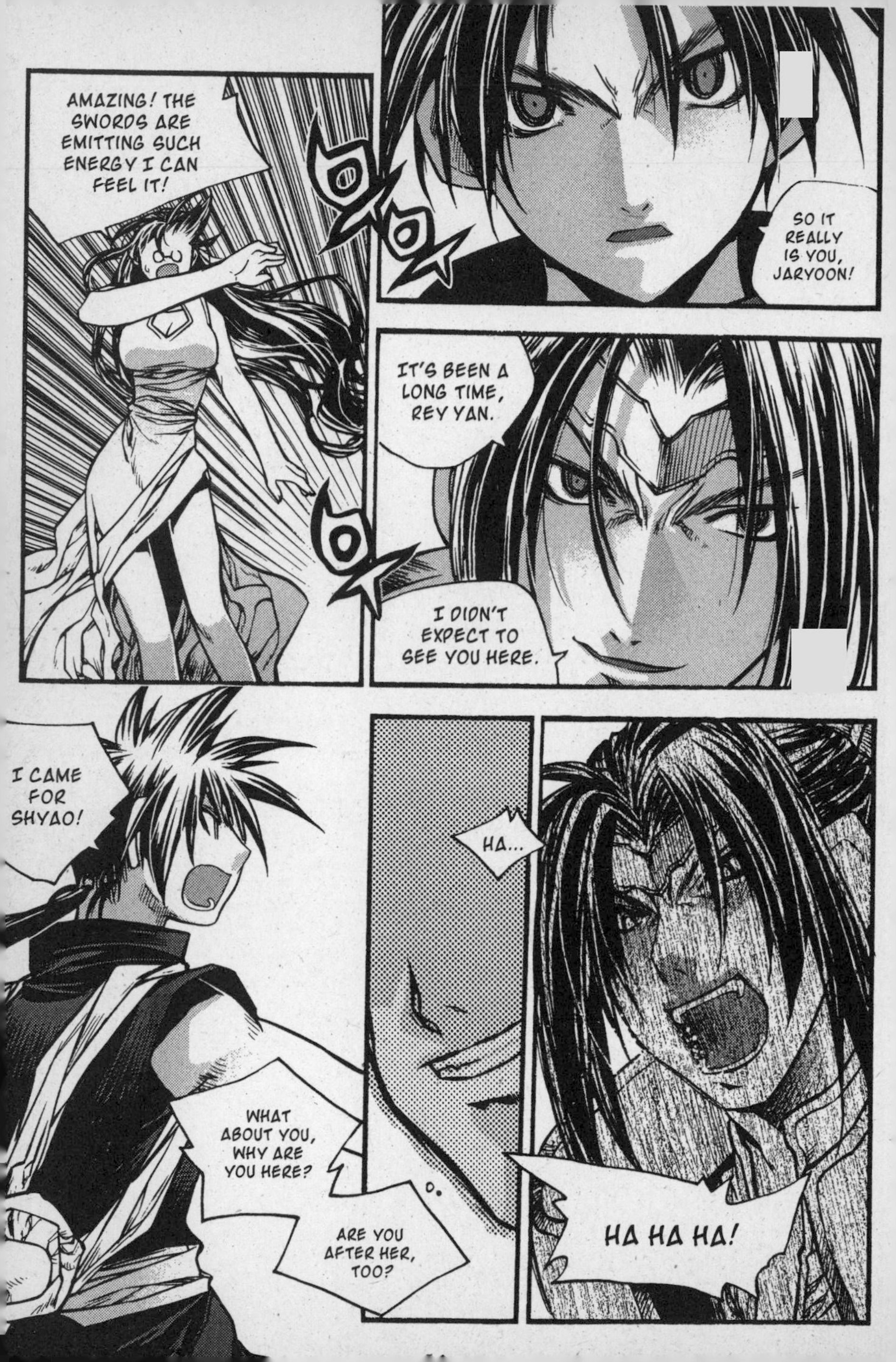

AMAZING! THE SWORDS ARE EMITTING SUCH ENERGY I CAN FEEL IT!
SO IT REALLY IS YOU, JARYOON!
IT'S BEEN A LONG TIME, REY YAN.
I DIDN'T EXPECT TO SEE YOU HERE.
I CAME FOR SHYAO!
WHAT ABOUT YOU, WHY ARE YOU HERE?
ARE YOU AFTER HER, TOO?
HA...
HA HA HA!

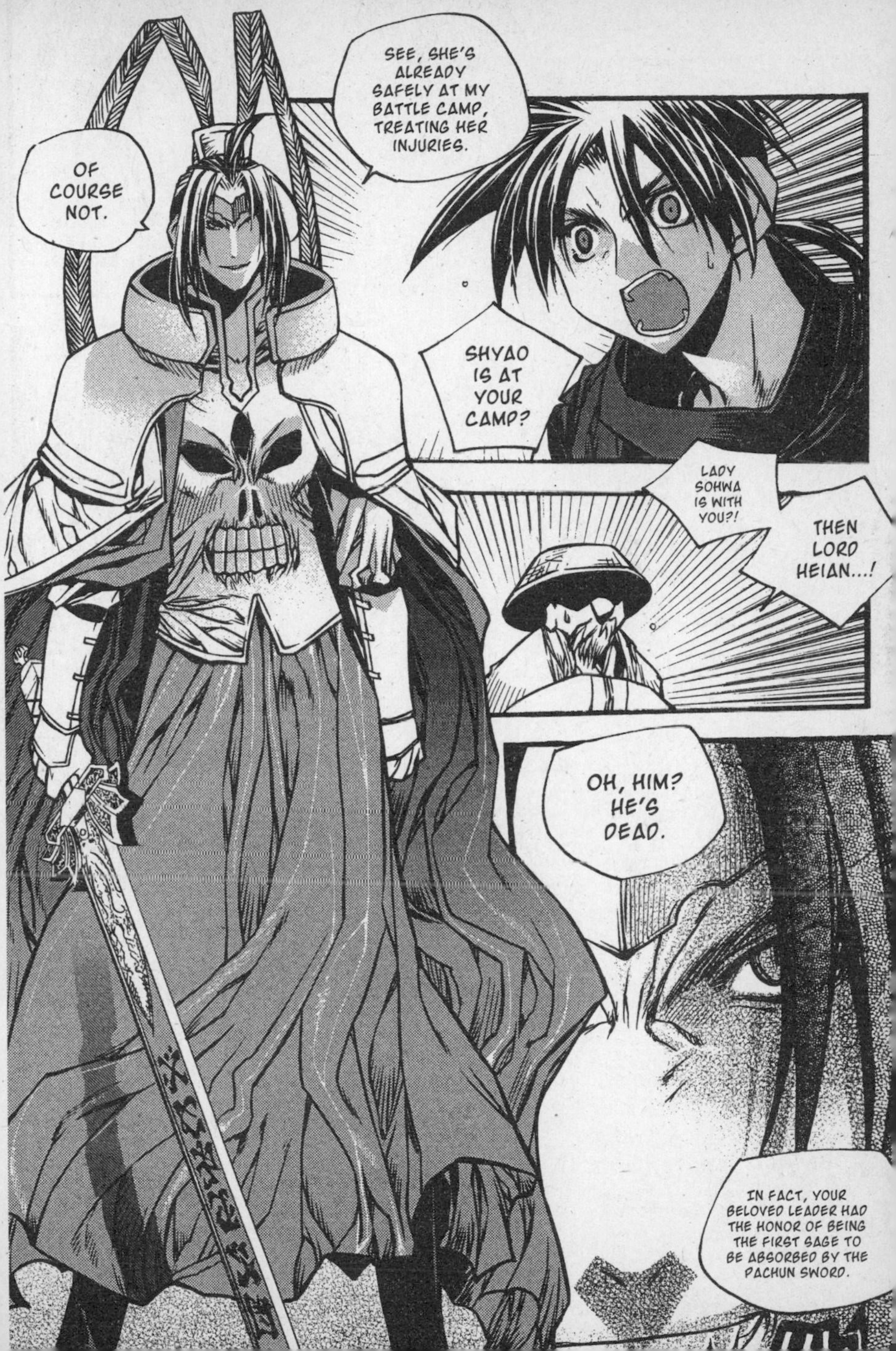
OF COURSE NOT.
SEE, SHE'S ALREADY SAFELY AT MY BATTLE CAMP, TREATING HER INJURIES.
SHYAO IS AT YOUR CAMP?
LADY SOHWA IS WITH YOU?!
THEN LORD HEIAN...!
OH, HIM? HE'S DEAD.
IN FACT, YOUR BELOVED LEADER HAD THE HONOR OF BEING THE FIRST SAGE TO BE ABSORBED BY THE PACHUN SWORD.

I DON'T BELIEVE YOU...

YOU LIE!

NO...

THERE'S NO WAY LORD HEIAN FELL UNDER YOUR SWORD.

...LOOK!

THE SWORD IS EMITTING THE MIGHTY FORCE OF A HEAVENLY SAGE!

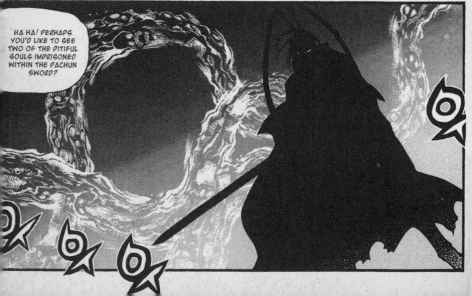

HA HA! PERHAPS YOU'D LIKE TO SEE TWO OF THE PITIFUL SOULS IMPRISONED WITHIN THE PACHUN SWORD?

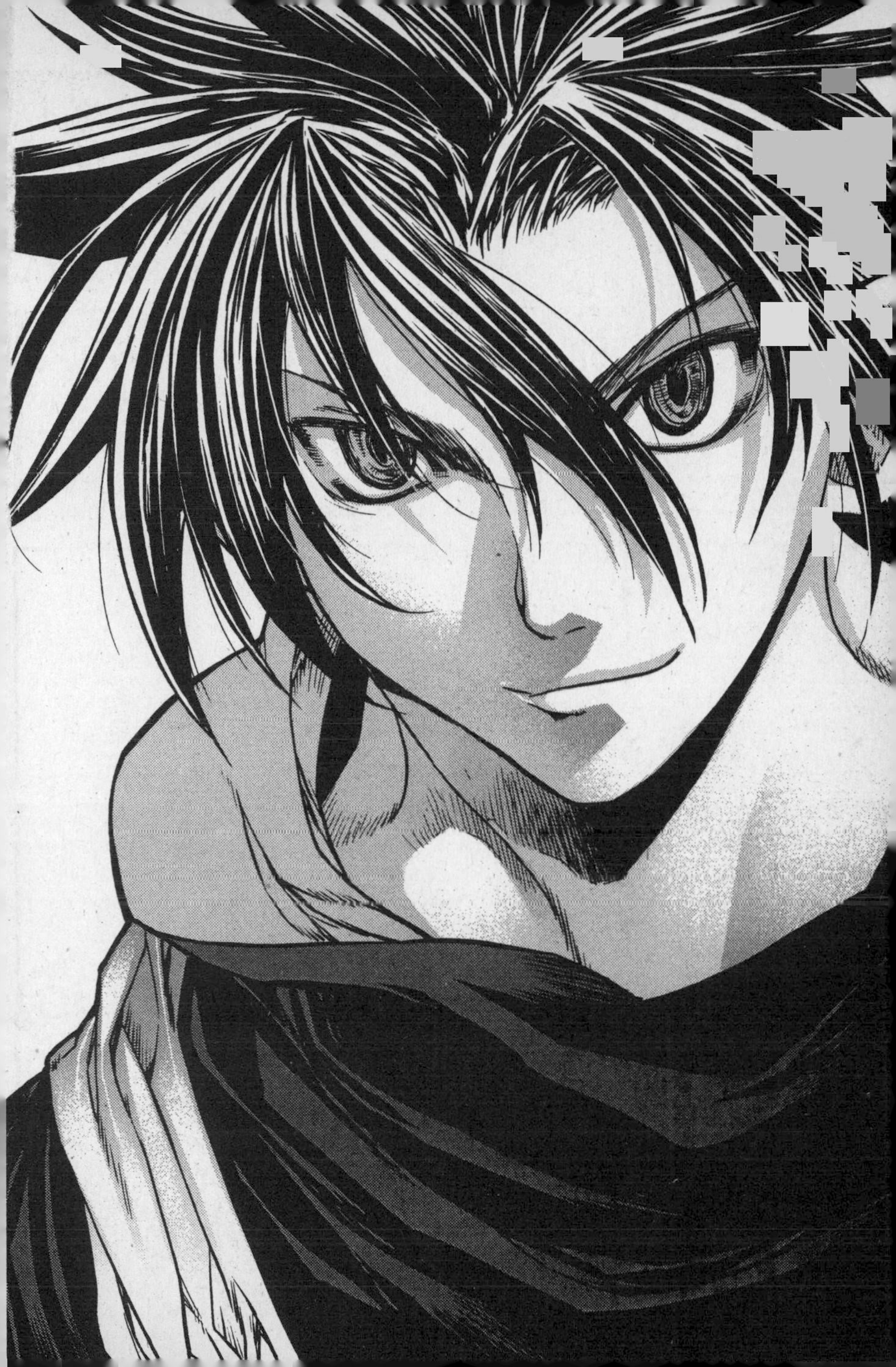

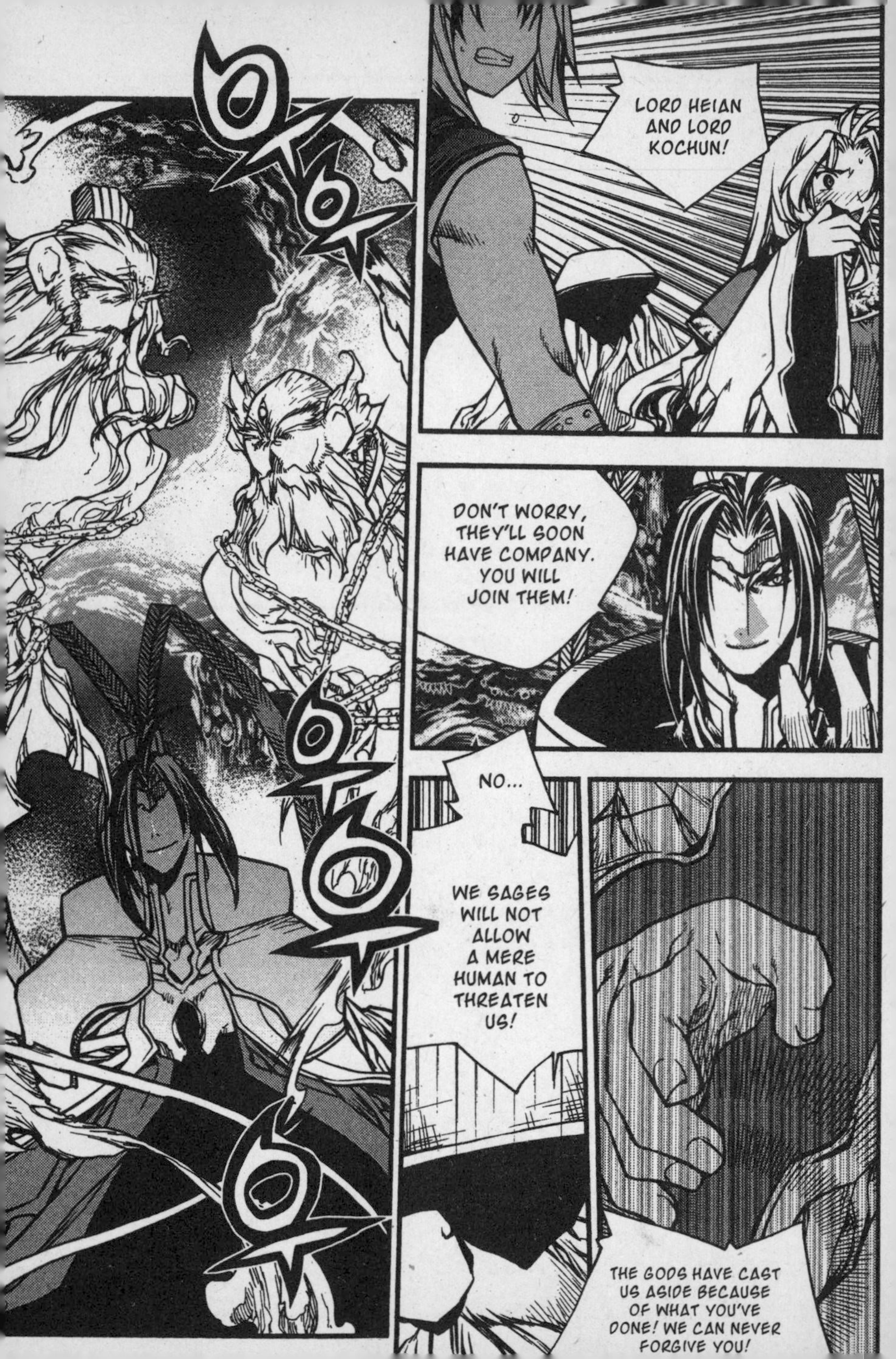
LORD HEIAN AND LORD KOCHUN!
DON'T WORRY, THEY'LL SOON HAVE COMPANY. YOU WILL JOIN THEM!
NO...
WE SAGES WILL NOT ALLOW A MERE HUMAN TO THREATEN US!
THE GODS HAVE CAST US ASIDE BECAUSE OF WHAT YOU'VE DONE! WE CAN NEVER FORGIVE YOU!

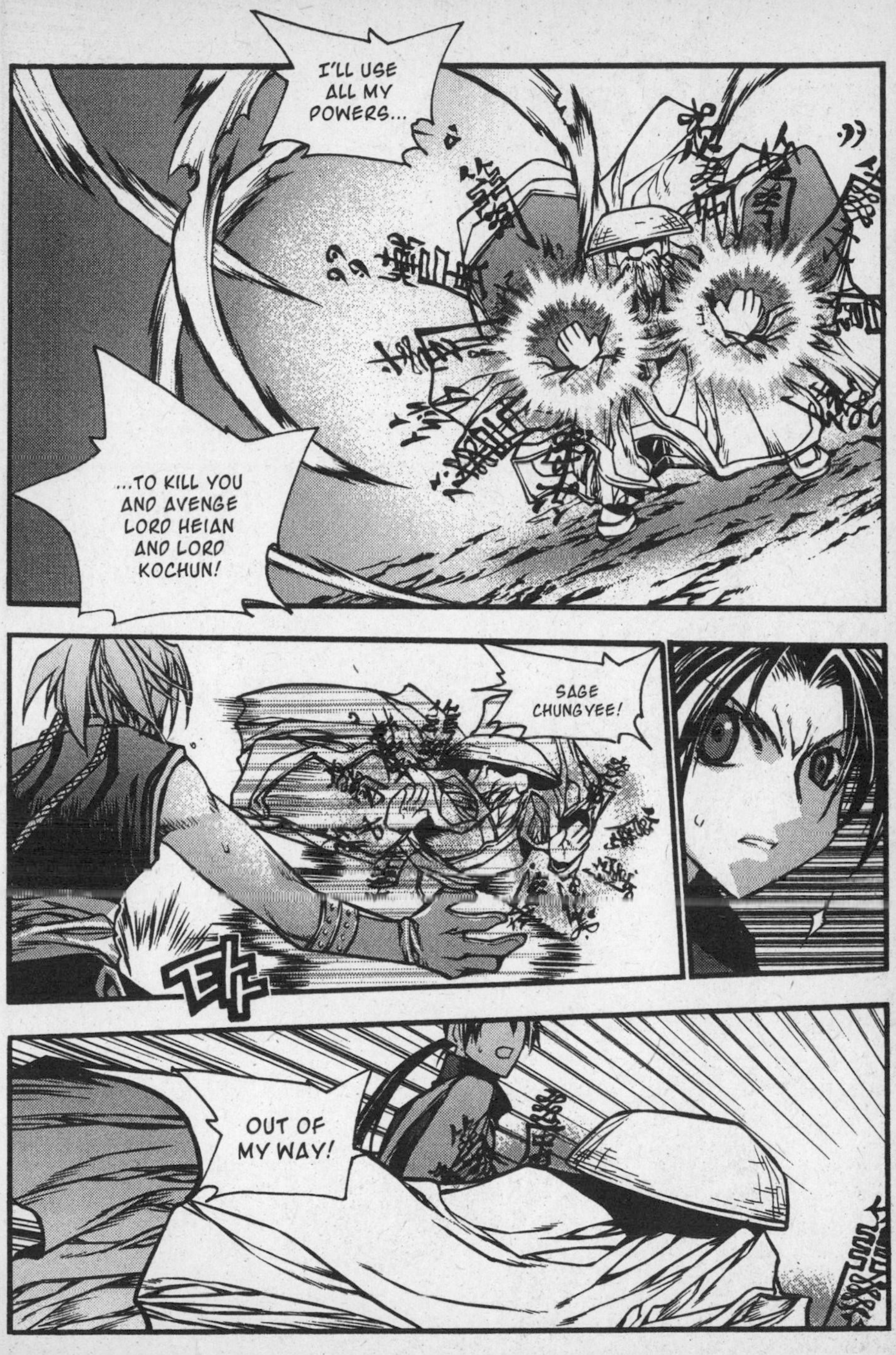
I'LL USE ALL MY POWERS...
...TO KILL YOU AND AVENGE LORD HEIAN AND LORD KOCHUN!
SAGE CHUNGYEE!
OUT OF MY WAY!

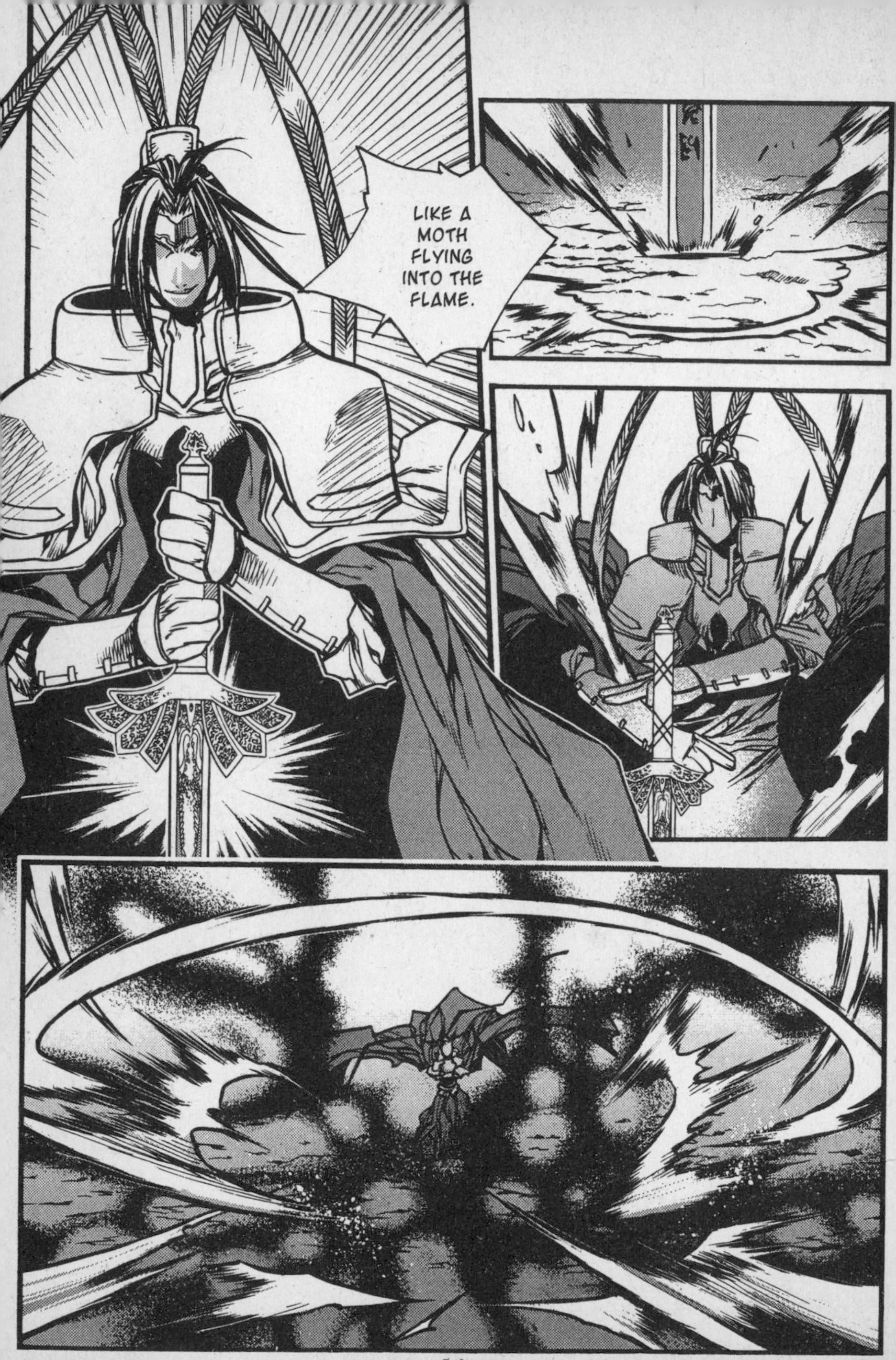
LIKE A MOTH FLYING INTO THE FLAME.

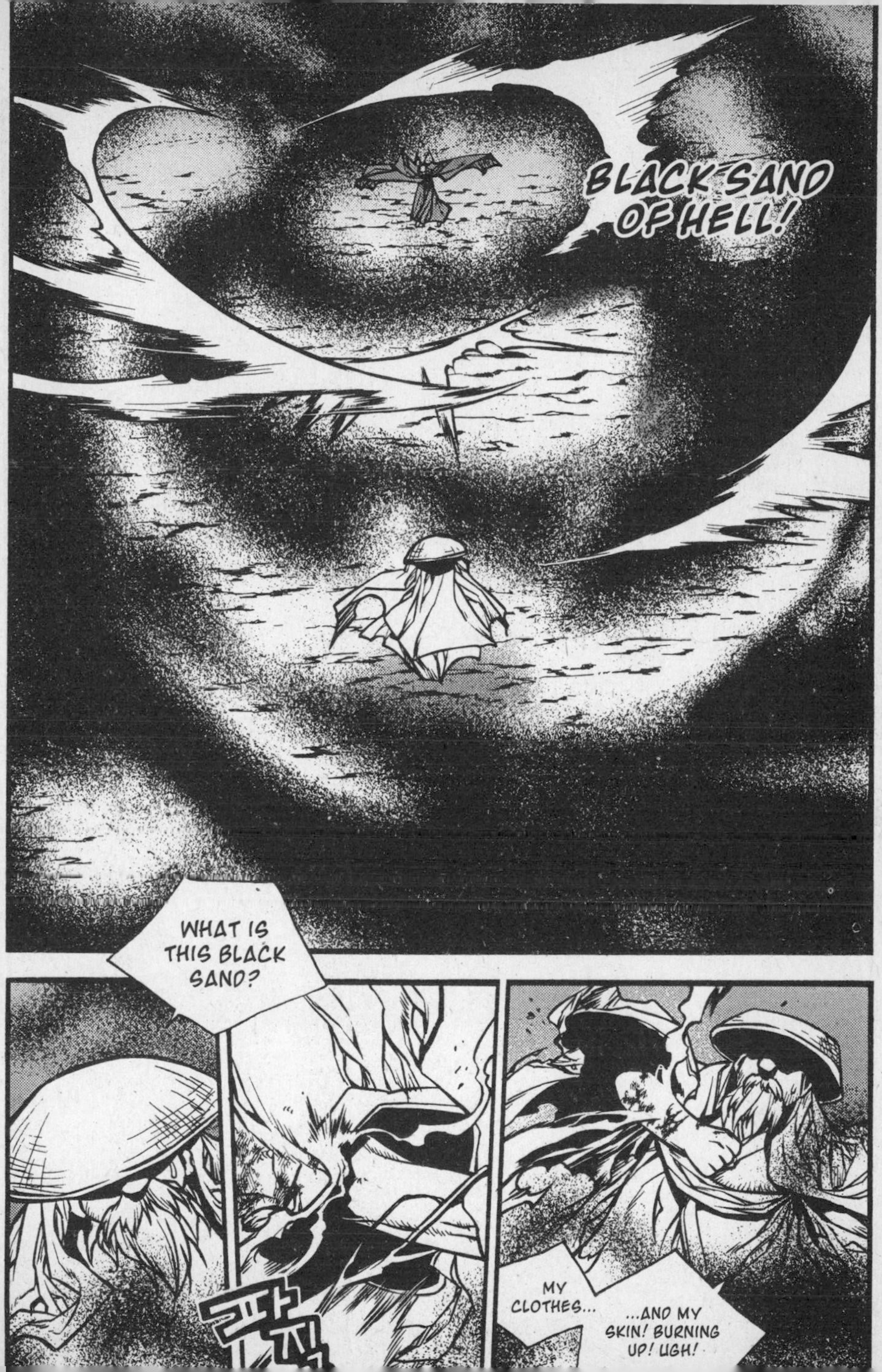
BLACK SAND OF HELL!
WHAT IS THIS BLACK SAND?
MY CLOTHES...
...AND MY SKIN! BURNING UP! UGH!

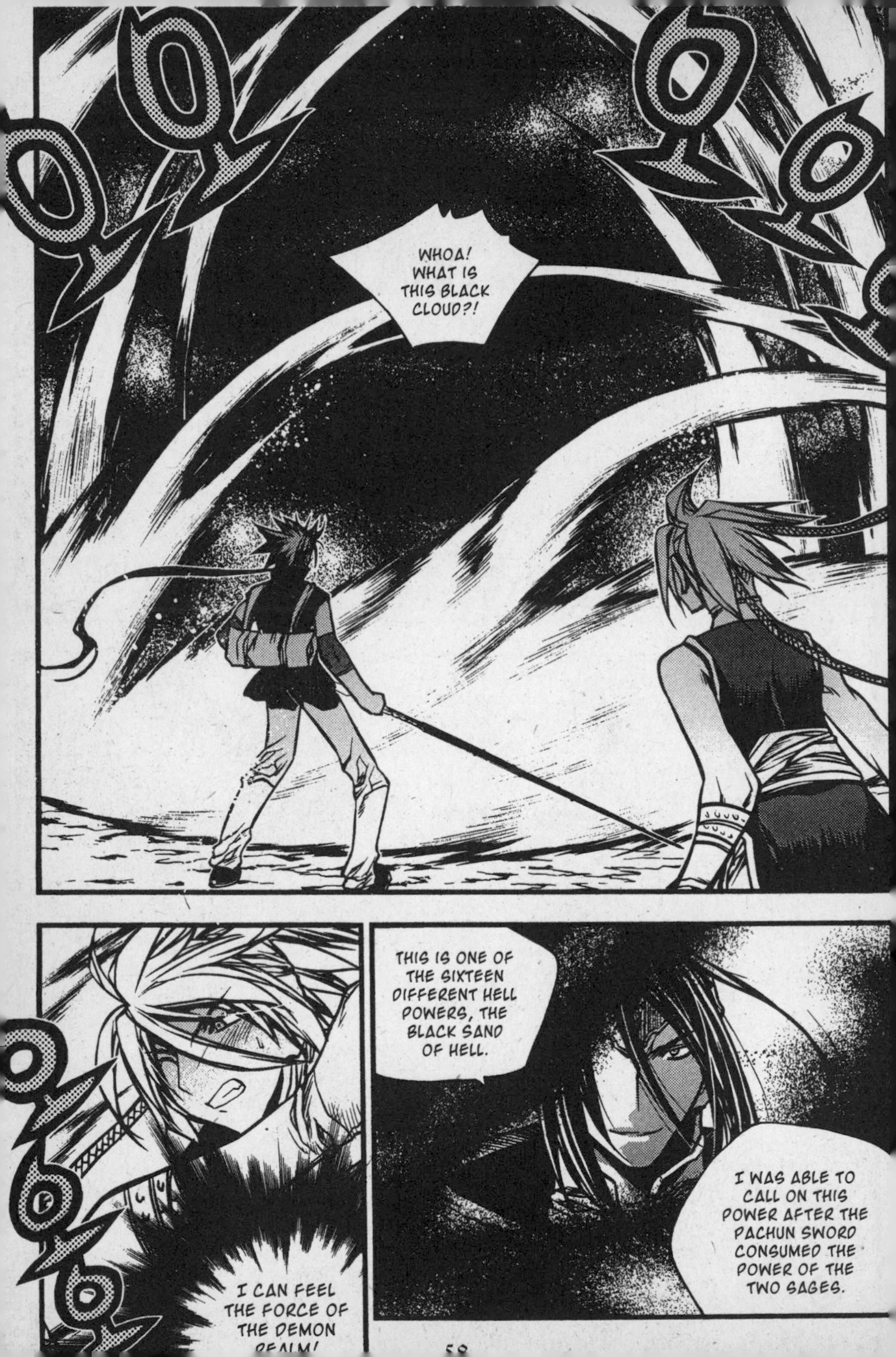
WHOA! WHAT IS THIS BLACK CLOUD?!
I CAN FEEL THE FORCE OF THE DEMON REALM!
THIS IS ONE OF THE SIXTEEN DIFFERENT HELL POWERS, THE BLACK SAND OF HELL.
I WAS ABLE TO CALL ON THIS POWER AFTER THE PACHUN SWORD CONSUMED THE POWER OF THE TWO SAGES.

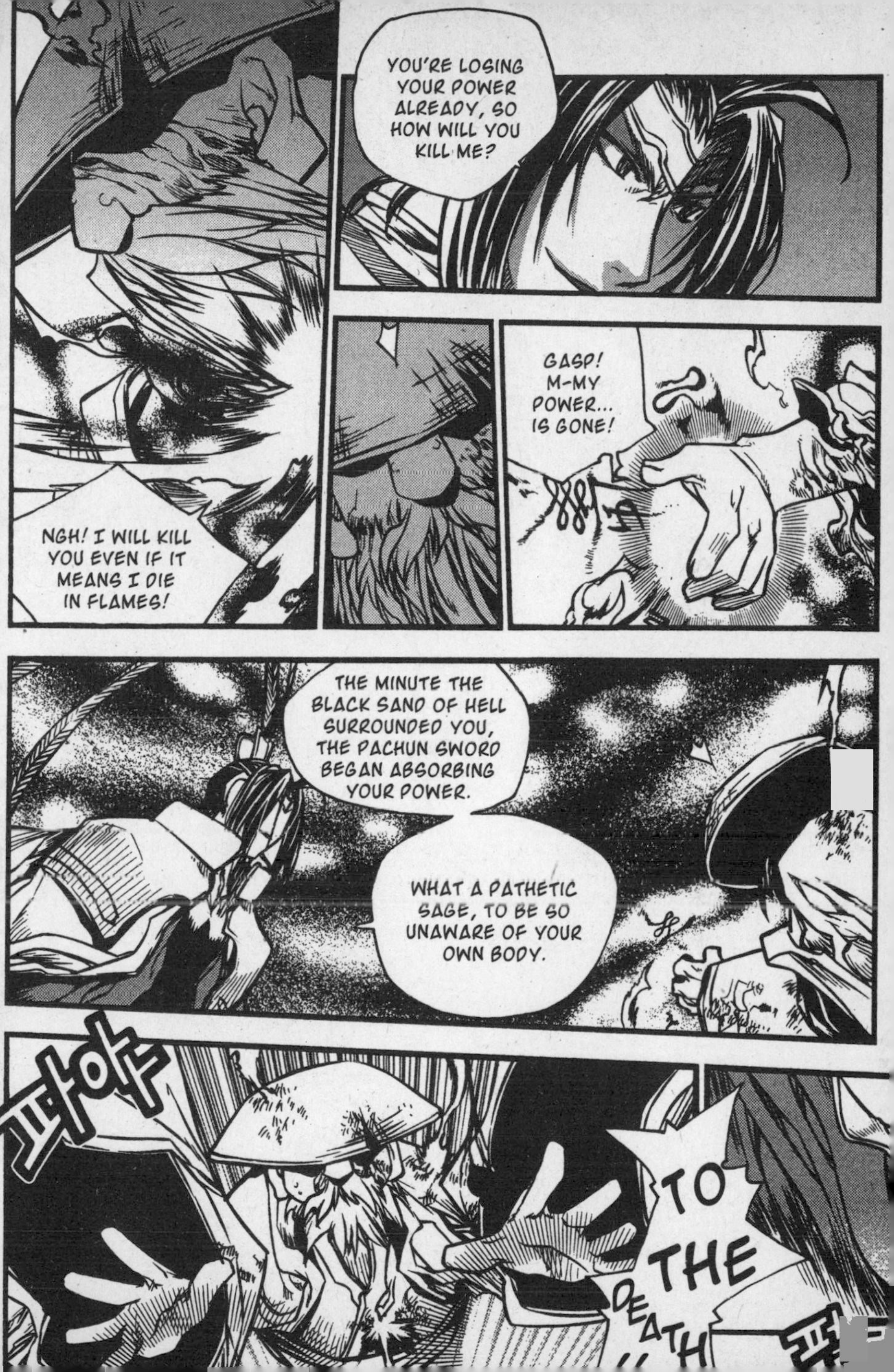
NGH! I WILL KILL YOU EVEN IF IT MEANS I DIE IN FLAMES!
YOU'RE LOSING YOUR POWER ALREADY, SO HOW WILL YOU KILL ME?
GASP! M-MY POWER... IS GONE!
THE MINUTE THE BLACK SAND OF HELL SURROUNDED YOU, THE PACHUN SWORD BEGAN ABSORBING YOUR POWER.
WHAT A PATHETIC SAGE, TO BE SO UNAWARE OF YOUR OWN BODY.
TO THE DEATH

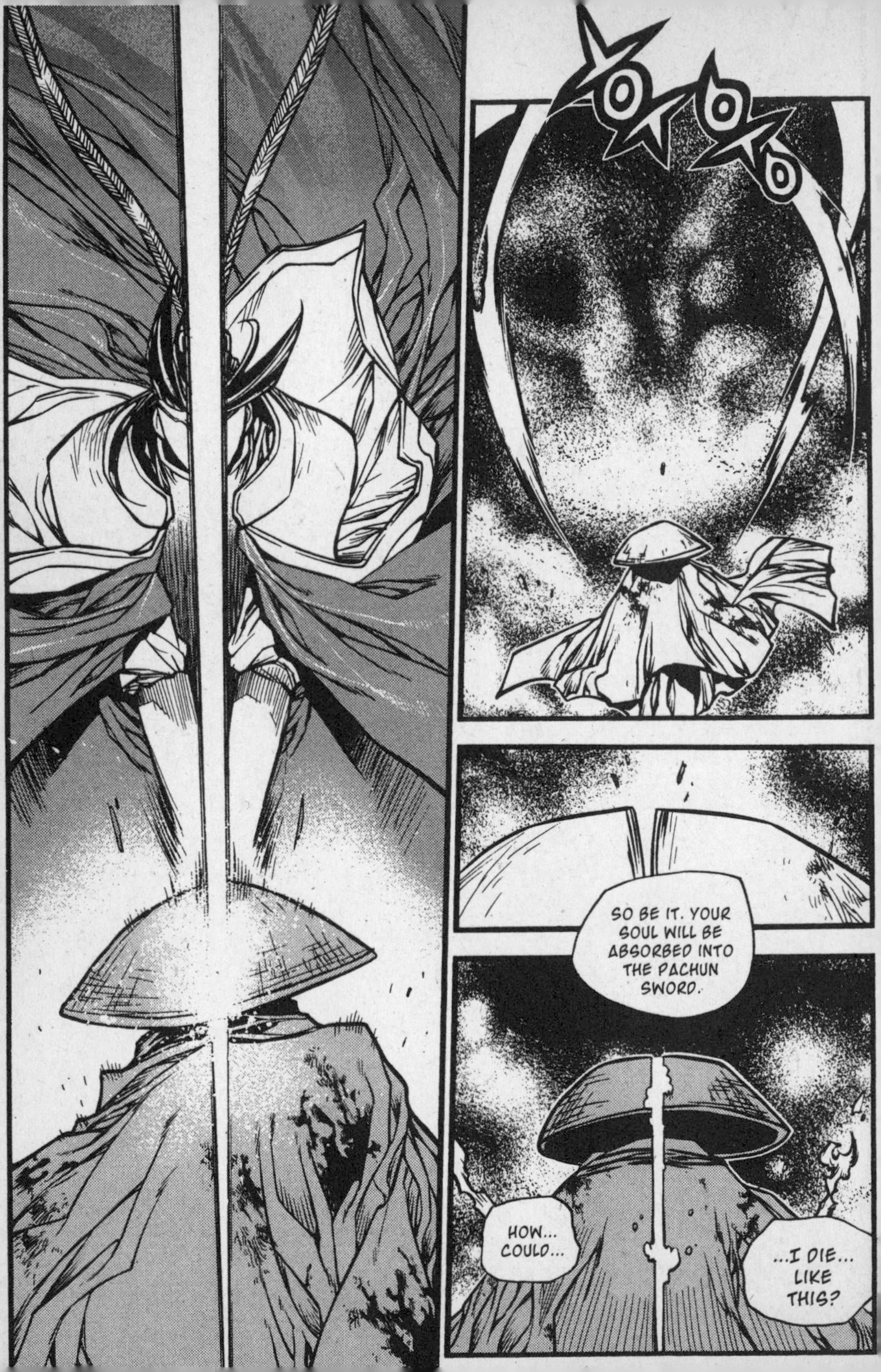
SO BE IT. YOUR SOUL WILL BE ABSORBED INTO THE PACHUN SWORD.
HOW... COULD...
...I DIE... LIKE THIS?

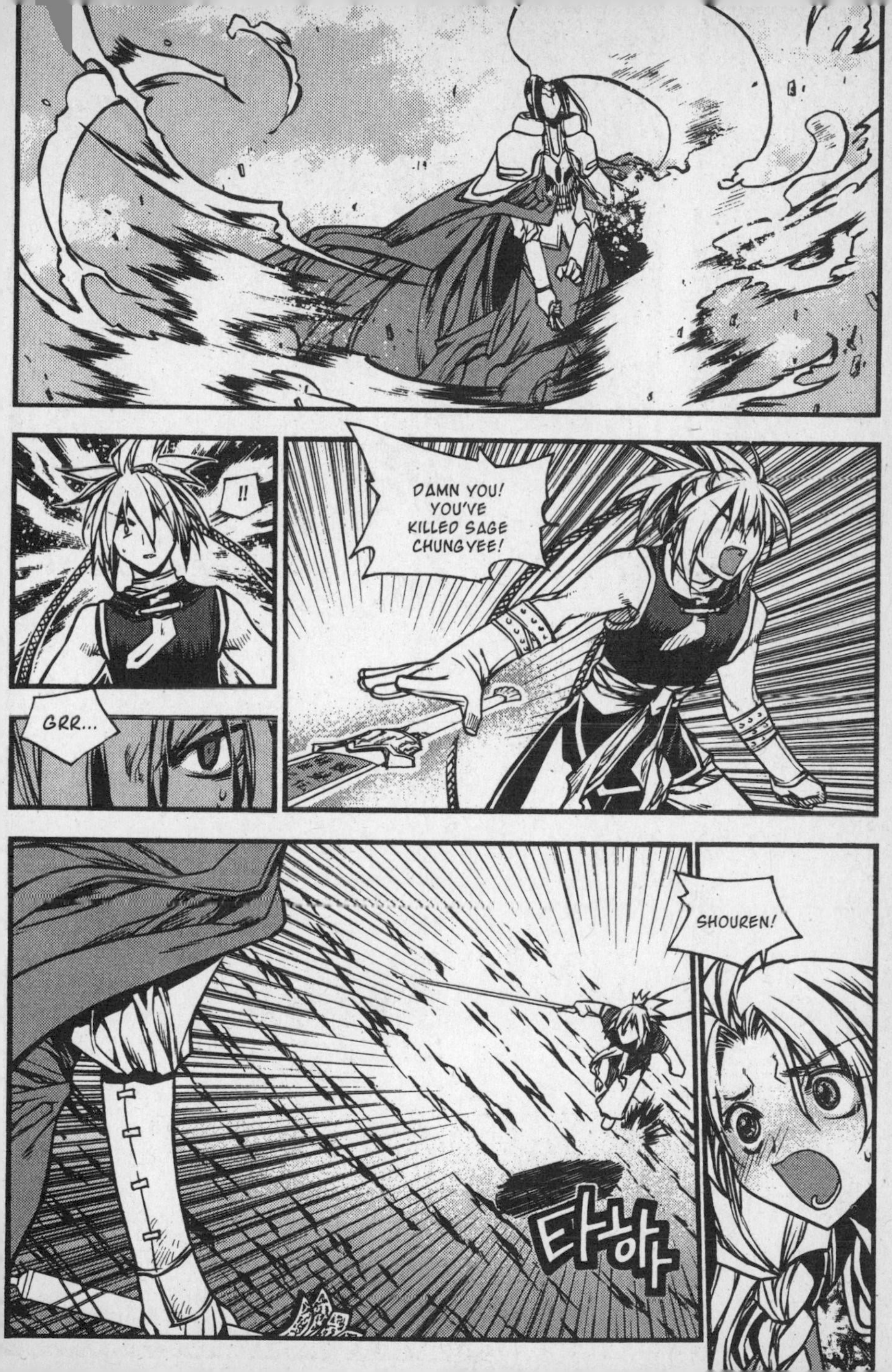
!!
DAMN YOU! YOU'VE KILLED SAGE CHUNGYEE!
GRR...
SHOUREN!
타하

MY, MY...

WHAT POWER YOU HAVE!

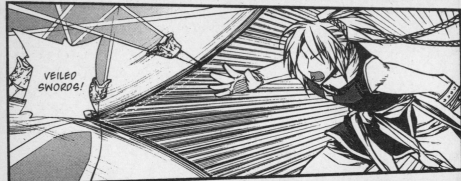

VEILED SWORDS!

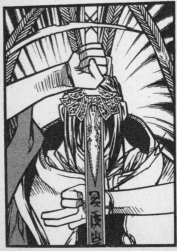

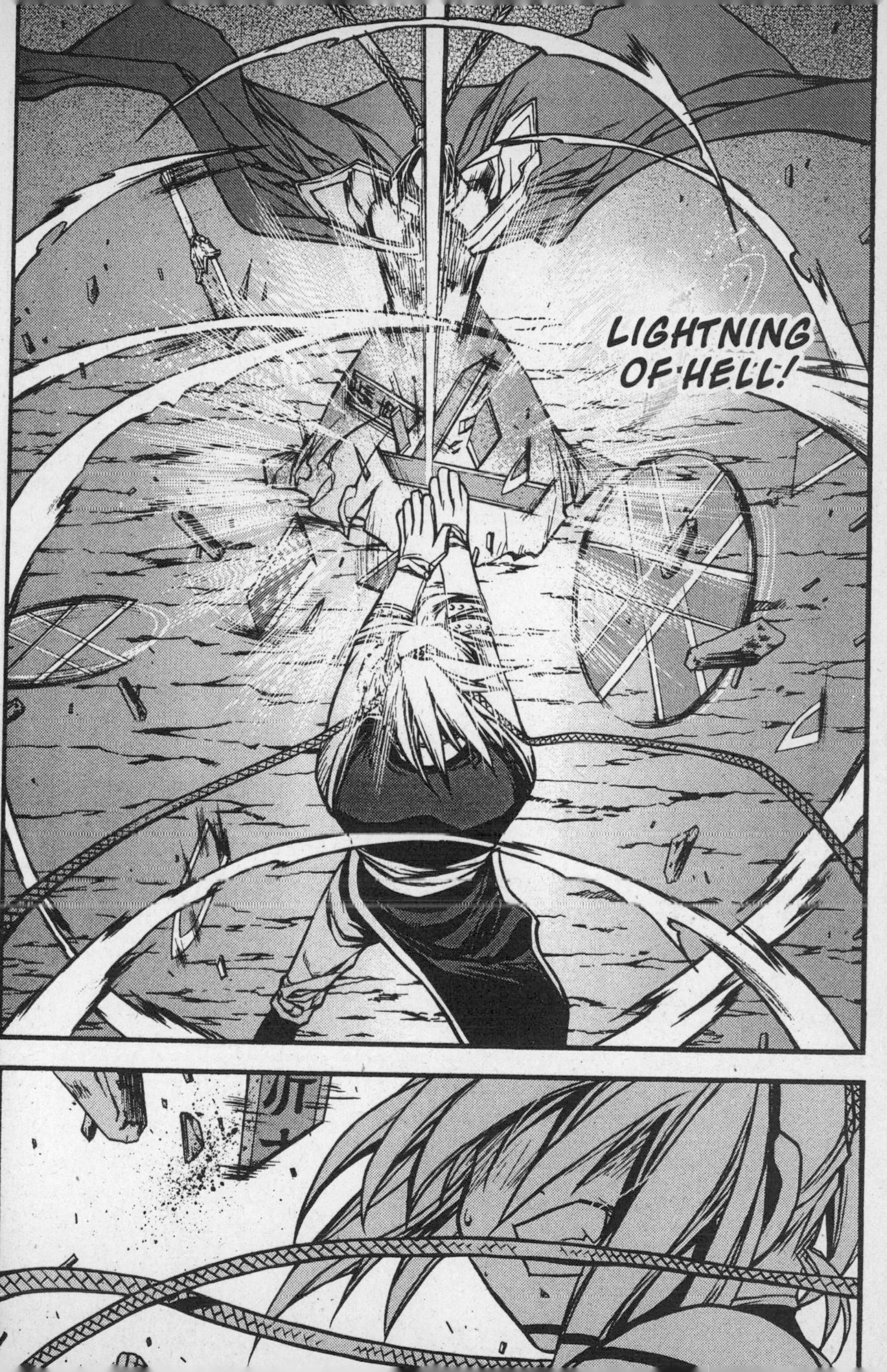
LIGHTNING OF HELL!

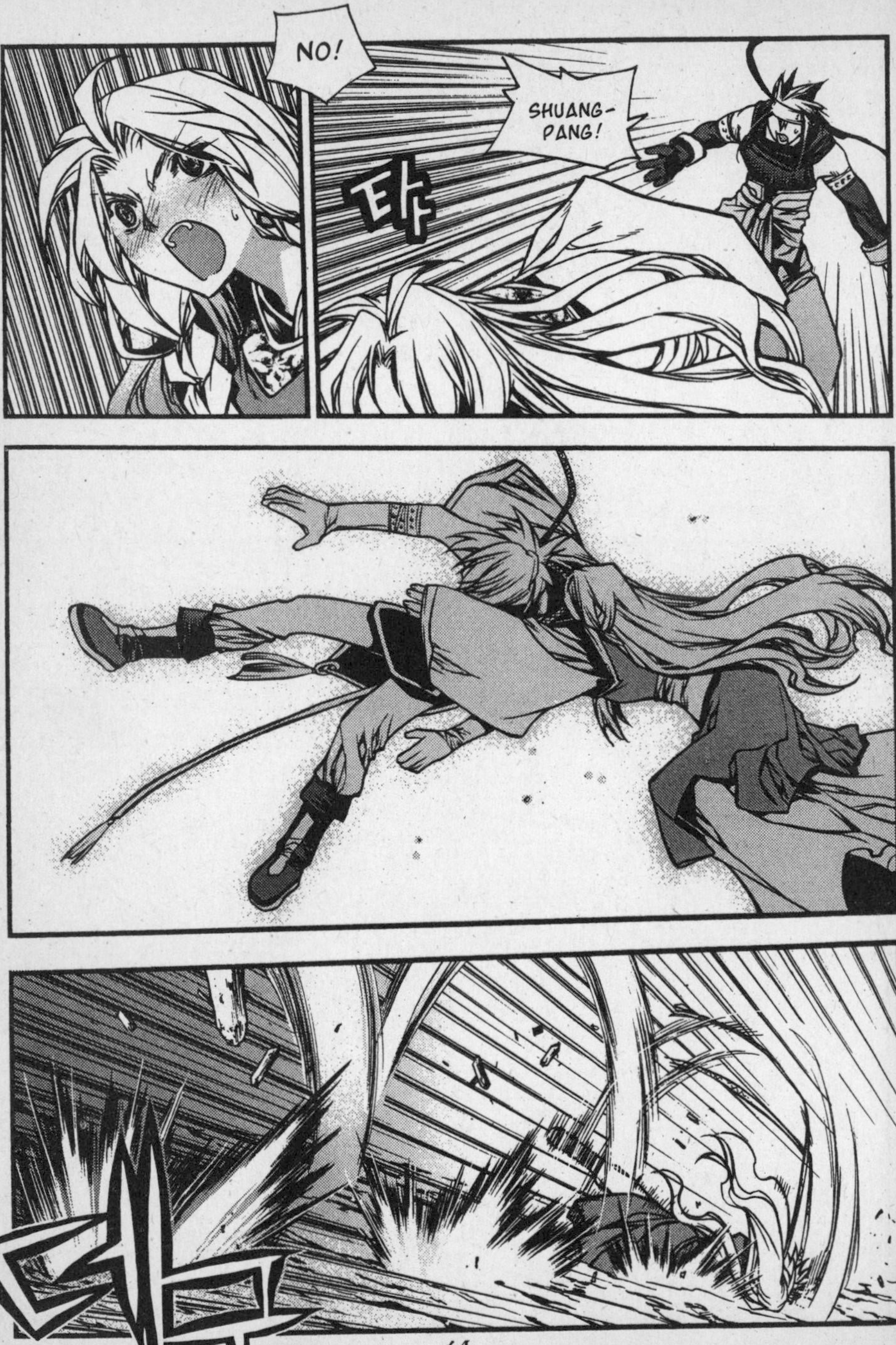
NO!
SHUANG-PANG!

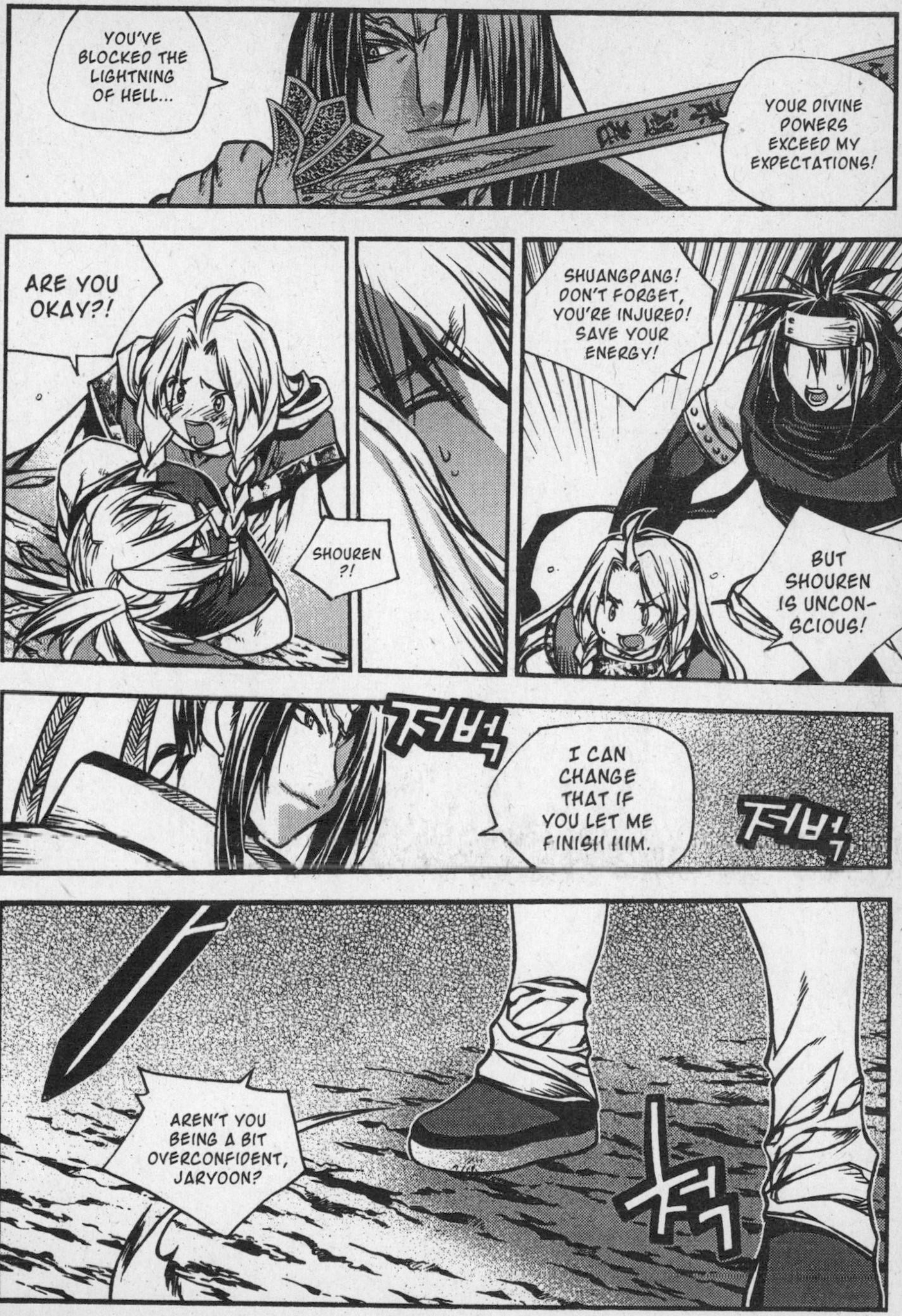
YOU'VE BLOCKED THE LIGHTNING OF HELL...
YOUR DIVINE POWERS EXCEED MY EXPECTATIONS!
ARE YOU OKAY?!
SHOUREN ?!
SHUANGPANG! DON'T FORGET, YOU'RE INJURED! SAVE YOUR ENERGY!
BUT SHOUREN IS UNCON-SCIOUS!
I CAN CHANGE THAT IF YOU LET ME FINISH HIM.
AREN'T YOU BEING A BIT OVERCONFIDENT, JARYOON?

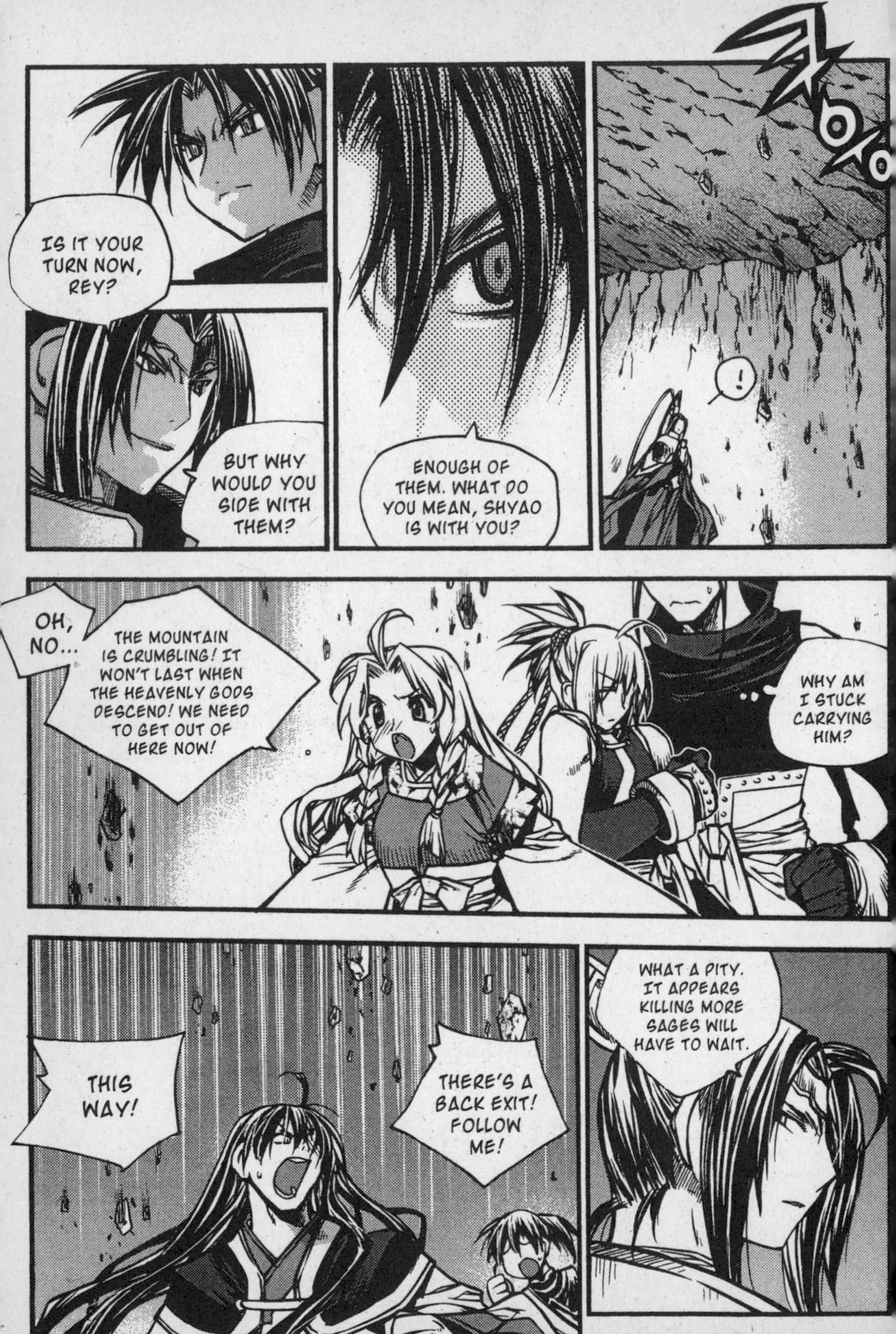
IS IT YOUR TURN NOW, REY?
BUT WHY WOULD YOU SIDE WITH THEM?
ENOUGH OF THEM. WHAT DO YOU MEAN, SHYAO IS WITH YOU?
!
OH, NO...
THE MOUNTAIN IS CRUMBLING! IT WON'T LAST WHEN THE HEAVENLY GODS DESCEND! WE NEED TO GET OUT OF HERE NOW!
WHY AM I STUCK CARRYING HIM?
THIS WAY!
THERE'S A BACK EXIT! FOLLOW ME!
WHAT A PITY. IT APPEARS KILLING MORE SAGES WILL HAVE TO WAIT.

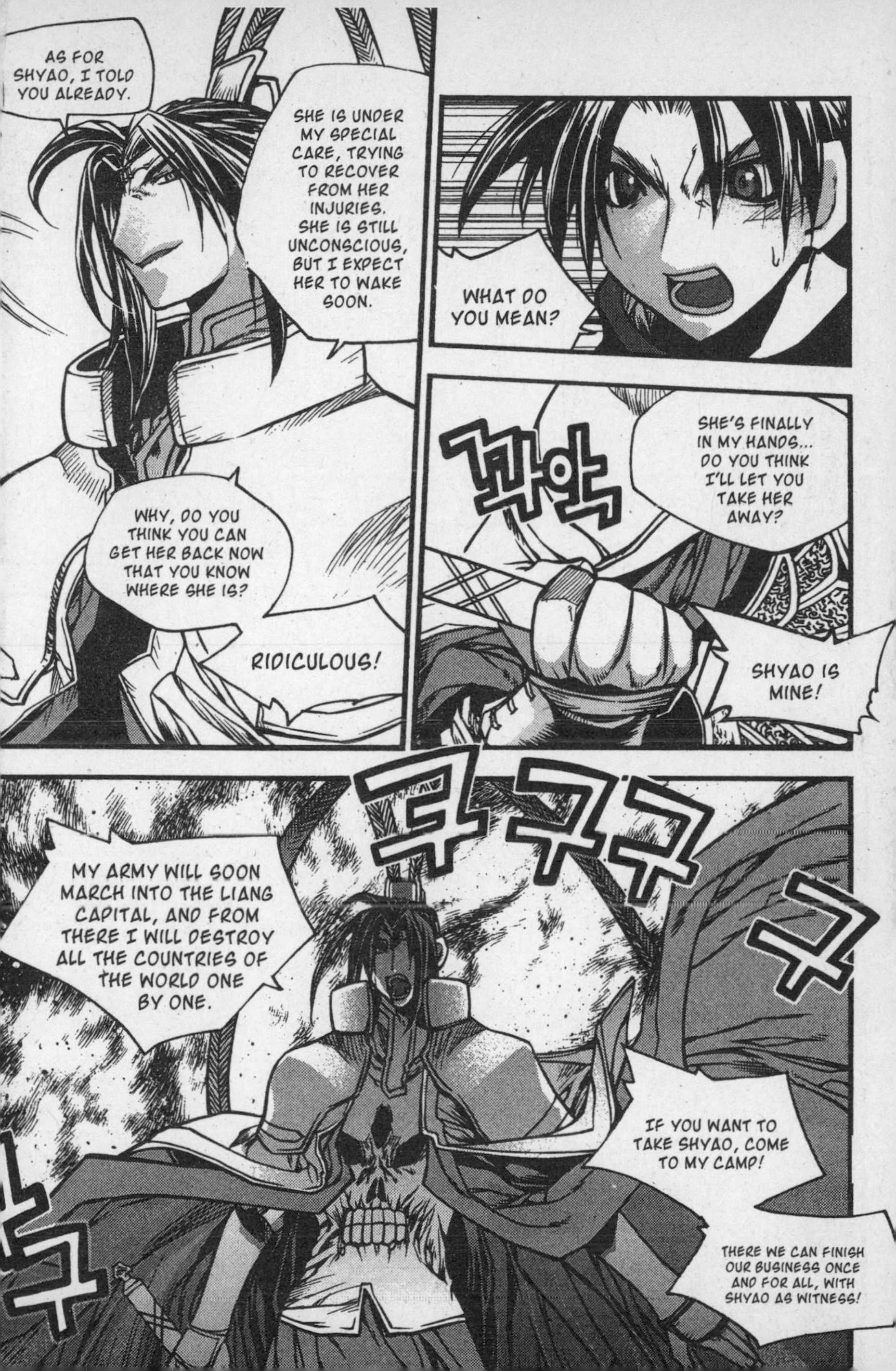
AS FOR SHYAO, I TOLD YOU ALREADY.
SHE IS UNDER MY SPECIAL CARE, TRYING TO RECOVER FROM HER INJURIES. SHE IS STILL UNCONSCIOUS, BUT I EXPECT HER TO WAKE SOON.
WHY, DO YOU THINK YOU CAN GET HER BACK NOW THAT YOU KNOW WHERE SHE IS?
RIDICULOUS!
WHAT DO YOU MEAN?
꽈악
SHE'S FINALLY IN MY HANDS... DO YOU THINK I'LL LET YOU TAKE HER AWAY?
SHYAO IS MINE!
쿠구구
MY ARMY WILL SOON MARCH INTO THE LIANG CAPITAL, AND FROM THERE I WILL DESTROY ALL THE COUNTRIES OF THE WORLD ONE BY ONE.
IF YOU WANT TO TAKE SHYAO, COME TO MY CAMP!
THERE WE CAN FINISH OUR BUSINESS ONCE AND FOR ALL, WITH SHYAO AS WITNESS!

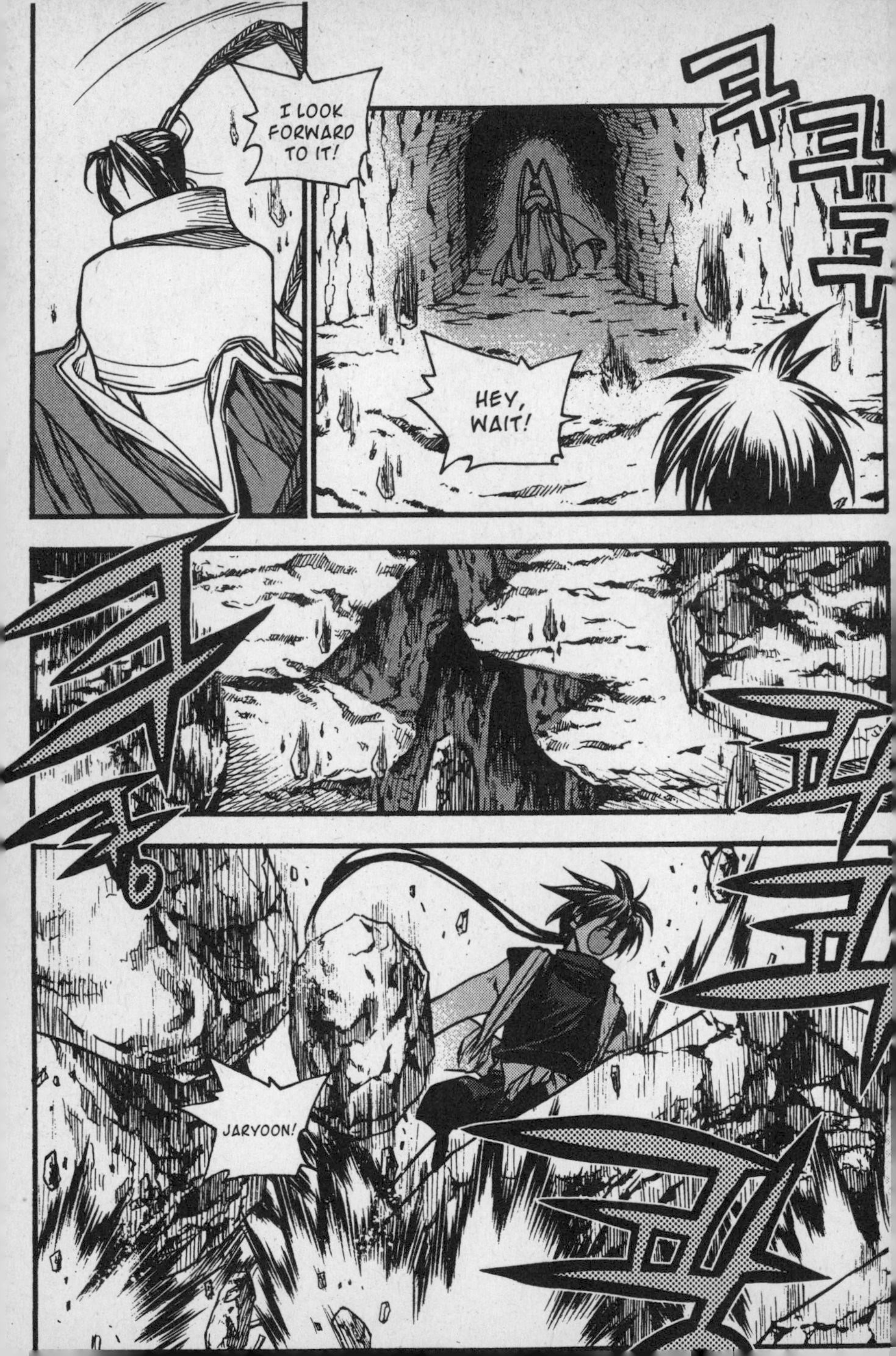
I LOOK FORWARD TO IT!
HEY, WAIT!
JARYOON!

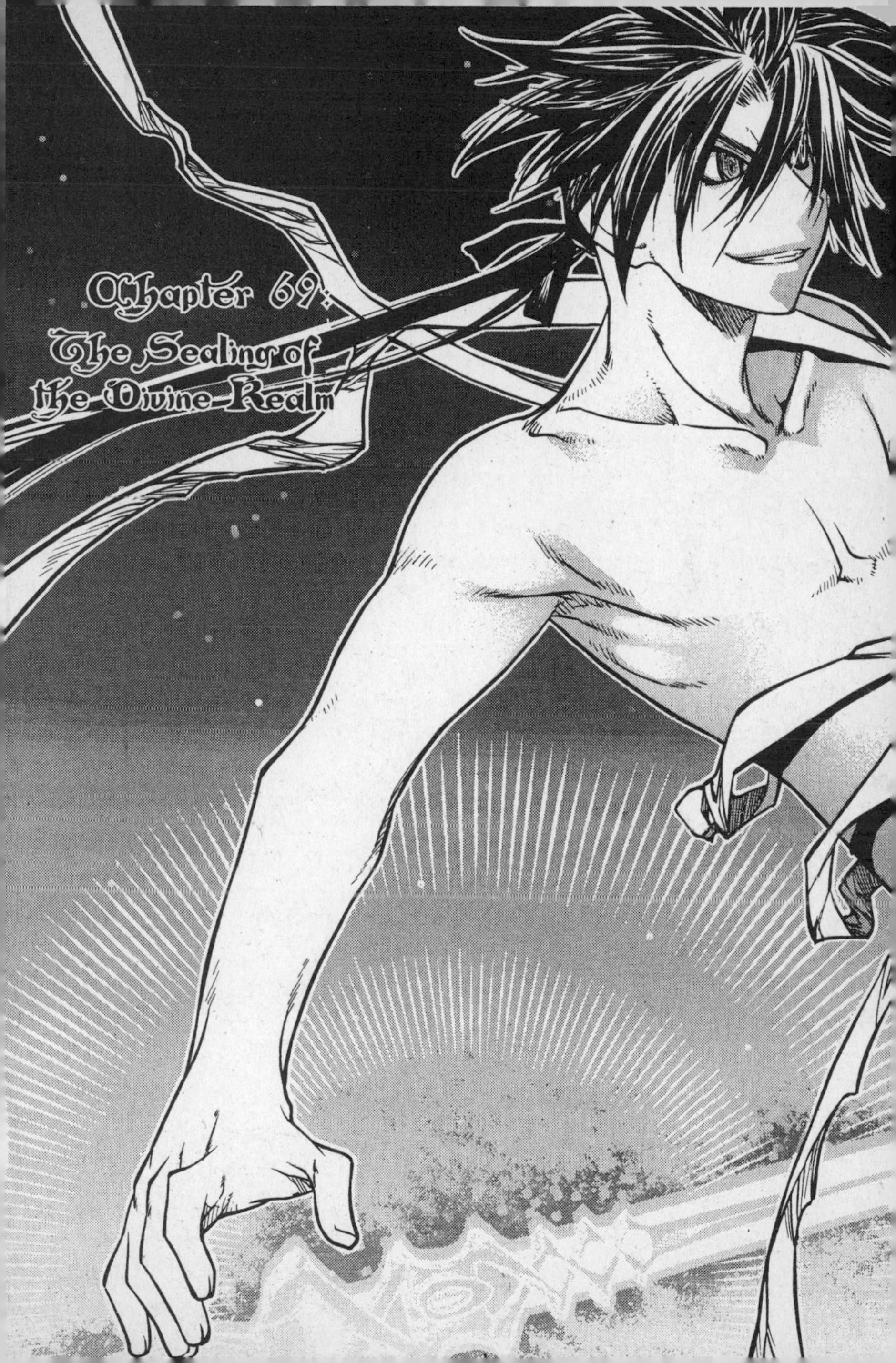
Chapter 69:
The Sealing of the Divine Realm

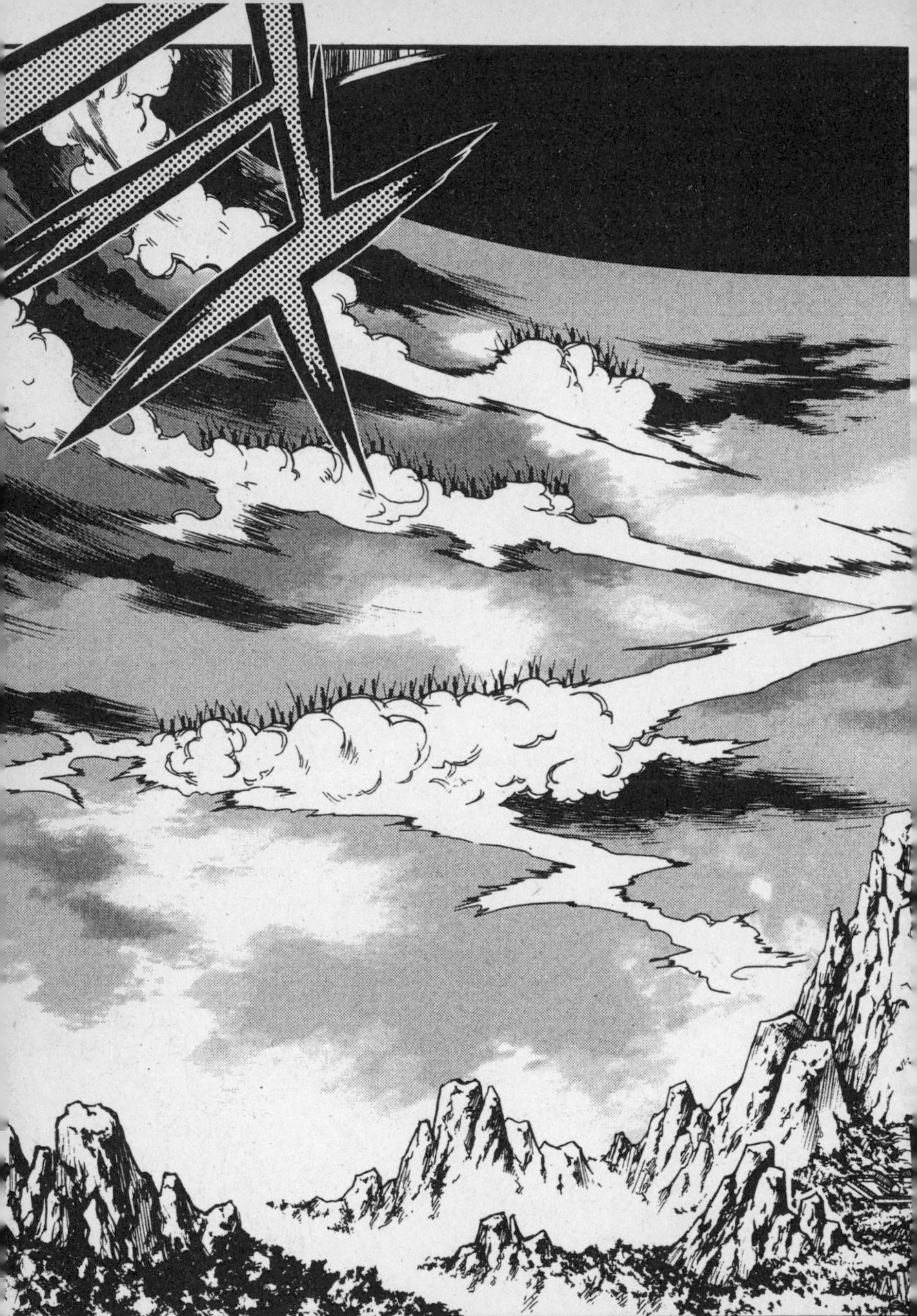

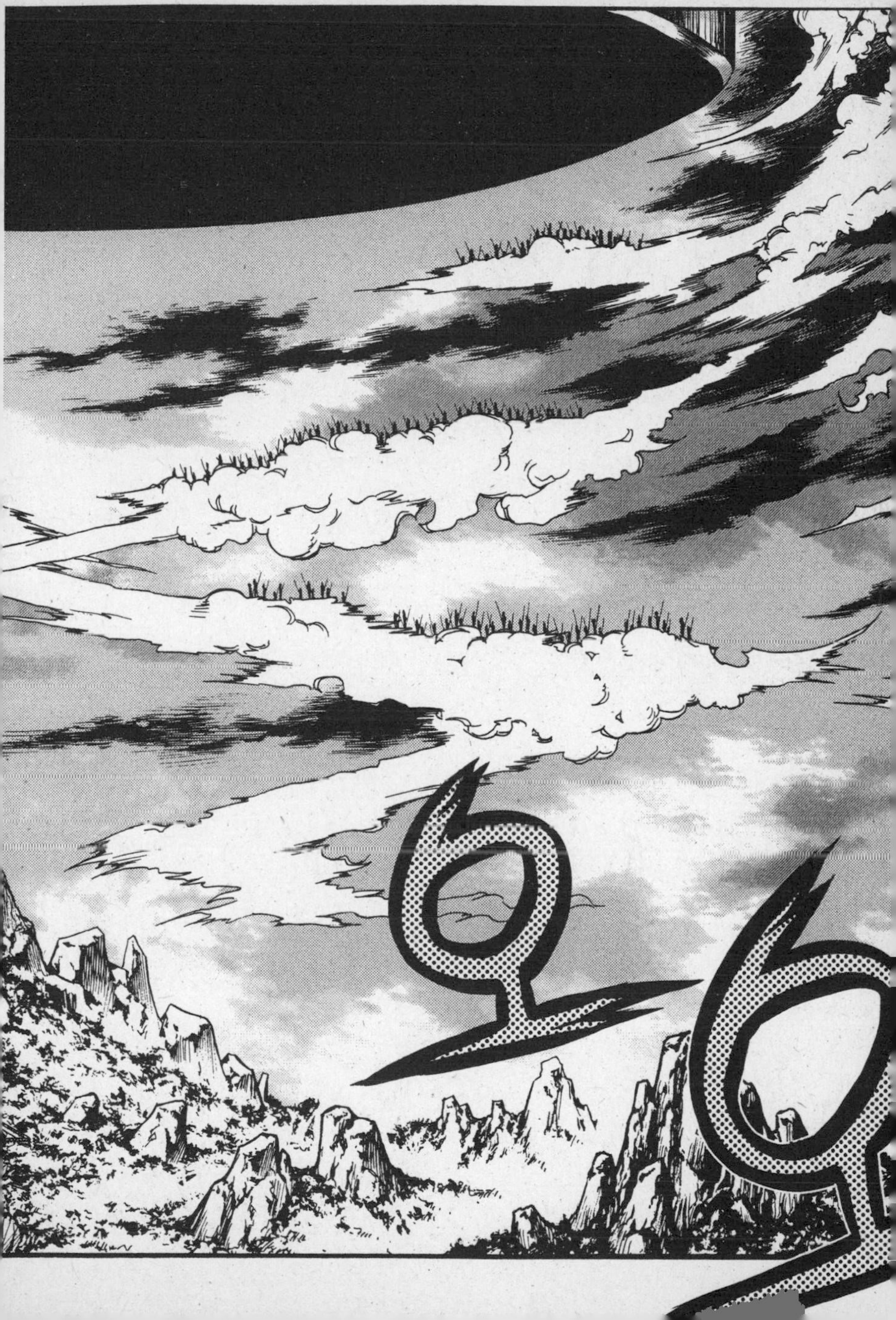

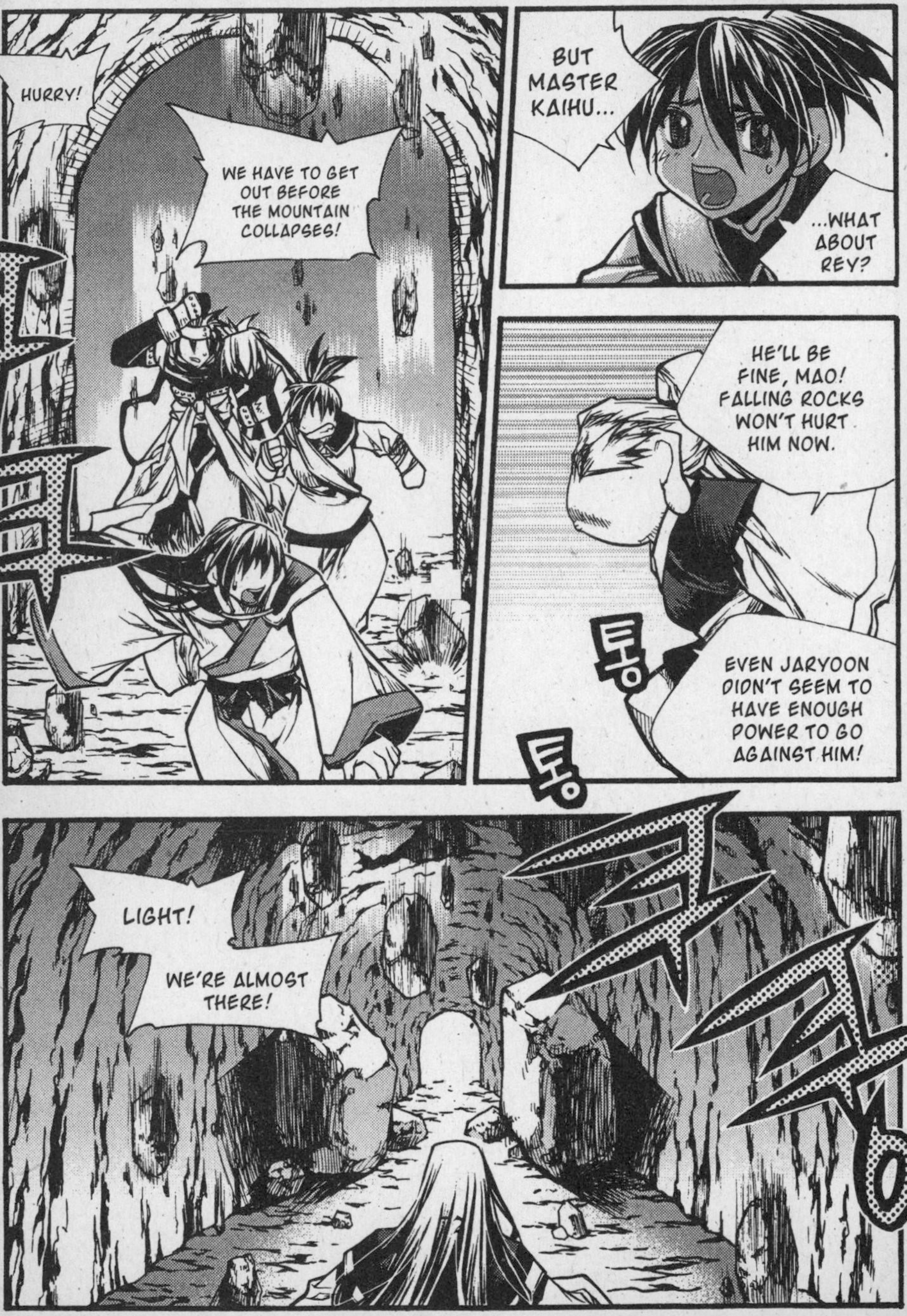
HURRY!
WE HAVE TO GET OUT BEFORE THE MOUNTAIN COLLAPSES!
BUT MASTER KAIHU...
...WHAT ABOUT REY?
HE'LL BE FINE, MAO! FALLING ROCKS WON'T HURT HIM NOW.
EVEN JARYOON DIDN'T SEEM TO HAVE ENOUGH POWER TO GO AGAINST HIM!
통
통
LIGHT!
WE'RE ALMOST THERE!

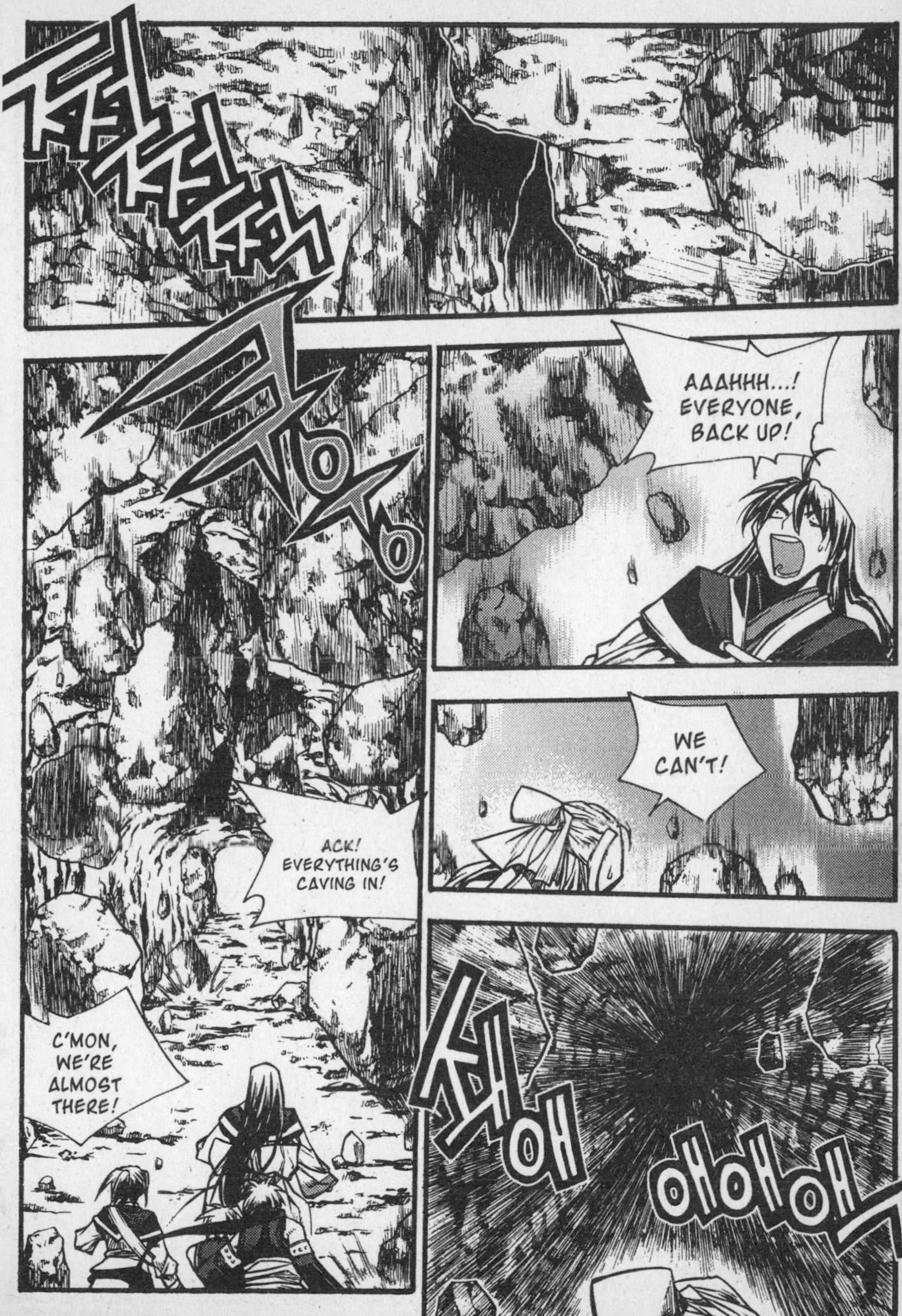
ACK! EVERYTHING'S CAVING IN!
C'MON, WE'RE ALMOST THERE!
AAAHHH...! EVERYONE, BACK UP!
WE CAN'T!

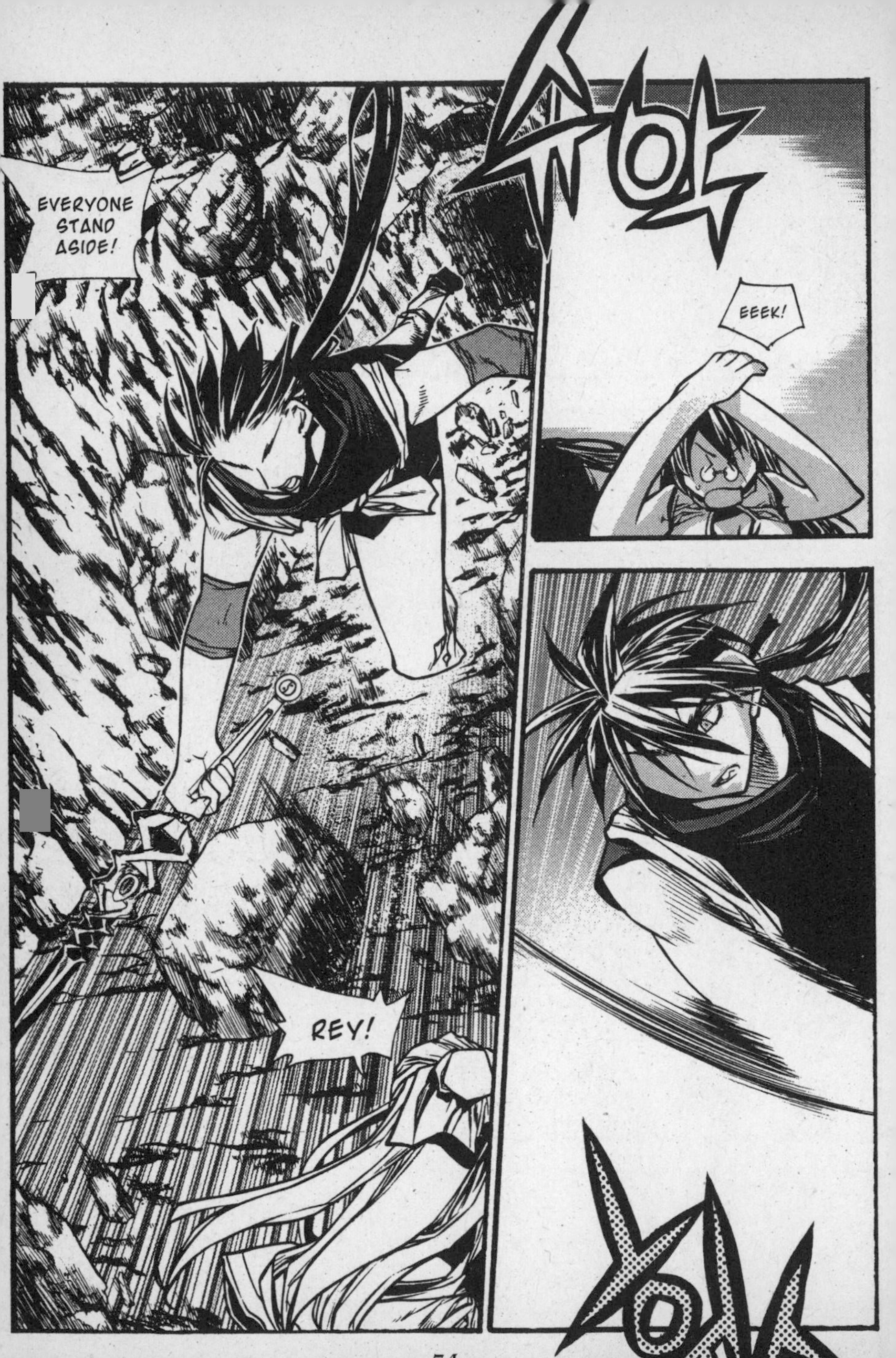
EVERYONE STAND ASIDE!
REY!
EEEK!

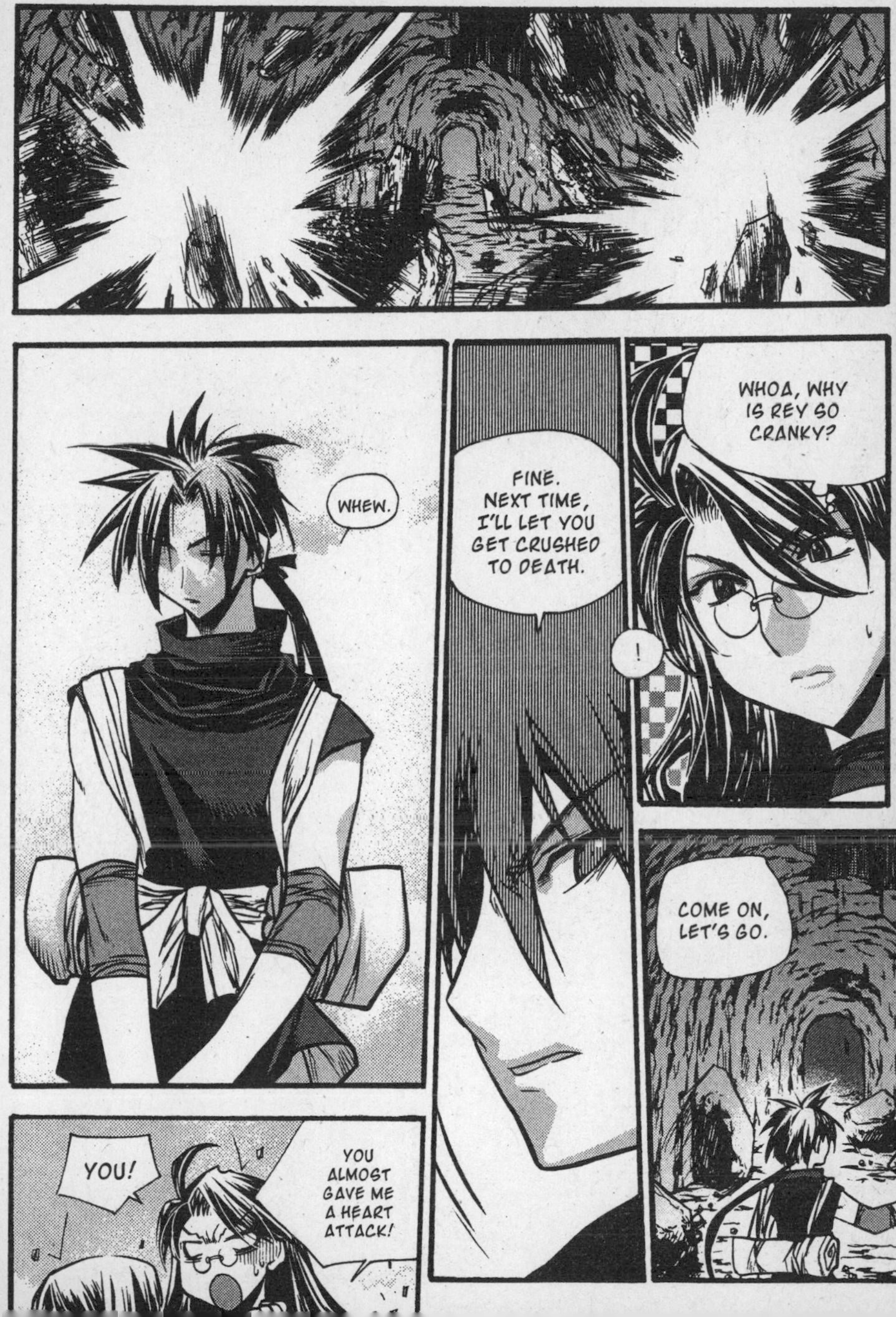
WHEW.
YOU!
YOU ALMOST GAVE ME A HEART ATTACK!
FINE. NEXT TIME, I'LL LET YOU GET CRUSHED TO DEATH.
WHOA, WHY IS REY SO CRANKY?
!
COME ON, LET'S GO.

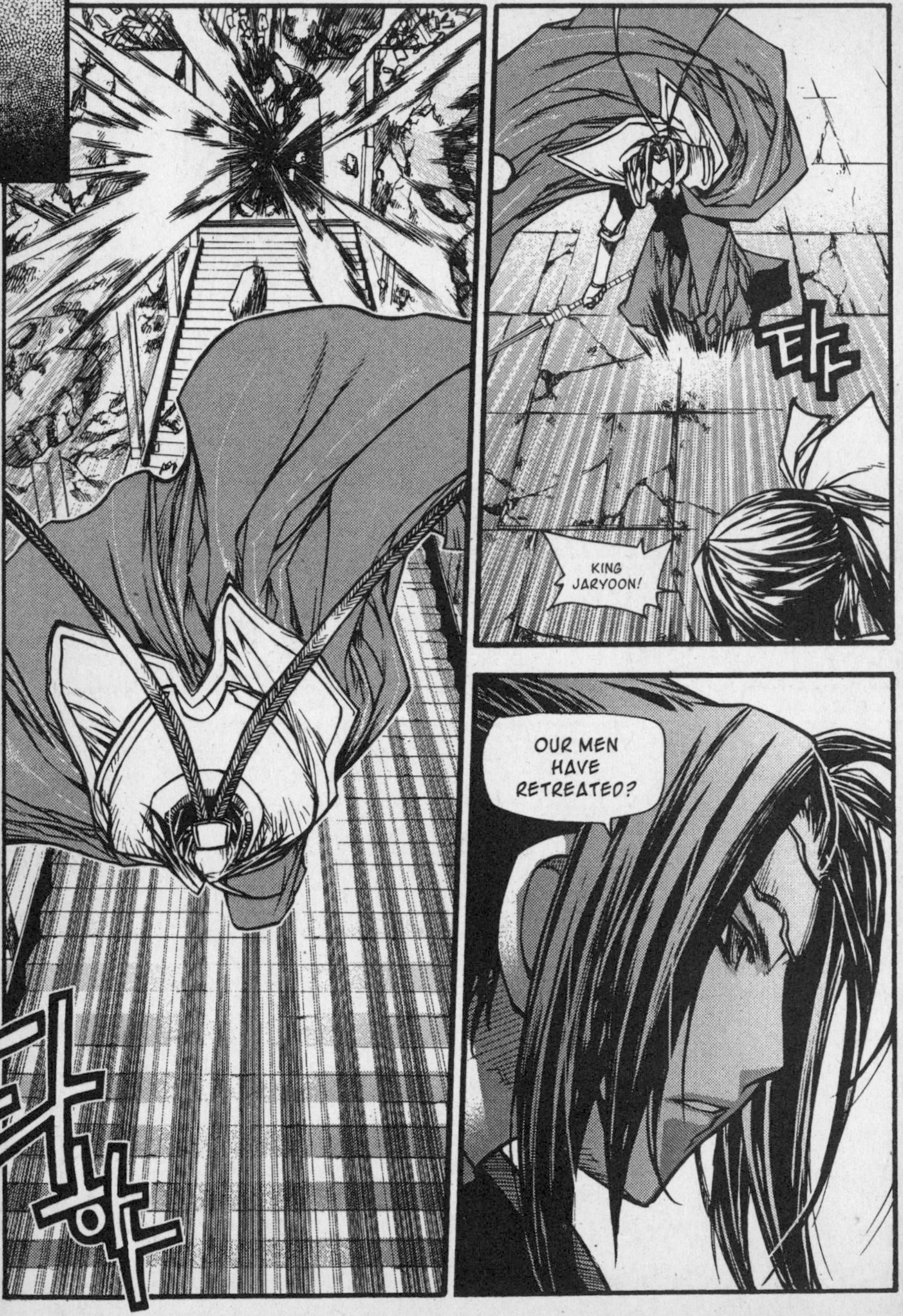
KING JARYOON!
OUR MEN HAVE RETREATED?

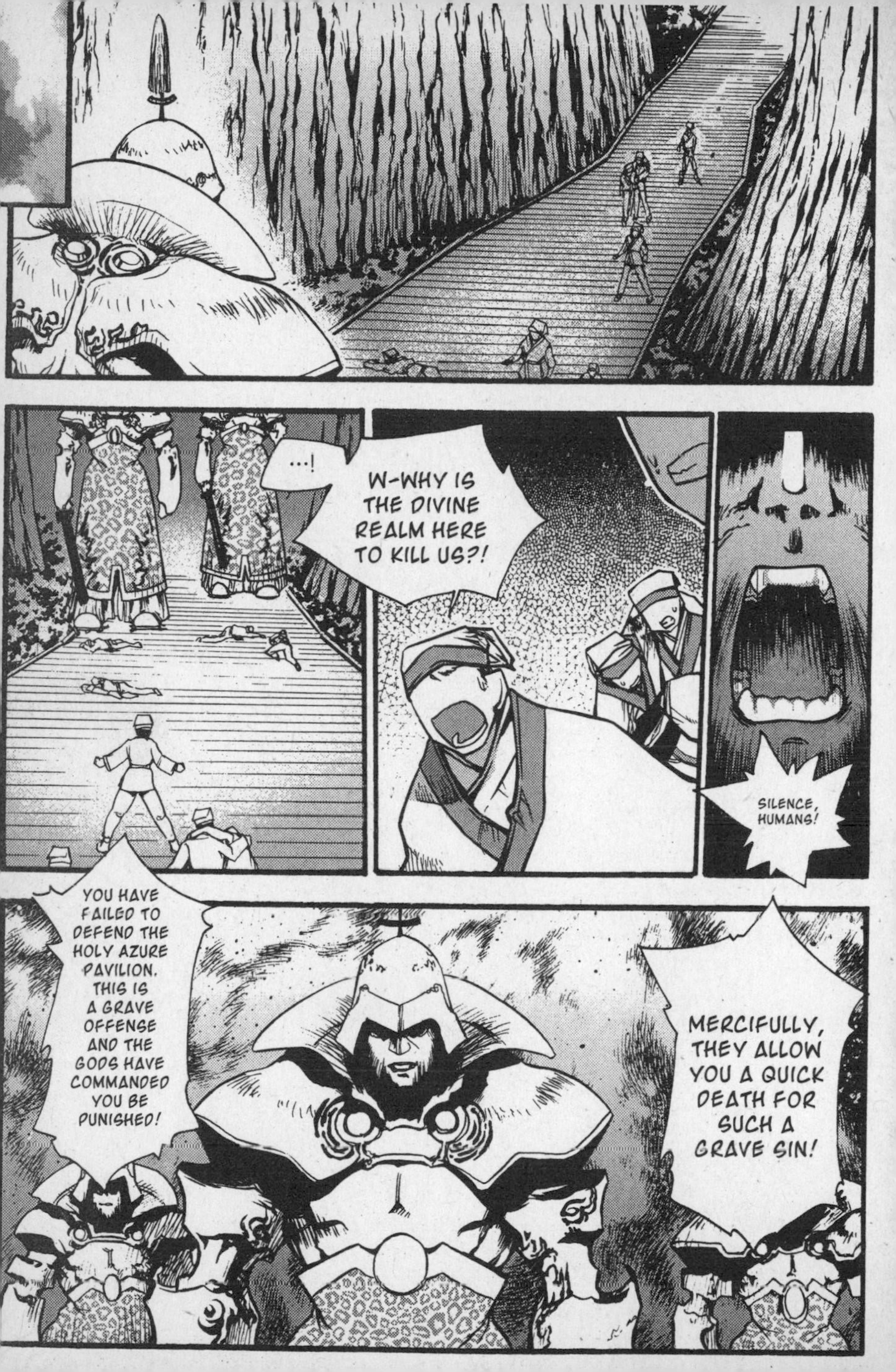
...!
W-WHY IS THE DIVINE REALM HERE TO KILL US?!
SILENCE, HUMANS!
YOU HAVE FAILED TO DEFEND THE HOLY AZURE PAVILION. THIS IS A GRAVE OFFENSE AND THE GODS HAVE COMMANDED YOU BE PUNISHED!
MERCIFULLY, THEY ALLOW YOU A QUICK DEATH FOR SUCH A GRAVE SIN!

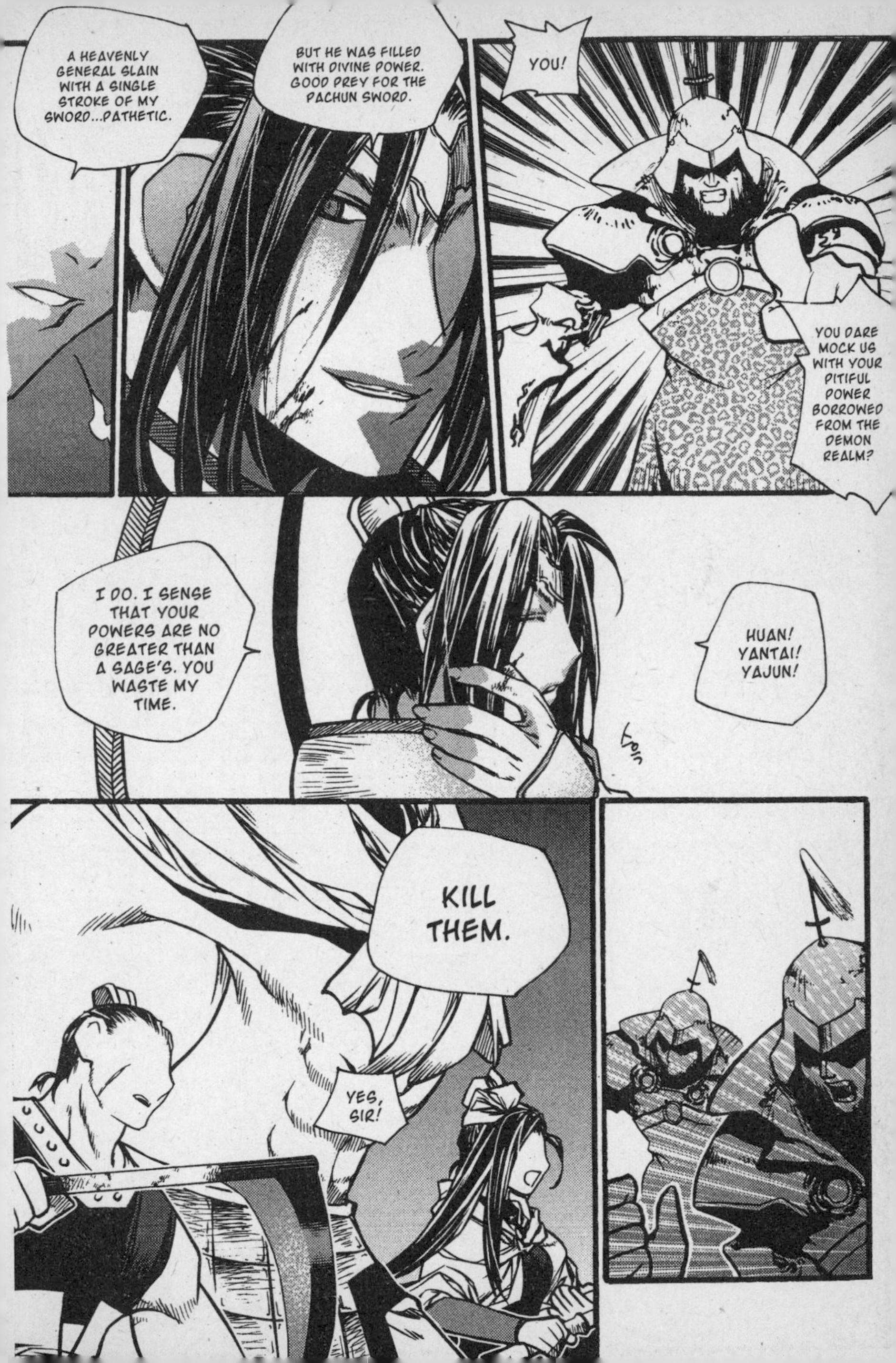
A HEAVENLY GENERAL SLAIN WITH A SINGLE STROKE OF MY SWORD...PATHETIC.
BUT HE WAS FILLED WITH DIVINE POWER. GOOD PREY FOR THE PACHUN SWORD.
YOU!
YOU DARE MOCK US WITH YOUR PITIFUL POWER BORROWED FROM THE DEMON REALM?
I DO. I SENSE THAT YOUR POWERS ARE NO GREATER THAN A SAGE'S. YOU WASTE MY TIME.
HUAN! YANTAI! YAJUN!
KILL THEM.
YES, SIR!

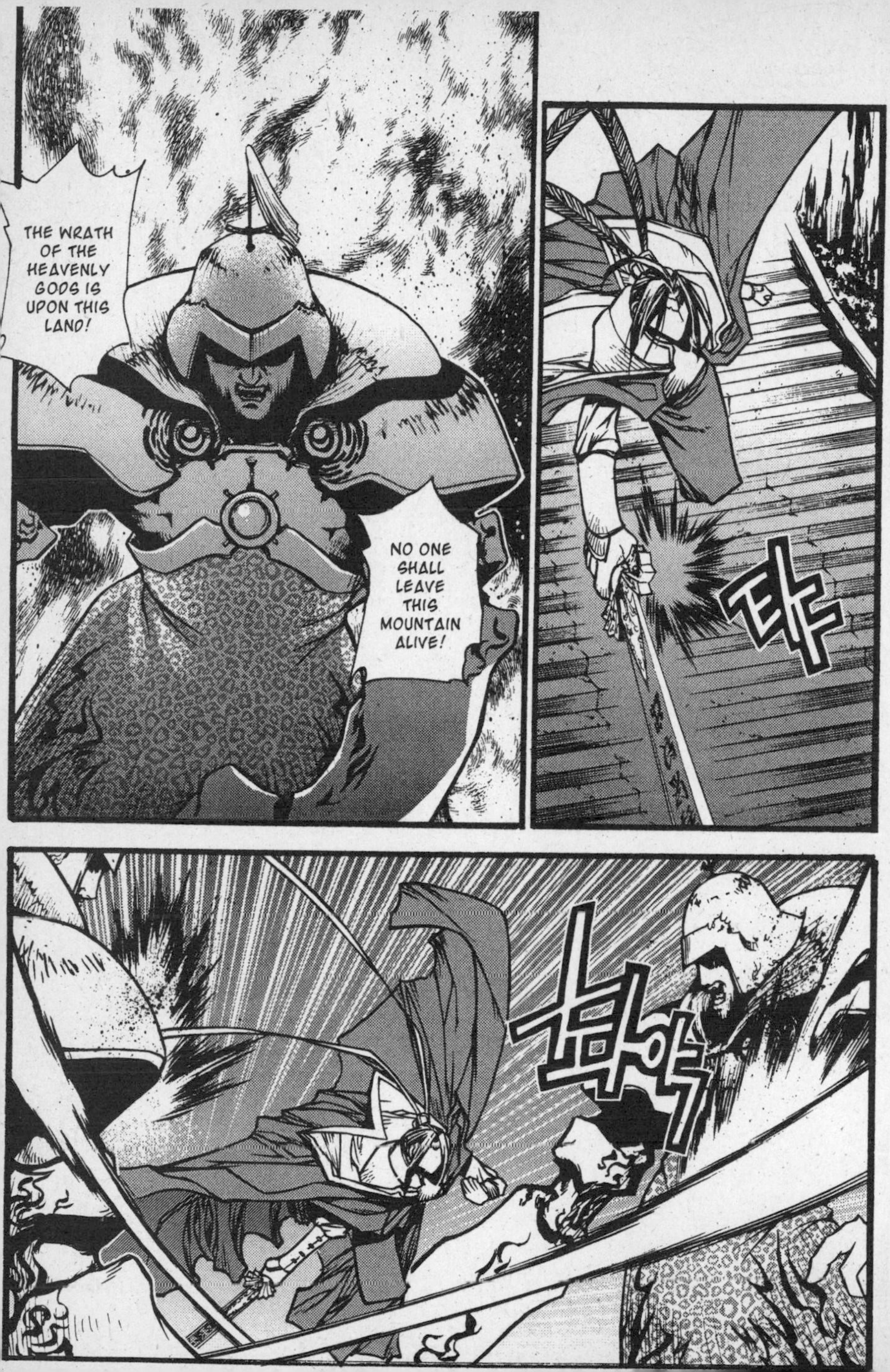
THE WRATH OF THE HEAVENLY GODS IS UPON THIS LAND!
NO ONE SHALL LEAVE THIS MOUNTAIN ALIVE!

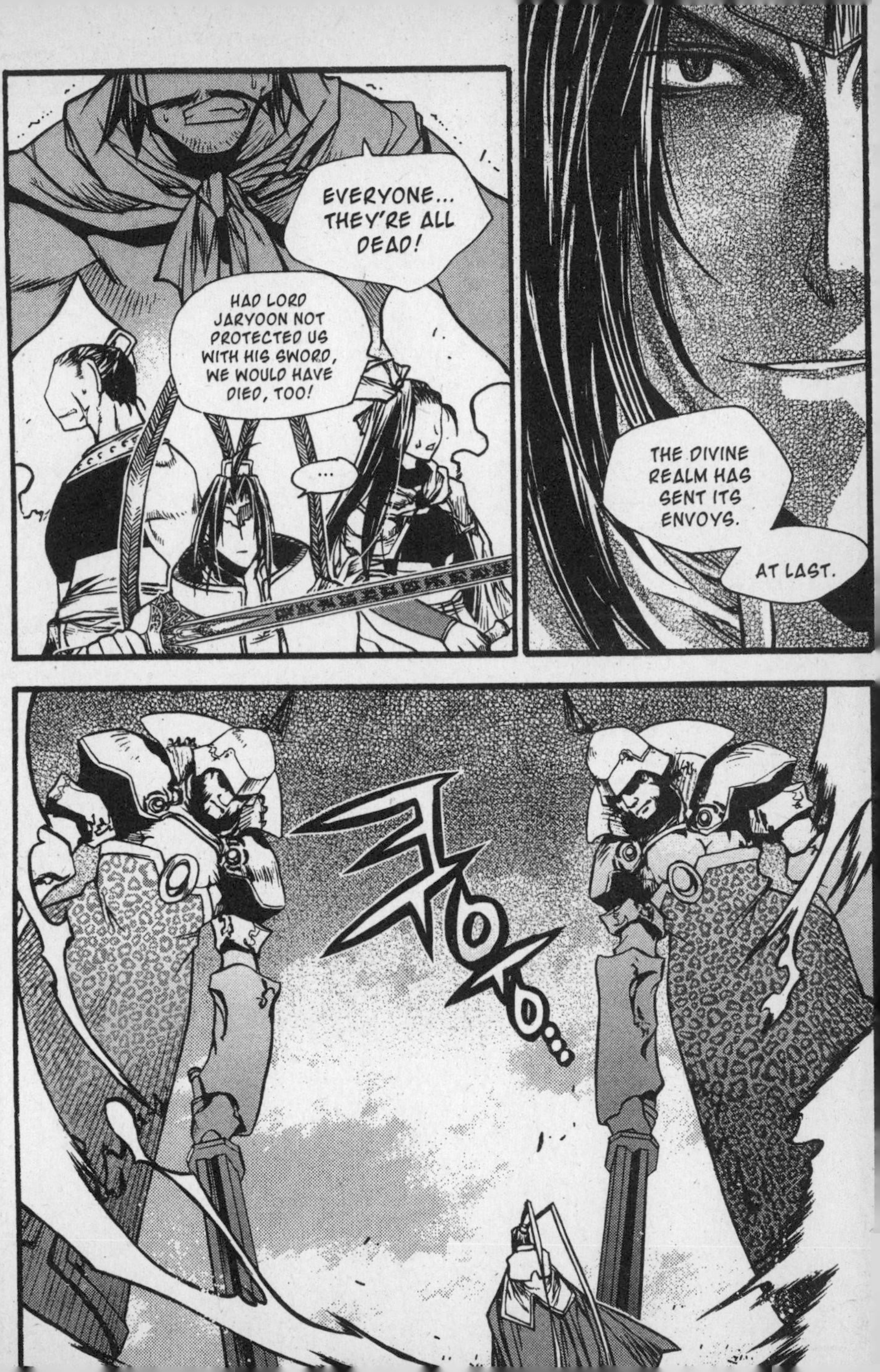
EVERYONE... THEY'RE ALL DEAD!
HAD LORD JARYOON NOT PROTECTED US WITH HIS SWORD, WE WOULD HAVE DIED, TOO!
...
THE DIVINE REALM HAS SENT ITS ENVOYS.
AT LAST.

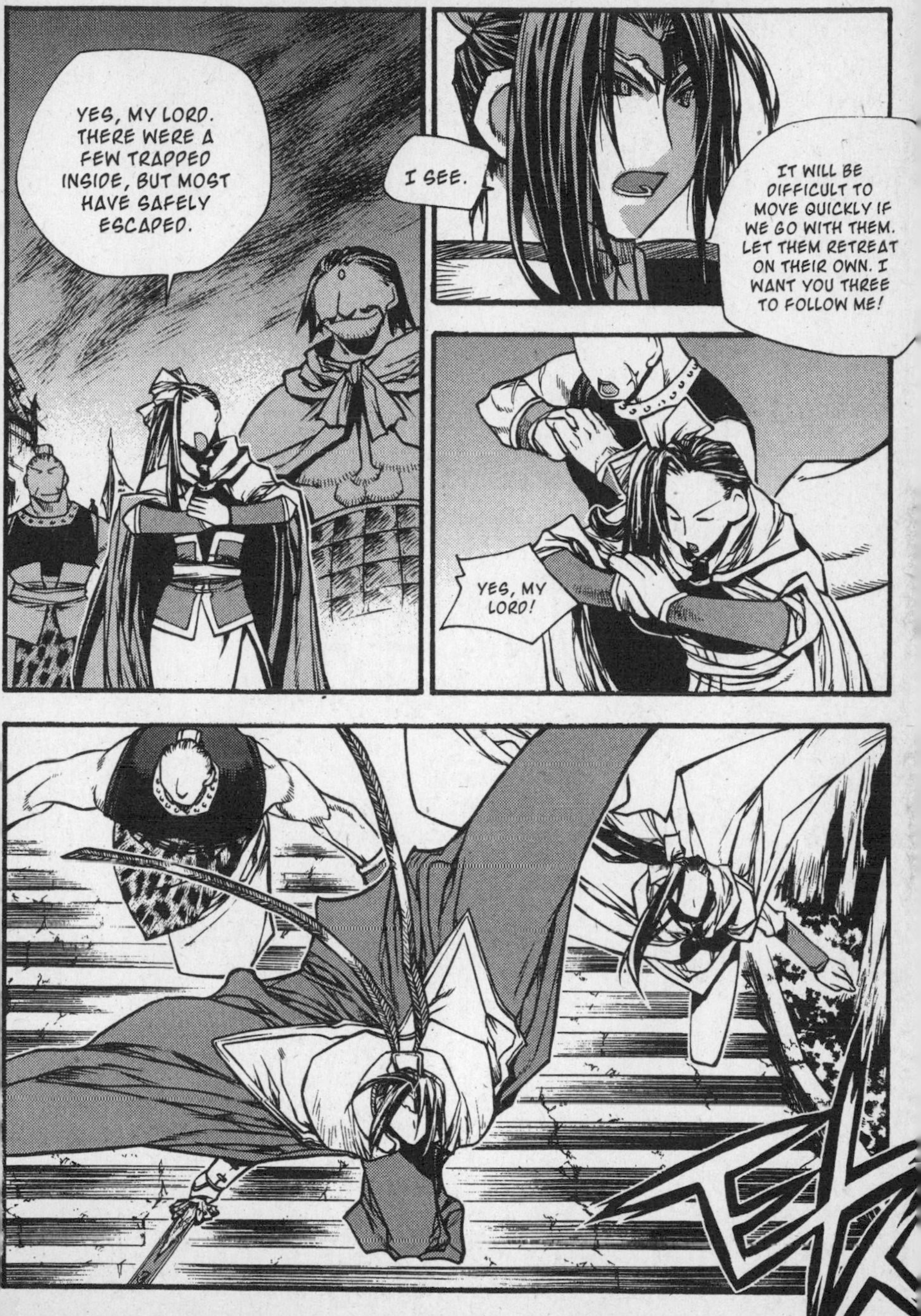
YES, MY LORD. THERE WERE A FEW TRAPPED INSIDE, BUT MOST HAVE SAFELY ESCAPED.
I SEE.
IT WILL BE DIFFICULT TO MOVE QUICKLY IF WE GO WITH THEM. LET THEM RETREAT ON THEIR OWN. I WANT YOU THREE TO FOLLOW ME!
YES, MY LORD!

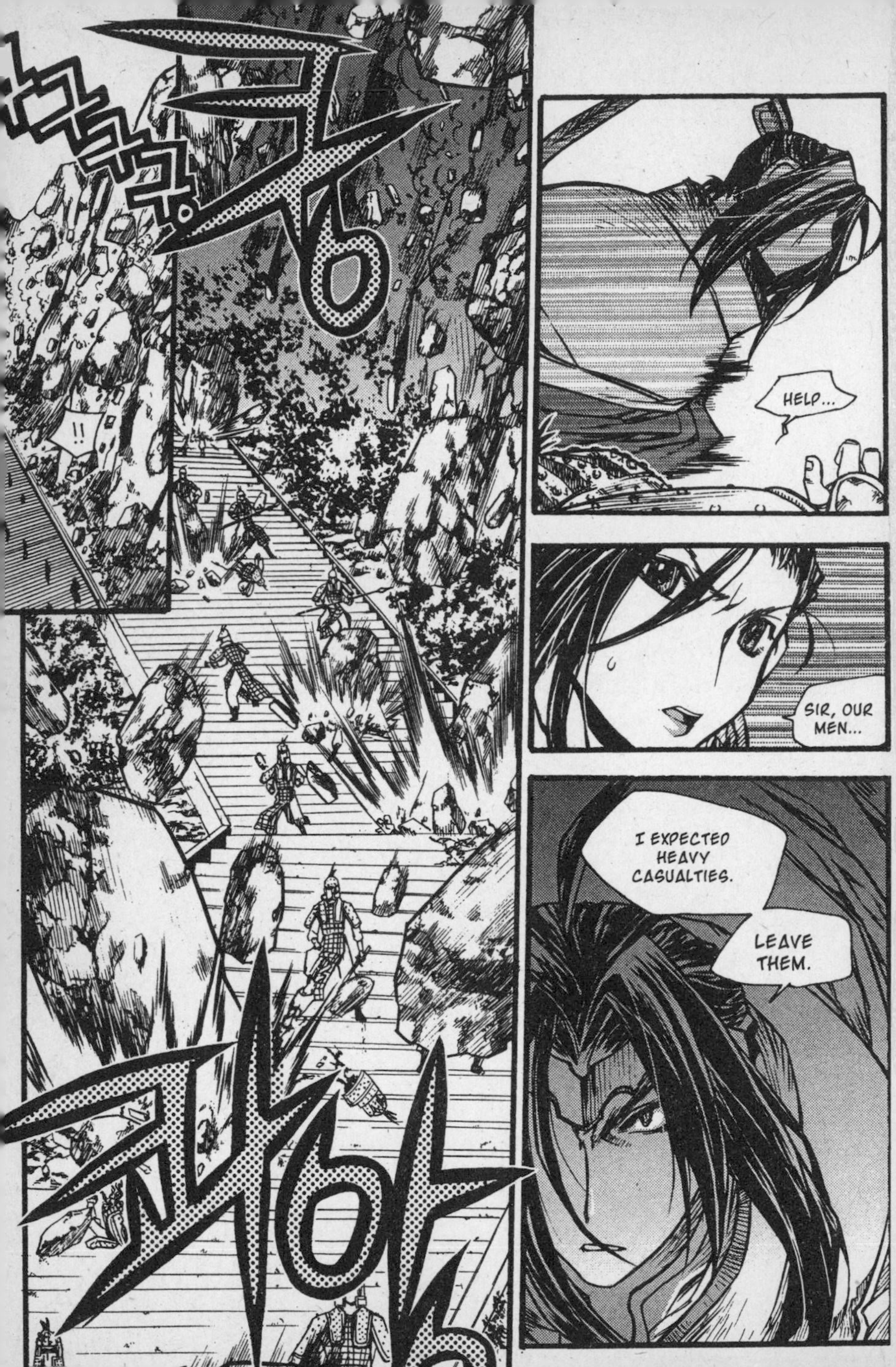
!!
HELP...
SIR, OUR MEN...
I EXPECTED HEAVY CASUALTIES.
LEAVE THEM.

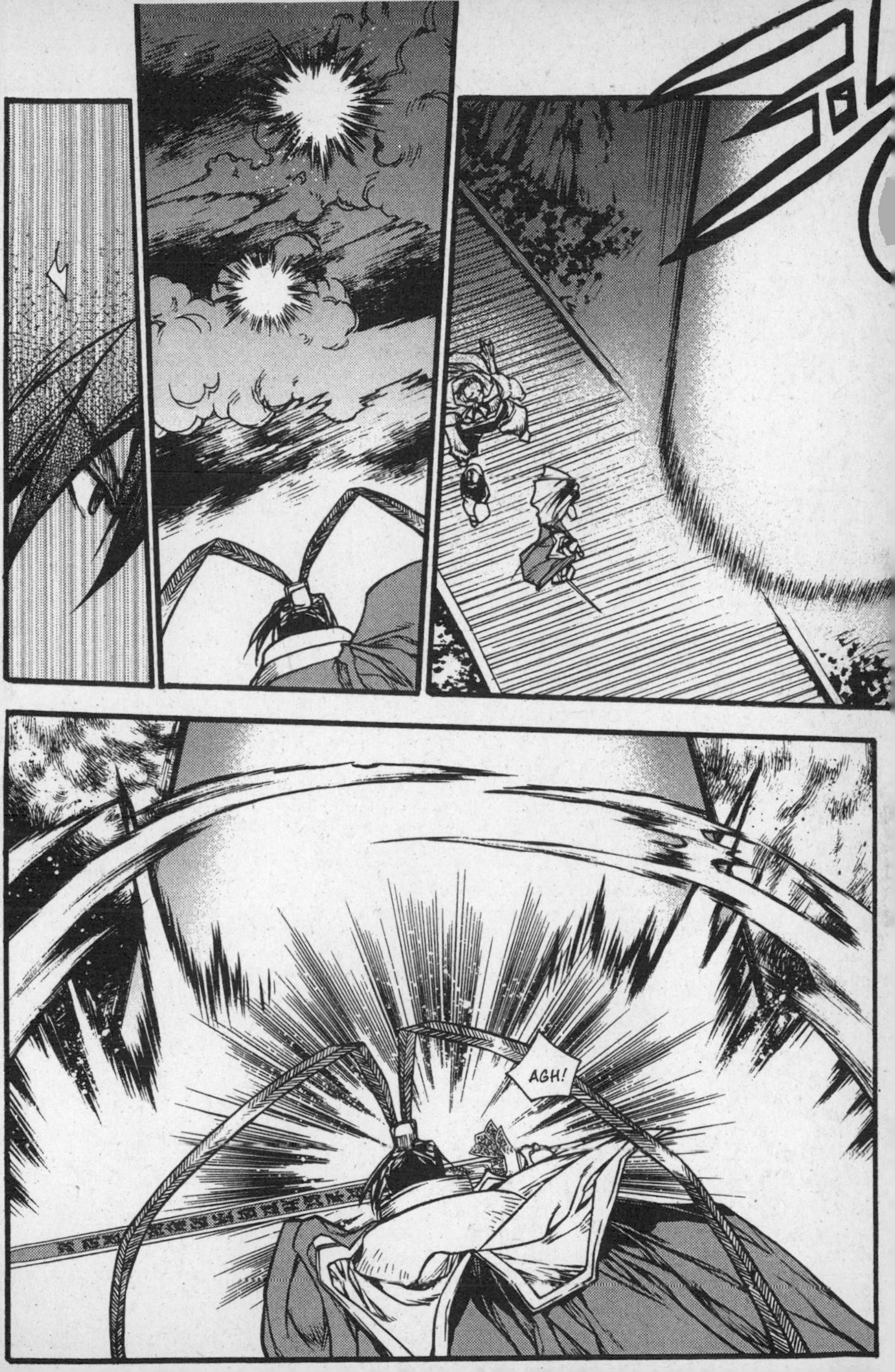
AGH!

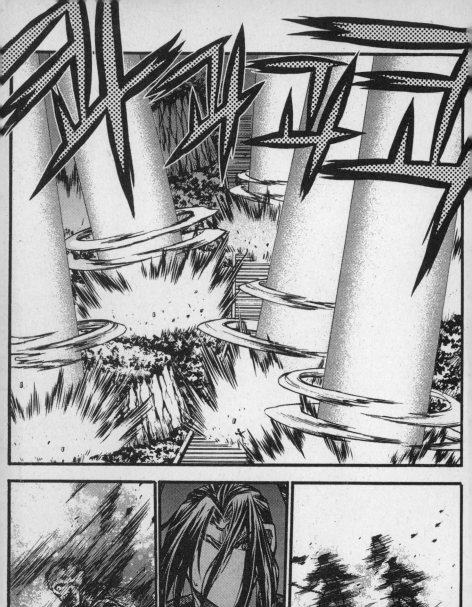

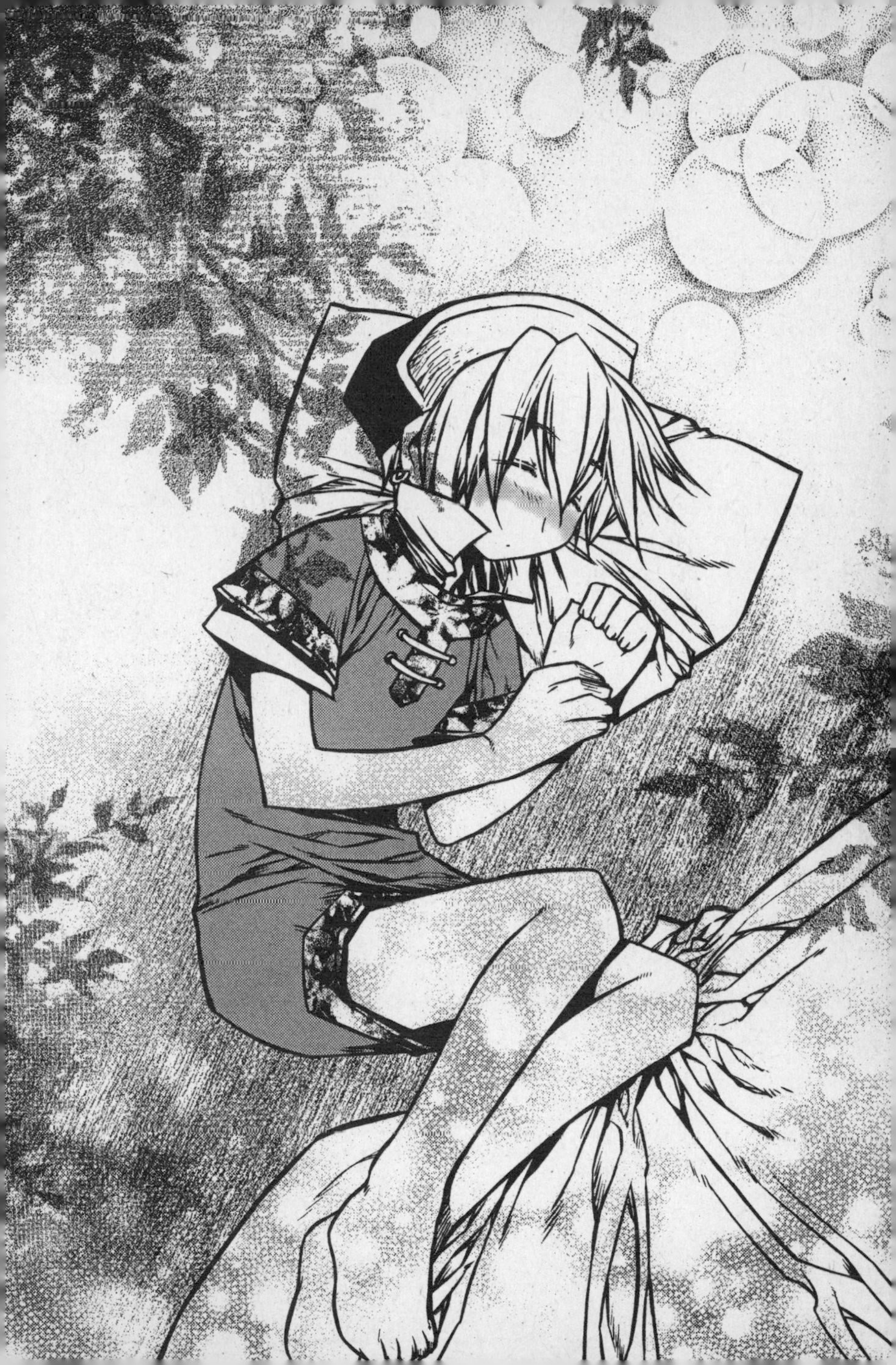

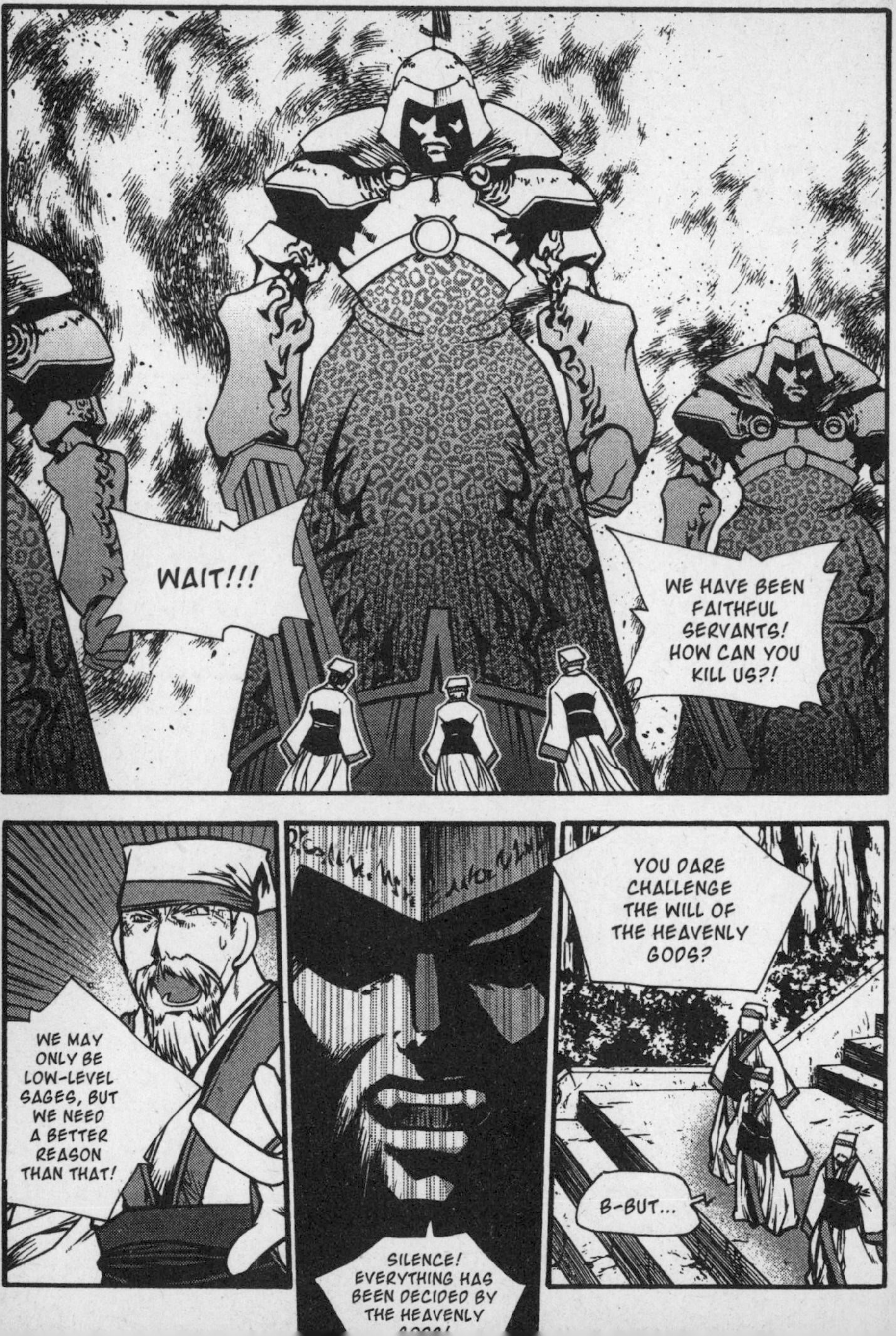
WAIT!!!
WE HAVE BEEN FAITHFUL SERVANTS! HOW CAN YOU KILL US?!
WE MAY ONLY BE LOW-LEVEL SAGES, BUT WE NEED A BETTER REASON THAN THAT!
SILENCE! EVERYTHING HAS BEEN DECIDED BY THE HEAVENLY
YOU DARE CHALLENGE THE WILL OF THE HEAVENLY GODS?
B-BUT...

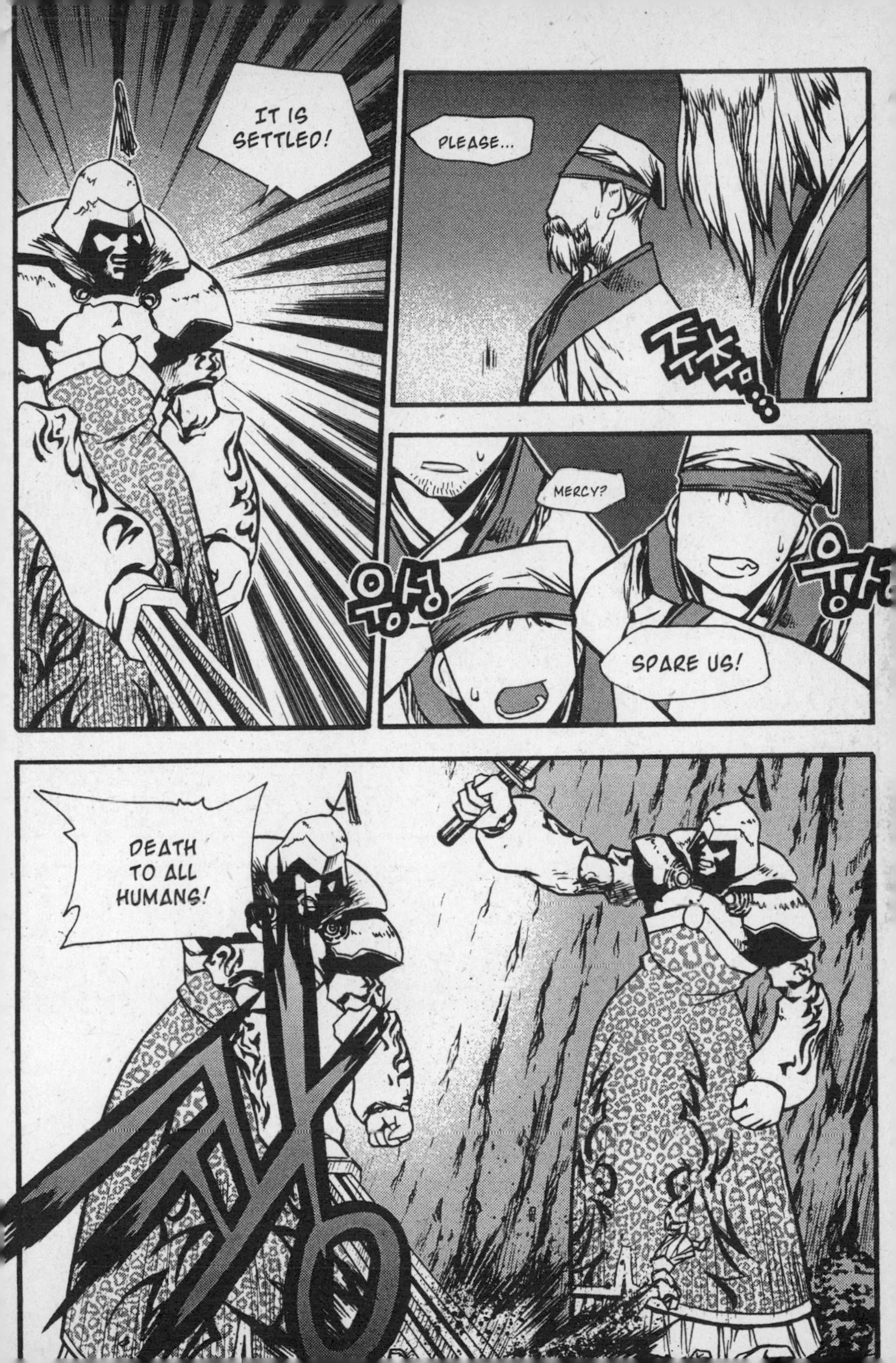
IT IS SETTLED!
PLEASE...
주춤...
MERCY?
웅성
SPARE US!
DEATH TO ALL HUMANS!

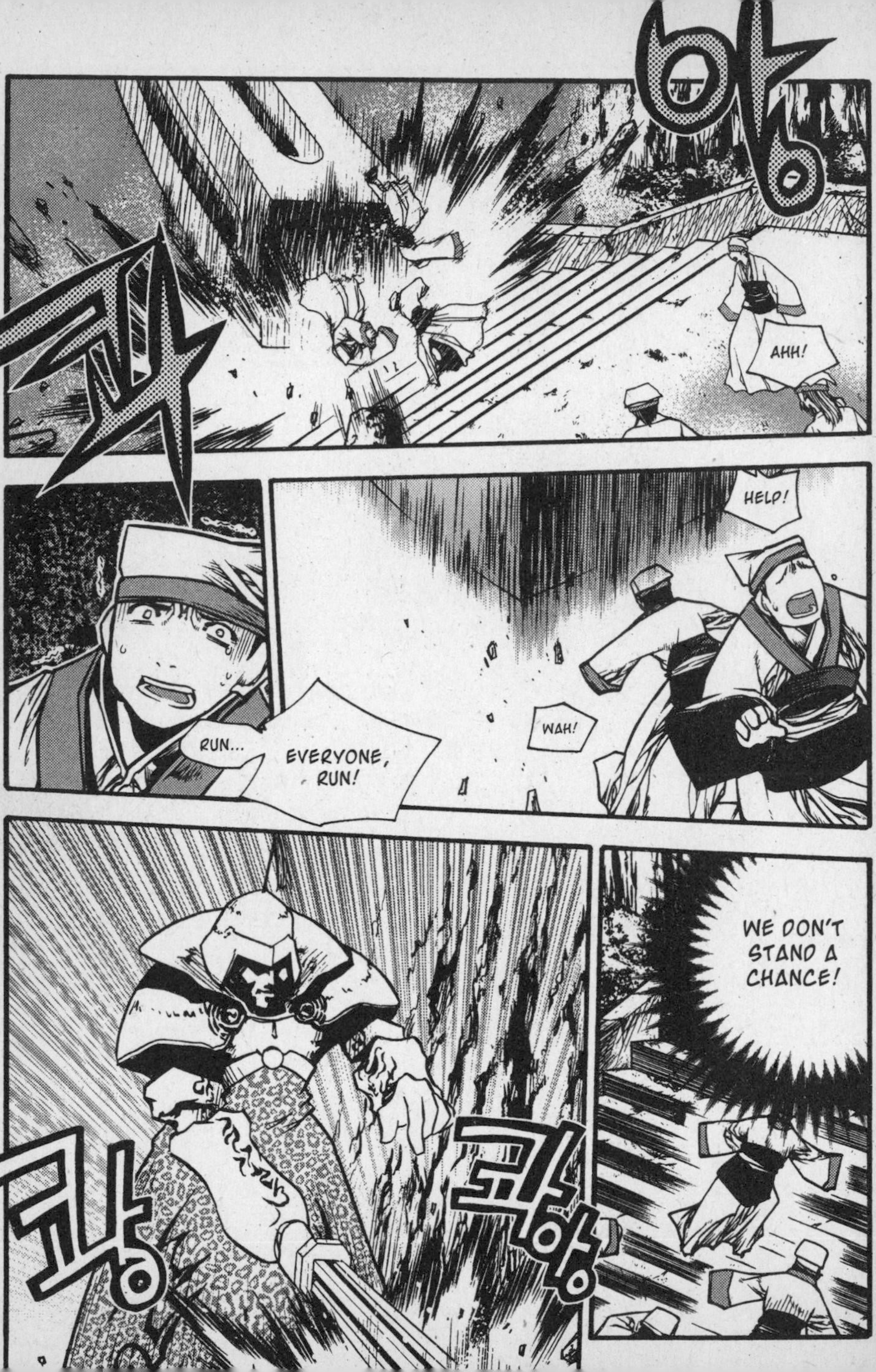
AHH!
RUN...
EVERYONE, RUN!
HELP!
WAH!
WE DON'T STAND A CHANCE!

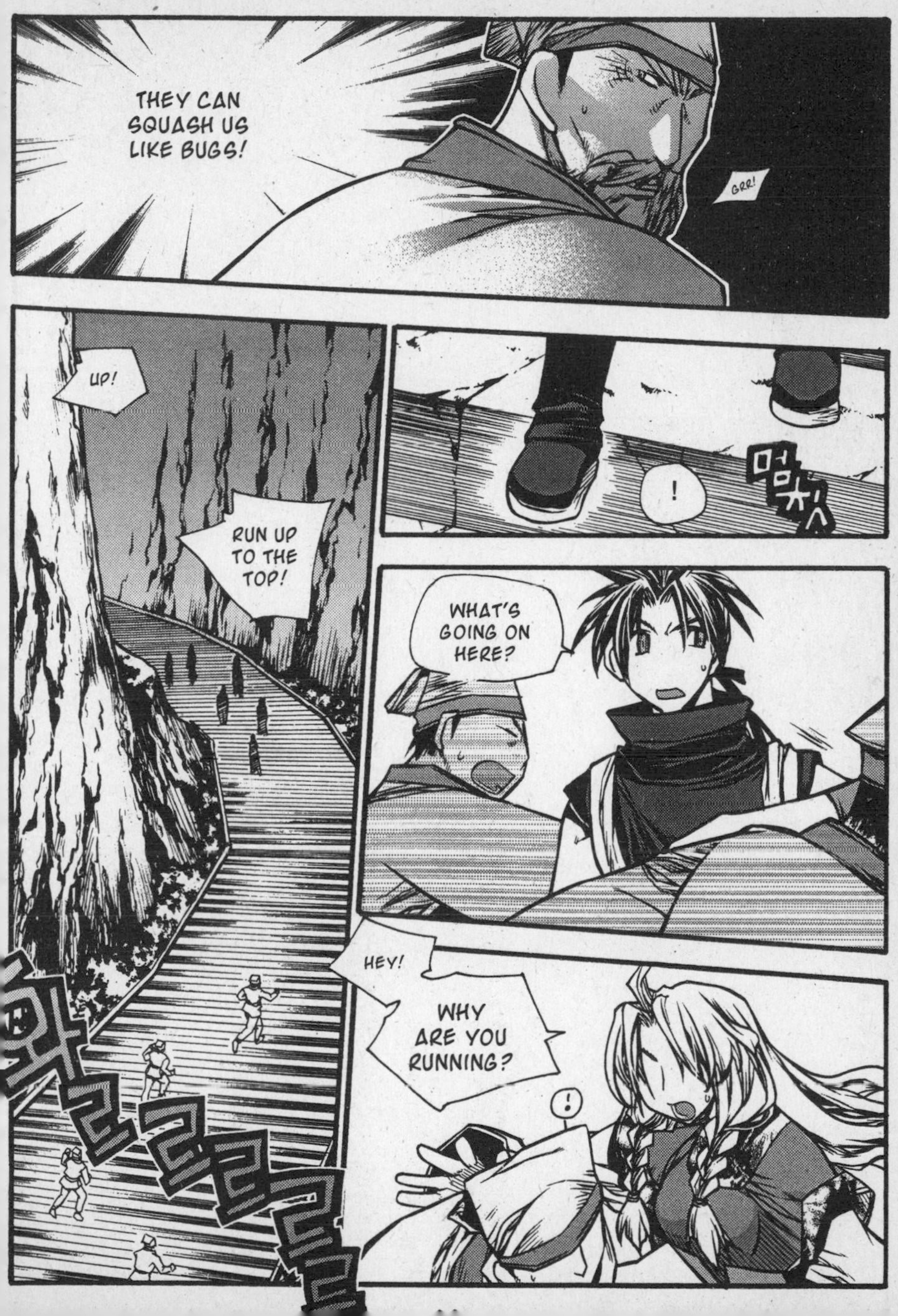
THEY CAN SQUASH US LIKE BUGS!
GRR!
UP!
RUN UP TO THE TOP!
!
WHAT'S GOING ON HERE?
HEY!
WHY ARE YOU RUNNING?
!

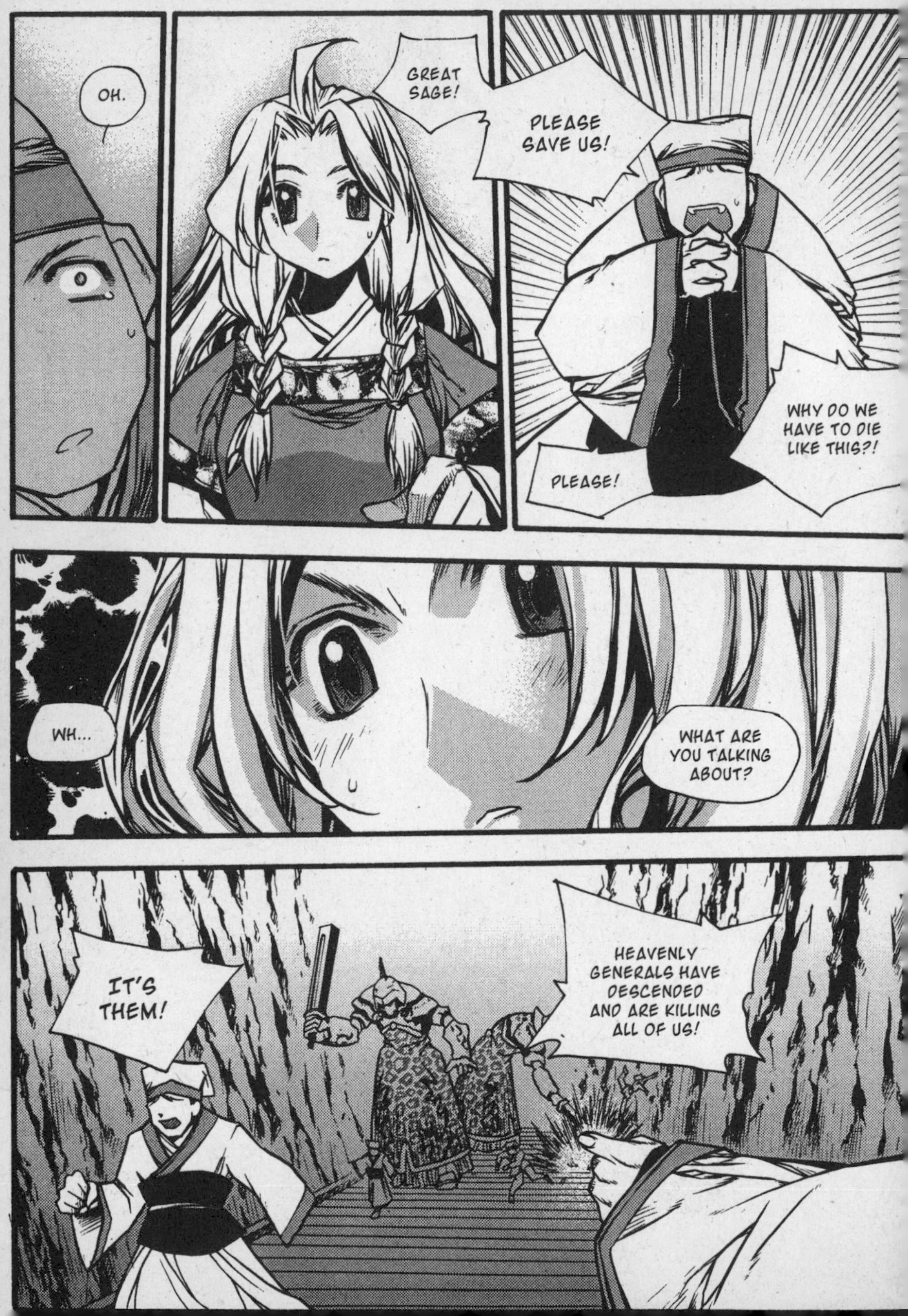
OH.
GREAT SAGE!
PLEASE SAVE US!
WHY DO WE HAVE TO DIE LIKE THIS?!
PLEASE!
WH...
WHAT ARE YOU TALKING ABOUT?
IT'S THEM!
HEAVENLY GENERALS HAVE DESCENDED AND ARE KILLING ALL OF US!

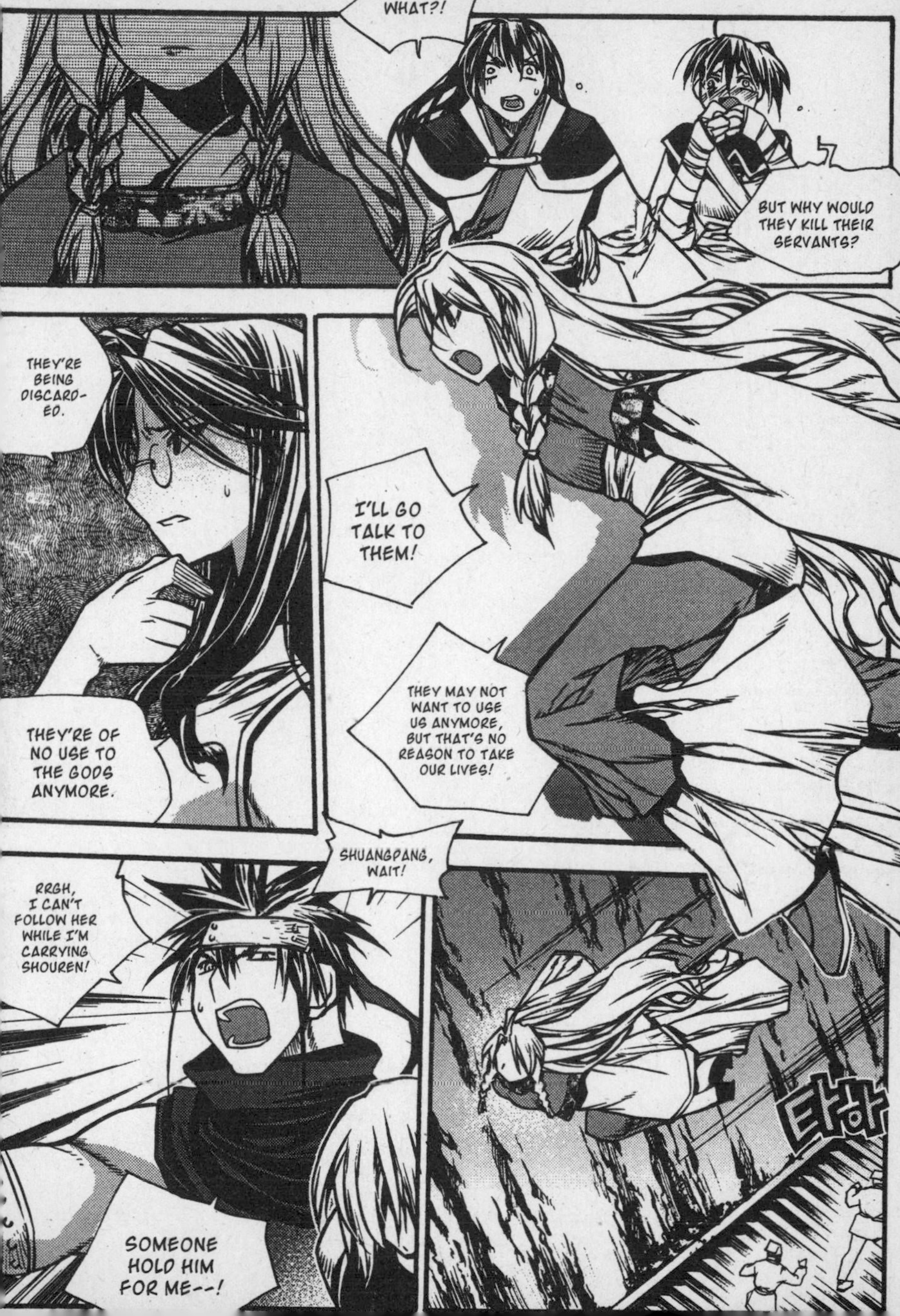
WHAT?!
BUT WHY WOULD THEY KILL THEIR SERVANTS?
THEY'RE BEING DISCARD-ED.
THEY'RE OF NO USE TO THE GODS ANYMORE.
I'LL GO TALK TO THEM!
THEY MAY NOT WANT TO USE US ANYMORE, BUT THAT'S NO REASON TO TAKE OUR LIVES!
SHUANGPANG, WAIT!
RRGH, I CAN'T FOLLOW HER WHILE I'M CARRYING SHOUREN!
SOMEONE HOLD HIM FOR ME--!
타아

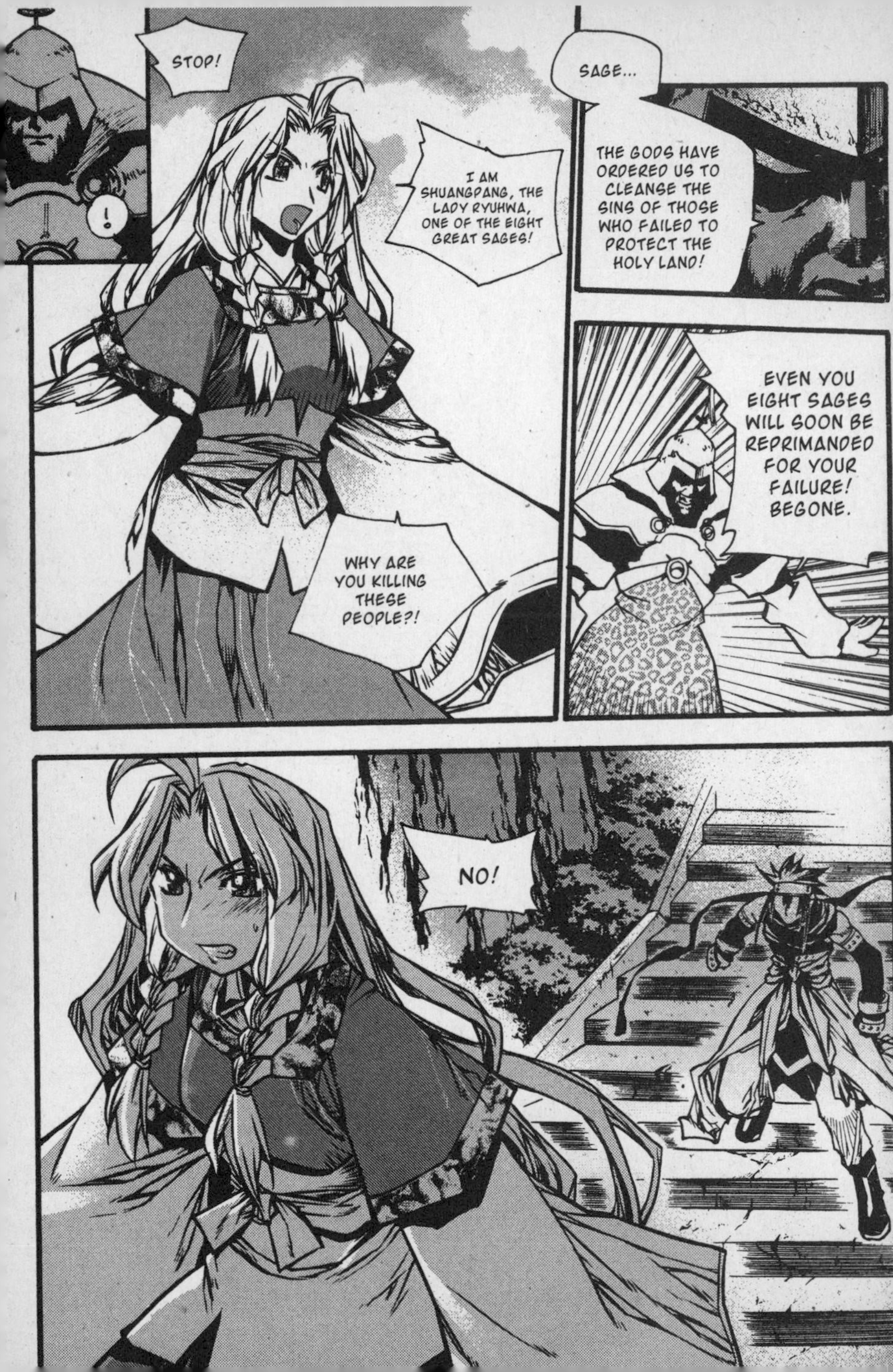

STOP!
!
I AM SHUANGPANG, THE LADY RYUHWA, ONE OF THE EIGHT GREAT SAGES!
WHY ARE YOU KILLING THESE PEOPLE?!
SAGE...
THE GODS HAVE ORDERED US TO CLEANSE THE SINS OF THOSE WHO FAILED TO PROTECT THE HOLY LAND!
EVEN YOU EIGHT SAGES WILL SOON BE REPRIMANDED FOR YOUR FAILURE! BEGONE.
NO!

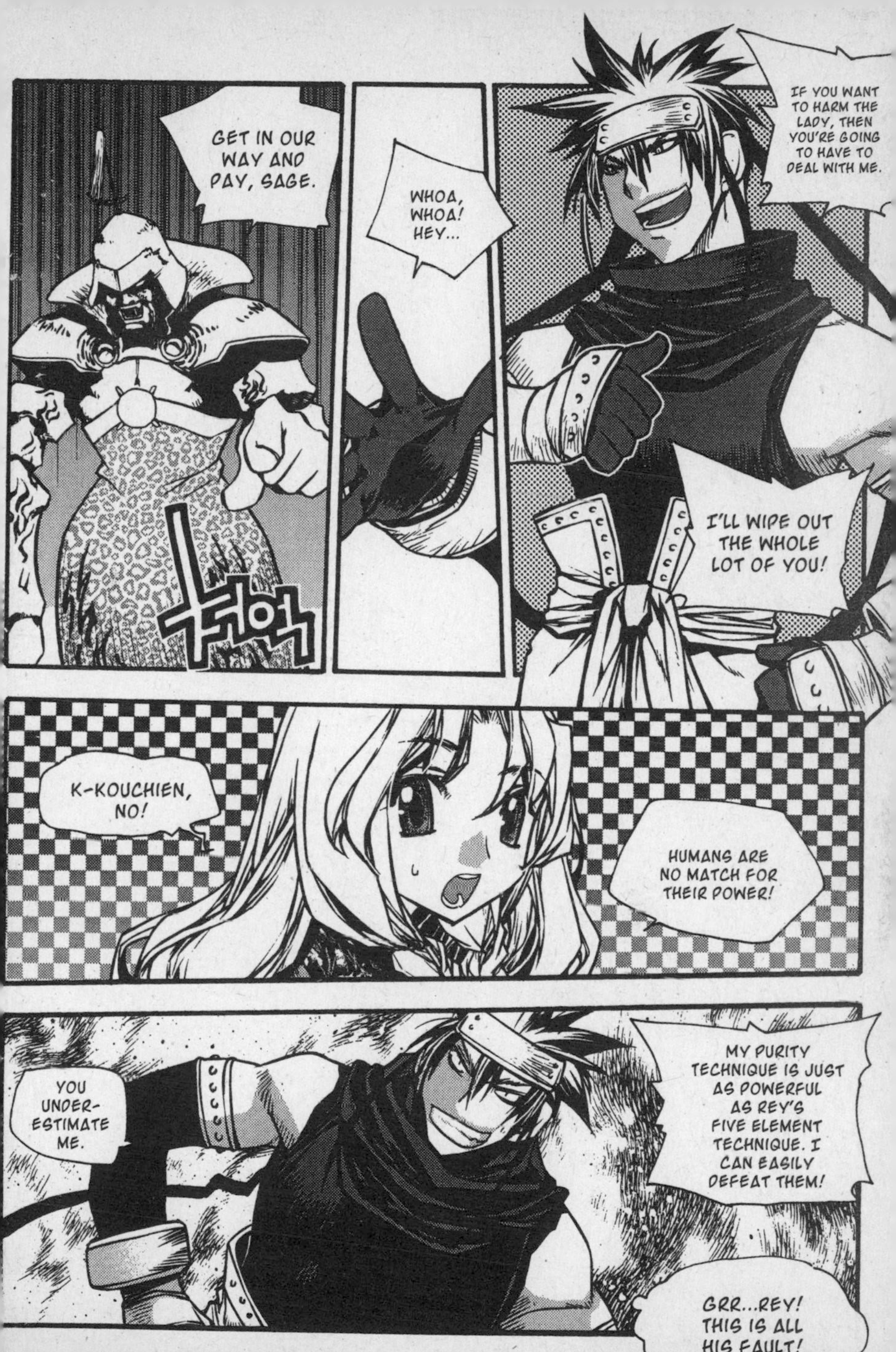
GET IN OUR WAY AND PAY, SAGE.
WHOA, WHOA! HEY...
IF YOU WANT TO HARM THE LADY, THEN YOU'RE GOING TO HAVE TO DEAL WITH ME.
I'LL WIPE OUT THE WHOLE LOT OF YOU!
K-KOUCHIEN, NO!
HUMANS ARE NO MATCH FOR THEIR POWER!
YOU UNDER-ESTIMATE ME.
MY PURITY TECHNIQUE IS JUST AS POWERFUL AS REY'S FIVE ELEMENT TECHNIQUE. I CAN EASILY DEFEAT THEM!
GRR...REY! THIS IS ALL HIS FAULT!

HYAAAA!!

PURITY TECHNIQUE~ PETALS OF FIRE!

YAA!

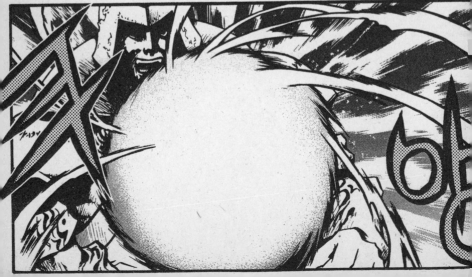

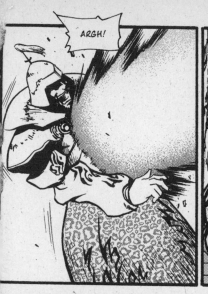

ARGH!

MY, WHAT A TEMPER KOUCHIEN HAS!

MOTHER.

I THINK WE NEED TO HELP HIM.

WE'D BETTER IF WE WANT TO LIVE, HUH?

SHISHAN WILL USE HER STRENGTH. I WILL USE MY POISON.

LET'S GO.

REY.

REY?

YOU NEED TO CLEAR THE WAY FOR US...

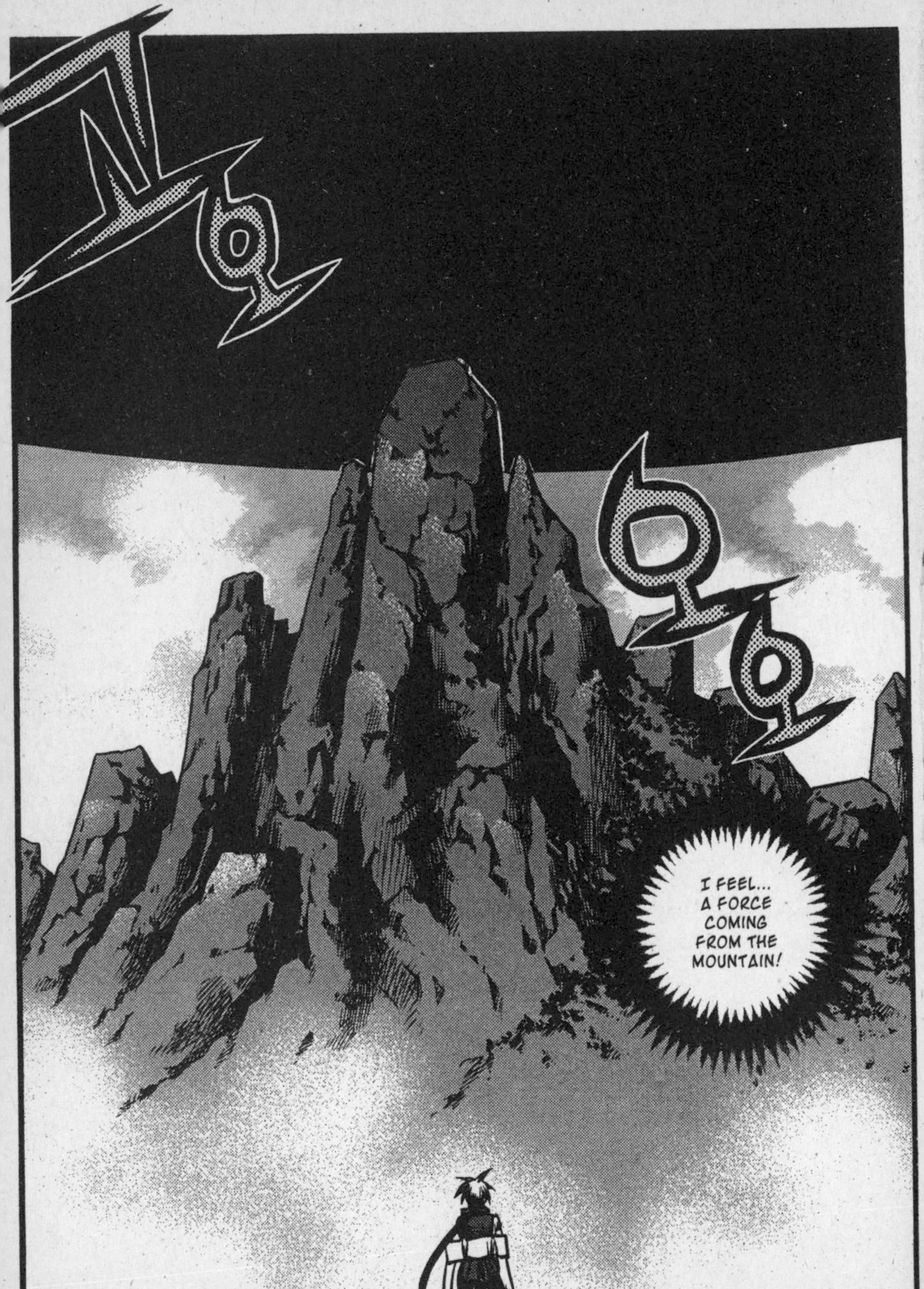
I FEEL... A FORCE COMING FROM THE MOUNTAIN!

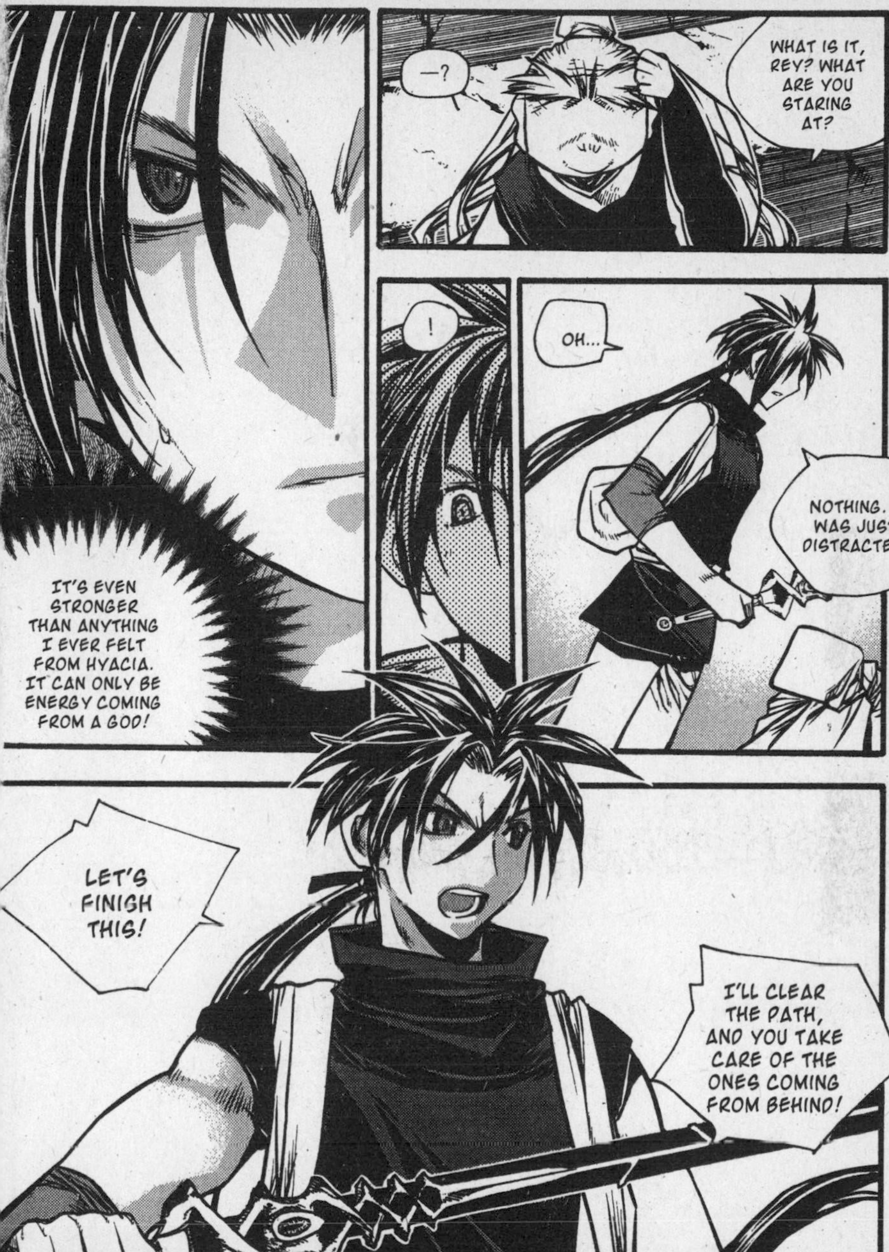
IT'S EVEN STRONGER THAN ANYTHING I EVER FELT FROM HYACIA. IT CAN ONLY BE ENERGY COMING FROM A GOD!
—?
WHAT IS IT, REY? WHAT ARE YOU STARING AT?
!
OH...
NOTHING. I WAS JUST DISTRACTED.
LET'S FINISH THIS!
I'LL CLEAR THE PATH, AND YOU TAKE CARE OF THE ONES COMING FROM BEHIND!

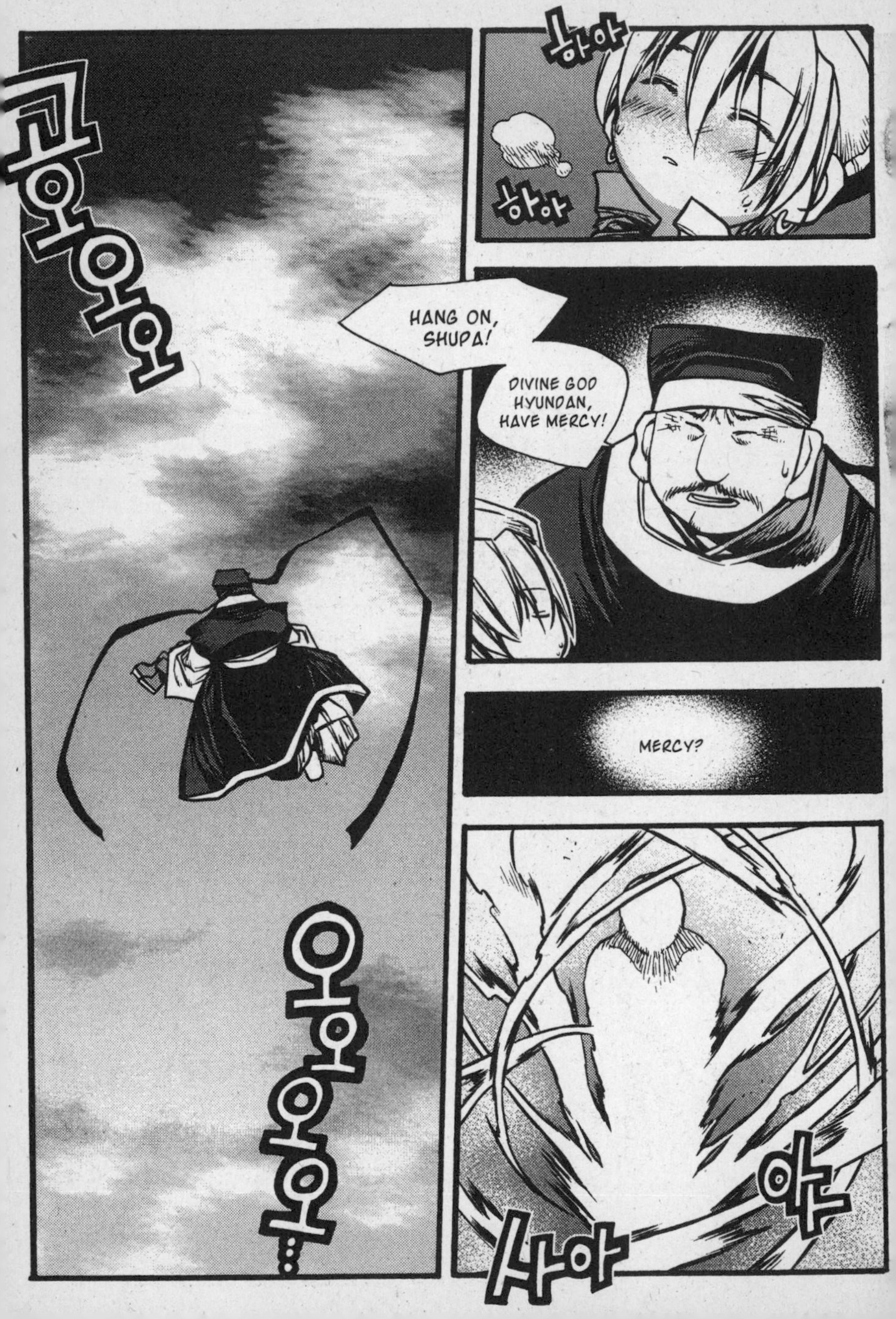
고오오오
오오오오…
하아
하아
HANG ON, SHUPA!
DIVINE GOD HYUNDAN, HAVE MERCY!
MERCY?
사아
아

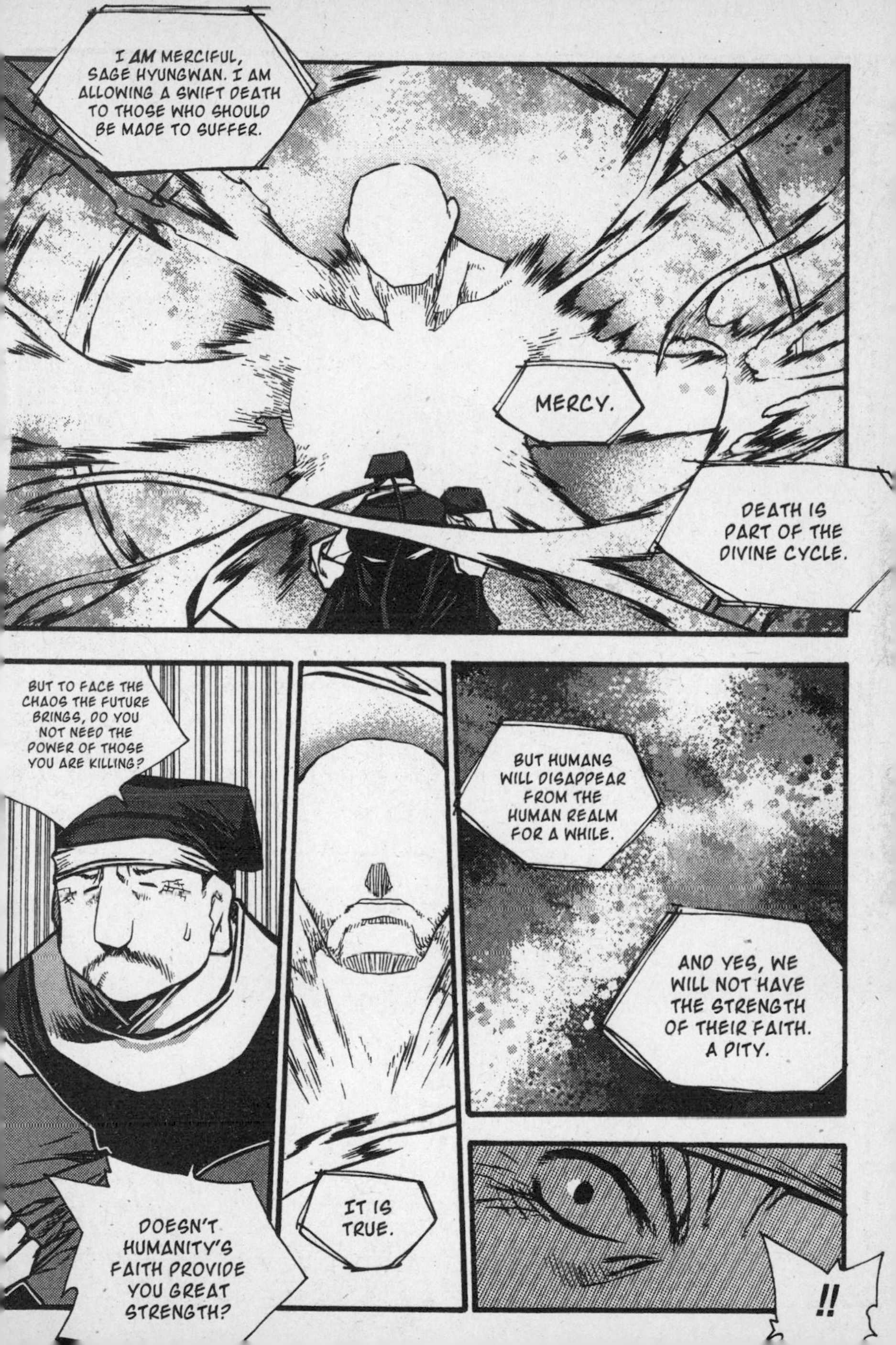
I AM MERCIFUL, SAGE HYUNGWAN. I AM ALLOWING A SWIFT DEATH TO THOSE WHO SHOULD BE MADE TO SUFFER.
MERCY.
DEATH IS PART OF THE DIVINE CYCLE.
BUT TO FACE THE CHAOS THE FUTURE BRINGS, DO YOU NOT NEED THE POWER OF THOSE YOU ARE KILLING?
DOESN'T HUMANITY'S FAITH PROVIDE YOU GREAT STRENGTH?
IT IS TRUE.
BUT HUMANS WILL DISAPPEAR FROM THE HUMAN REALM FOR A WHILE.
AND YES, WE WILL NOT HAVE THE STRENGTH OF THEIR FAITH. A PITY.
!!

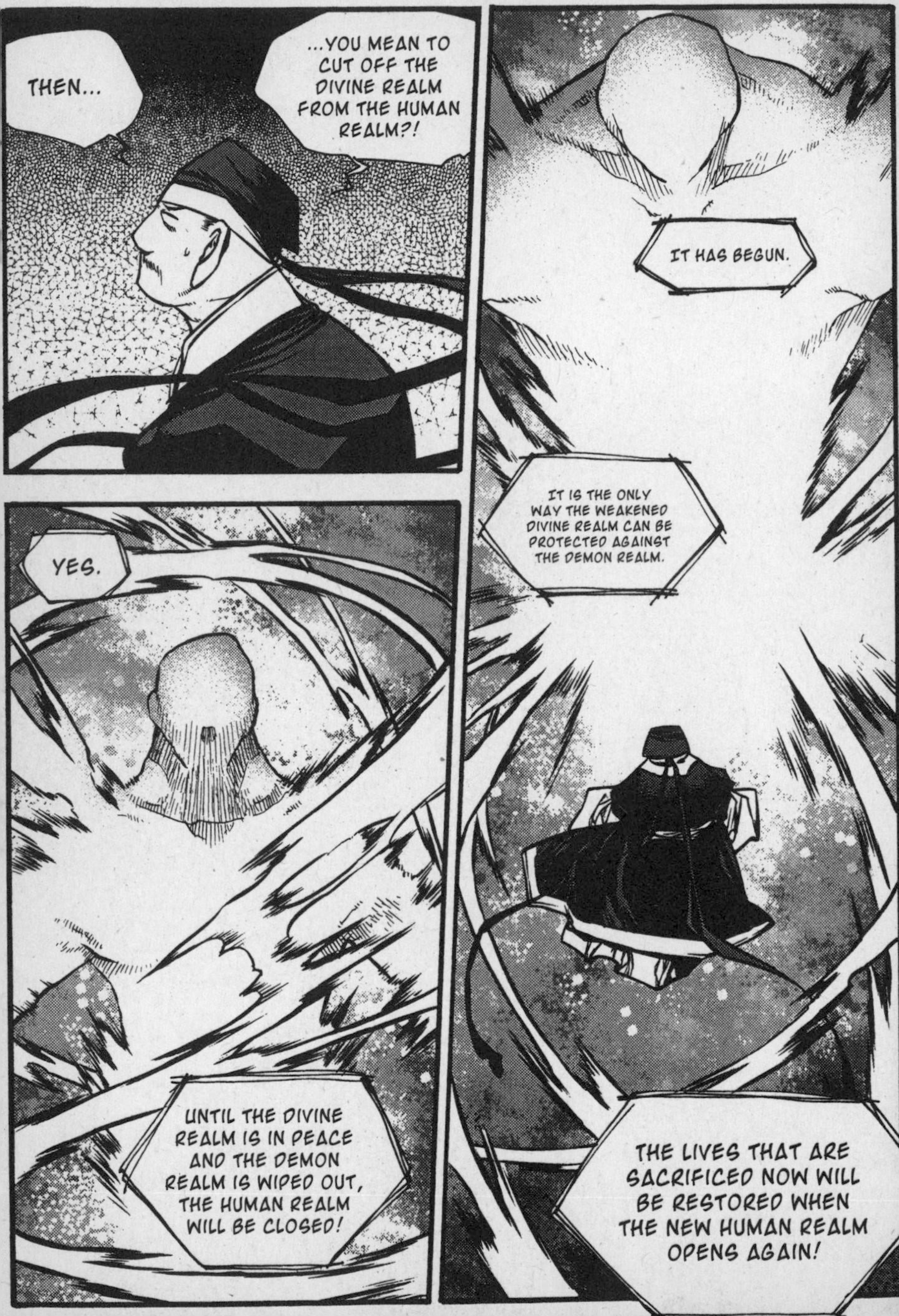
THEN...
...YOU MEAN TO CUT OFF THE DIVINE REALM FROM THE HUMAN REALM?!
YES.
UNTIL THE DIVINE REALM IS IN PEACE AND THE DEMON REALM IS WIPED OUT, THE HUMAN REALM WILL BE CLOSED!
IT HAS BEGUN.
IT IS THE ONLY WAY THE WEAKENED DIVINE REALM CAN BE PROTECTED AGAINST THE DEMON REALM.
THE LIVES THAT ARE SACRIFICED NOW WILL BE RESTORED WHEN THE NEW HUMAN REALM OPENS AGAIN!

Chapter 70: Hyunbing and Gumno

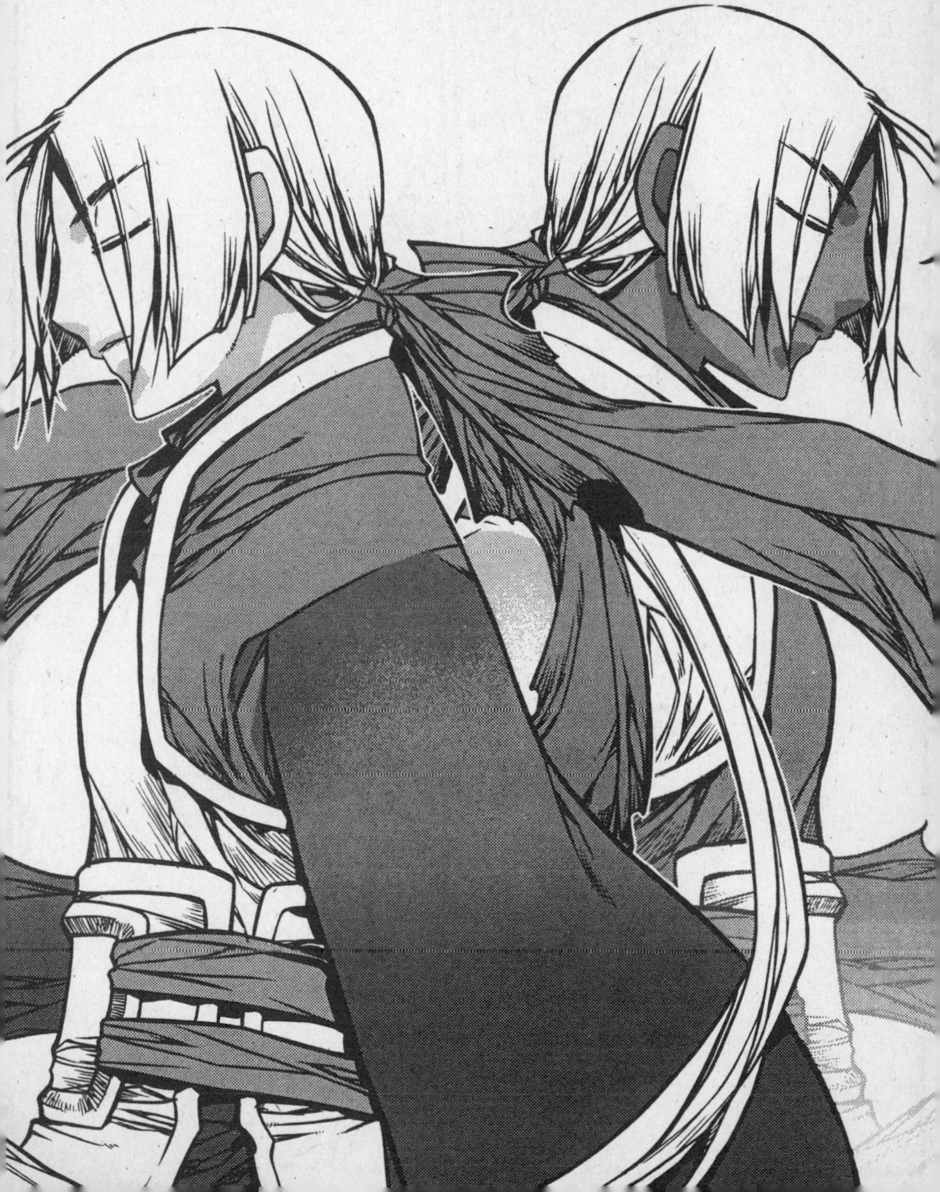

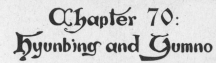

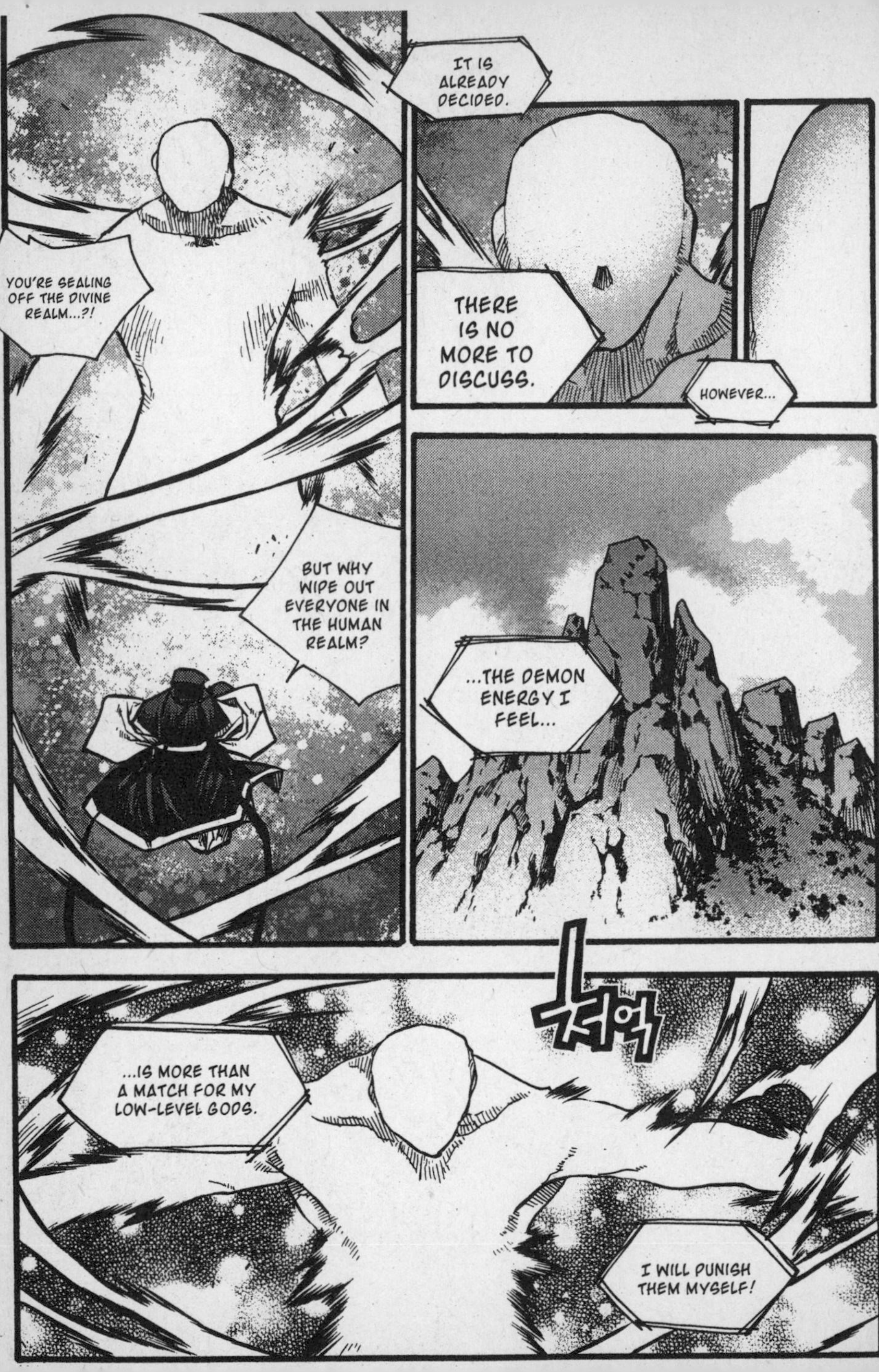
YOU'RE SEALING OFF THE DIVINE REALM...?!
BUT WHY WIPE OUT EVERYONE IN THE HUMAN REALM?
IT IS ALREADY DECIDED.
THERE IS NO MORE TO DISCUSS.
HOWEVER...
...THE DEMON ENERGY I FEEL...
...IS MORE THAN A MATCH FOR MY LOW-LEVEL GODS.
척억
I WILL PUNISH THEM MYSELF!

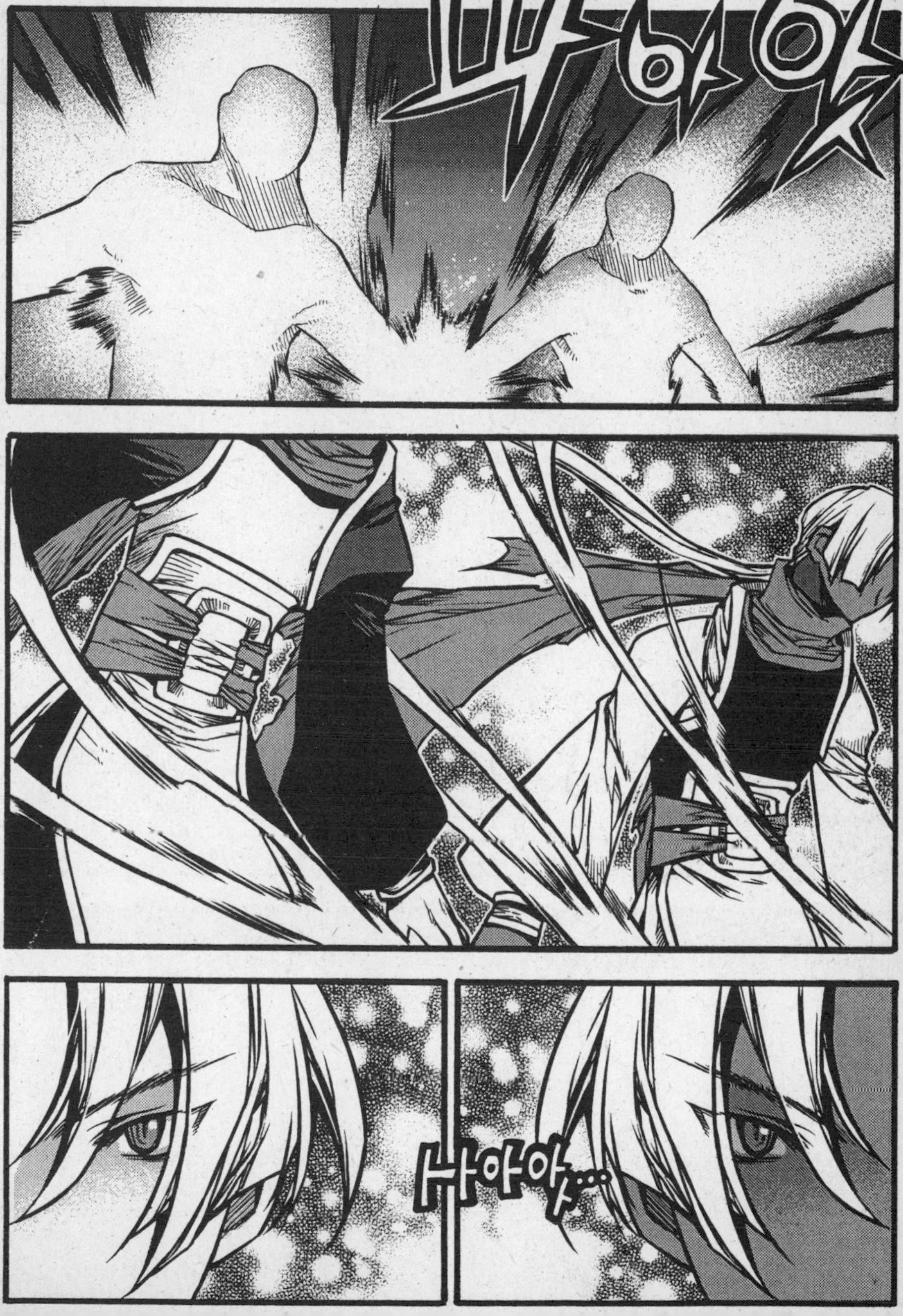
파앗앗
나아아…

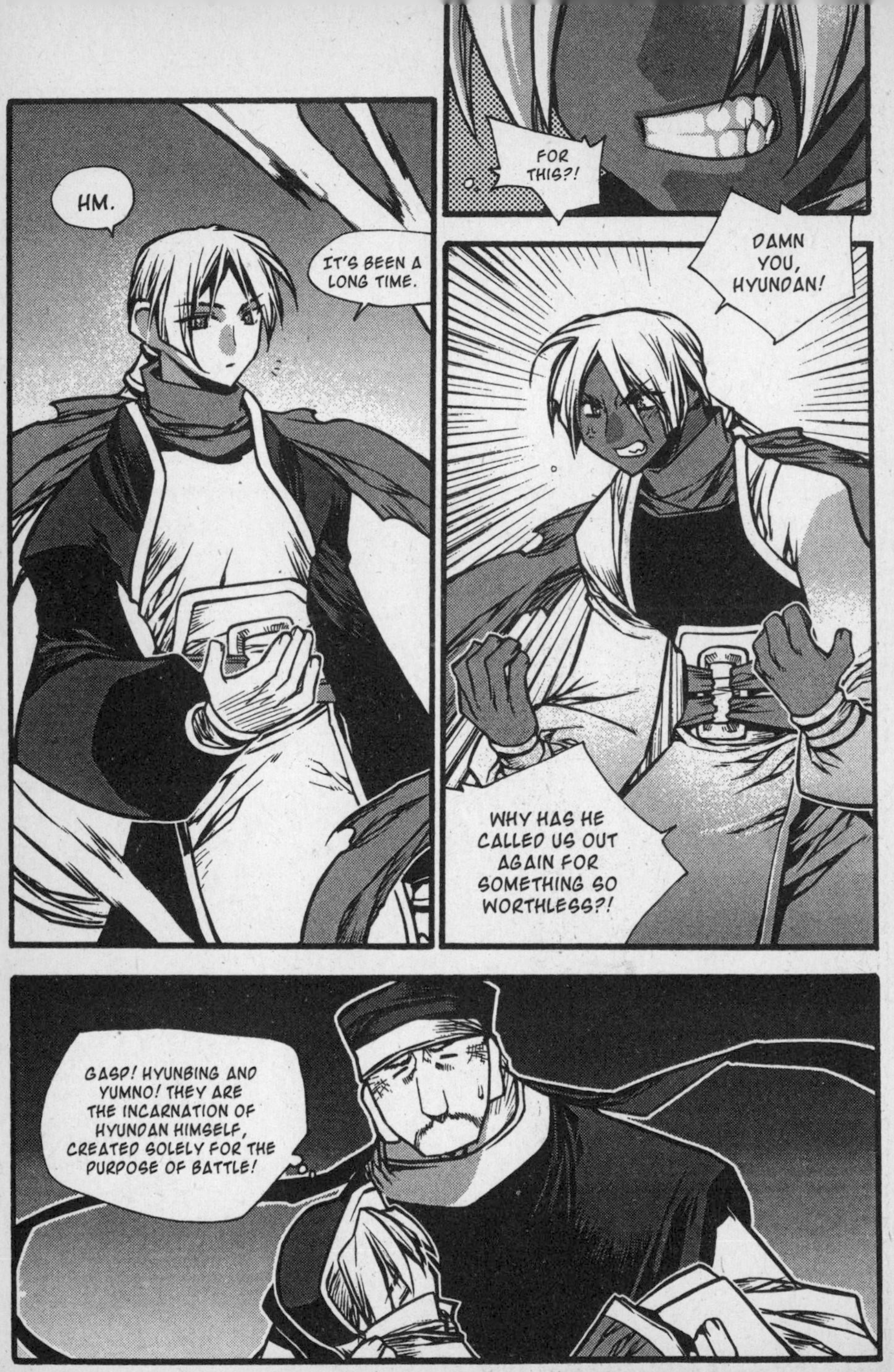
HM.
IT'S BEEN A LONG TIME.
FOR THIS?!
DAMN YOU, HYUNDAN!
WHY HAS HE CALLED US OUT AGAIN FOR SOMETHING SO WORTHLESS?!
GASP! HYUNBING AND YUMNO! THEY ARE THE INCARNATION OF HYUNDAN HIMSELF, CREATED SOLELY FOR THE PURPOSE OF BATTLE!

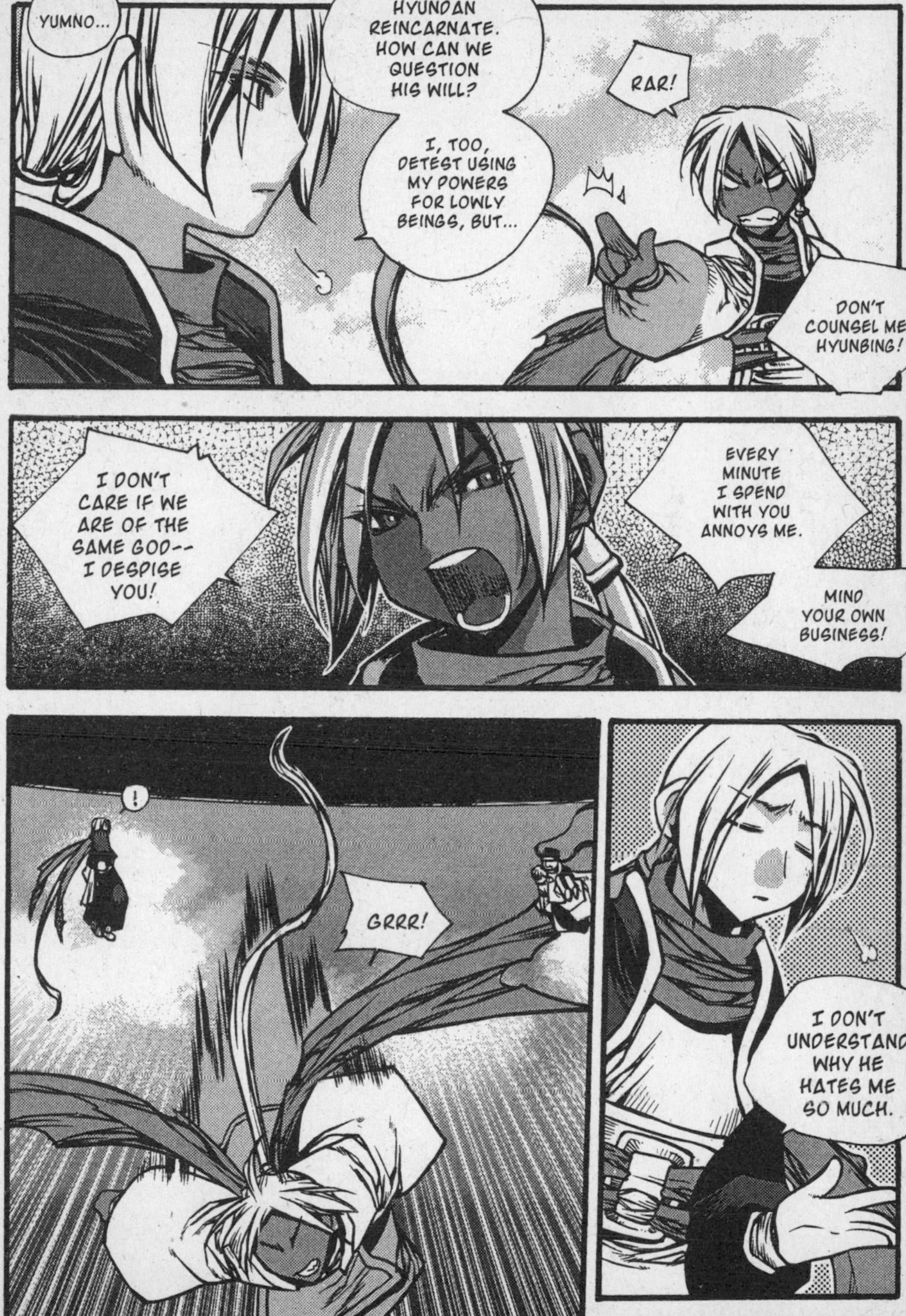
YUMNO...
WE ARE HYUNDAN REINCARNATE. HOW CAN WE QUESTION HIS WILL?
I, TOO, DETEST USING MY POWERS FOR LOWLY BEINGS, BUT...
RAR!
DON'T COUNSEL ME, HYUNBING!
I DON'T CARE IF WE ARE OF THE SAME GOD-- I DESPISE YOU!
EVERY MINUTE I SPEND WITH YOU ANNOYS ME.
MIND YOUR OWN BUSINESS!
!
GRRR!
I DON'T UNDERSTAND WHY HE HATES ME SO MUCH.

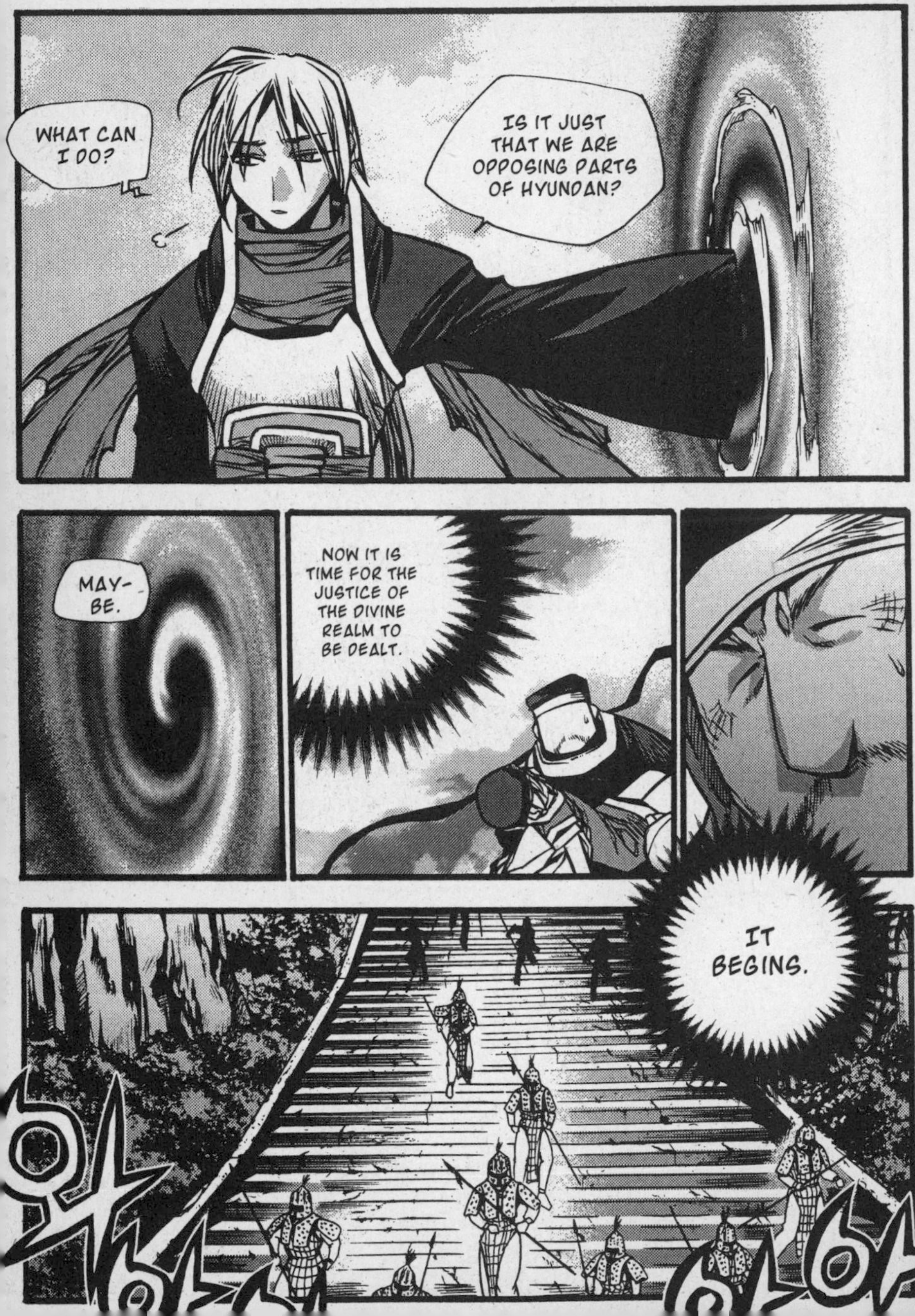
WHAT CAN I DO?
IS IT JUST THAT WE ARE OPPOSING PARTS OF HYUNDAN?
MAY-BE.
NOW IT IS TIME FOR THE JUSTICE OF THE DIVINE REALM TO BE DEALT.
IT BEGINS.

HA!

AAACK!

THESE HUMANS ARE PERSISTENT!

THEY ATTACK US KNOWING THAT THEIR WEAPONS ARE NO MATCH FOR US.

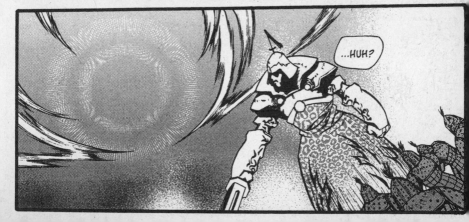

...HUH?

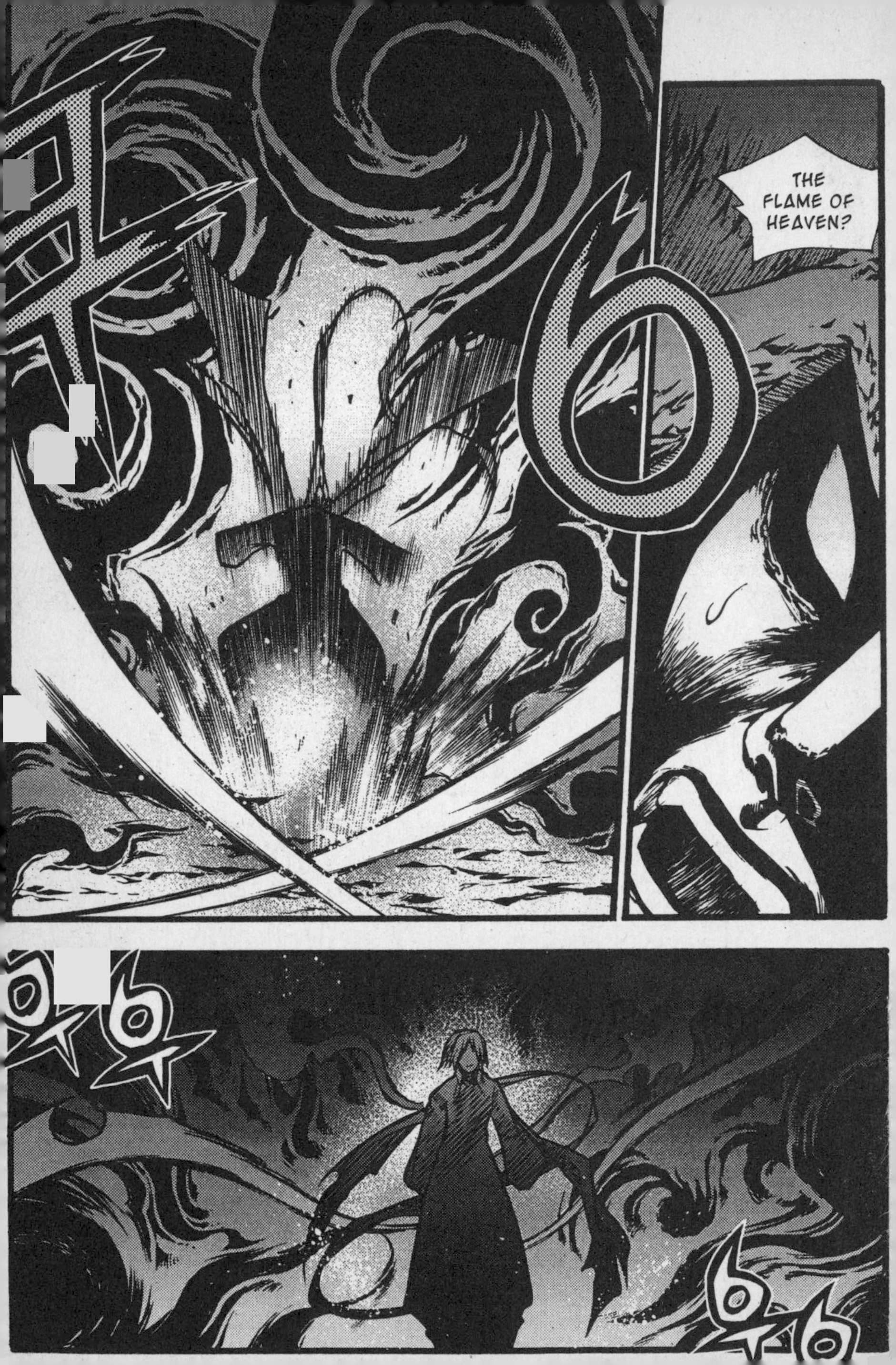
THE FLAME OF HEAVEN?

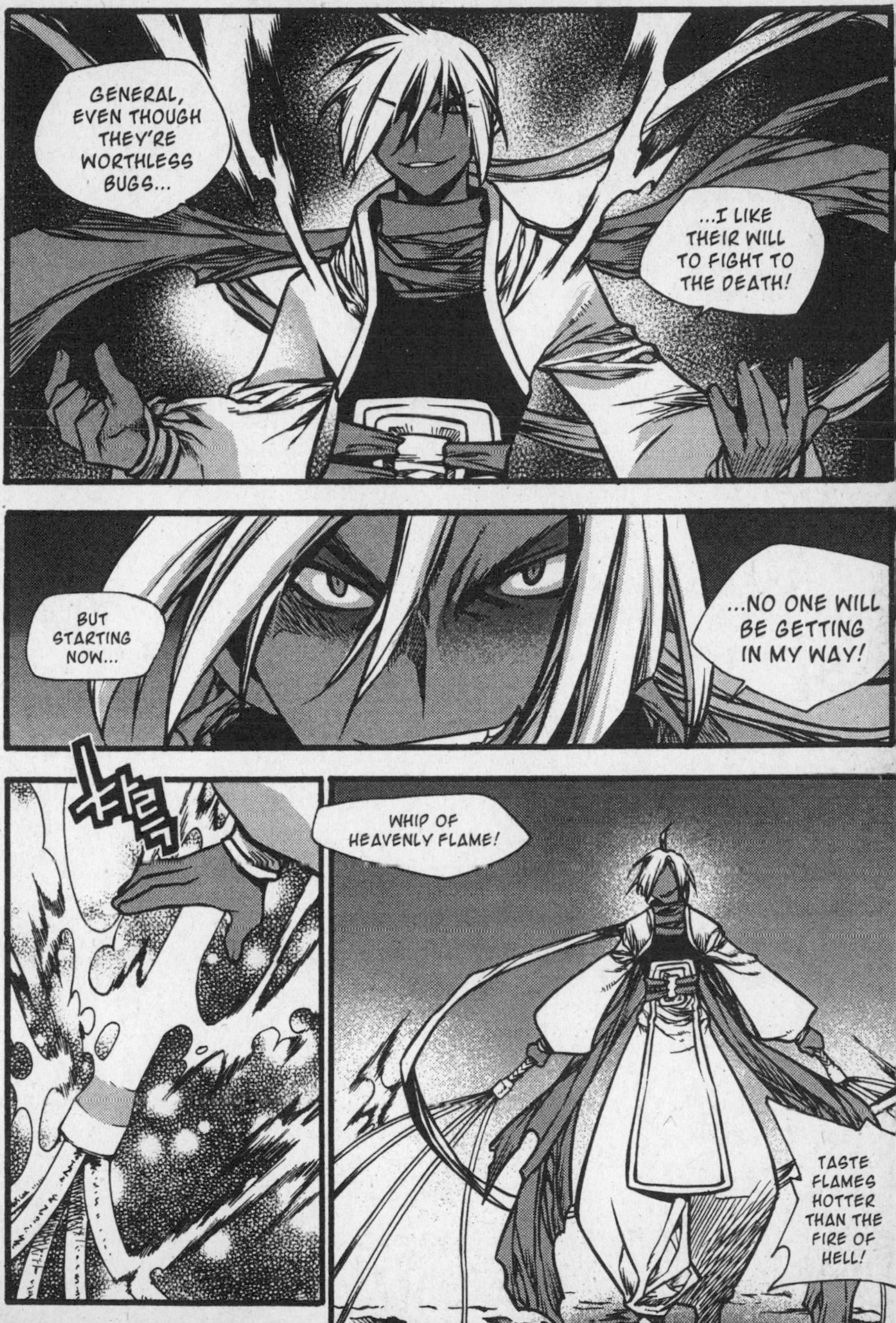
GENERAL, EVEN THOUGH THEY'RE WORTHLESS BUGS...
...I LIKE THEIR WILL TO FIGHT TO THE DEATH!
BUT STARTING NOW...
...NO ONE WILL BE GETTING IN MY WAY!
WHIP OF HEAVENLY FLAME!
TASTE FLAMES HOTTER THAN THE FIRE OF HELL!

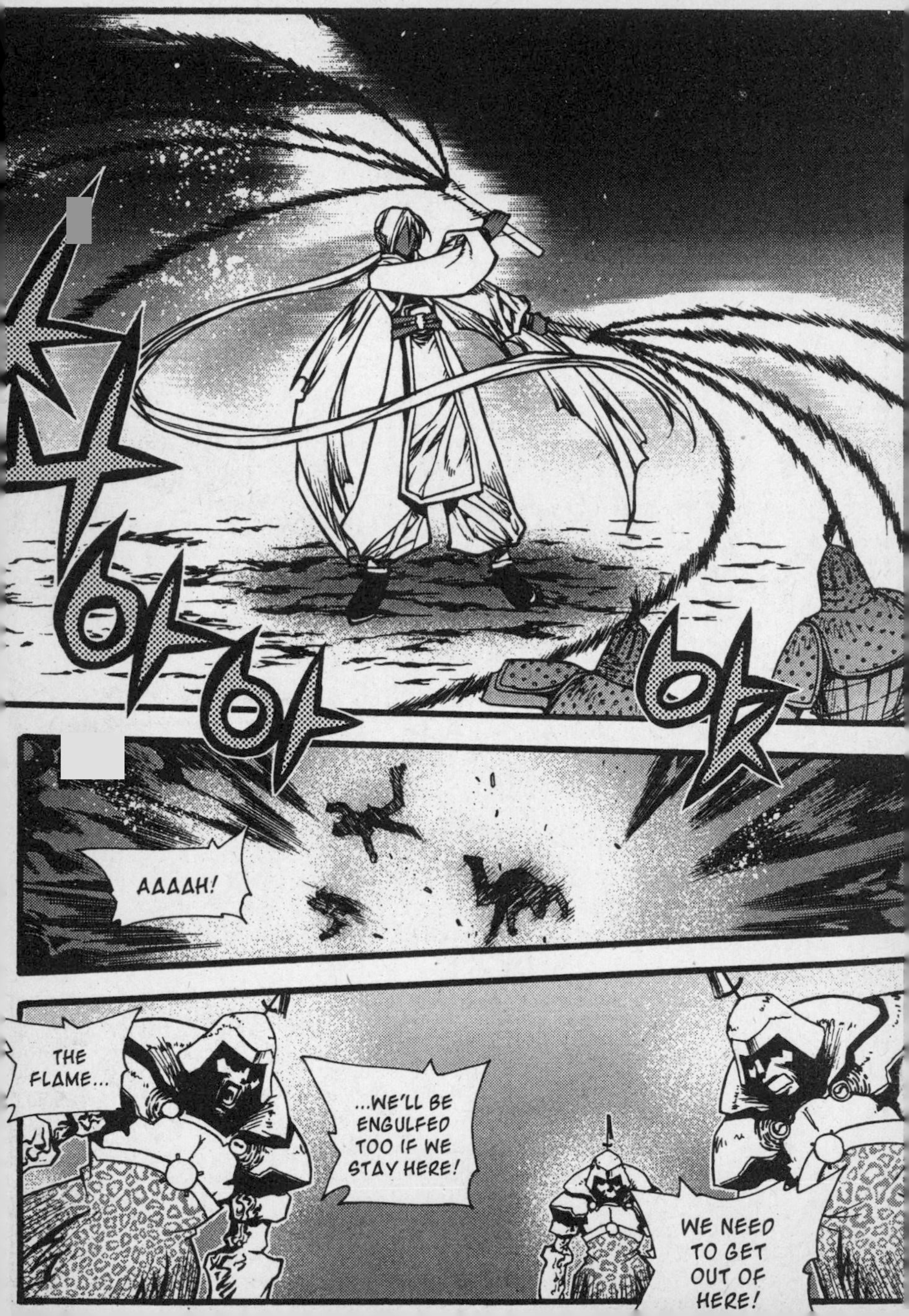
AAAAH!
THE FLAME...
...WE'LL BE ENGULFED TOO IF WE STAY HERE!
WE NEED TO GET OUT OF HERE!

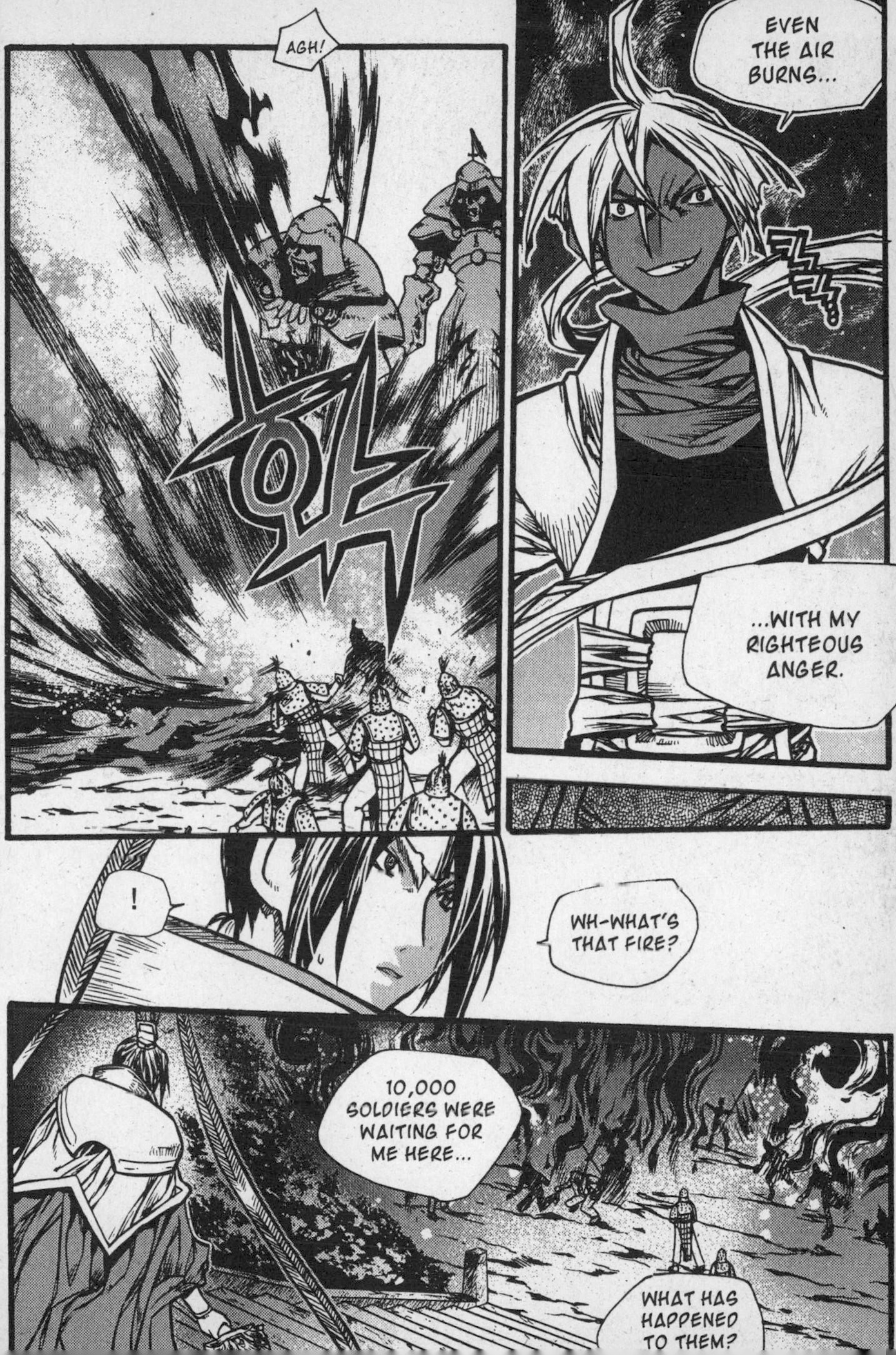
AGH!
EVEN THE AIR BURNS...
...WITH MY RIGHTEOUS ANGER.
!
WH-WHAT'S THAT FIRE?
10,000 SOLDIERS WERE WAITING FOR ME HERE...
WHAT HAS HAPPENED TO THEM?

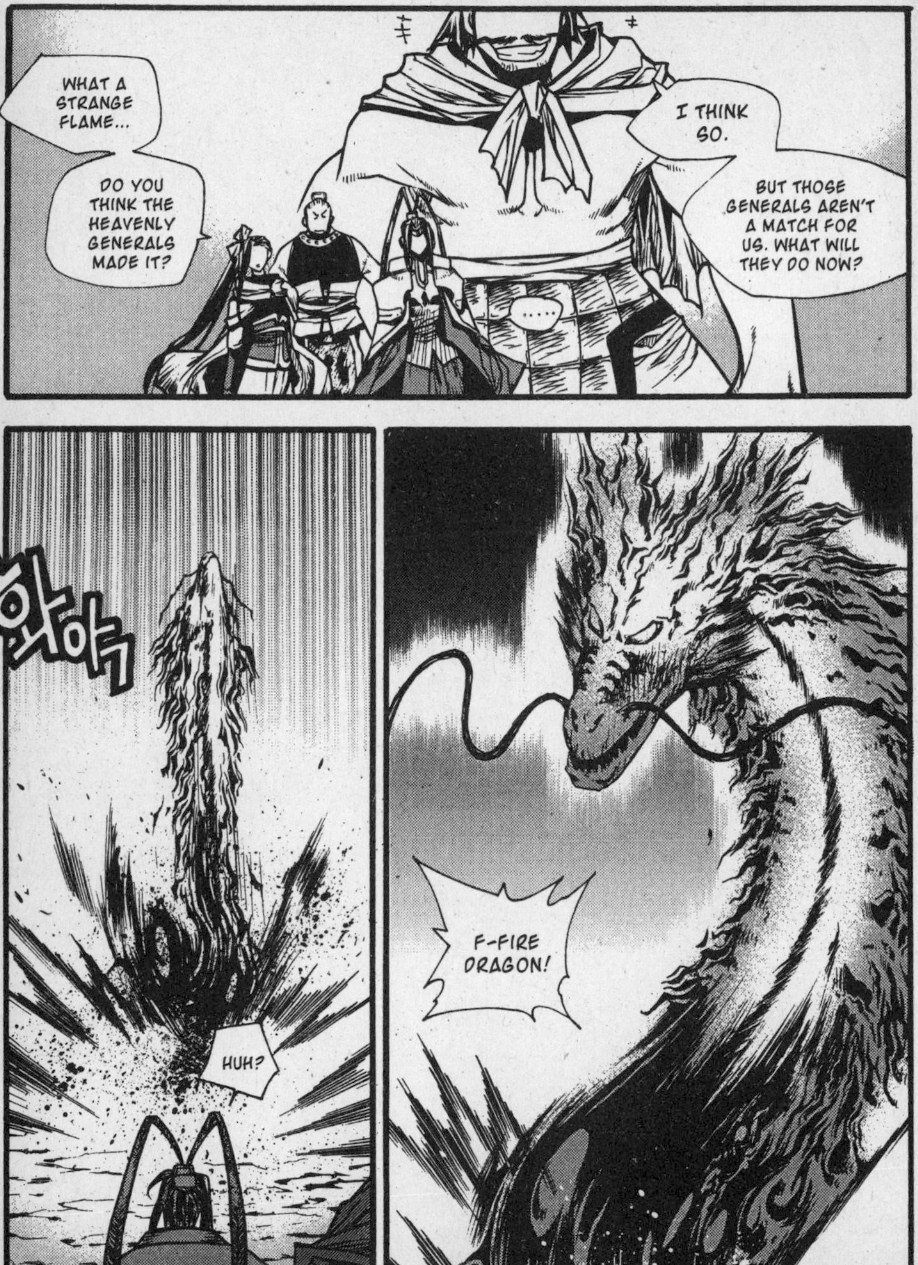
WHAT A STRANGE FLAME...
DO YOU THINK THE HEAVENLY GENERALS MADE IT?
.....
I THINK SO.
BUT THOSE GENERALS AREN'T A MATCH FOR US. WHAT WILL THEY DO NOW?
HUH?
F-FIRE DRAGON!

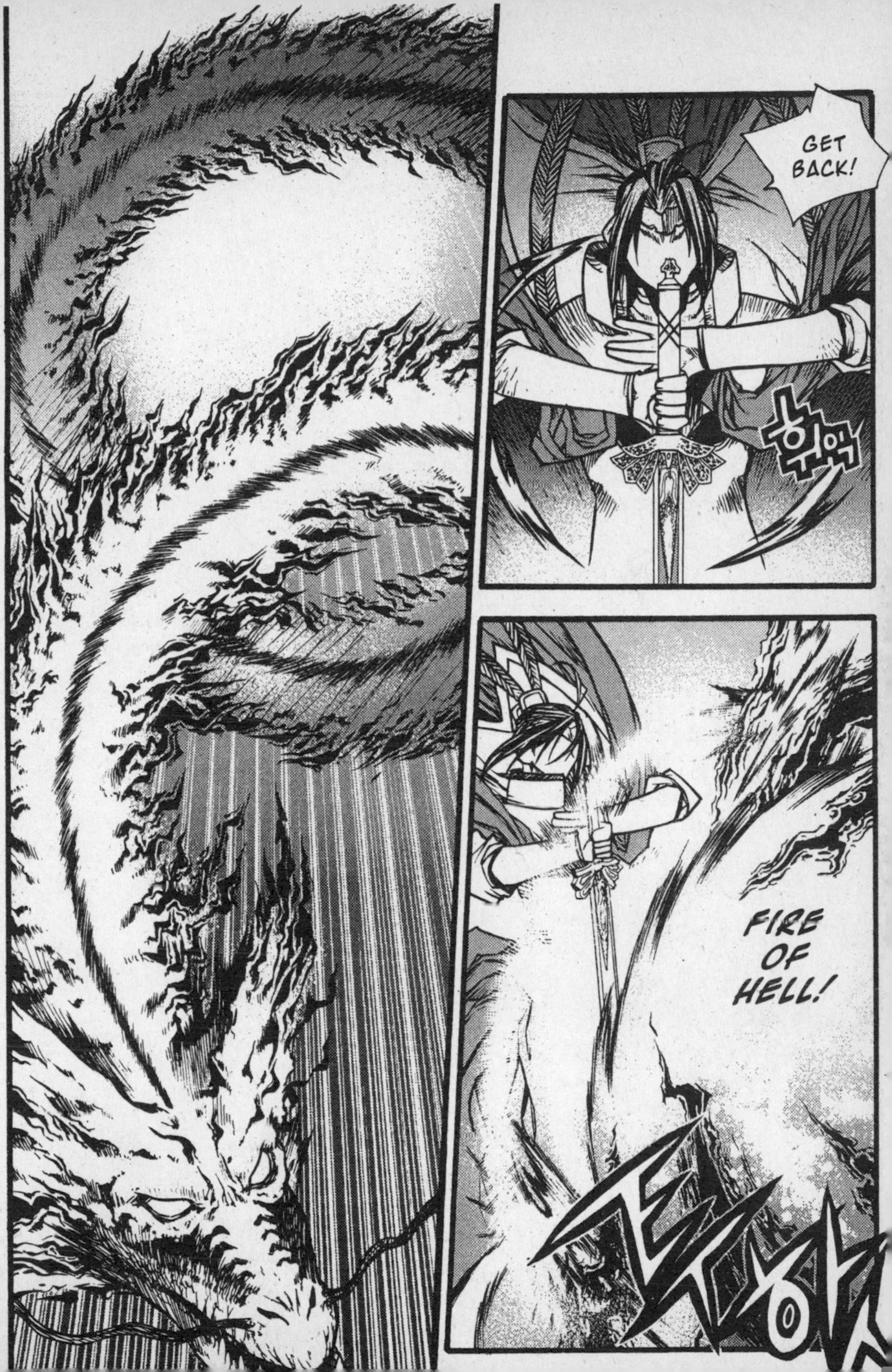
GET BACK!
FIRE OF HELL!

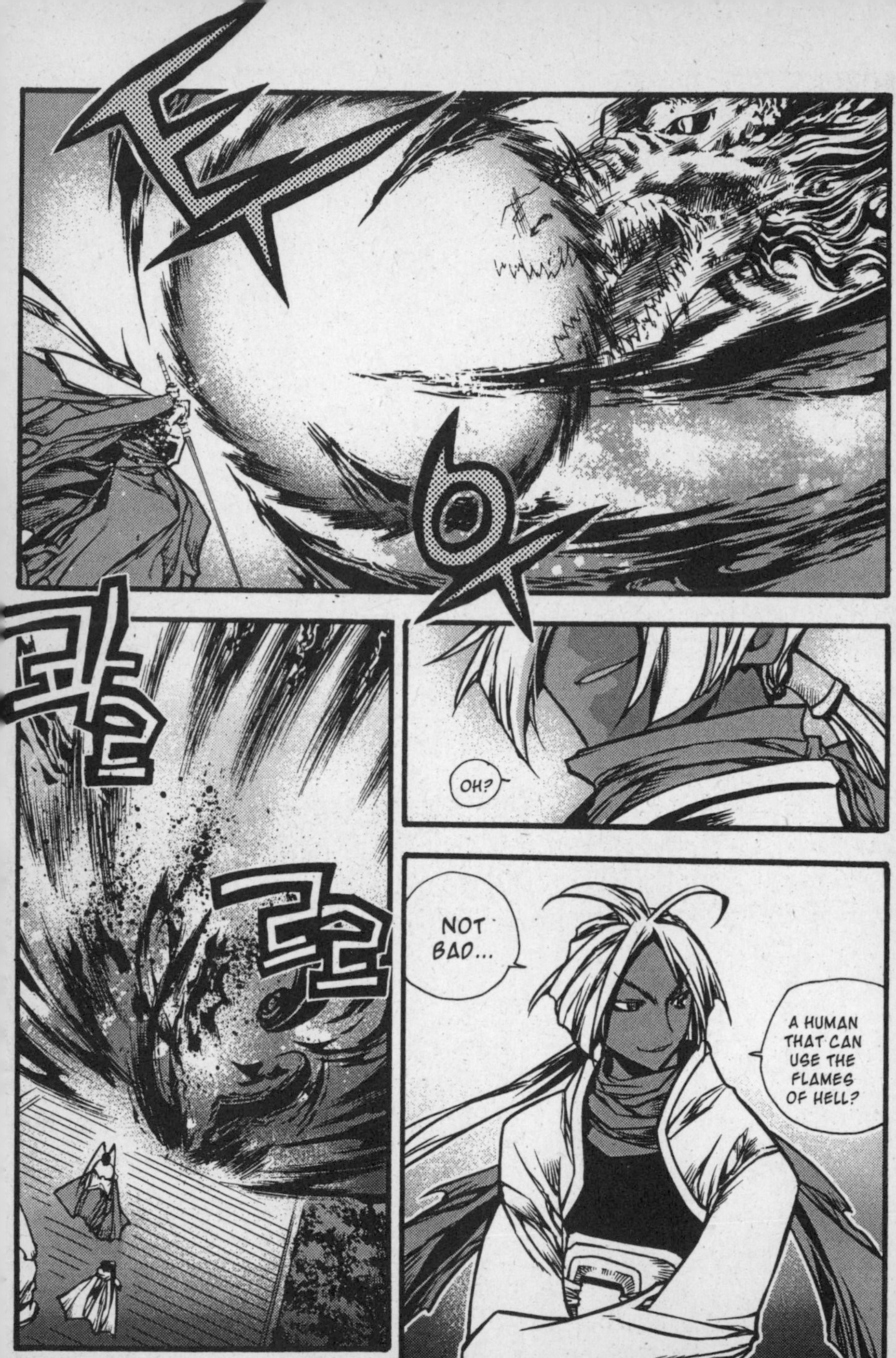
OH?
NOT BAD...
A HUMAN THAT CAN USE THE FLAMES OF HELL?

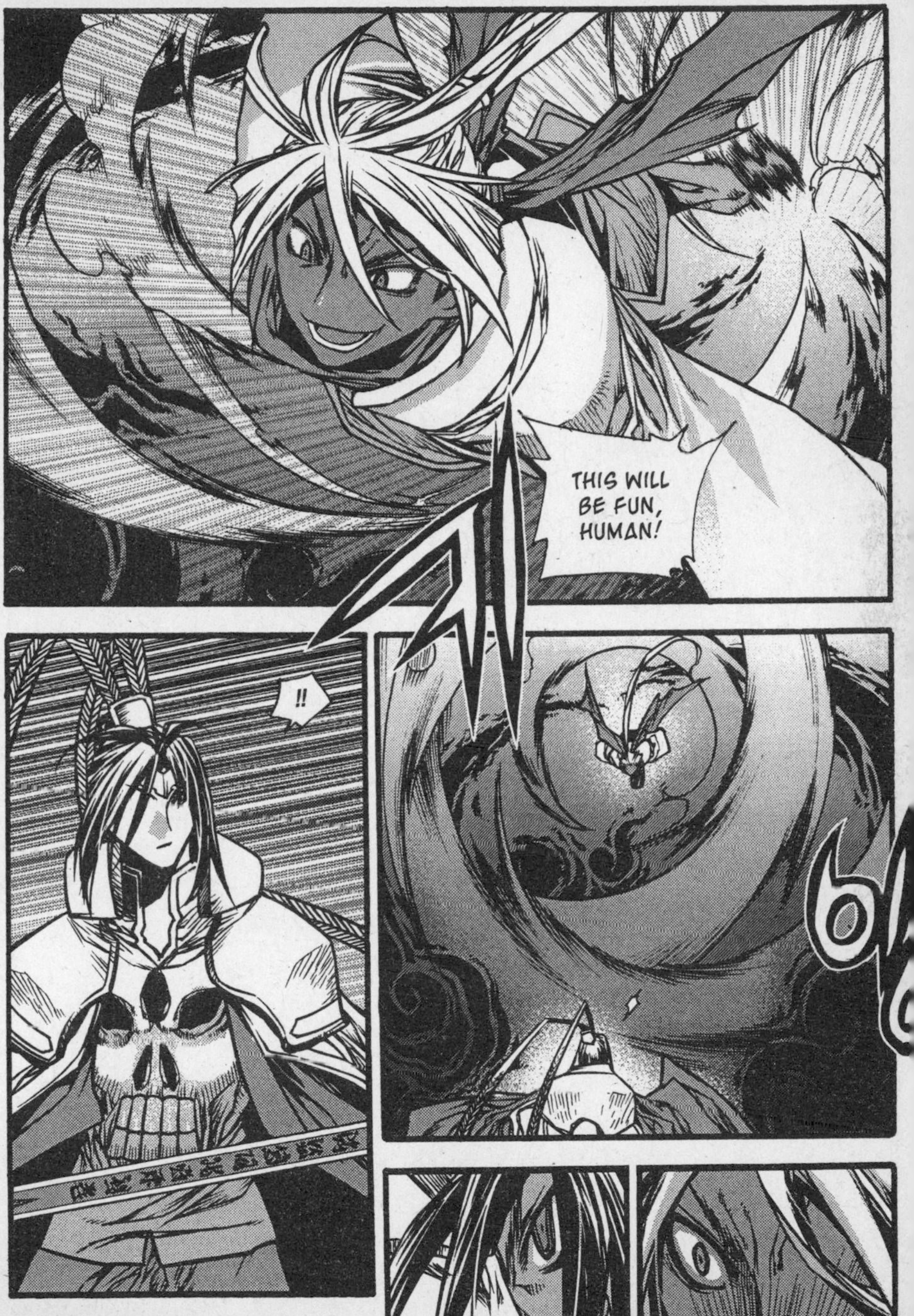
THIS WILL BE FUN, HUMAN!
!!

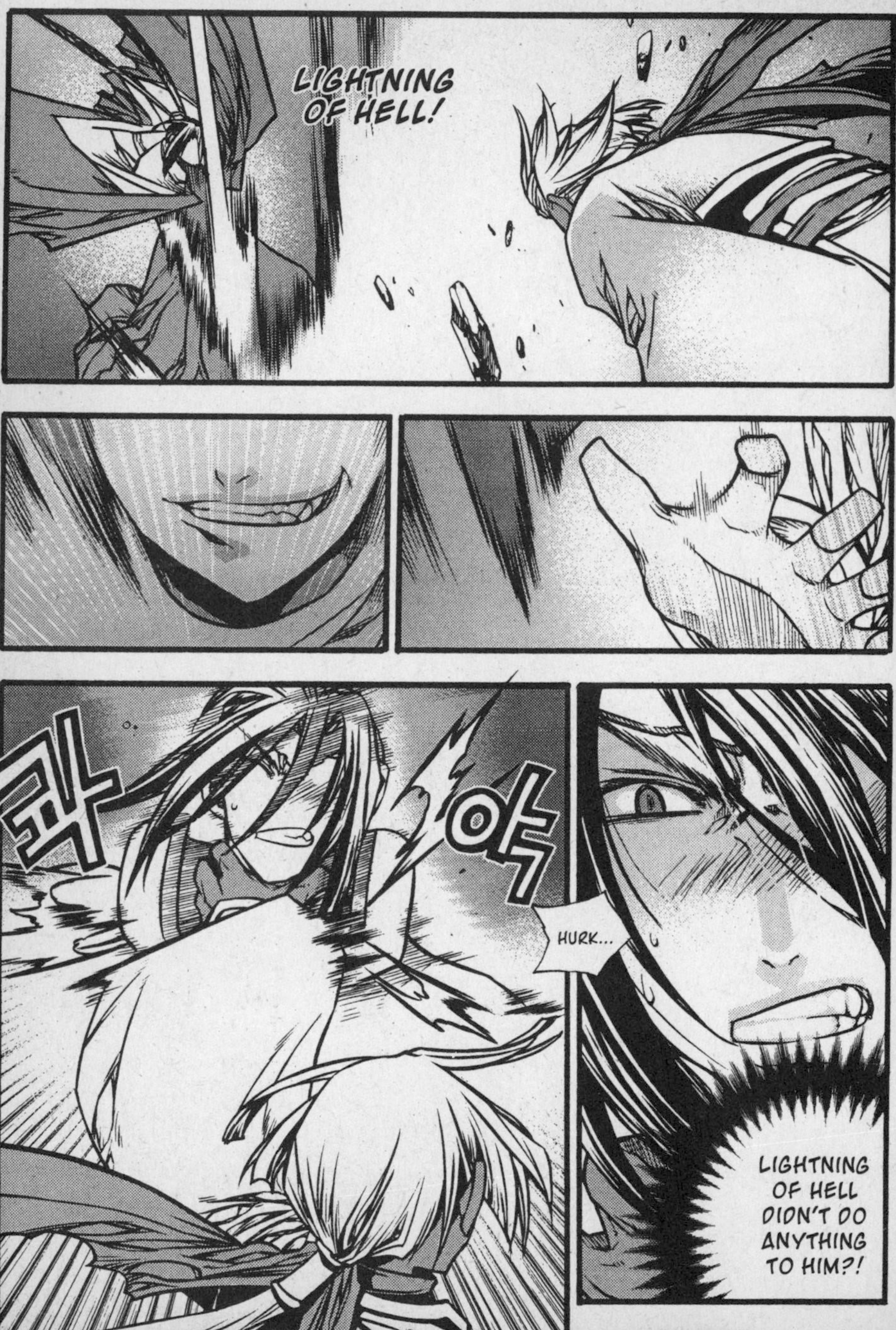
LIGHTNING OF HELL!
HURK...
LIGHTNING OF HELL DIDN'T DO ANYTHING TO HIM?!

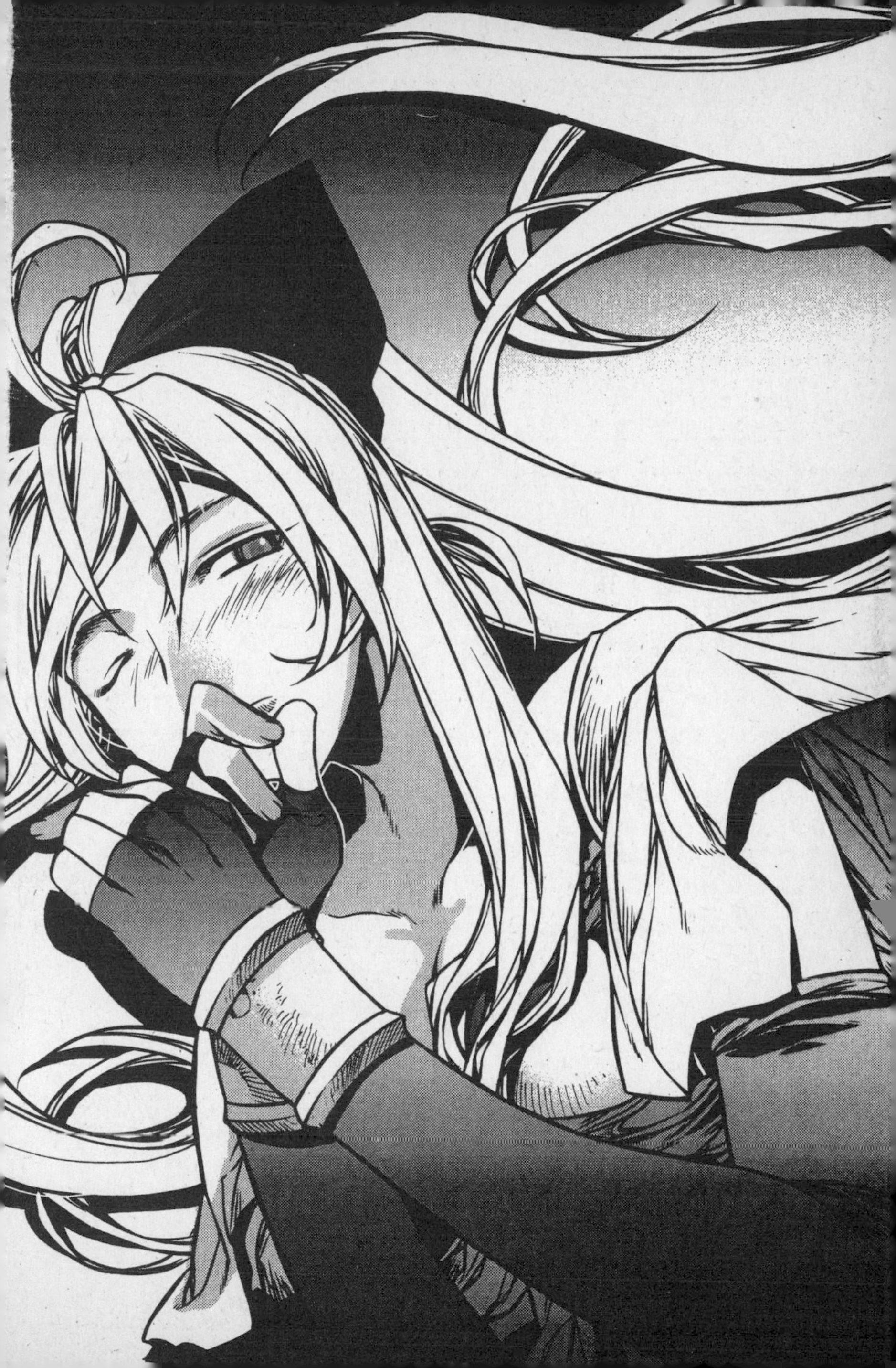

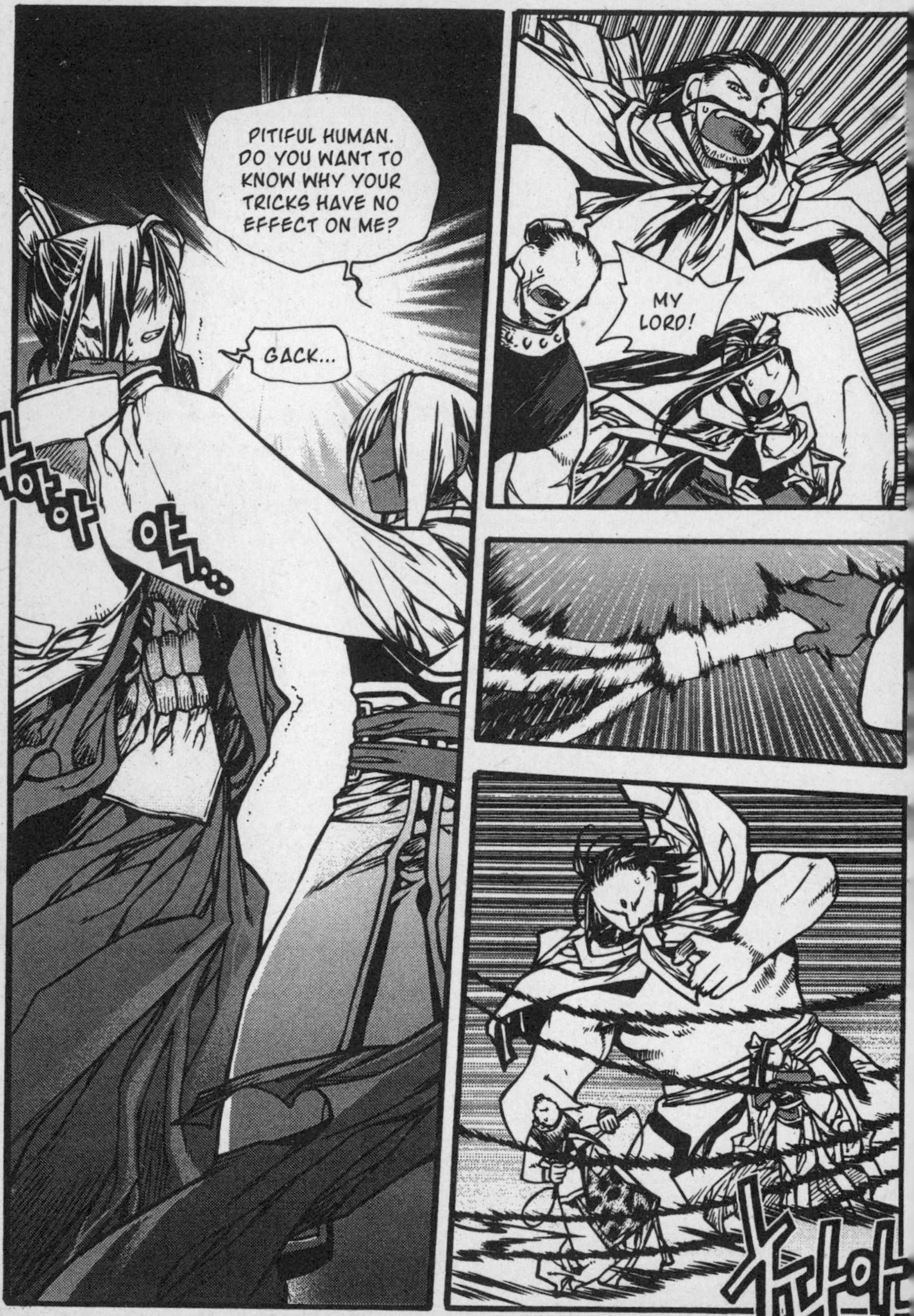
PITIFUL HUMAN. DO YOU WANT TO KNOW WHY YOUR TRICKS HAVE NO EFFECT ON ME?
GACK...
MY LORD!

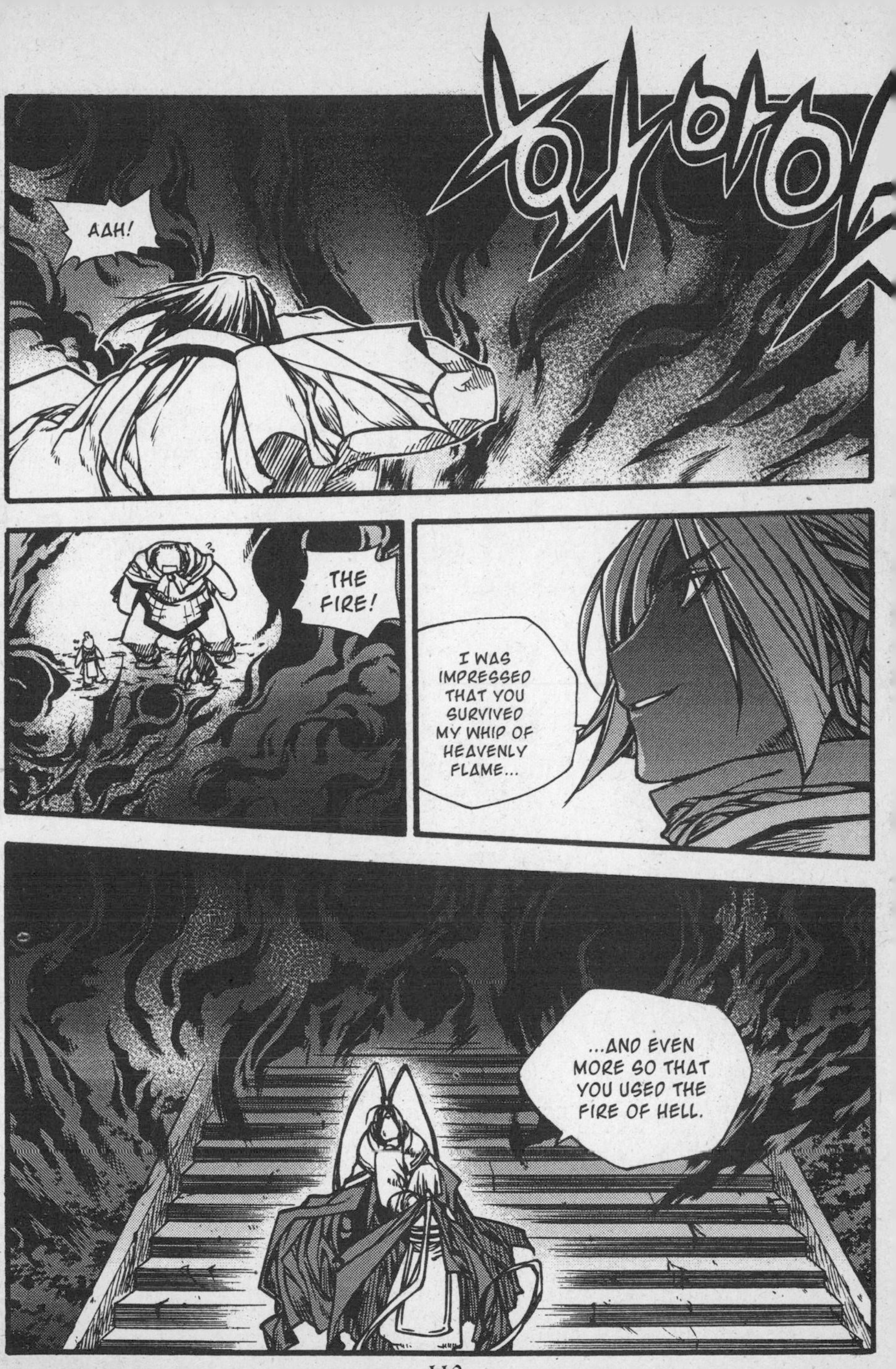
AAH!
THE FIRE!
I WAS IMPRESSED THAT YOU SURVIVED MY WHIP OF HEAVENLY FLAME...
...AND EVEN MORE SO THAT YOU USED THE FIRE OF HELL.

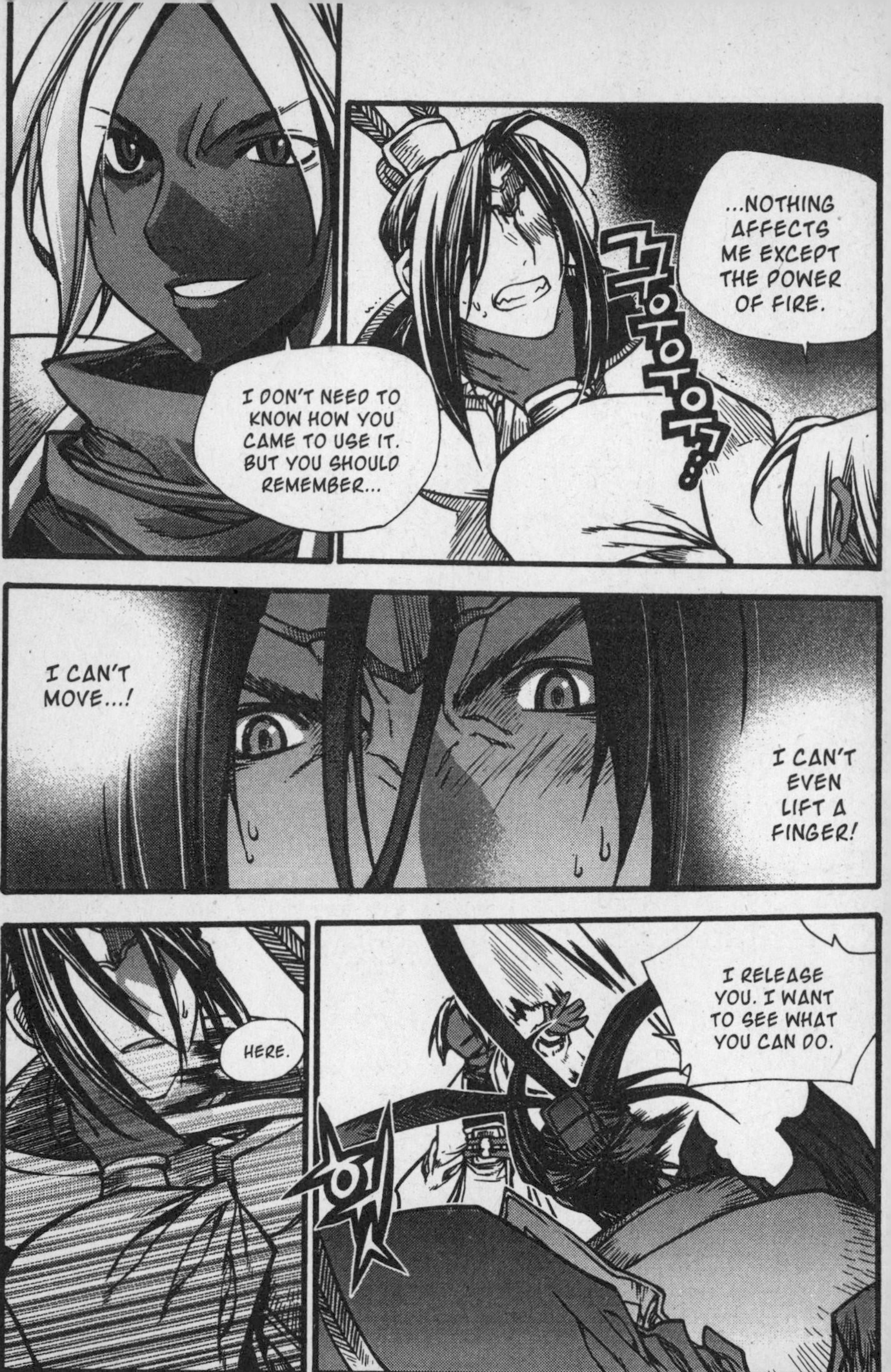
I DON'T NEED TO KNOW HOW YOU CAME TO USE IT. BUT YOU SHOULD REMEMBER...
...NOTHING AFFECTS ME EXCEPT THE POWER OF FIRE.
I CAN'T MOVE...!
I CAN'T EVEN LIFT A FINGER!
HERE.
I RELEASE YOU. I WANT TO SEE WHAT YOU CAN DO.

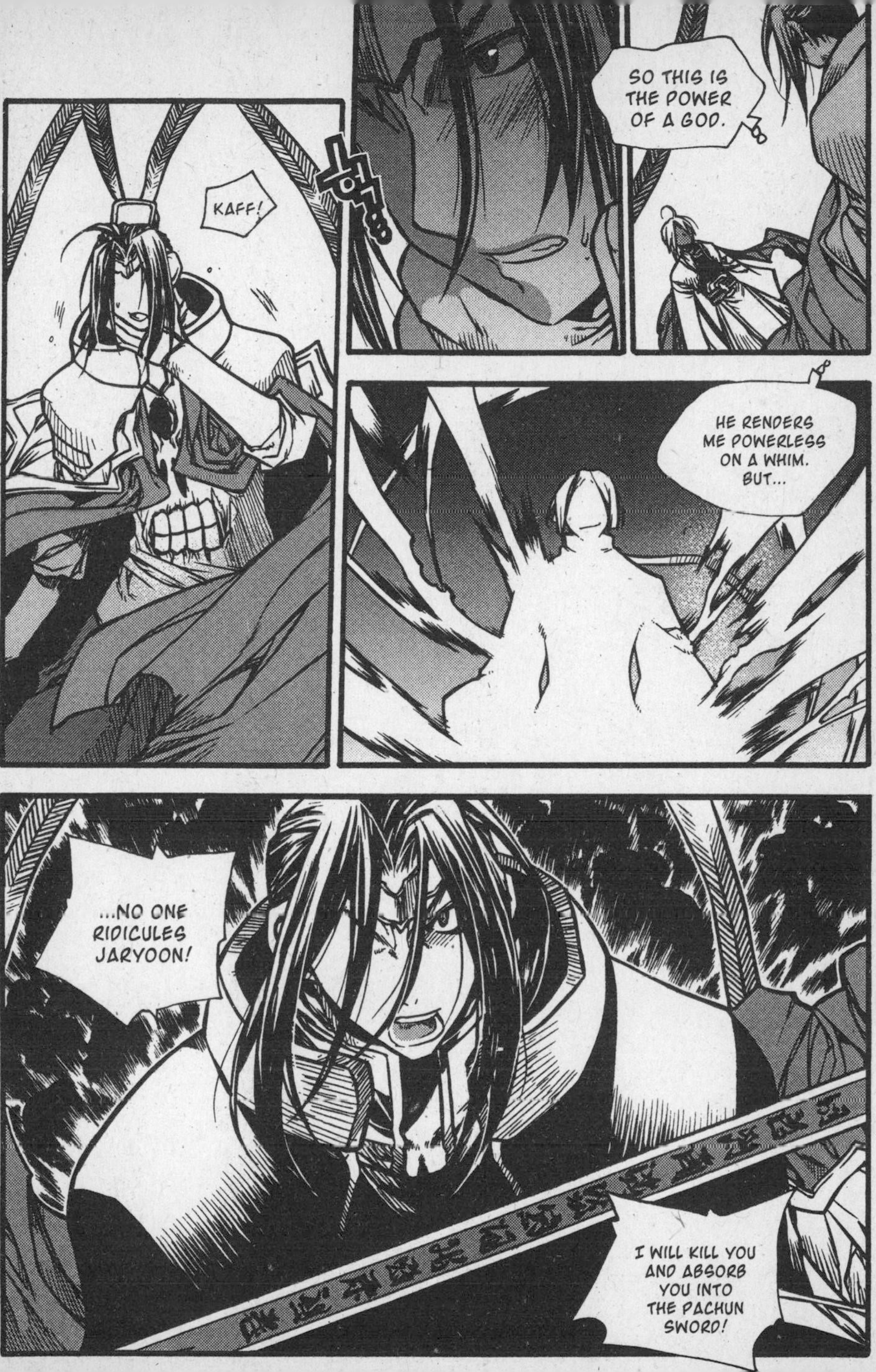
KAFF!
SO THIS IS THE POWER OF A GOD.
HE RENDERS ME POWERLESS ON A WHIM. BUT...
...NO ONE RIDICULES JARYOON!
I WILL KILL YOU AND ABSORB YOU INTO THE PACHUN SWORD!

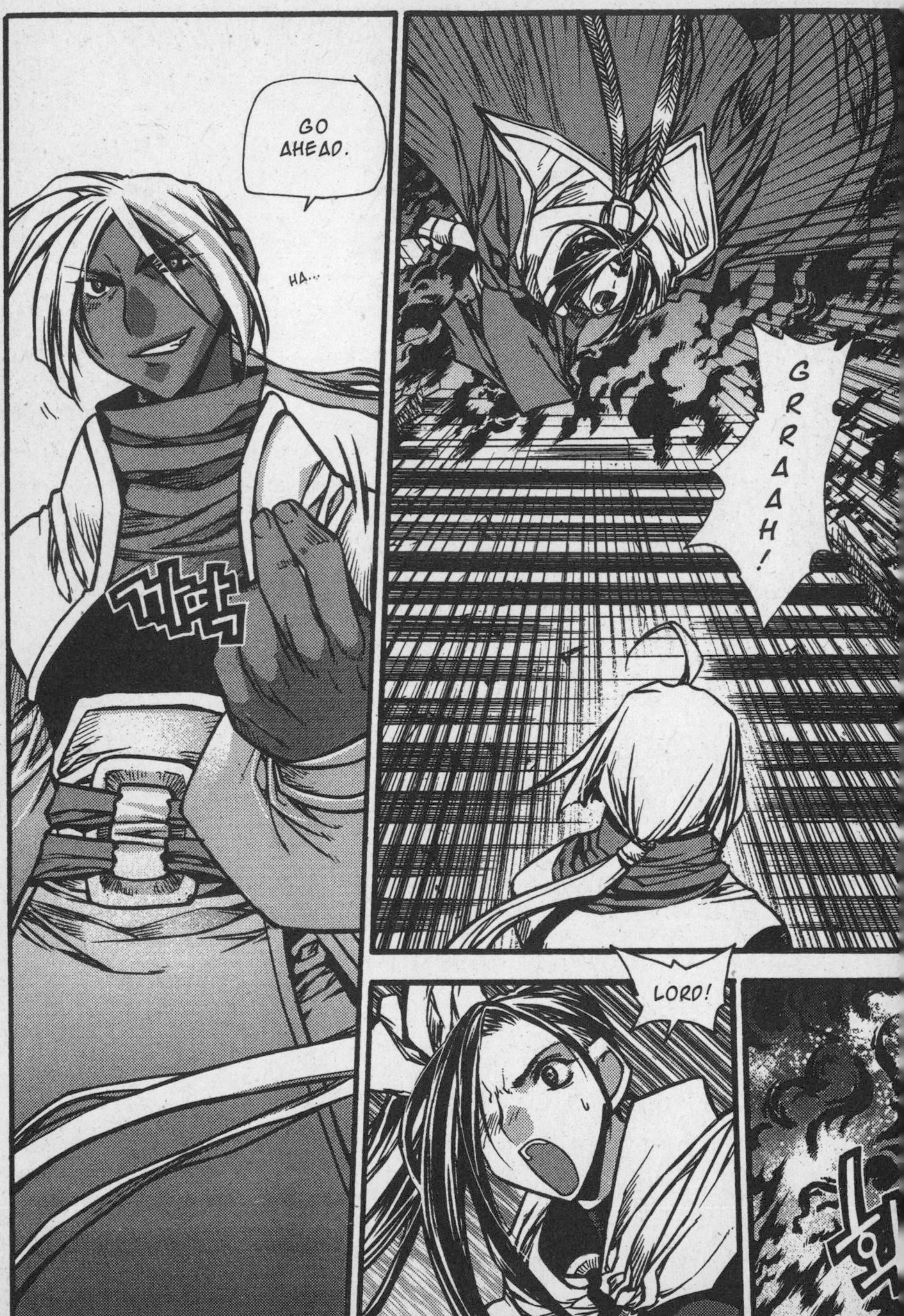
GO AHEAD.
HA...
GRRAAH!
LORD!

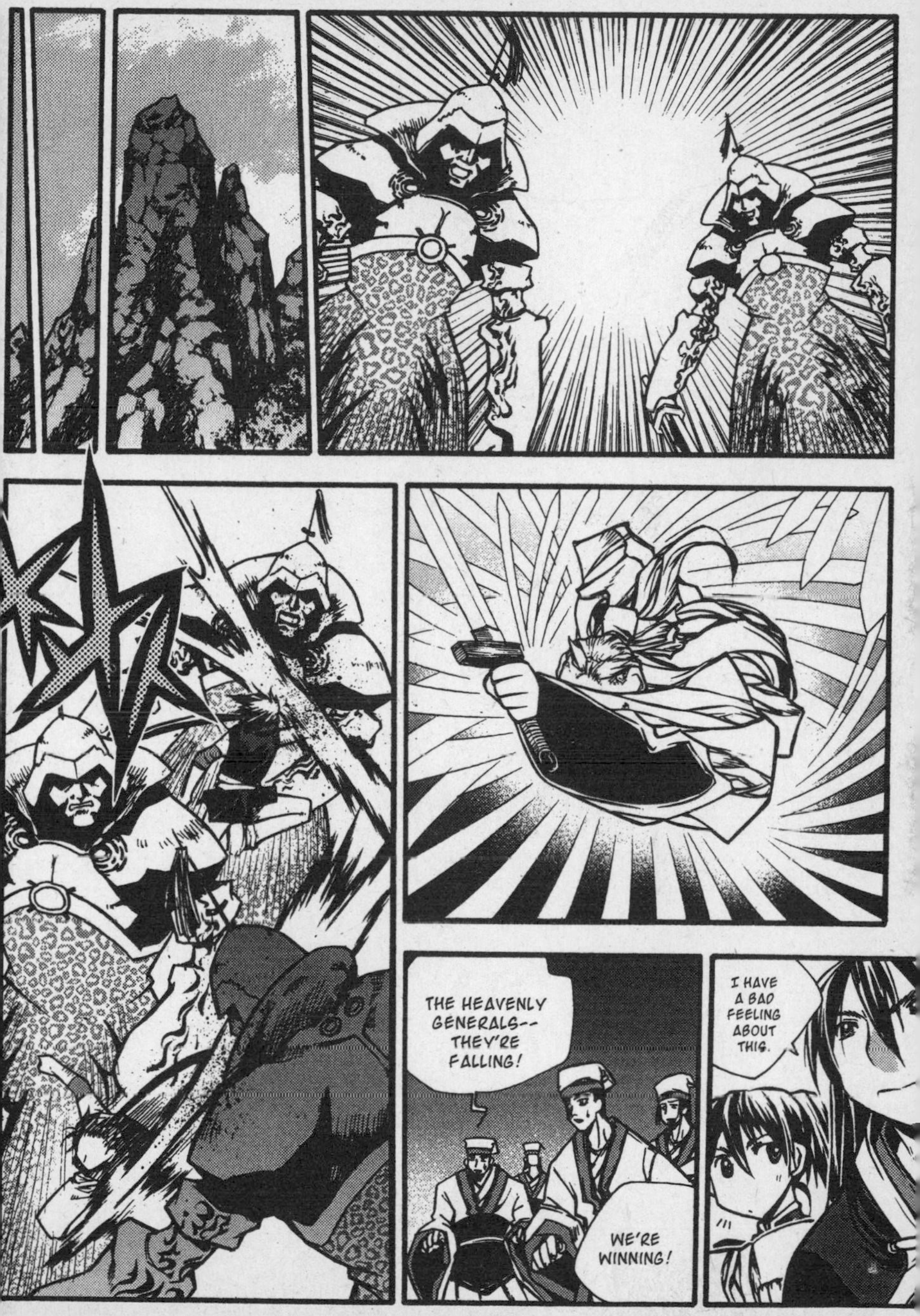
THE HEAVENLY GENERALS-- THEY'RE FALLING!
WE'RE WINNING!
I HAVE A BAD FEELING ABOUT THIS.

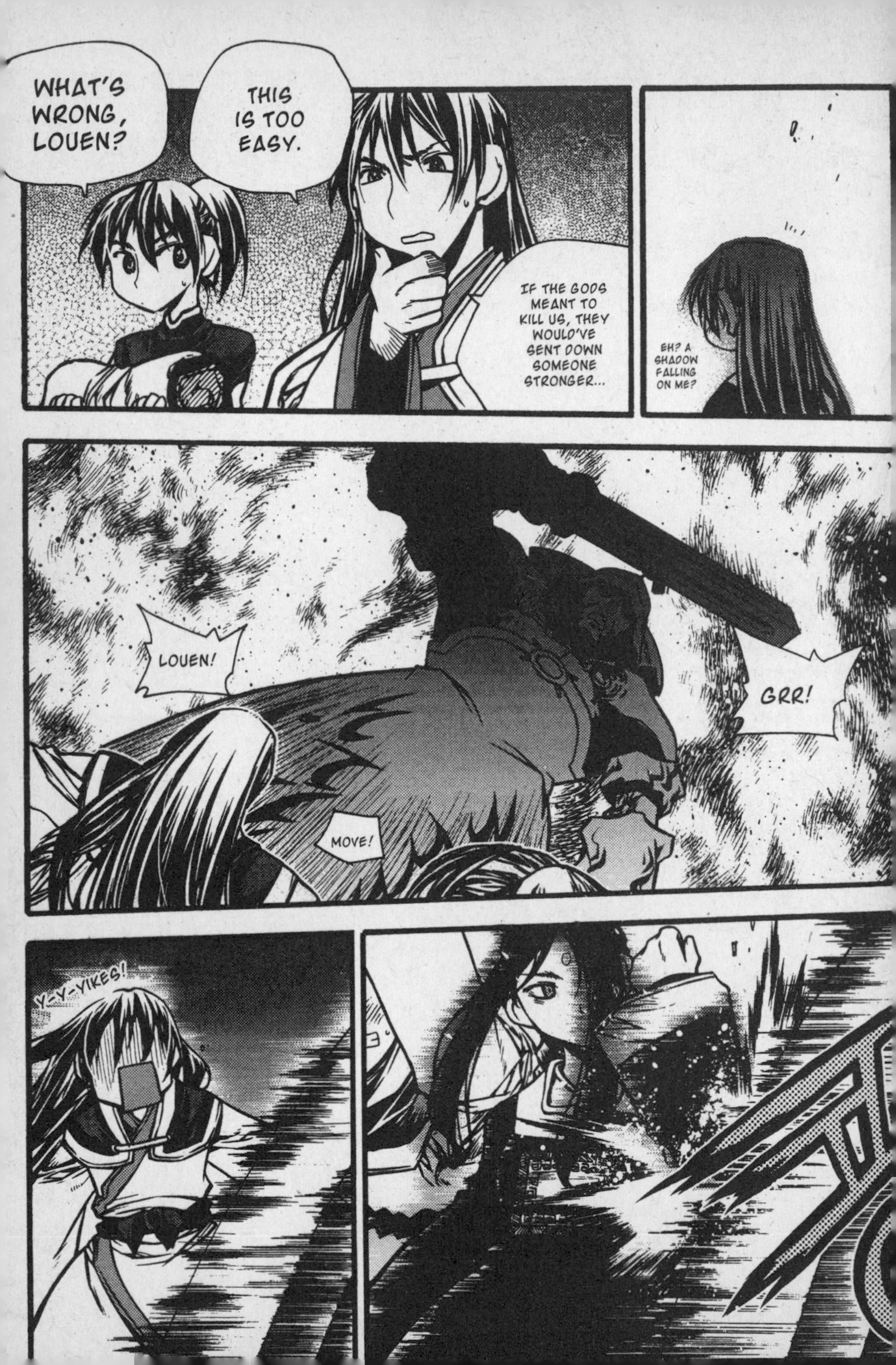
WHAT'S WRONG, LOUEN?
THIS IS TOO EASY.
IF THE GODS MEANT TO KILL US, THEY WOULD'VE SENT DOWN SOMEONE STRONGER...
!?
EH? A SHADOW FALLING ON ME?
LOUEN!
GRR!
MOVE!
Y-Y-YIKES!

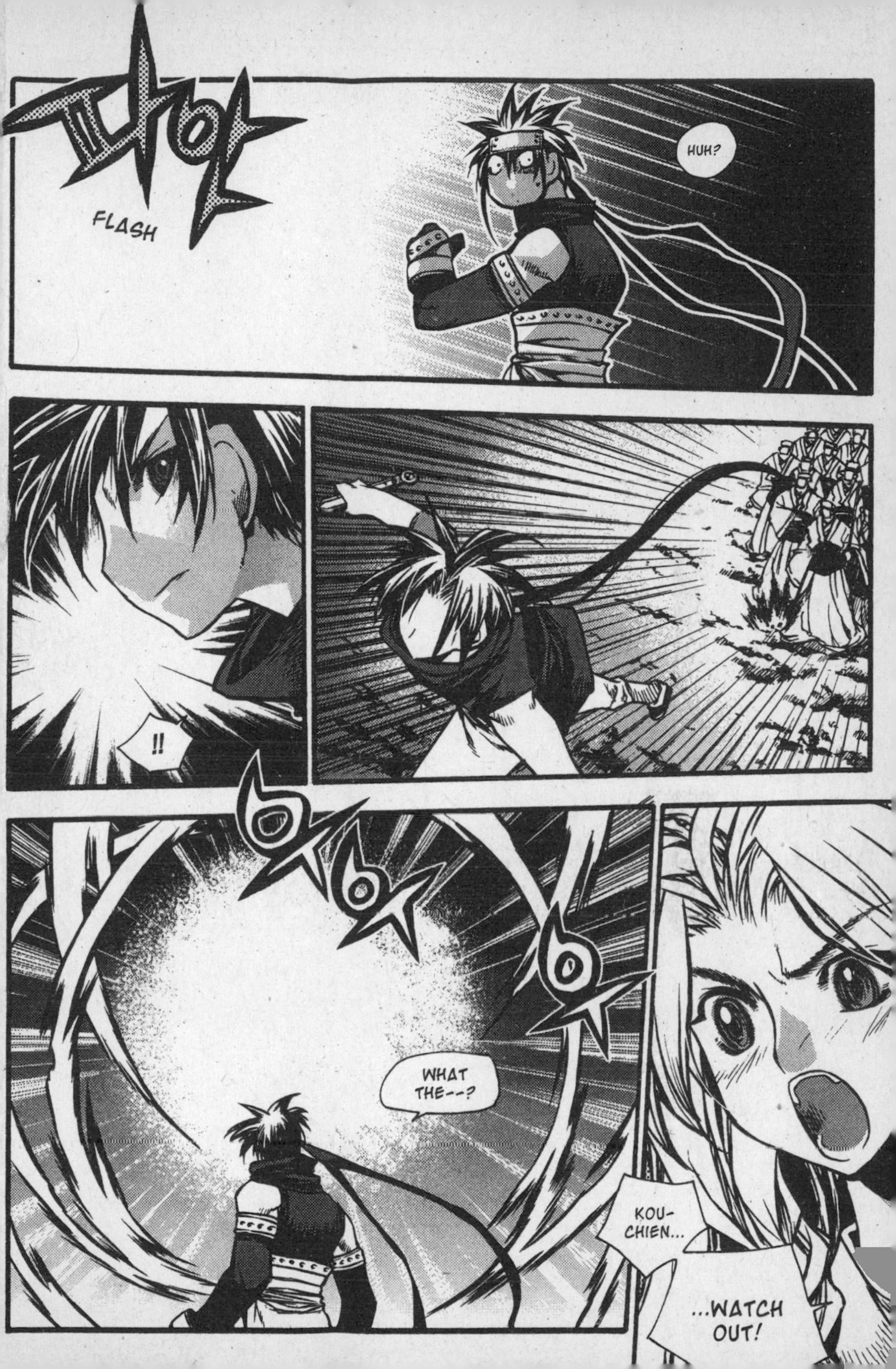
FLASH
HUH?
!!
WHAT THE--?
KOU-CHIEN...
...WATCH OUT!

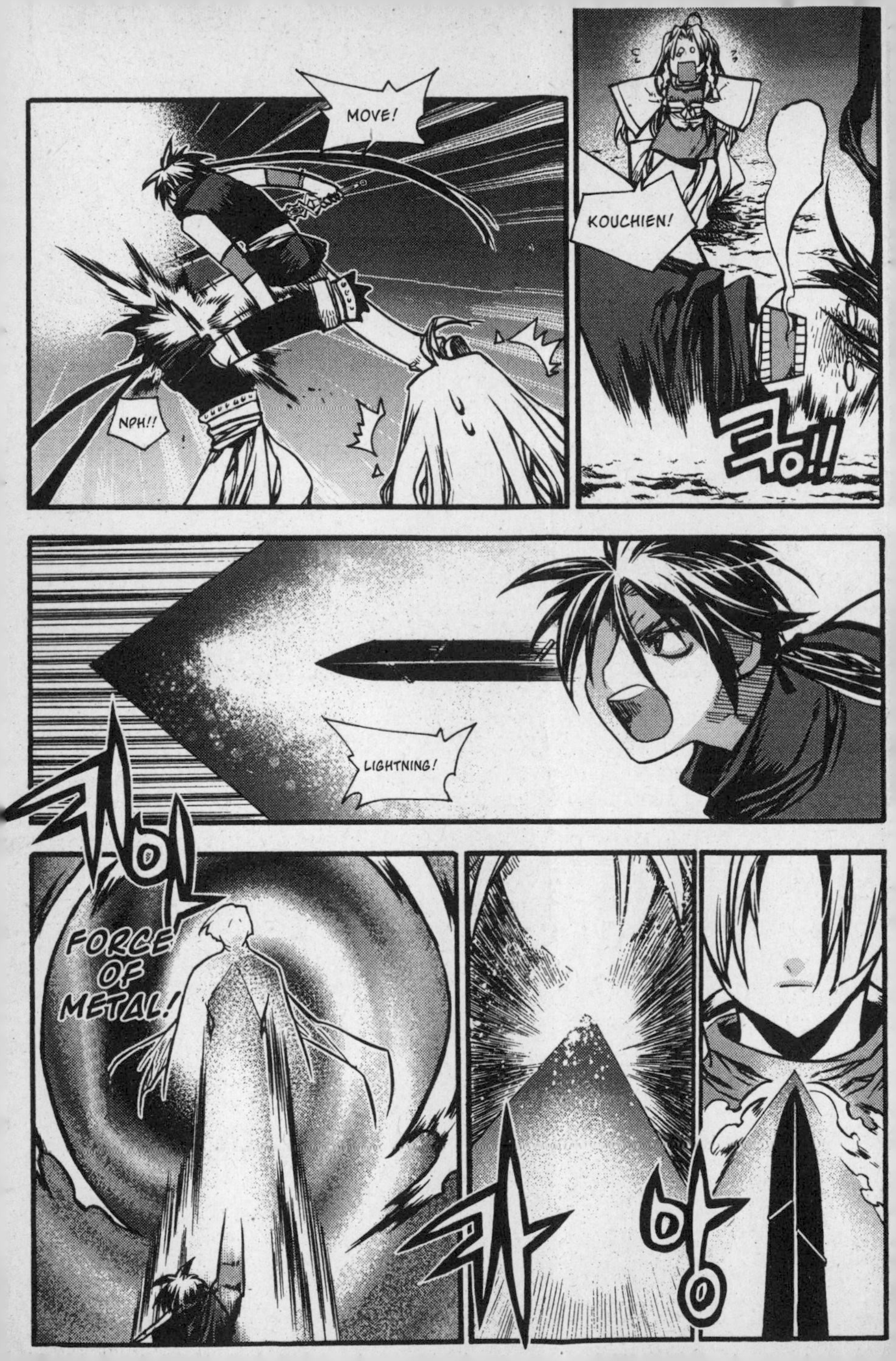
MOVE!
NPH!!
KOUCHIEN!
LIGHTNING!
FORCE OF METAL!

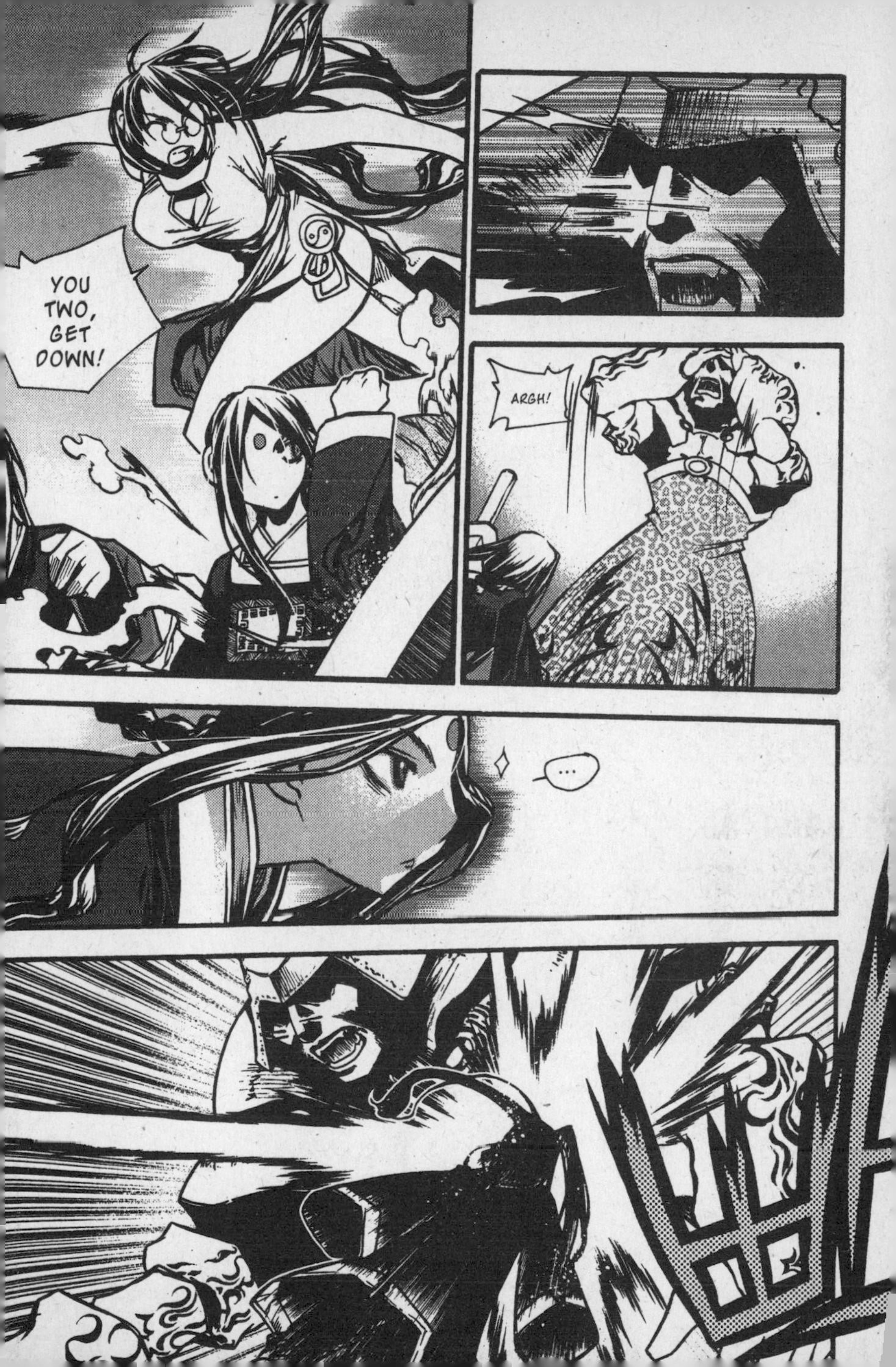
YOU TWO, GET DOWN!
ARGH!
...

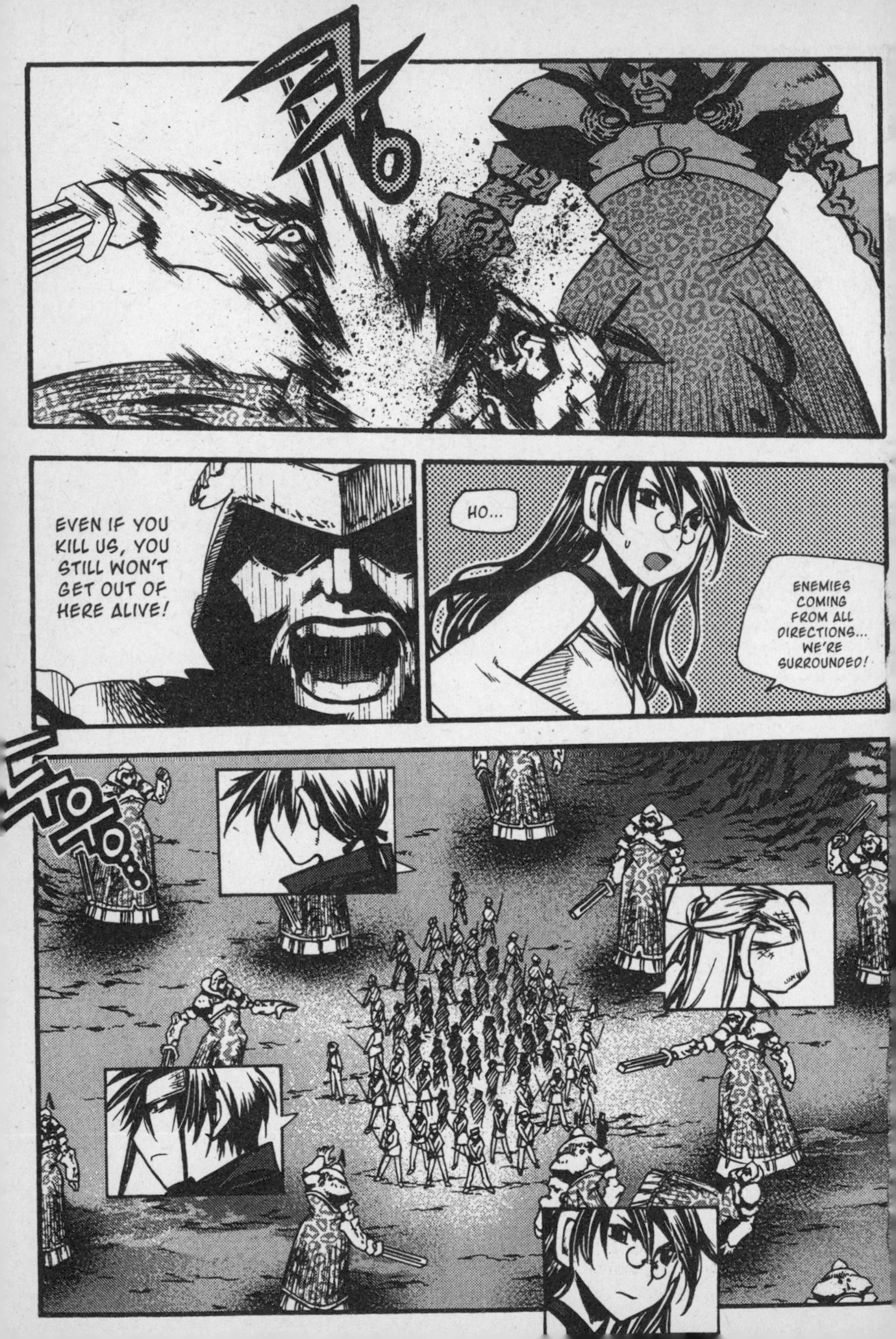
EVEN IF YOU KILL US, YOU STILL WON'T GET OUT OF HERE ALIVE!
HO...
ENEMIES COMING FROM ALL DIRECTIONS... WE'RE SURROUNDED!

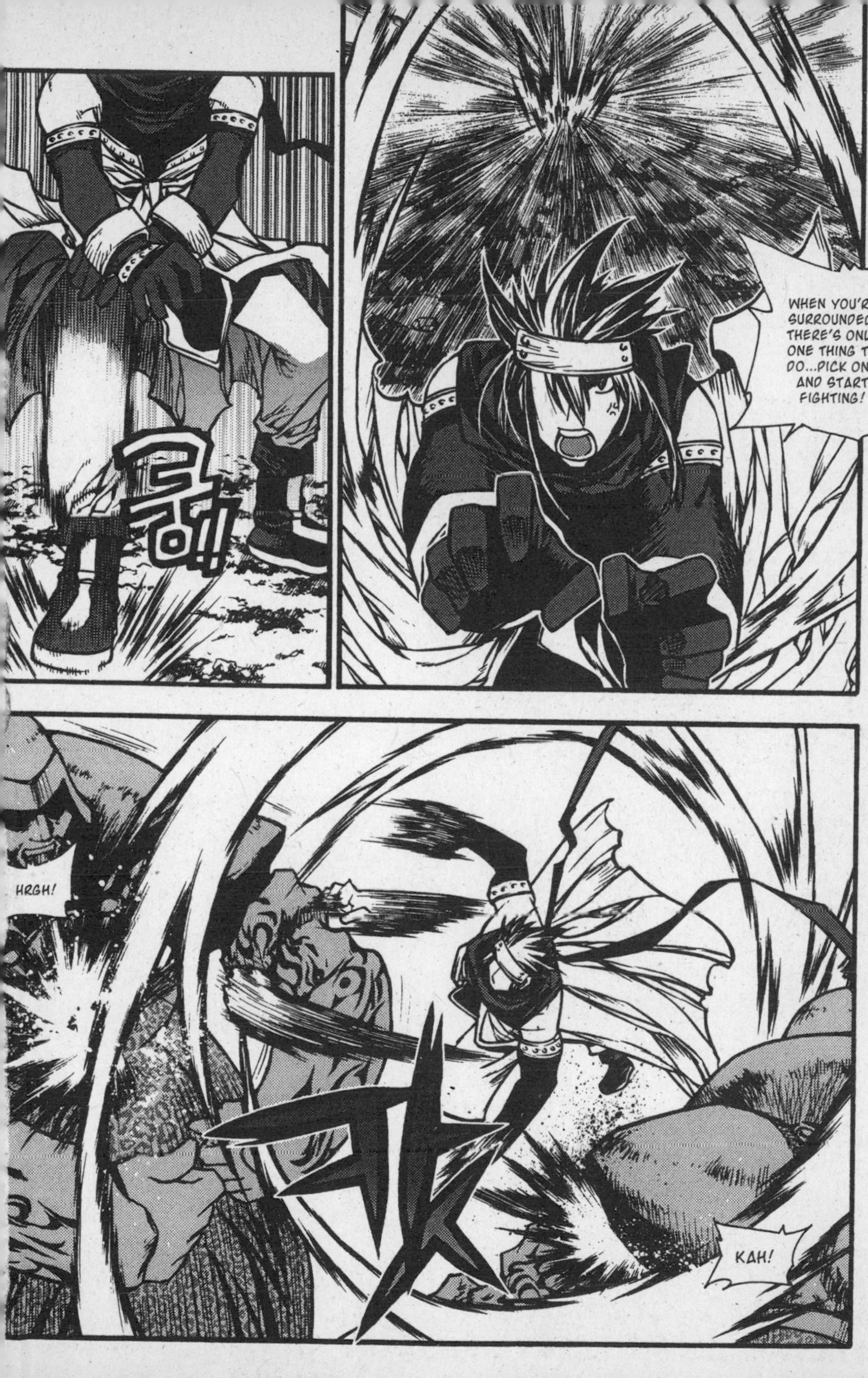
WHEN YOU'RE SURROUNDED, THERE'S ONLY ONE THING TO DO...PICK ONE AND START FIGHTING!
HRGH!
KAH!

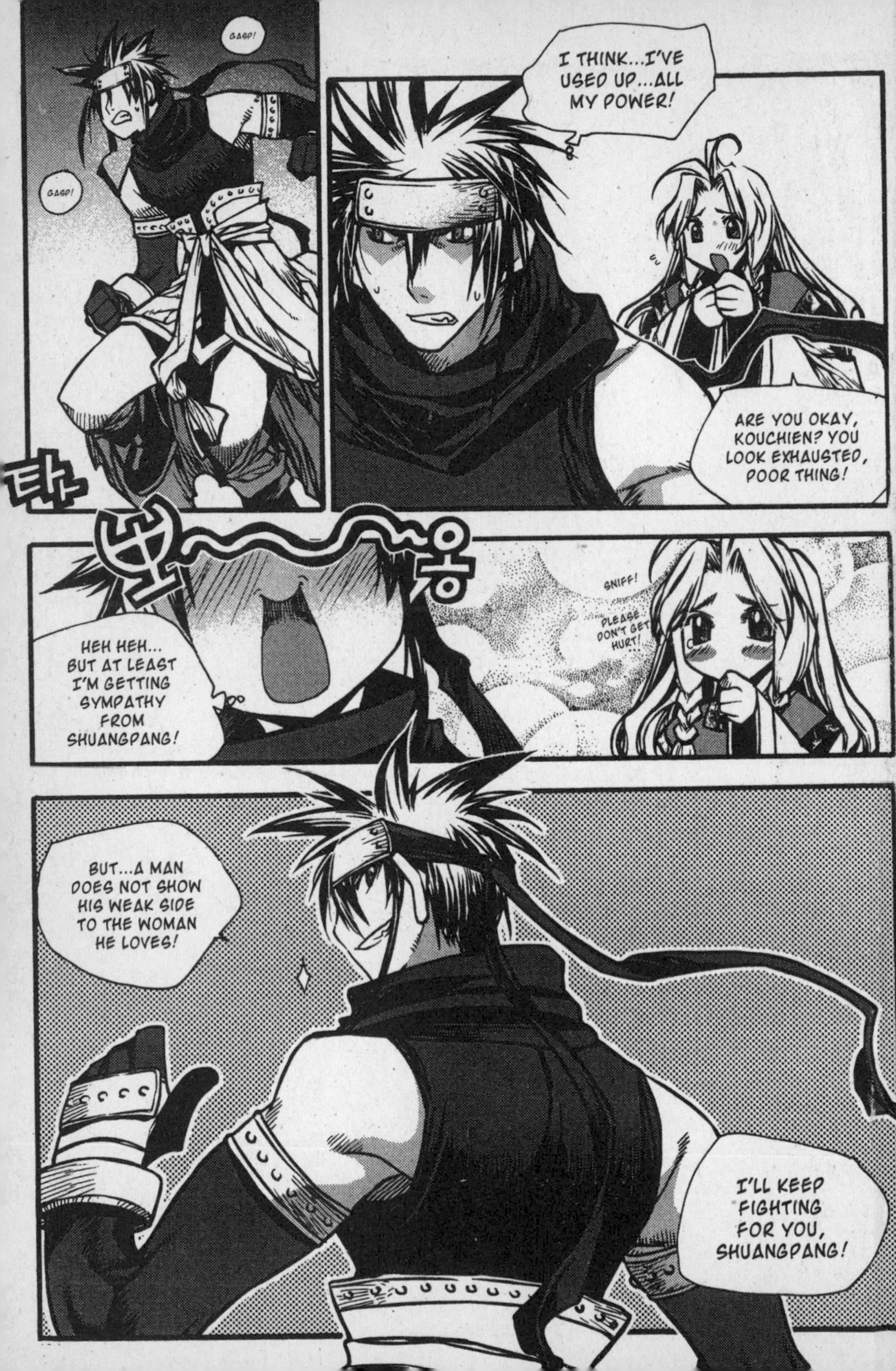
GASP!
GASP!
I THINK...I'VE USED UP...ALL MY POWER!
ARE YOU OKAY, KOUCHIEN? YOU LOOK EXHAUSTED, POOR THING!
탁
보~~~옹
HEH HEH... BUT AT LEAST I'M GETTING SYMPATHY FROM SHUANGPANG!
SNIFF!
PLEASE DON'T GET HURT!
BUT...A MAN DOES NOT SHOW HIS WEAK SIDE TO THE WOMAN HE LOVES!
I'LL KEEP FIGHTING FOR YOU, SHUANGPANG!

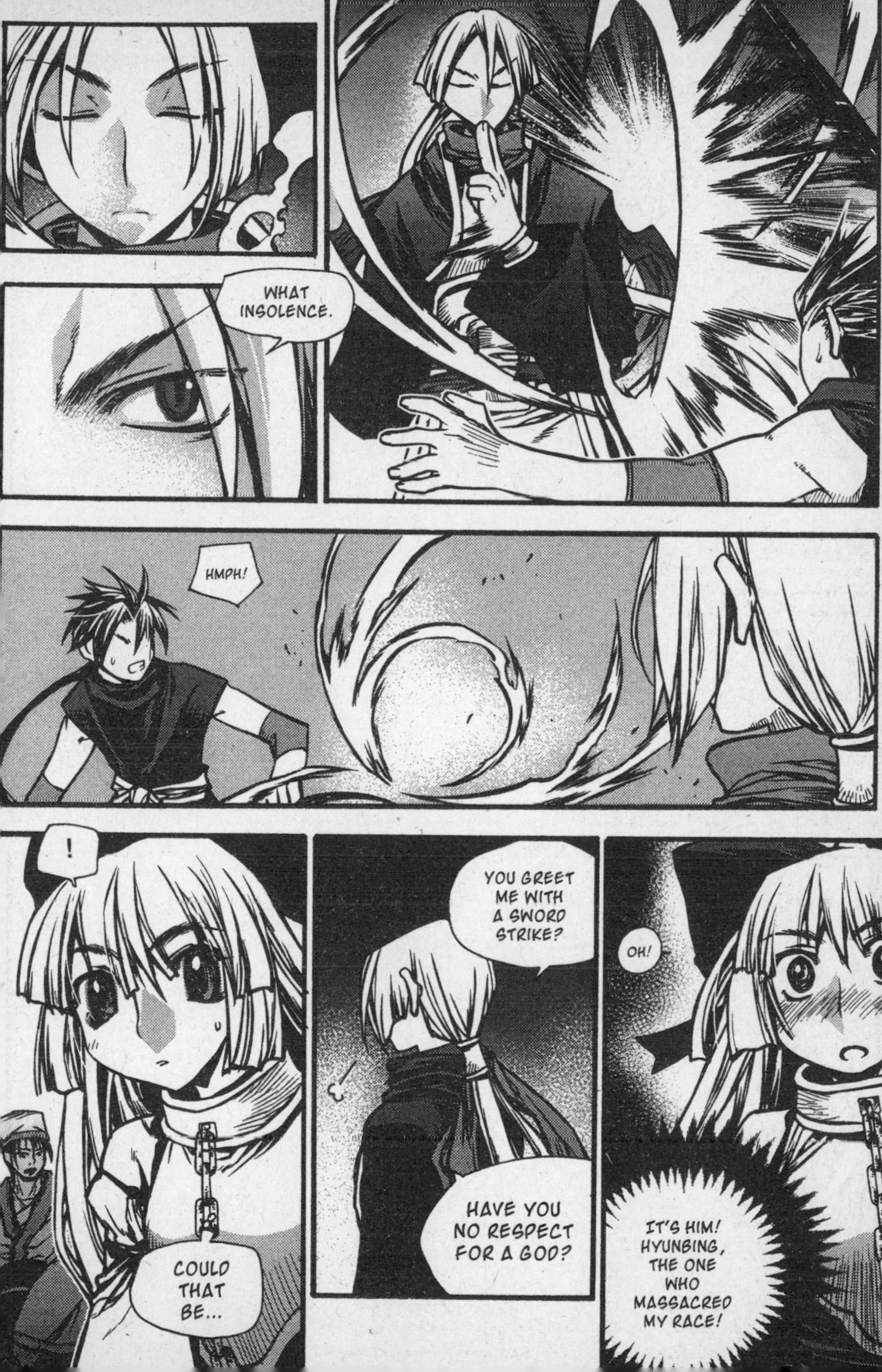
WHAT INSOLENCE.
HMPH!
!
COULD THAT BE...
YOU GREET ME WITH A SWORD STRIKE?
HAVE YOU NO RESPECT FOR A GOD?
OH!
IT'S HIM! HYUNBING, THE ONE WHO MASSACRED MY RACE!

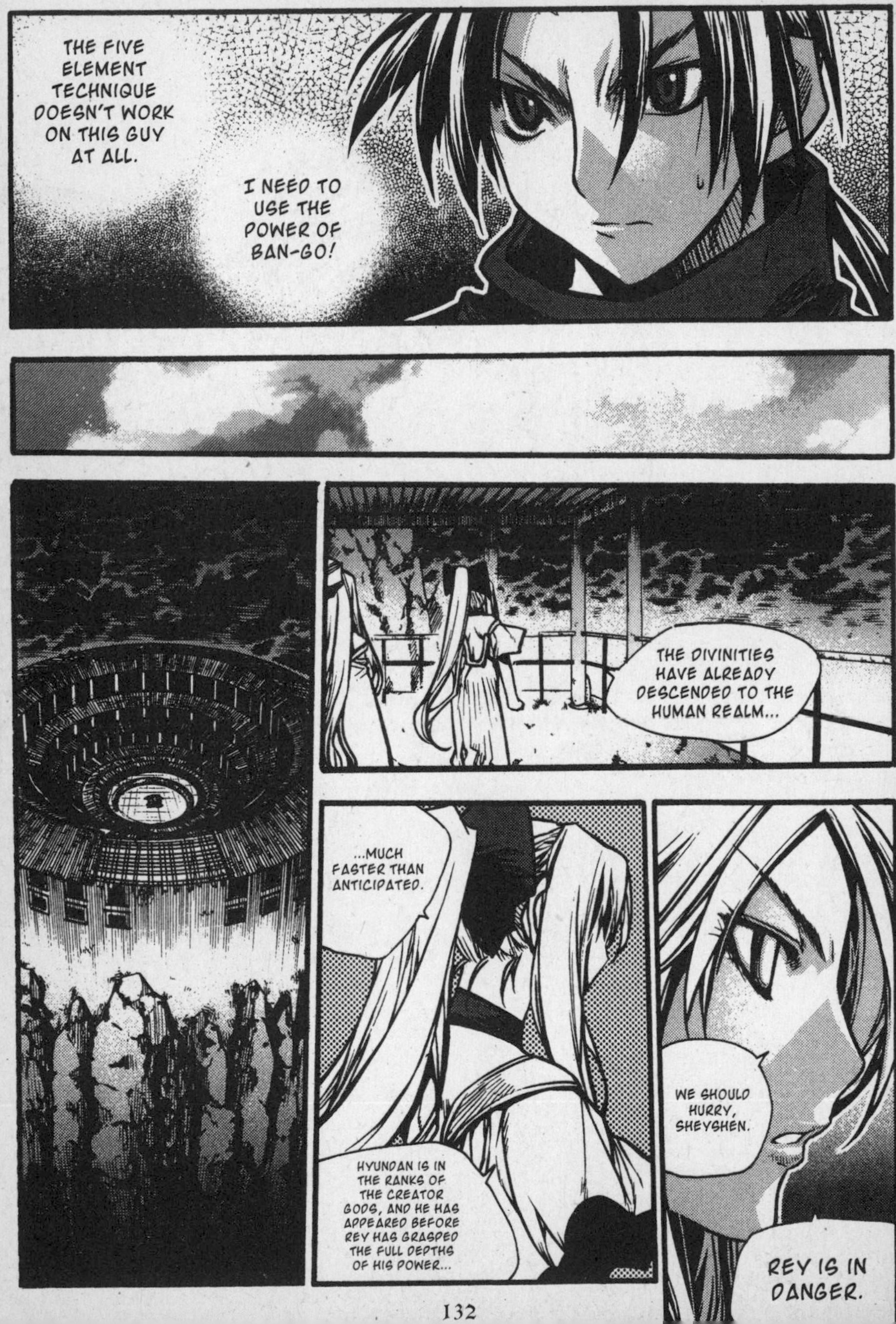
THE FIVE ELEMENT TECHNIQUE DOESN'T WORK ON THIS GUY AT ALL.
I NEED TO USE THE POWER OF BAN-GO!
THE DIVINITIES HAVE ALREADY DESCENDED TO THE HUMAN REALM...
...MUCH FASTER THAN ANTICIPATED.
HYUNDAN IS IN THE RANKS OF THE CREATOR GODS, AND HE HAS APPEARED BEFORE REY HAS GRASPED THE FULL DEPTHS OF HIS POWER...
WE SHOULD HURRY, SHEYSHEN.
REY IS IN DANGER.

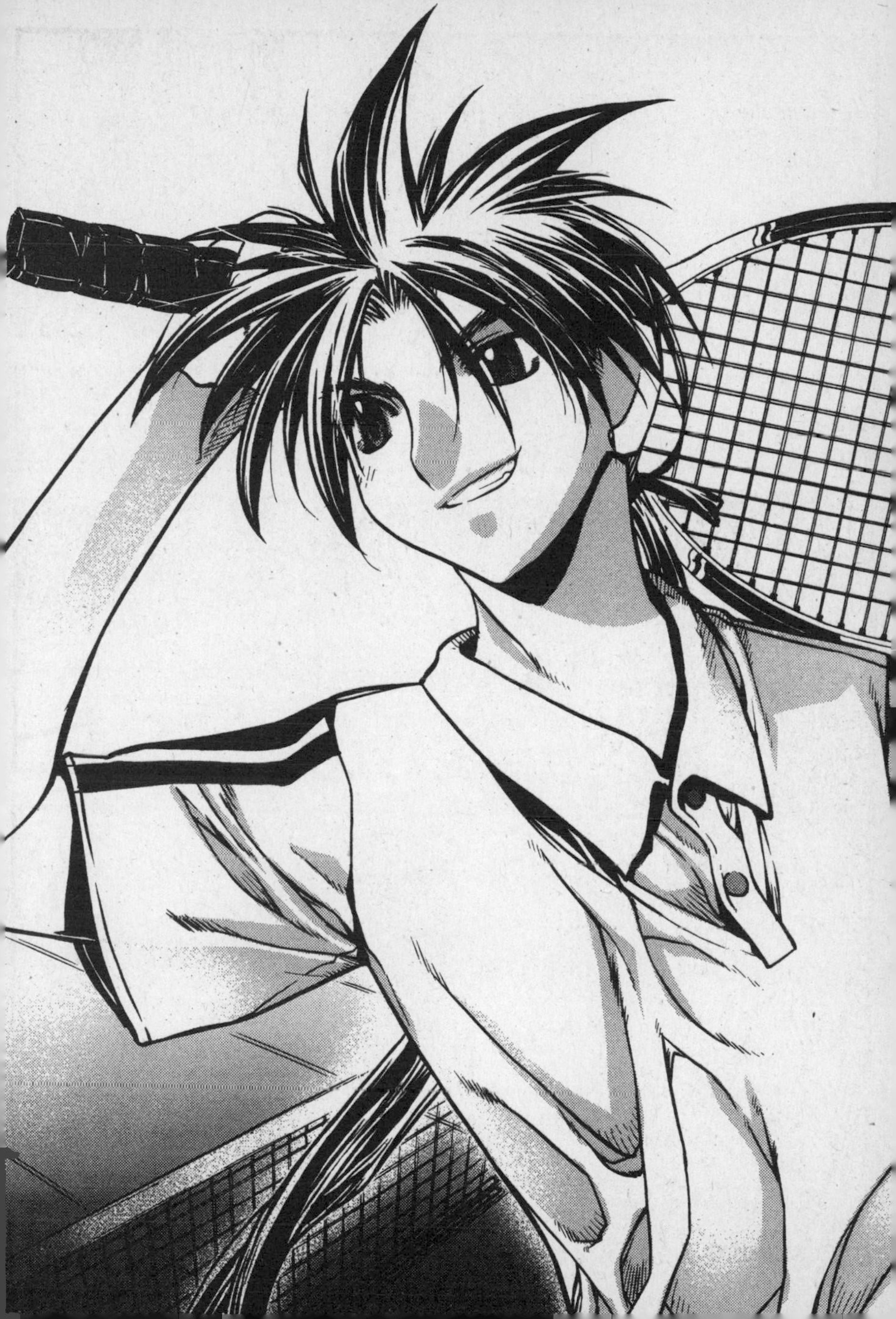

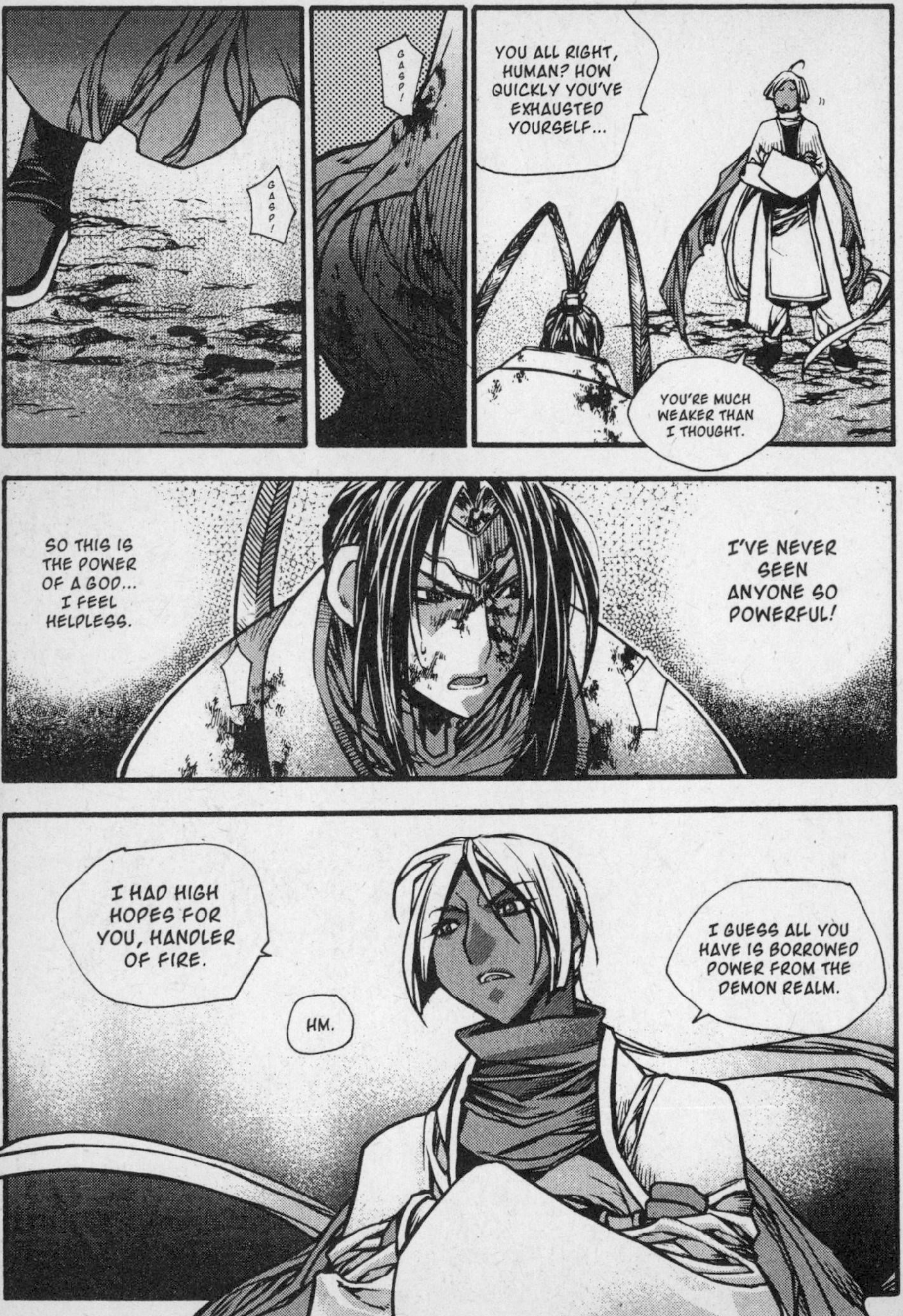
GASP!
GASP!
YOU ALL RIGHT, HUMAN? HOW QUICKLY YOU'VE EXHAUSTED YOURSELF...
YOU'RE MUCH WEAKER THAN I THOUGHT.
SO THIS IS THE POWER OF A GOD... I FEEL HELPLESS.
I'VE NEVER SEEN ANYONE SO POWERFUL!
I HAD HIGH HOPES FOR YOU, HANDLER OF FIRE.
HM.
I GUESS ALL YOU HAVE IS BORROWED POWER FROM THE DEMON REALM.

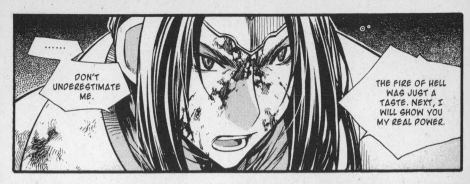

......

DON'T UNDERESTIMATE ME.

THE FIRE OF HELL WAS JUST A TASTE. NEXT, I WILL SHOW YOU MY REAL POWER.

I TAKE IT YOU HAVE KILLED MANY?

WHAT ARE YOU MUTTERING ABOUT? OF COURSE I'VE KILLED MANY.

HA.

BOTH YOU AND I...

...WE'RE HARDENED WARRIORS.

WHICH IS WHY I NOW SUMMON THE ULTIMATE HEAT OF HELL!

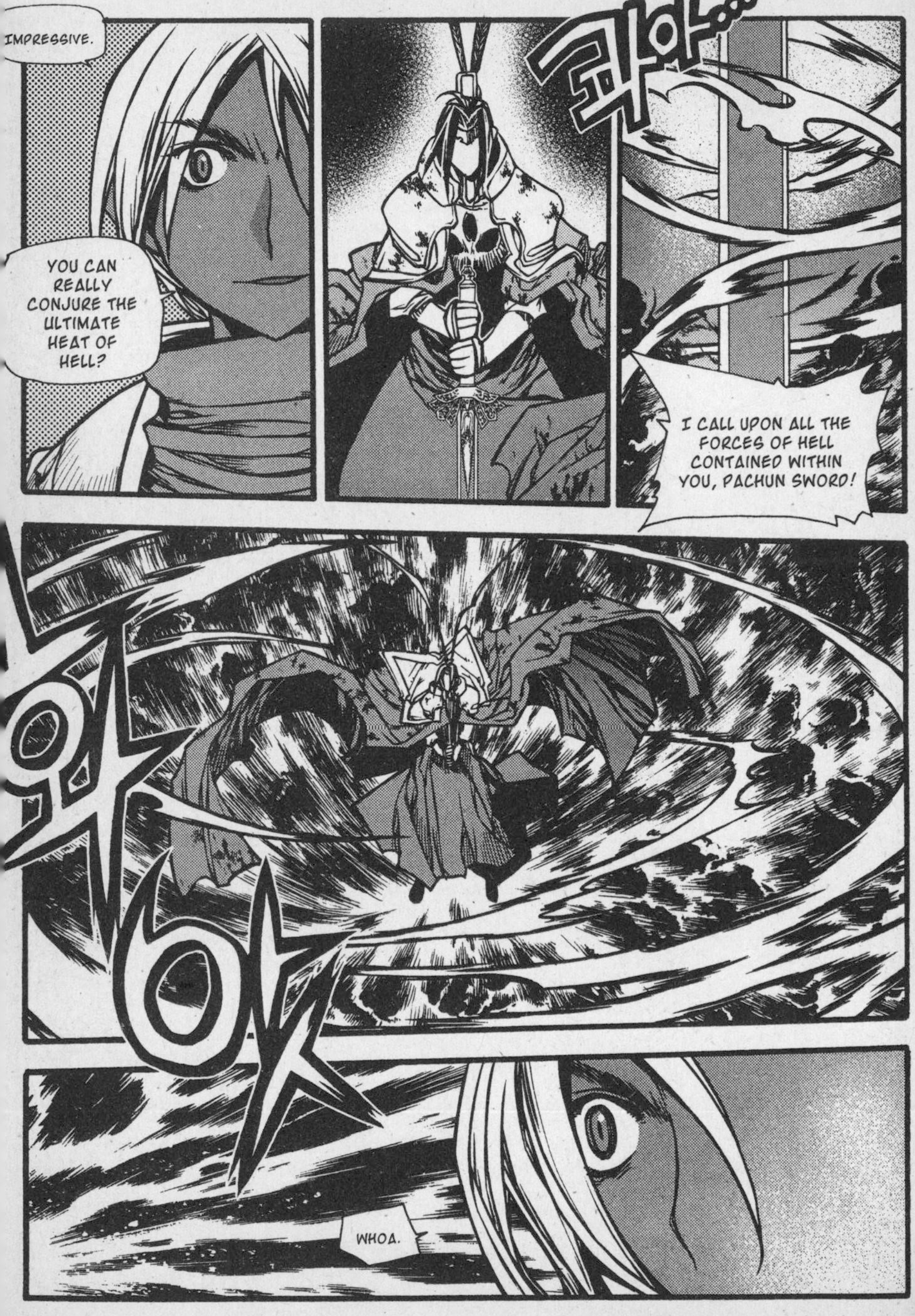
IMPRESSIVE.
YOU CAN REALLY CONJURE THE ULTIMATE HEAT OF HELL?
콰아...
I CALL UPON ALL THE FORCES OF HELL CONTAINED WITHIN YOU, PACHUN SWORD!
WHOA.

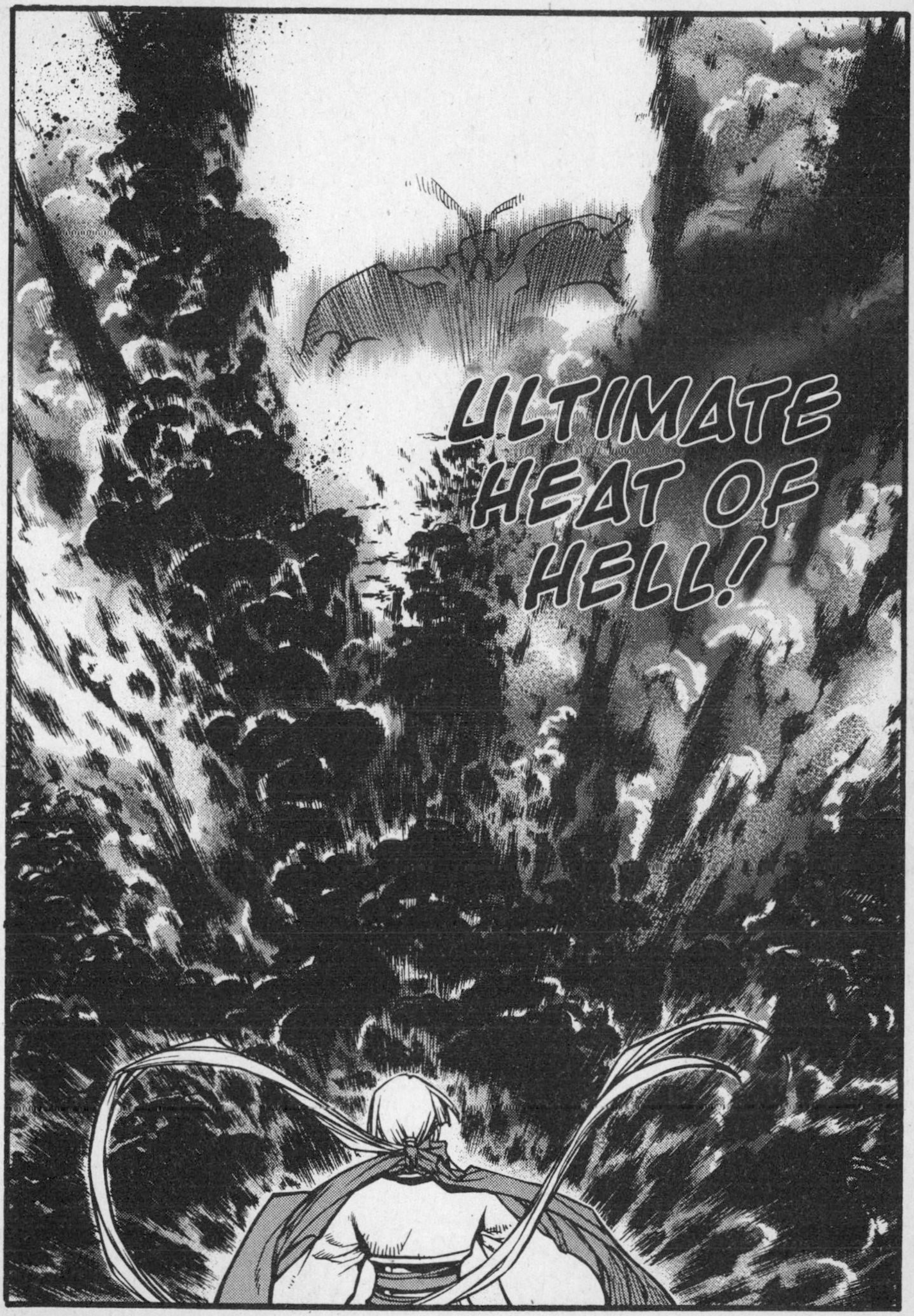
ULTIMATE HEAT OF HELL!

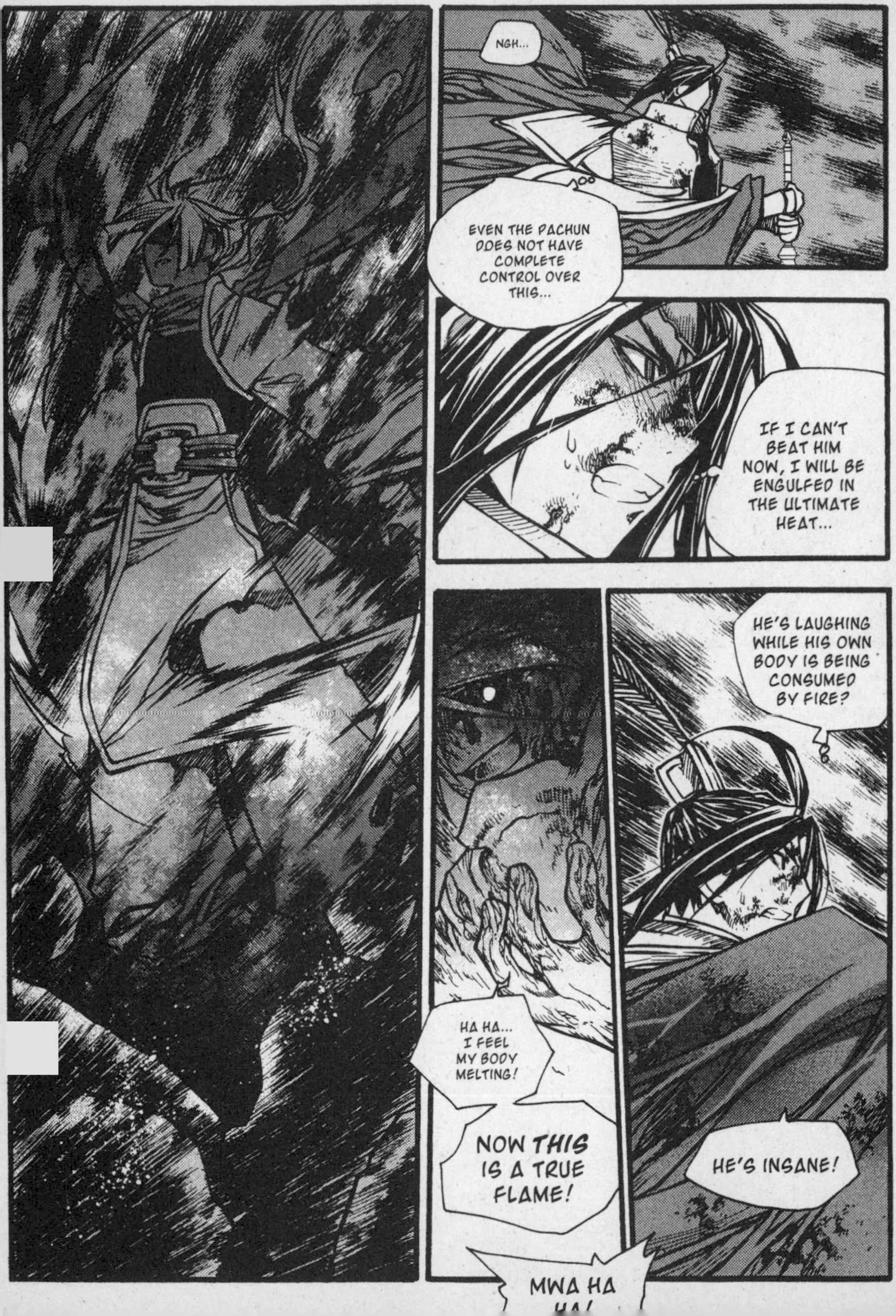
NGH...
EVEN THE PACHUN DOES NOT HAVE COMPLETE CONTROL OVER THIS...
IF I CAN'T BEAT HIM NOW, I WILL BE ENGULFED IN THE ULTIMATE HEAT...
HA HA... I FEEL MY BODY MELTING!
NOW THIS IS A TRUE FLAME!
MWA HA HA!
HE'S LAUGHING WHILE HIS OWN BODY IS BEING CONSUMED BY FIRE?
HE'S INSANE!

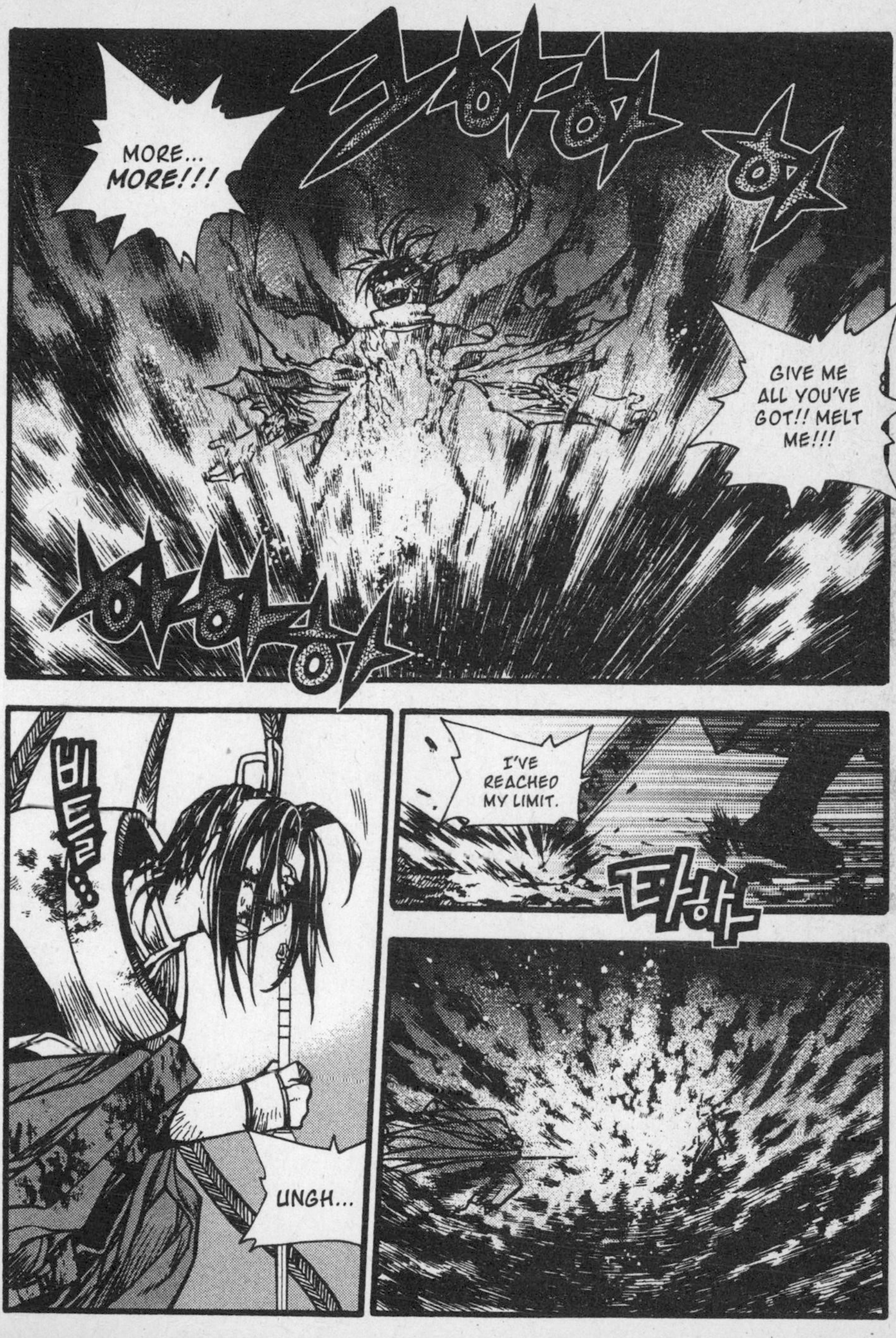
MORE... MORE!!!
GIVE ME ALL YOU'VE GOT!! MELT ME!!!
비틀..
UNGH...
I'VE REACHED MY LIMIT.

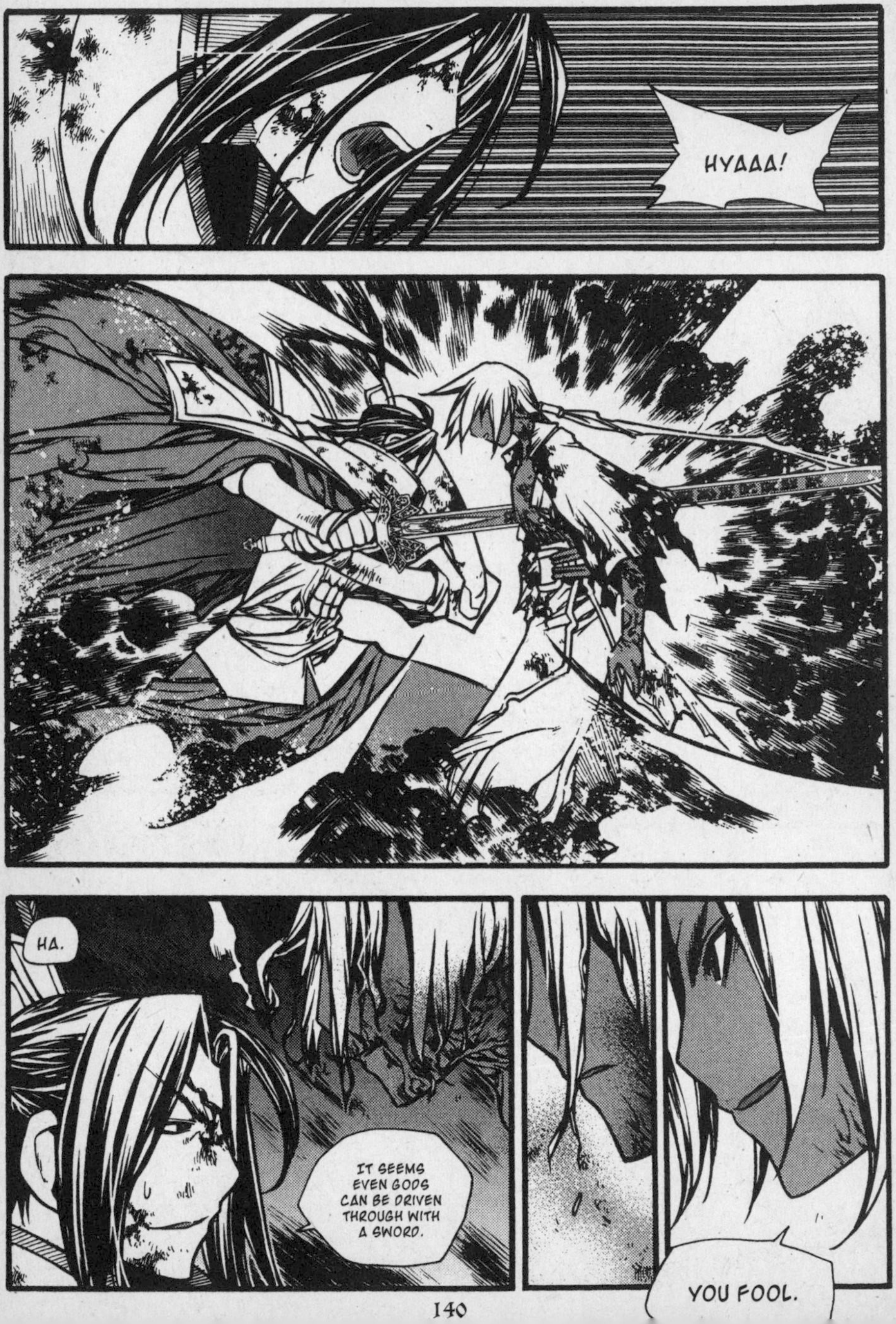
HYAAA!
HA.
IT SEEMS EVEN GODS CAN BE DRIVEN THROUGH WITH A SWORD.
YOU FOOL.

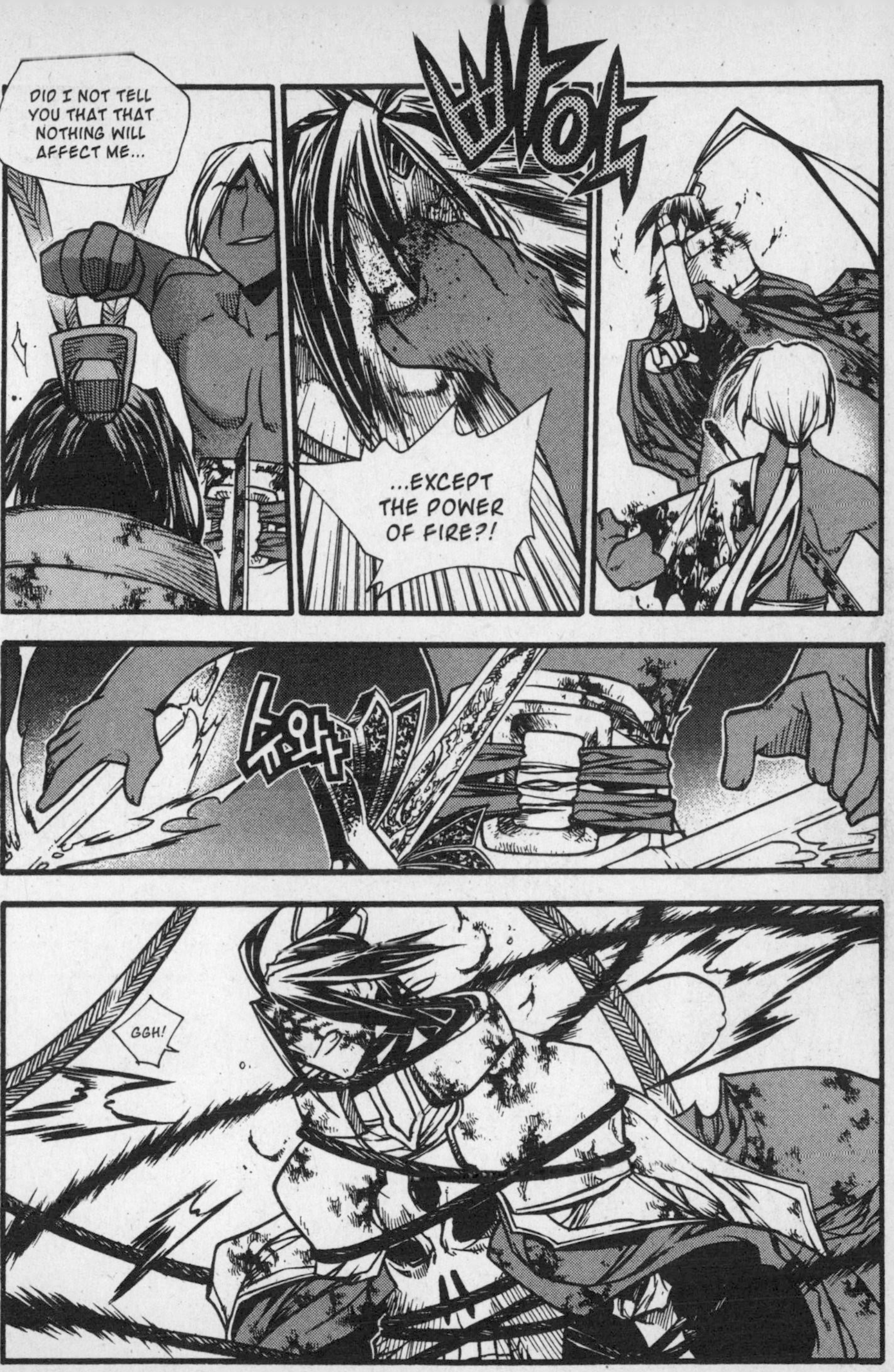
DID I NOT TELL YOU THAT THAT NOTHING WILL AFFECT ME...
...EXCEPT THE POWER OF FIRE?!
GGH!

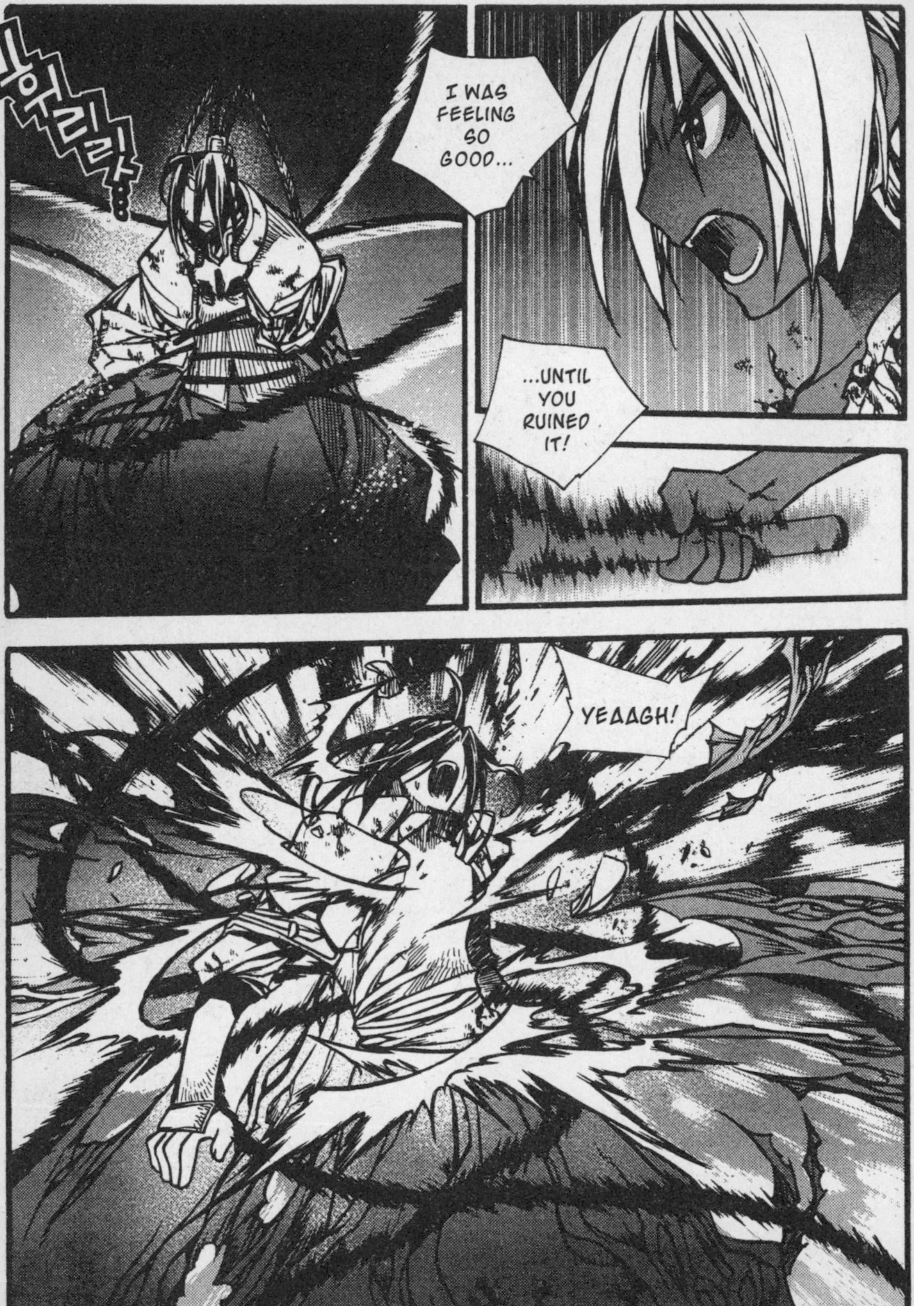
휘리라...
I WAS FEELING SO GOOD...
...UNTIL YOU RUINED IT!
YEAAGH!

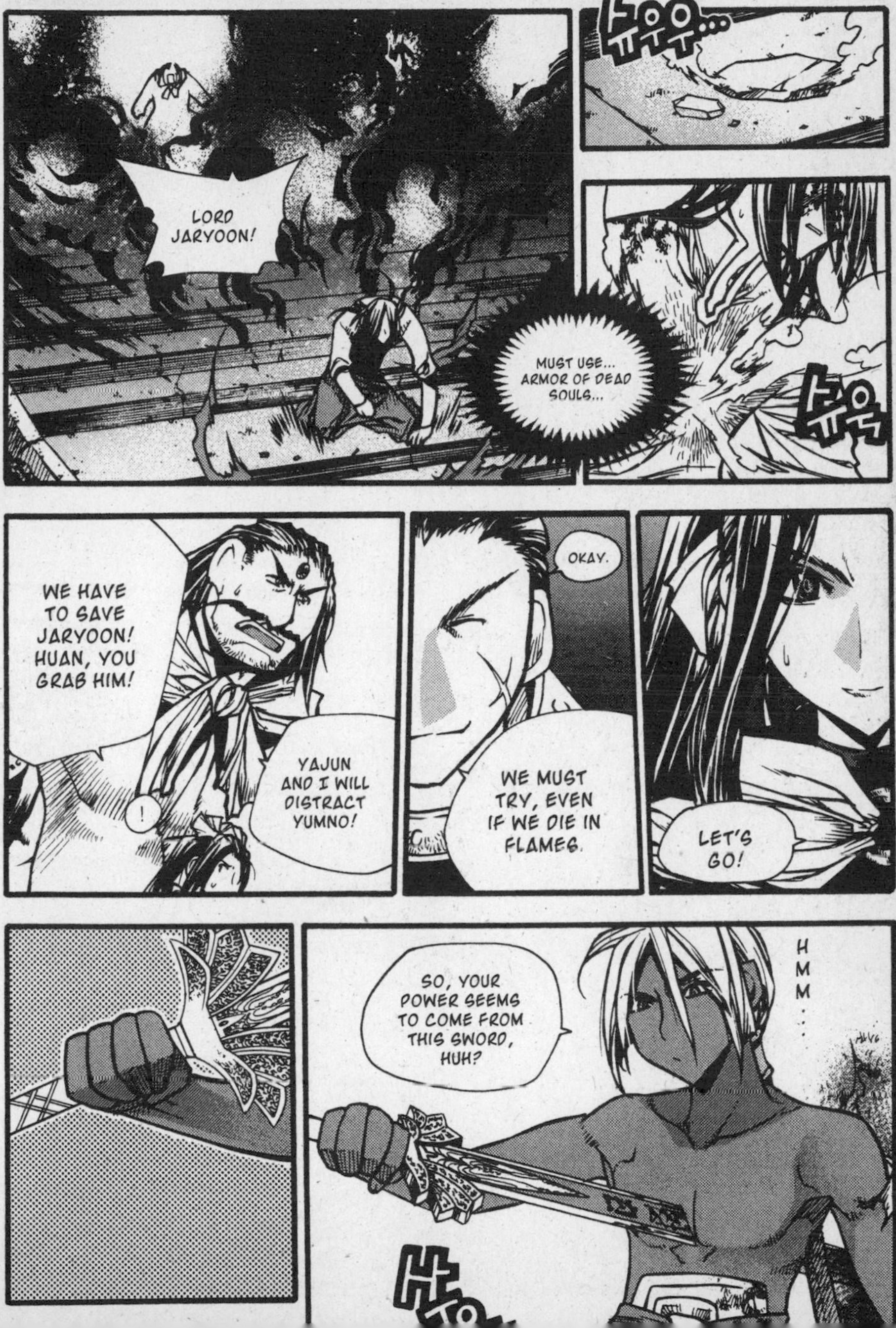

LORD JARYOON!
MUST USE... ARMOR OF DEAD SOULS...
WE HAVE TO SAVE JARYOON! HUAN, YOU GRAB HIM!
!
YAJUN AND I WILL DISTRACT YUMNO!
OKAY.
WE MUST TRY, EVEN IF WE DIE IN FLAMES.
LET'S GO!
SO, YOUR POWER SEEMS TO COME FROM THIS SWORD, HUH?
HMM...

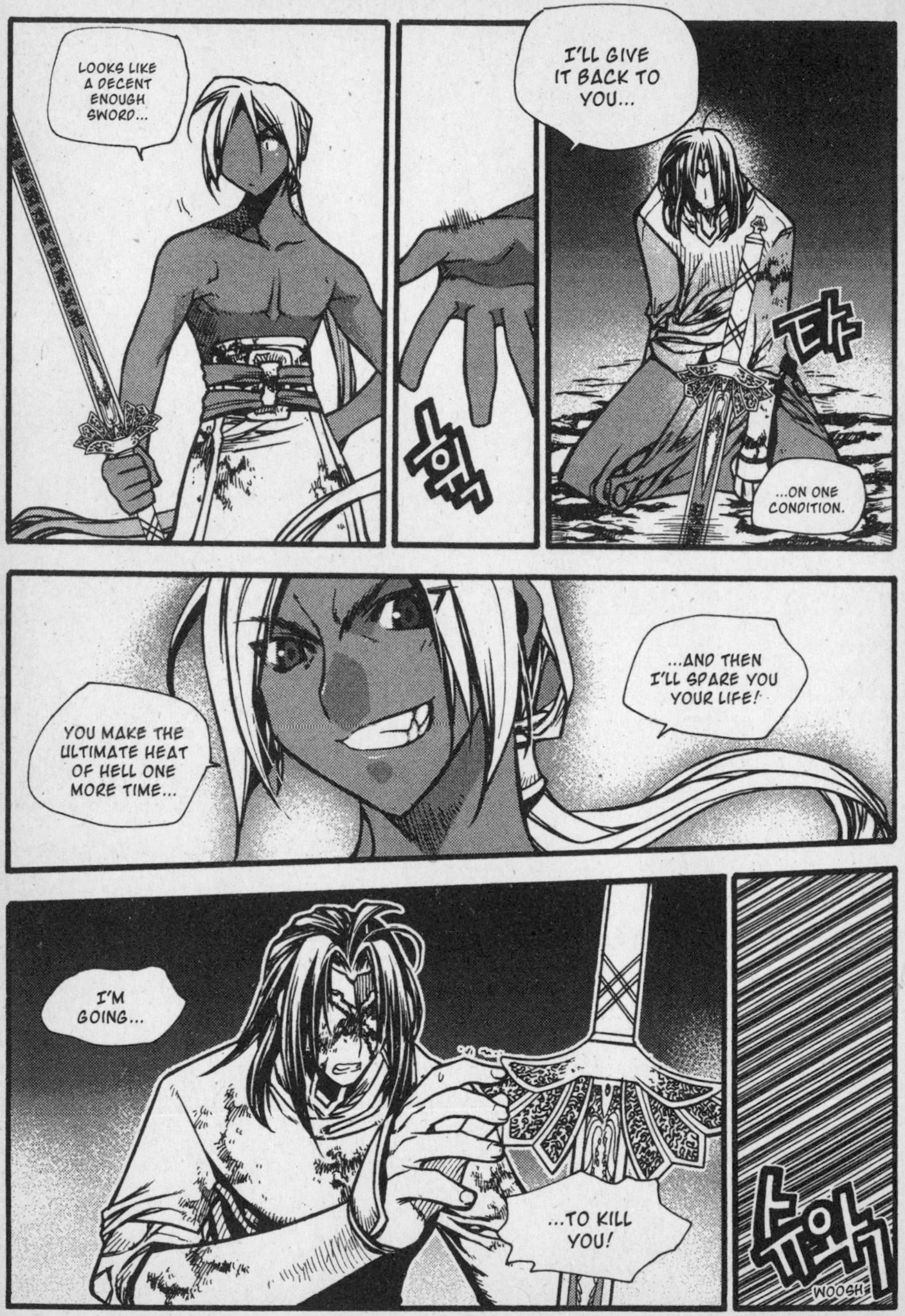
LOOKS LIKE A DECENT ENOUGH SWORD...
I'LL GIVE IT BACK TO YOU...
...ON ONE CONDITION.
YOU MAKE THE ULTIMATE HEAT OF HELL ONE MORE TIME...
...AND THEN I'LL SPARE YOU YOUR LIFE!
I'M GOING...
...TO KILL YOU!
WOOSH

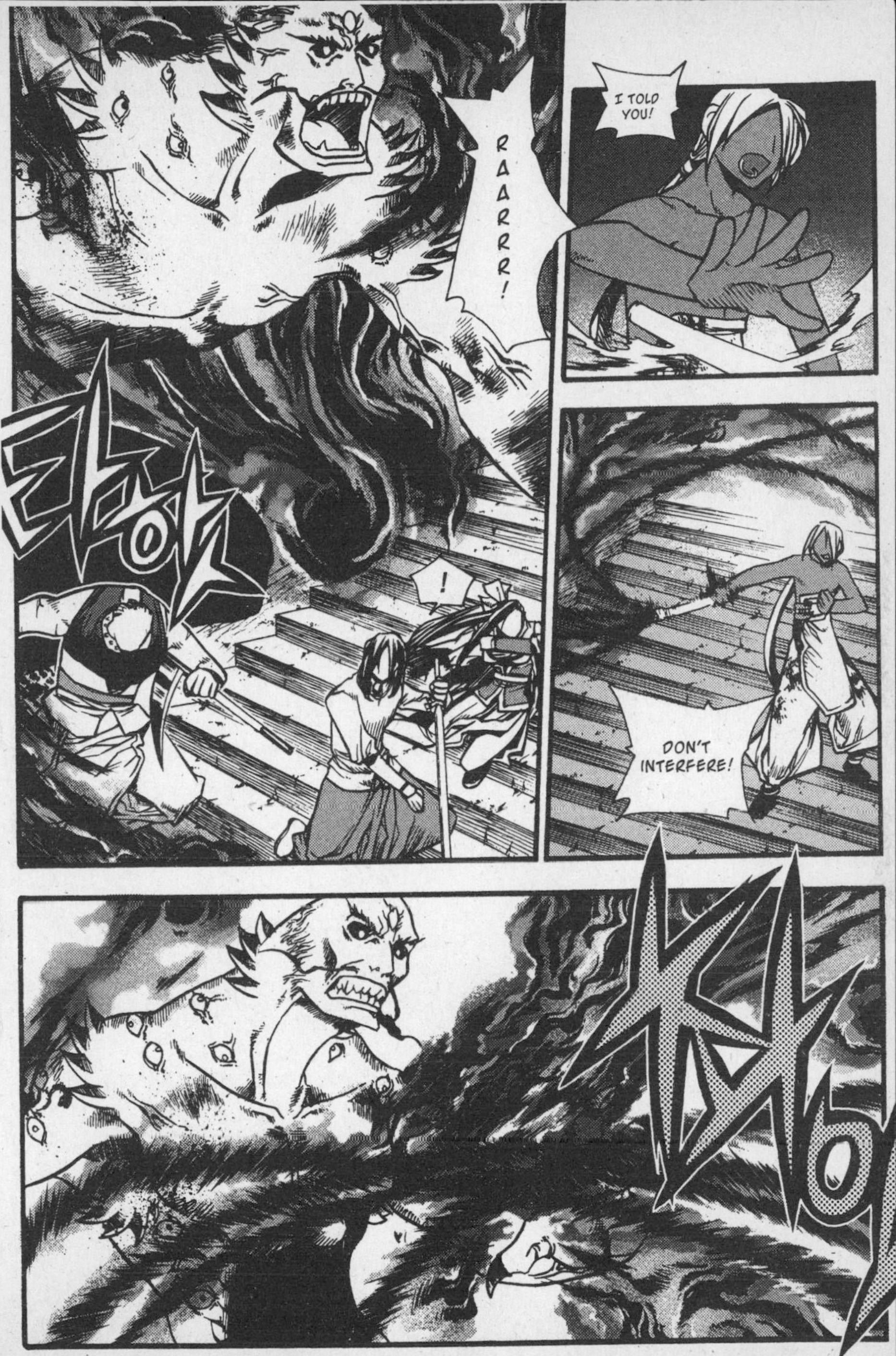
RAAARRR!
!
I TOLD YOU!
DON'T INTERFERE!

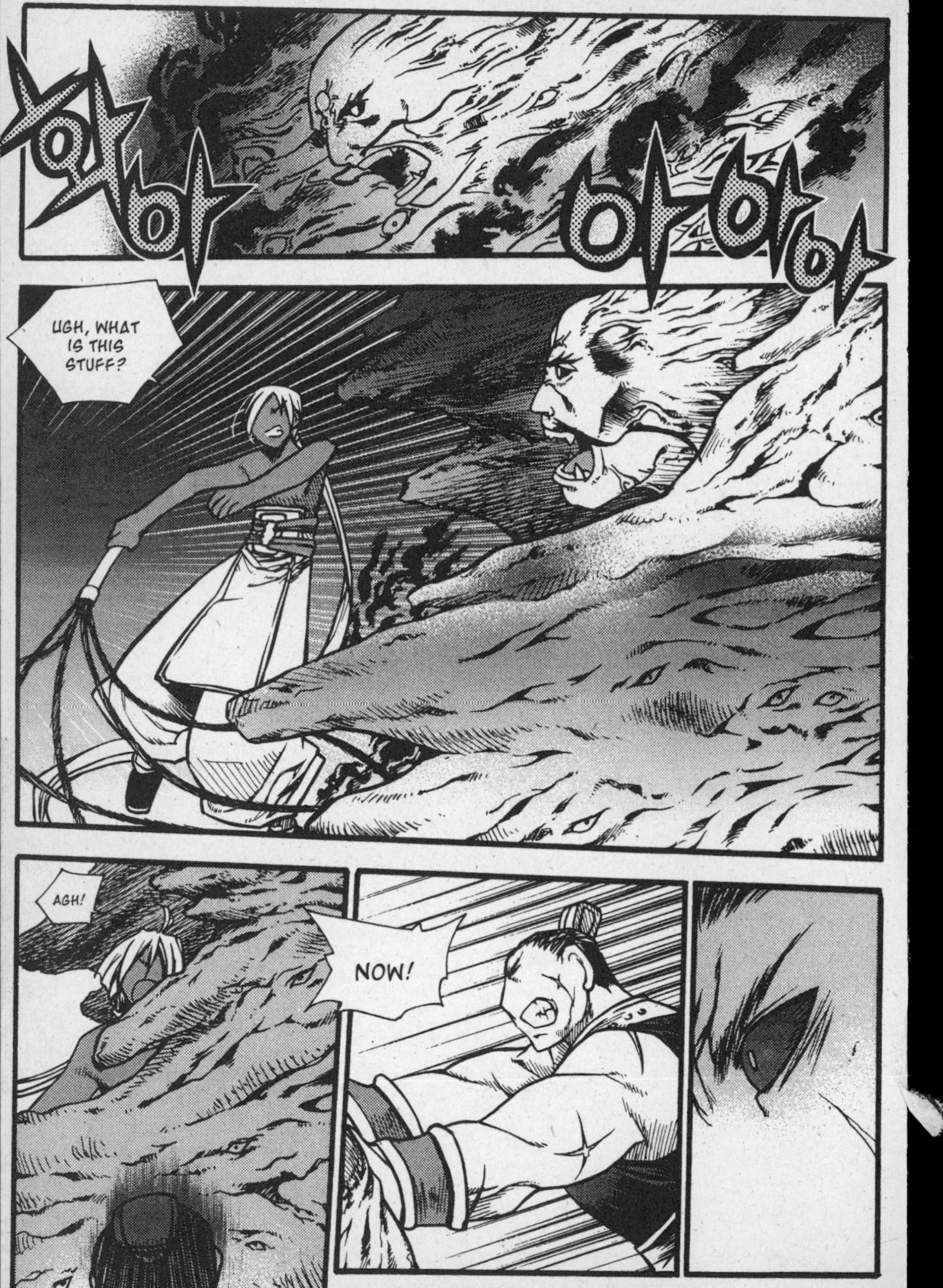
와아
아아아아
UGH, WHAT IS THIS STUFF?
AGH!
NOW!

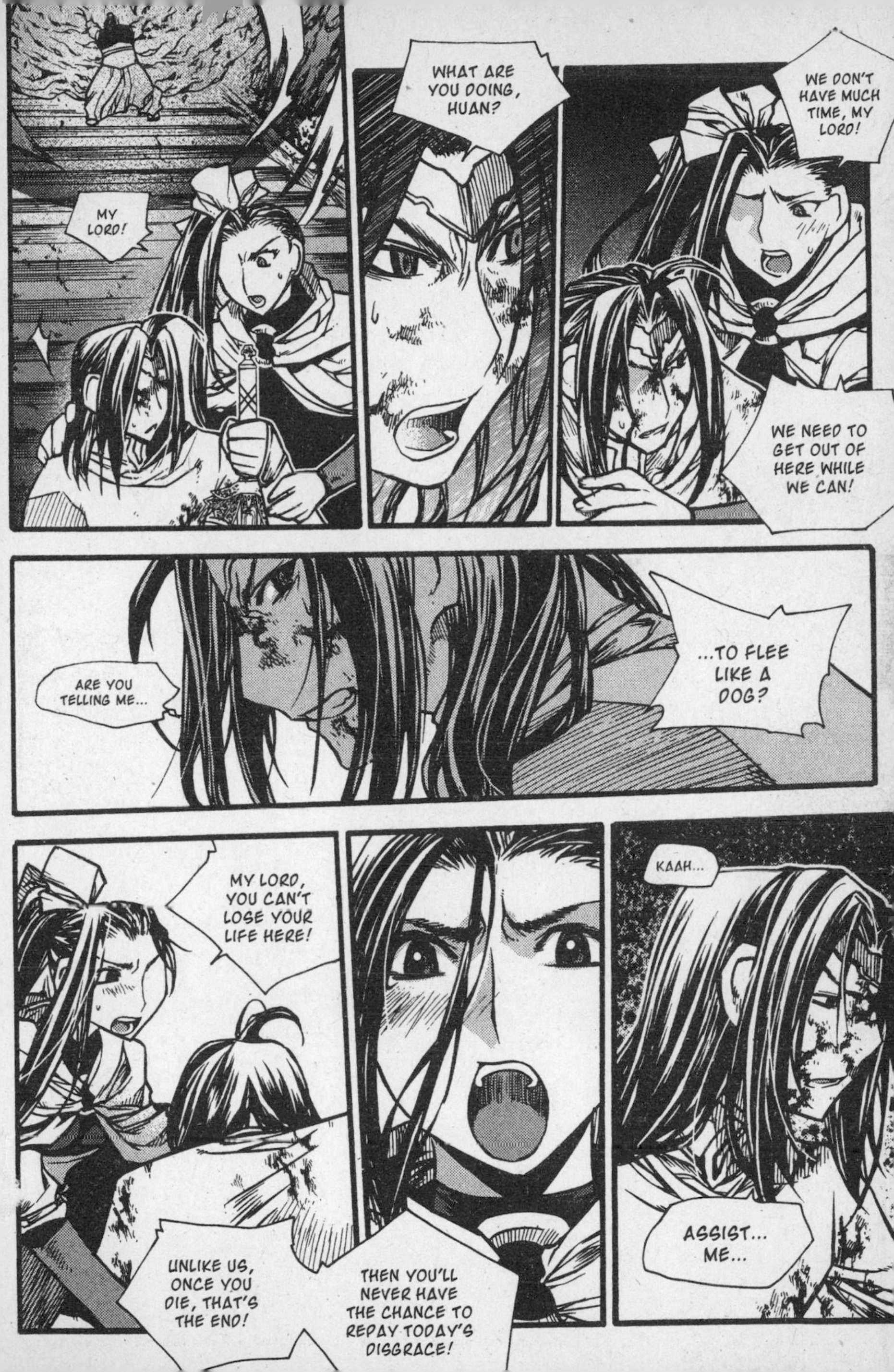
MY LORD!
WHAT ARE YOU DOING, HUAN?
WE DON'T HAVE MUCH TIME, MY LORD!
WE NEED TO GET OUT OF HERE WHILE WE CAN!
ARE YOU TELLING ME...
...TO FLEE LIKE A DOG?
MY LORD, YOU CAN'T LOSE YOUR LIFE HERE!
UNLIKE US, ONCE YOU DIE, THAT'S THE END!
THEN YOU'LL NEVER HAVE THE CHANCE TO REPAY TODAY'S DISGRACE!
KAAH...
ASSIST... ME...

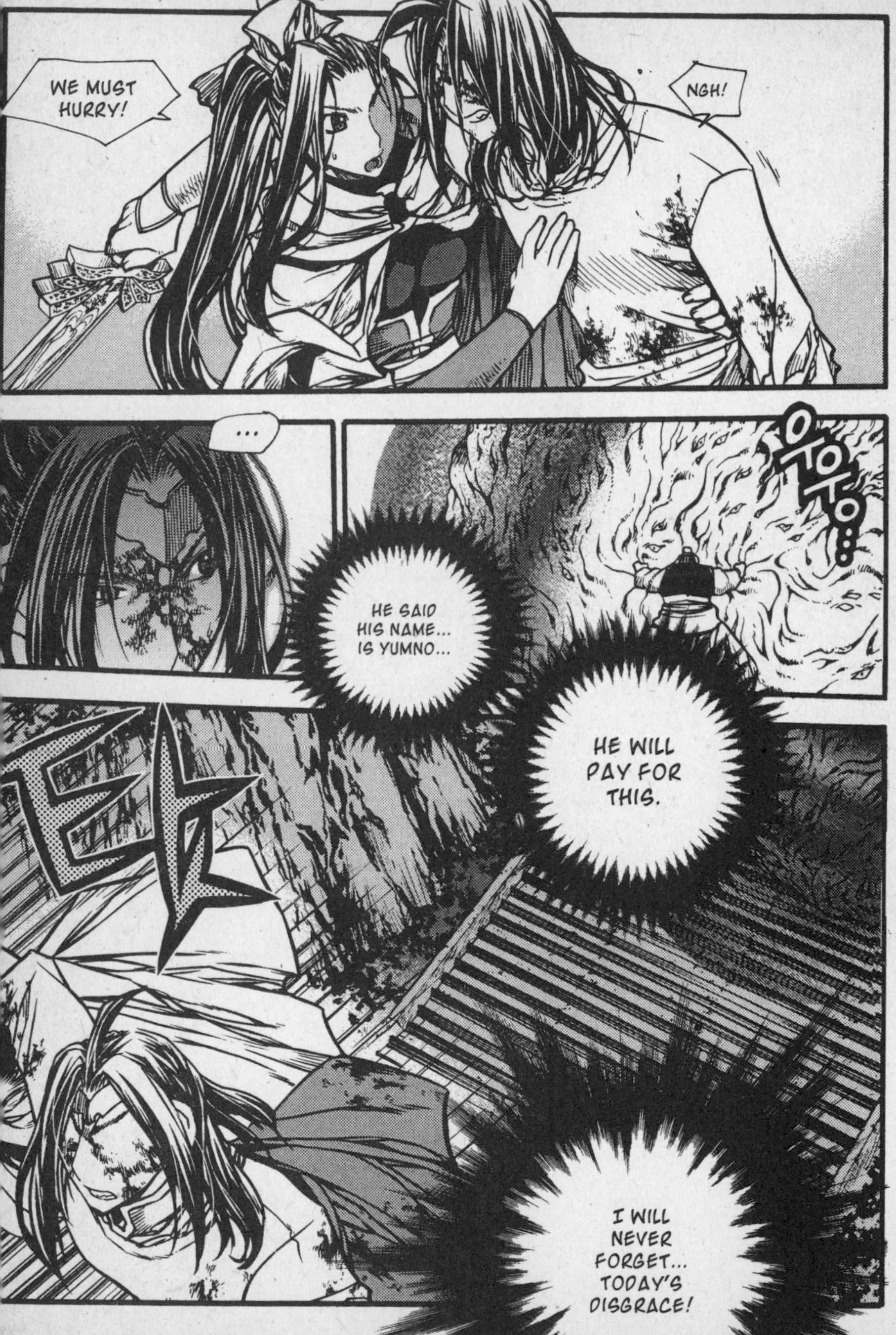
NGH!
WE MUST HURRY!
OTOTO...
...
HE SAID HIS NAME... IS YUMNO...
HE WILL PAY FOR THIS.
I WILL NEVER FORGET... TODAY'S DISGRACE!

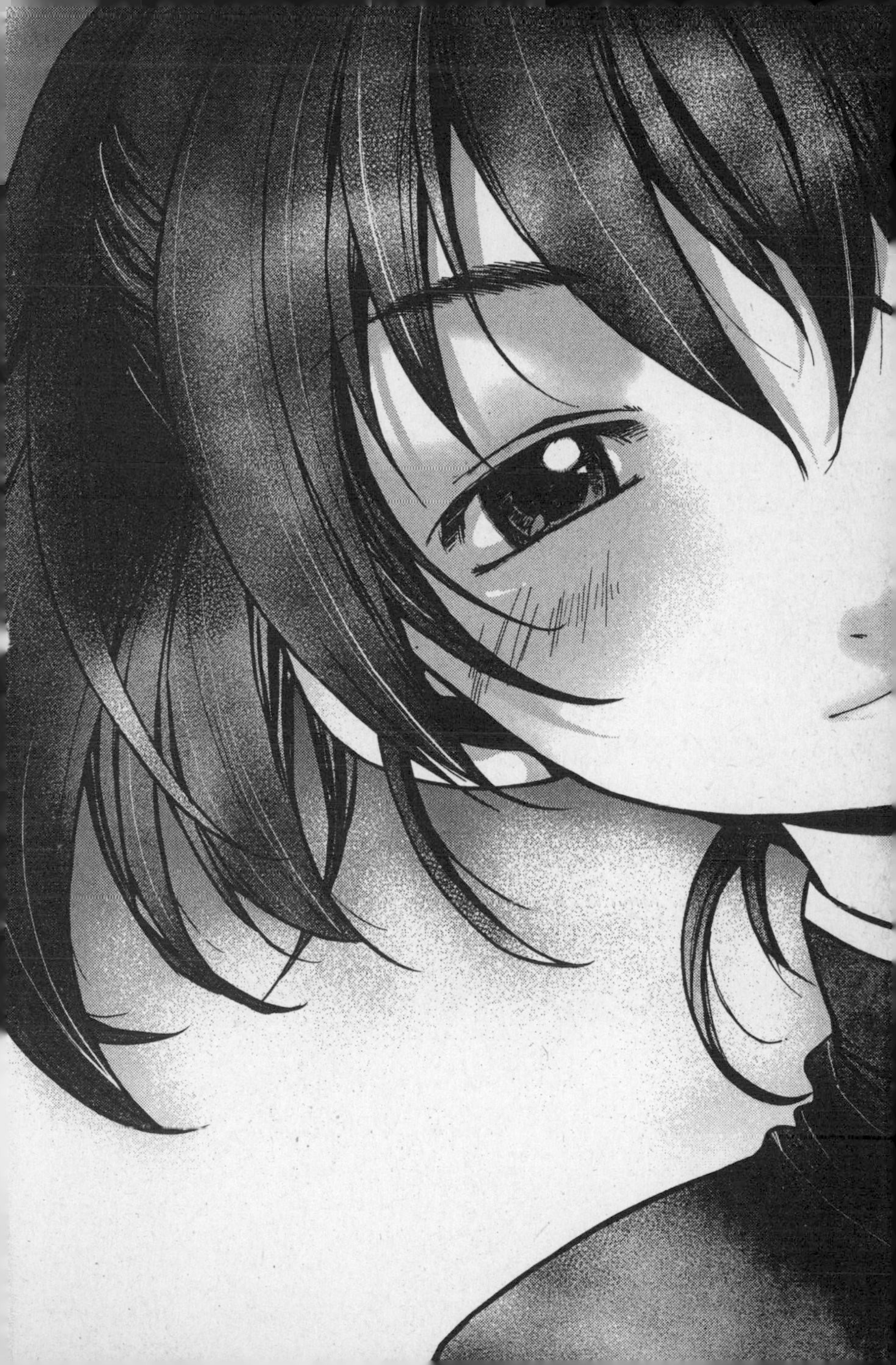

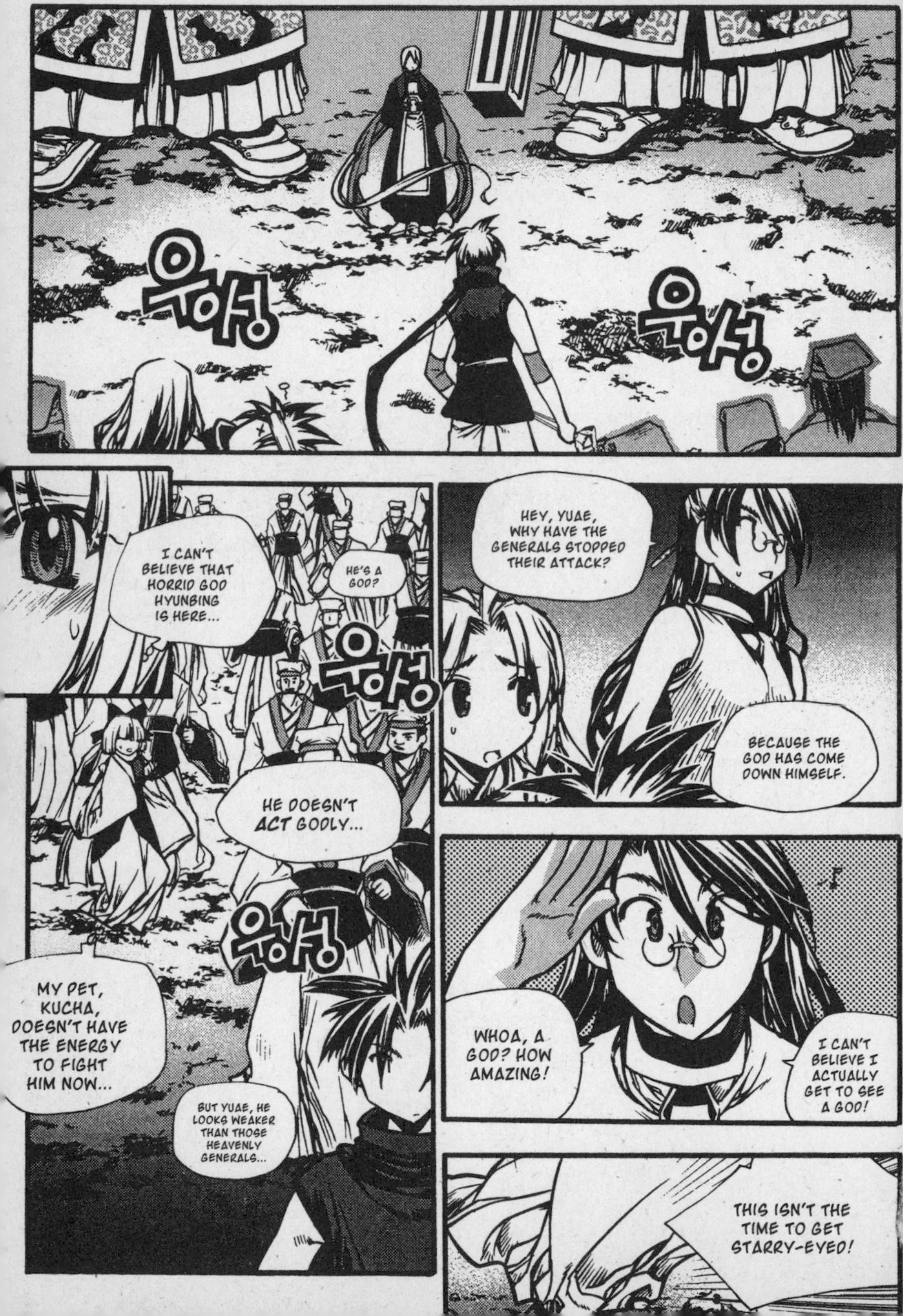
우앙
우앙
I CAN'T BELIEVE THAT HORRID GOD HYUNBING IS HERE...
HE'S A GOD?
우앙
HE DOESN'T ACT GODLY...
우앙
MY PET, KUCHA, DOESN'T HAVE THE ENERGY TO FIGHT HIM NOW...
BUT YUAE, HE LOOKS WEAKER THAN THOSE HEAVENLY GENERALS...
HEY, YUAE, WHY HAVE THE GENERALS STOPPED THEIR ATTACK?
BECAUSE THE GOD HAS COME DOWN HIMSELF.
WHOA, A GOD? HOW AMAZING!
I CAN'T BELIEVE I ACTUALLY GET TO SEE A GOD!
THIS ISN'T THE TIME TO GET STARRY-EYED!

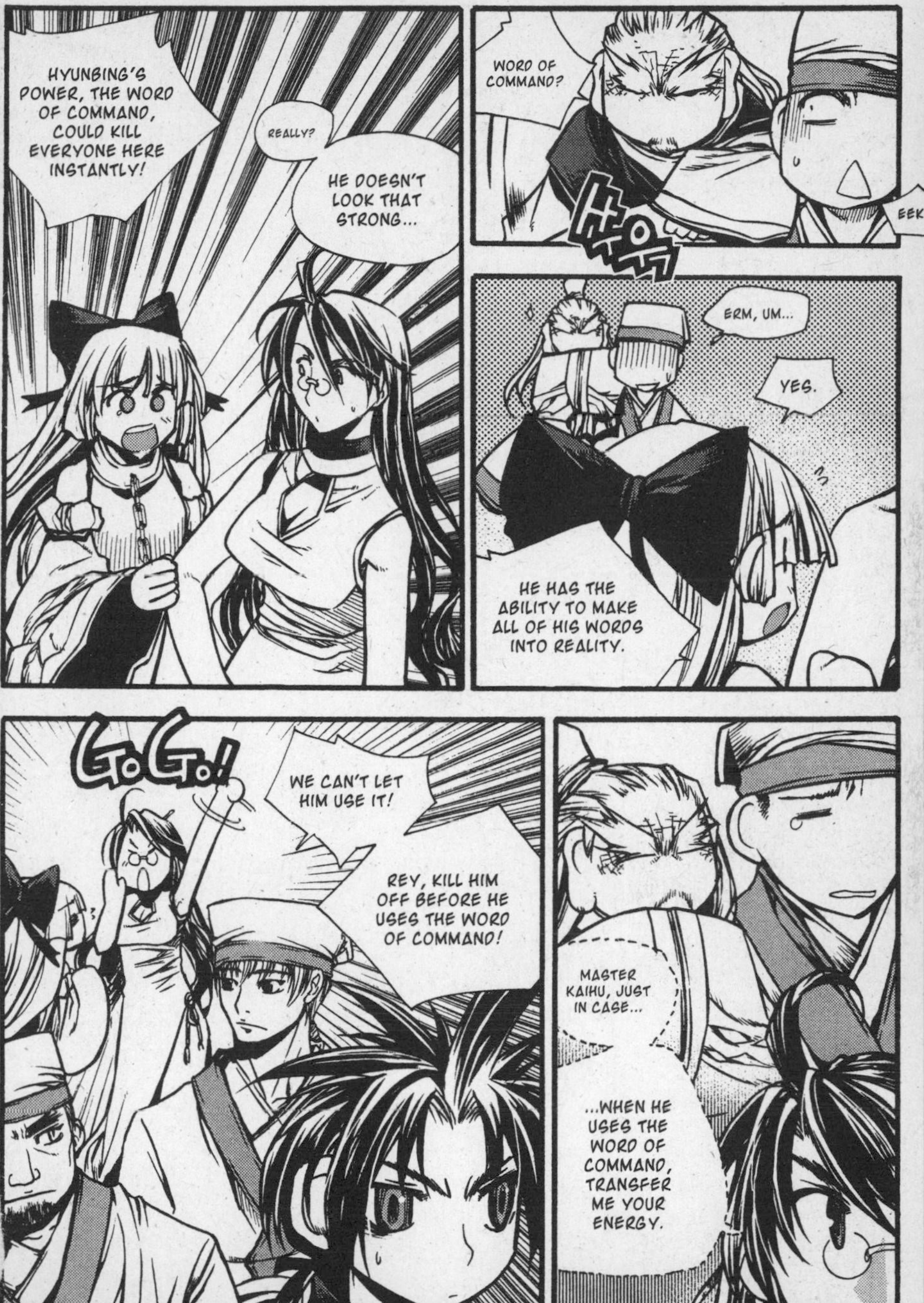

HYUNBING'S POWER, THE WORD OF COMMAND, COULD KILL EVERYONE HERE INSTANTLY!
REALLY?
HE DOESN'T LOOK THAT STRONG...
WORD OF COMMAND?
EEK
ERM, UM...
YES.
HE HAS THE ABILITY TO MAKE ALL OF HIS WORDS INTO REALITY.
GO GO!
WE CAN'T LET HIM USE IT!
REY, KILL HIM OFF BEFORE HE USES THE WORD OF COMMAND!
MASTER KAIHU, JUST IN CASE...
...WHEN HE USES THE WORD OF COMMAND, TRANSFER ME YOUR ENERGY.

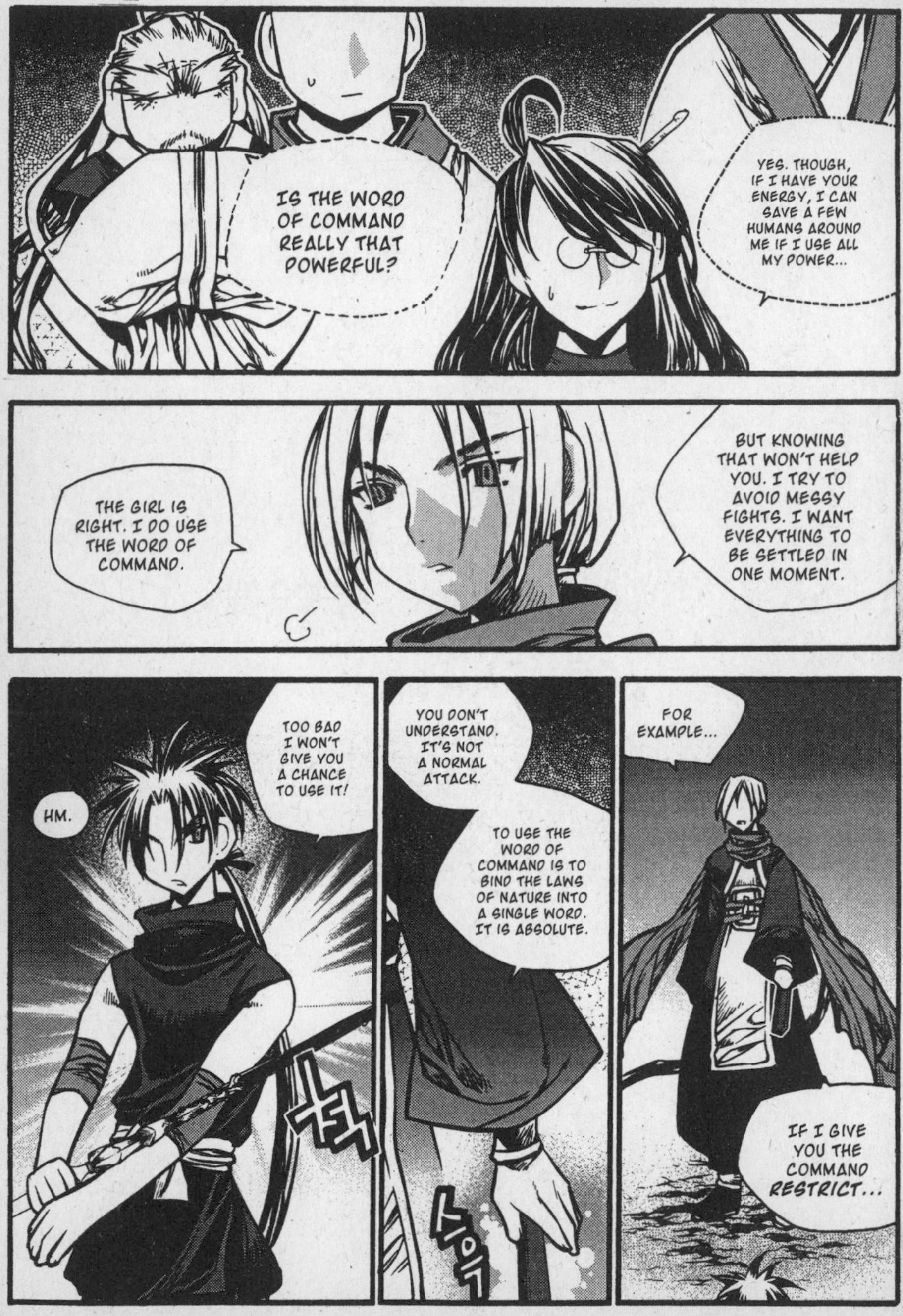
IS THE WORD OF COMMAND REALLY THAT POWERFUL?
YES. THOUGH, IF I HAVE YOUR ENERGY, I CAN SAVE A FEW HUMANS AROUND ME IF I USE ALL MY POWER...
THE GIRL IS RIGHT. I DO USE THE WORD OF COMMAND.
BUT KNOWING THAT WON'T HELP YOU. I TRY TO AVOID MESSY FIGHTS. I WANT EVERYTHING TO BE SETTLED IN ONE MOMENT.
TOO BAD I WON'T GIVE YOU A CHANCE TO USE IT!
HM.
YOU DON'T UNDERSTAND. IT'S NOT A NORMAL ATTACK.
TO USE THE WORD OF COMMAND IS TO BIND THE LAWS OF NATURE INTO A SINGLE WORD. IT IS ABSOLUTE.
FOR EXAMPLE...
IF I GIVE YOU THE COMMAND **RESTRICT**...

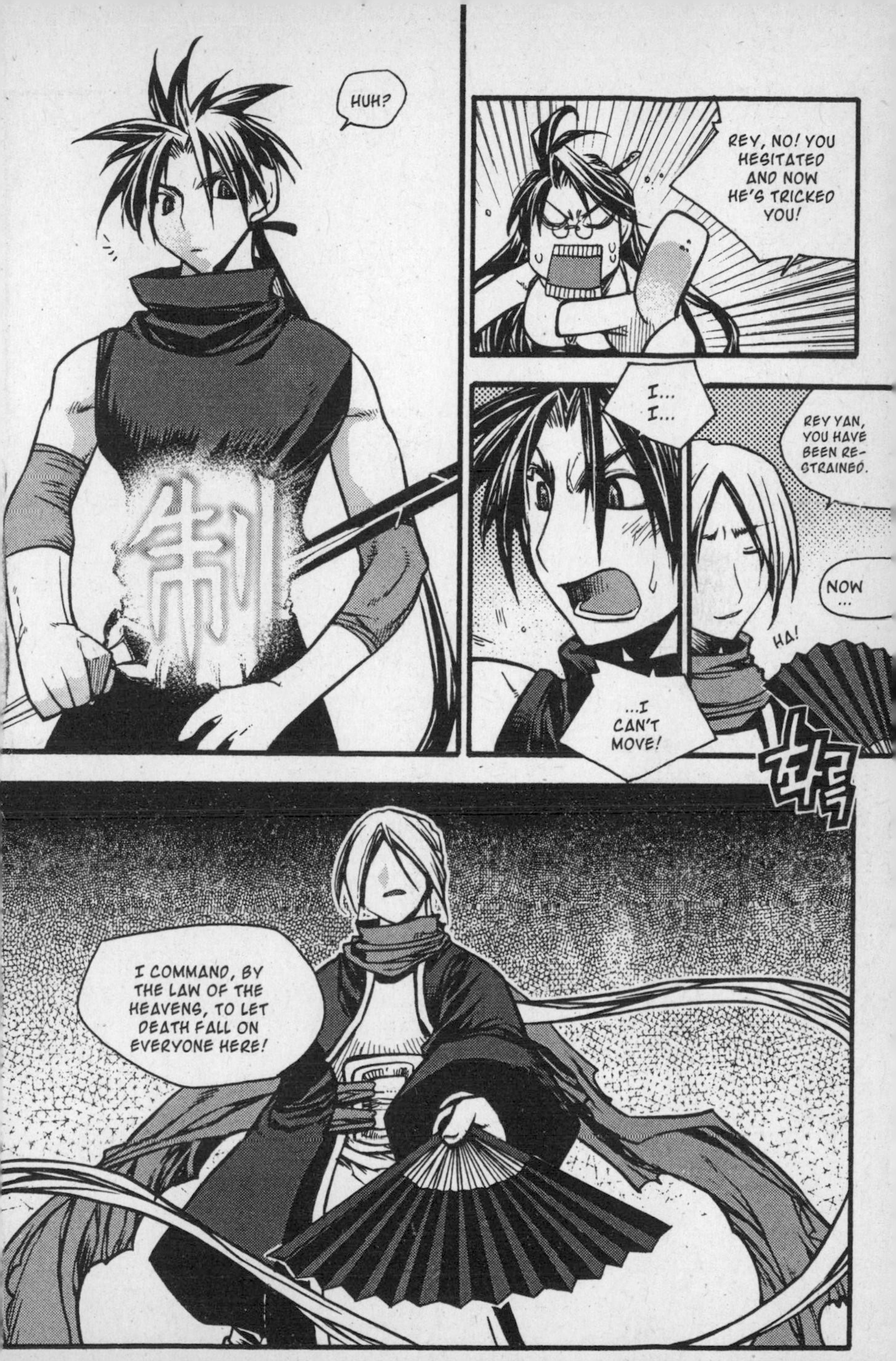
HUH?
REY, NO! YOU HESITATED AND NOW HE'S TRICKED YOU!
I... I...
REY YAN, YOU HAVE BEEN RE-STRAINED.
NOW ...
HA!
...I CAN'T MOVE!
I COMMAND, BY THE LAW OF THE HEAVENS, TO LET DEATH FALL ON EVERYONE HERE!

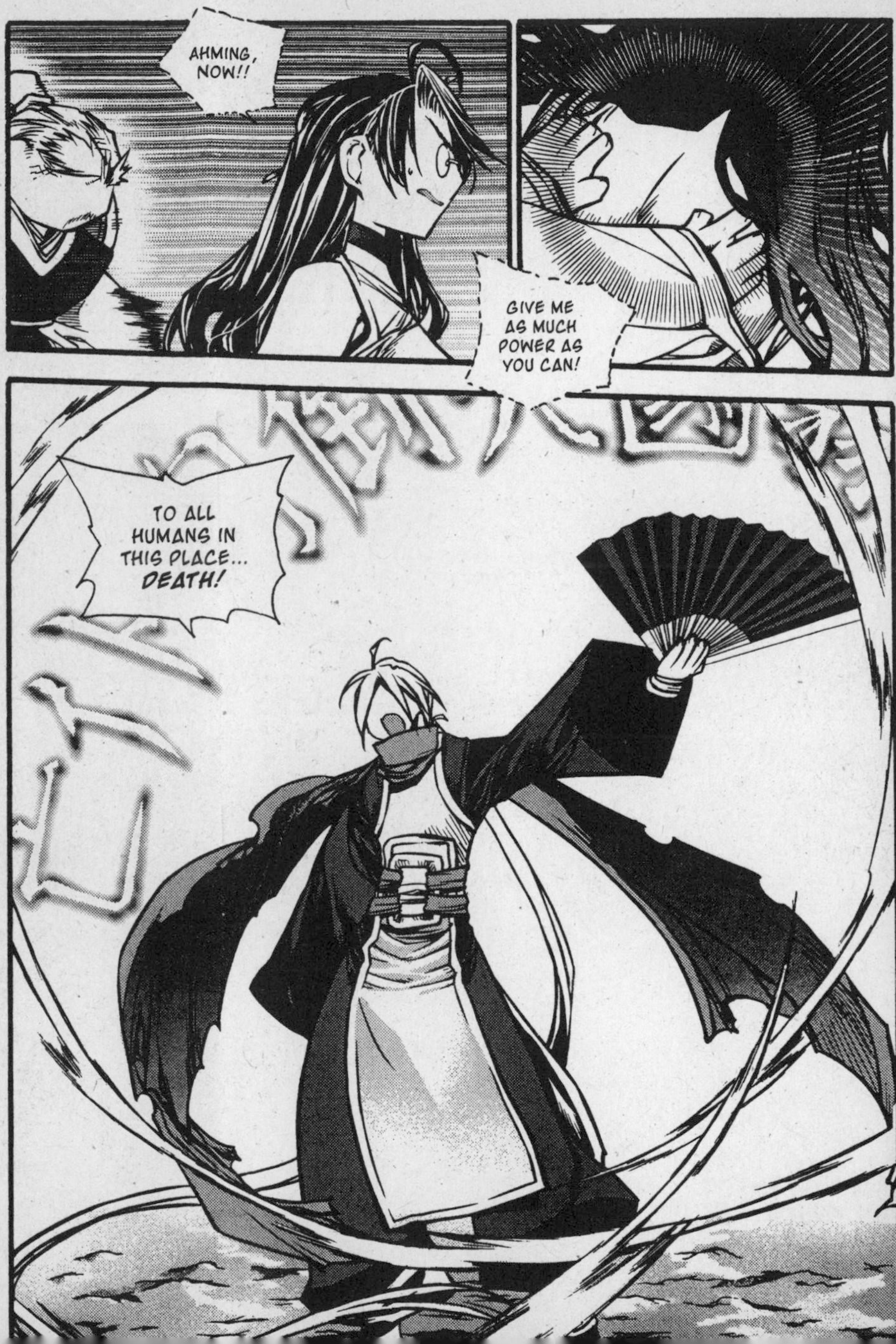
AHMING, NOW!!
GIVE ME AS MUCH POWER AS YOU CAN!
TO ALL HUMANS IN THIS PLACE... DEATH!

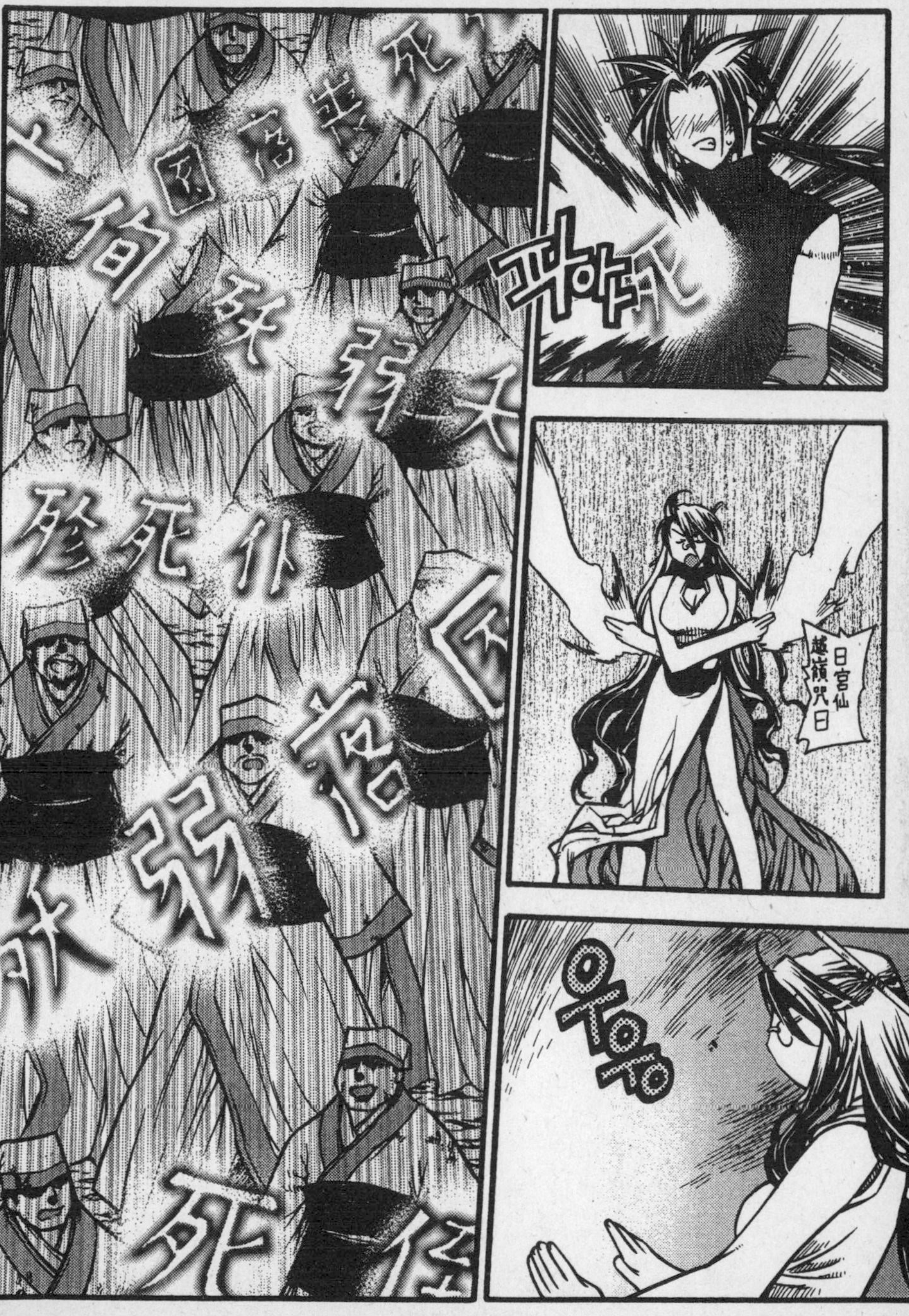
파아앗
日宮仙
越嶺咒日
우우웅

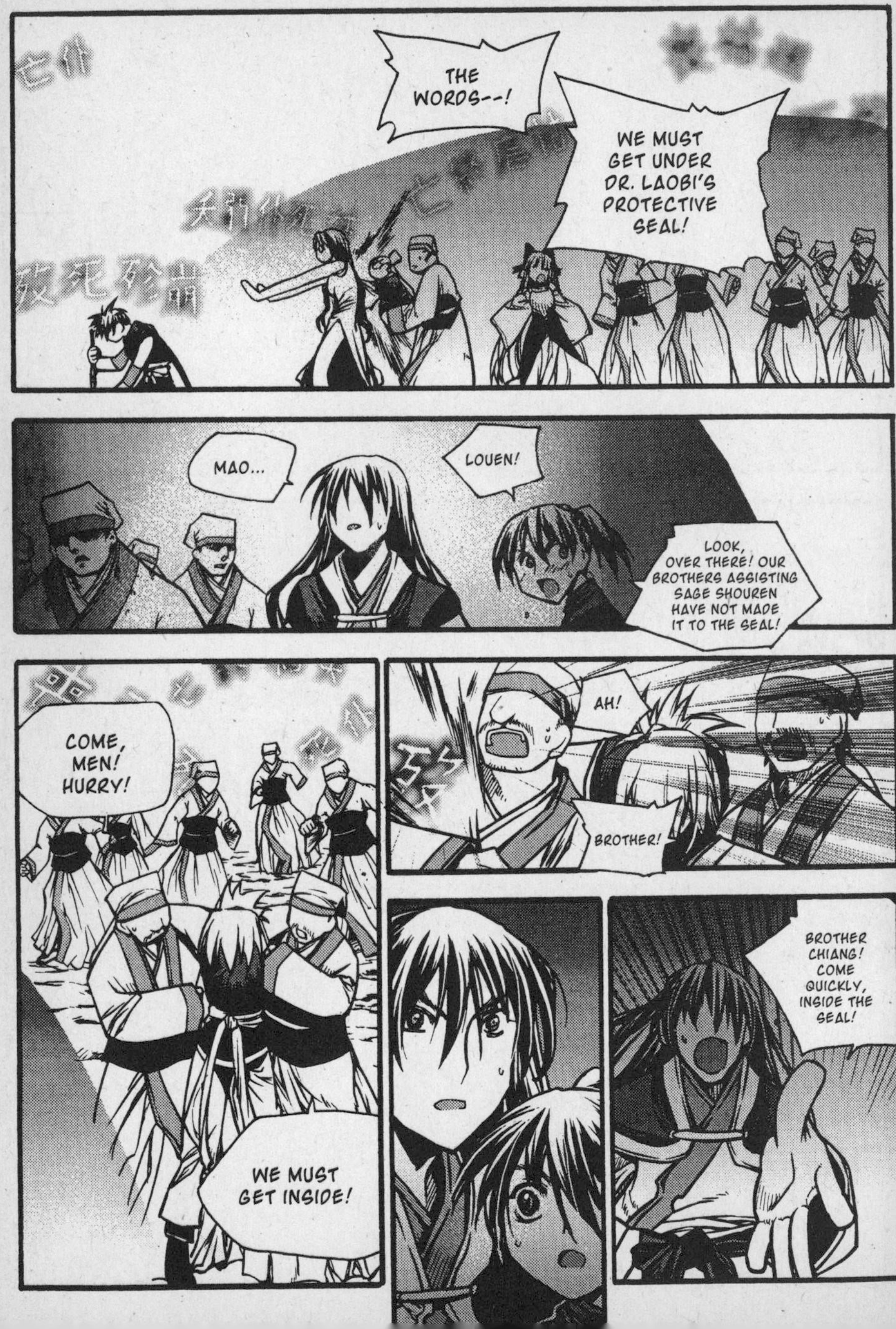
THE WORDS--!
WE MUST GET UNDER DR. LAOBI'S PROTECTIVE SEAL!
MAO...
LOUEN!
LOOK, OVER THERE! OUR BROTHERS ASSISTING SAGE SHOUREN HAVE NOT MADE IT TO THE SEAL!
COME, MEN! HURRY!
WE MUST GET INSIDE!
AH!
BROTHER!
BROTHER CHIANG! COME QUICKLY, INSIDE THE SEAL!

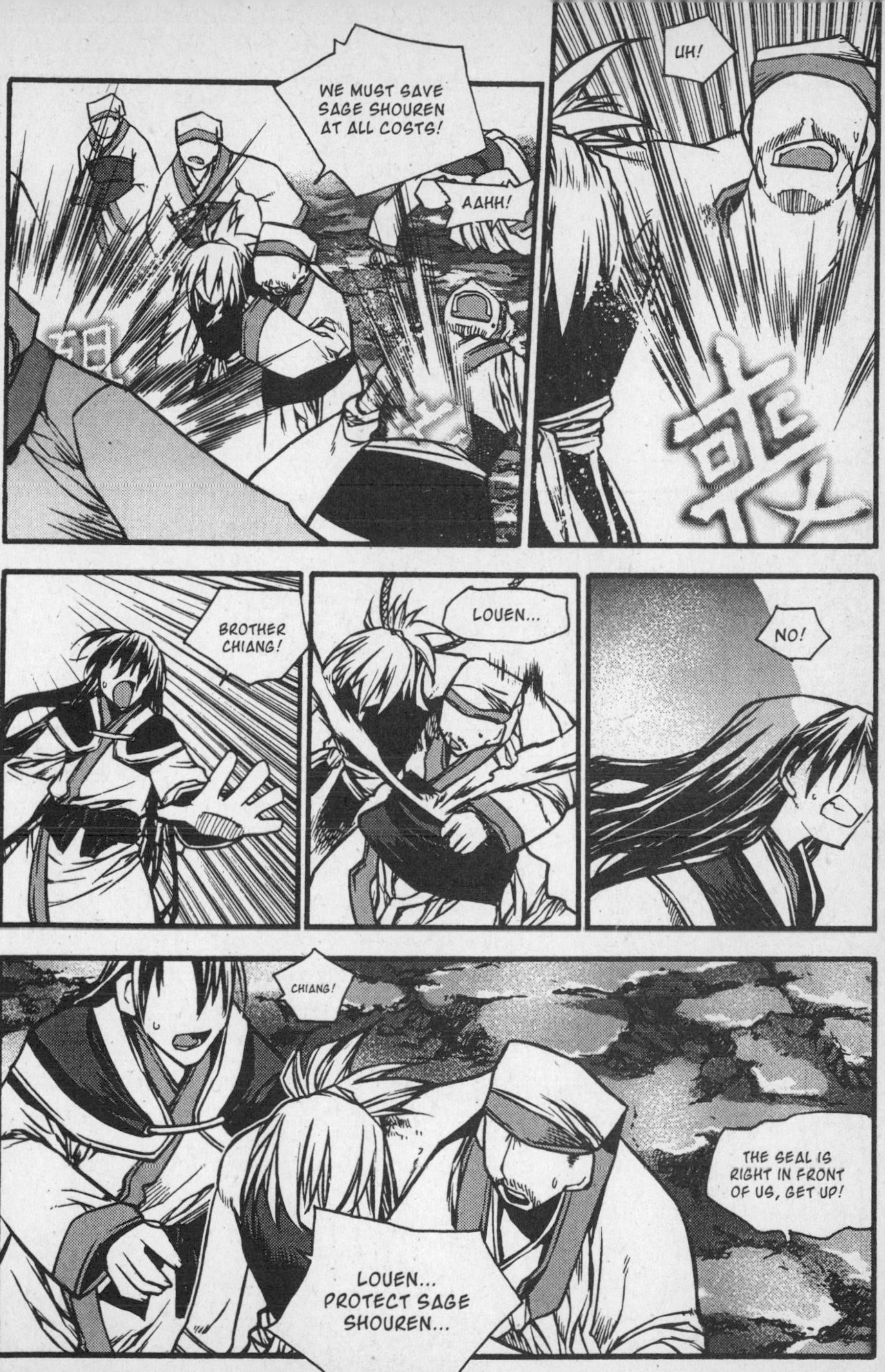
WE MUST SAVE SAGE SHOUREN AT ALL COSTS!
AAHH!
UH!
BROTHER CHIANG!
LOUEN...
NO!
CHIANG!
THE SEAL IS RIGHT IN FRONT OF US, GET UP!
LOUEN... PROTECT SAGE SHOUREN...

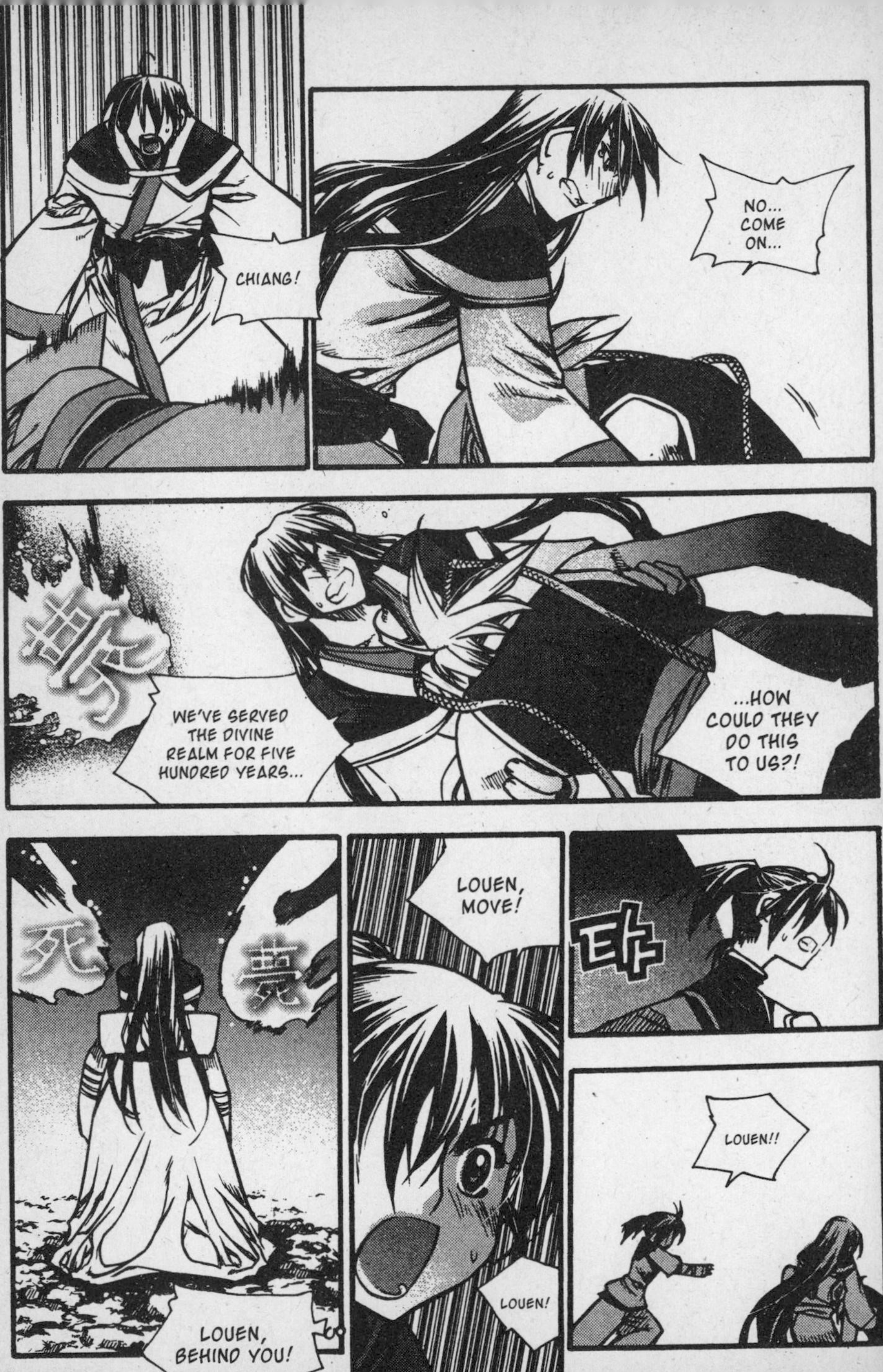
CHIANG!
NO... COME ON...
WE'VE SERVED THE DIVINE REALM FOR FIVE HUNDRED YEARS...
...HOW COULD THEY DO THIS TO US?!
LOUEN, BEHIND YOU!
LOUEN, MOVE!
LOUEN!
탁
LOUEN!!

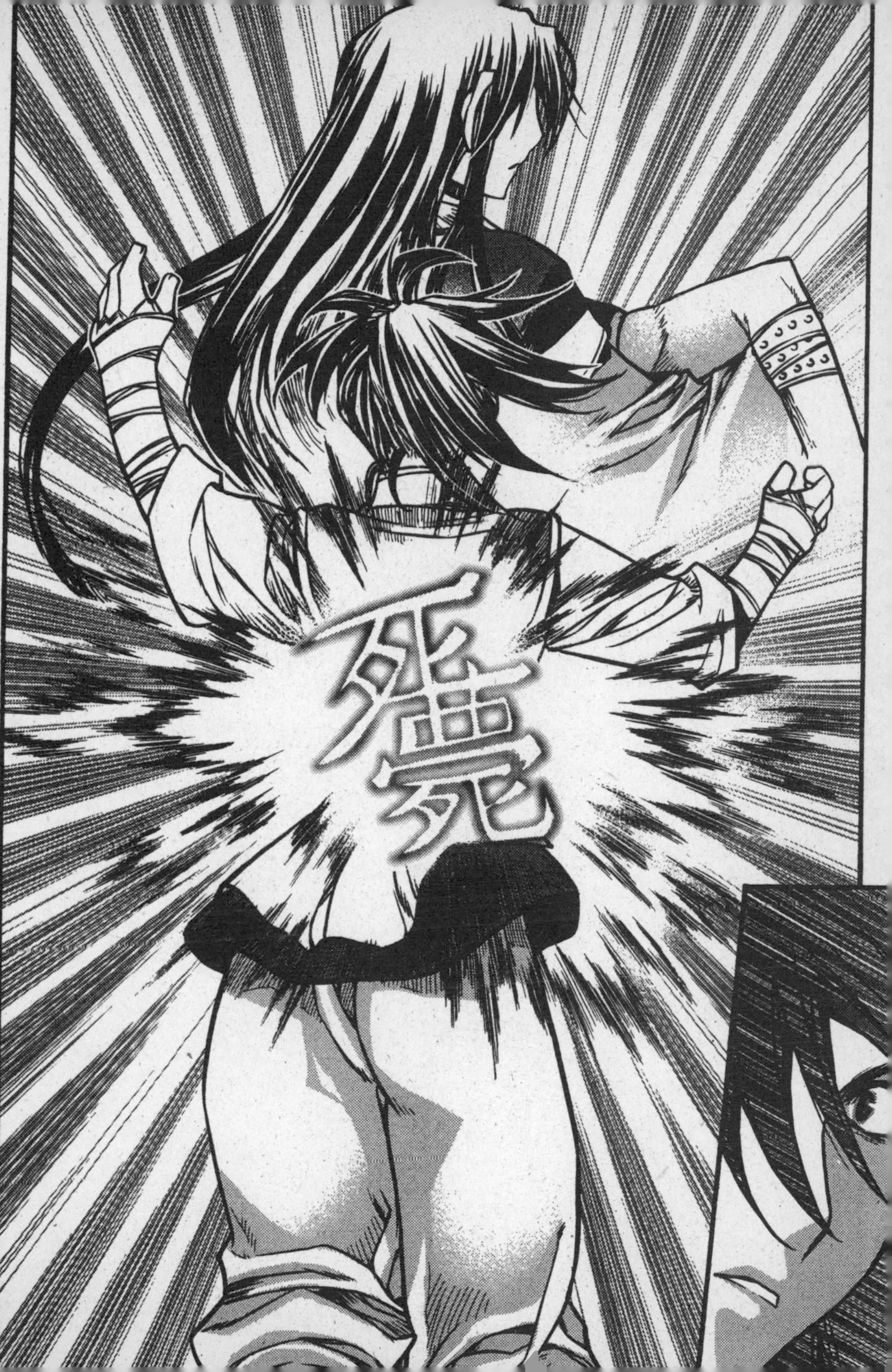

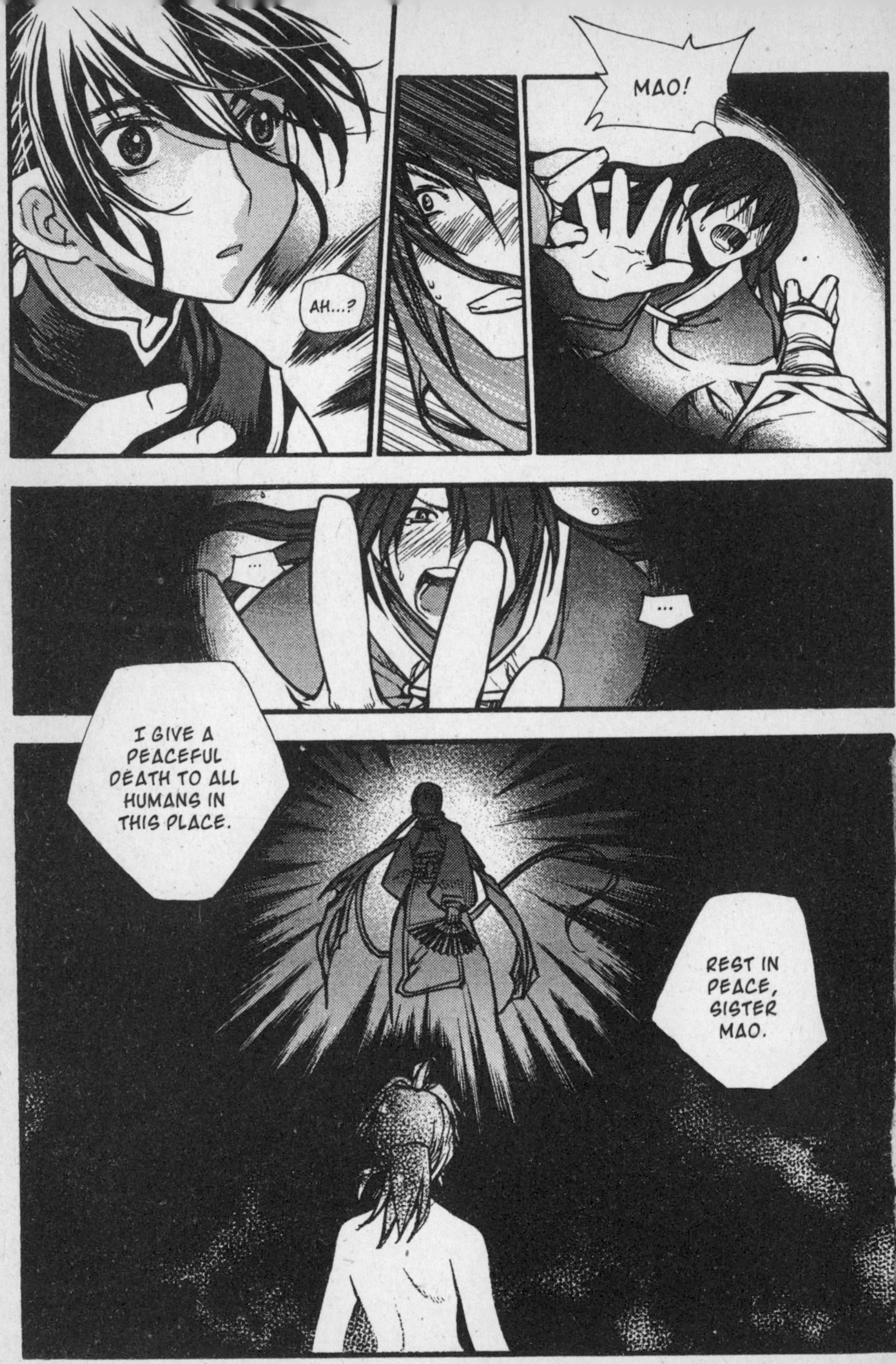
AH...?
MAO!
...
...
I GIVE A PEACEFUL DEATH TO ALL HUMANS IN THIS PLACE.
REST IN PEACE, SISTER MAO.

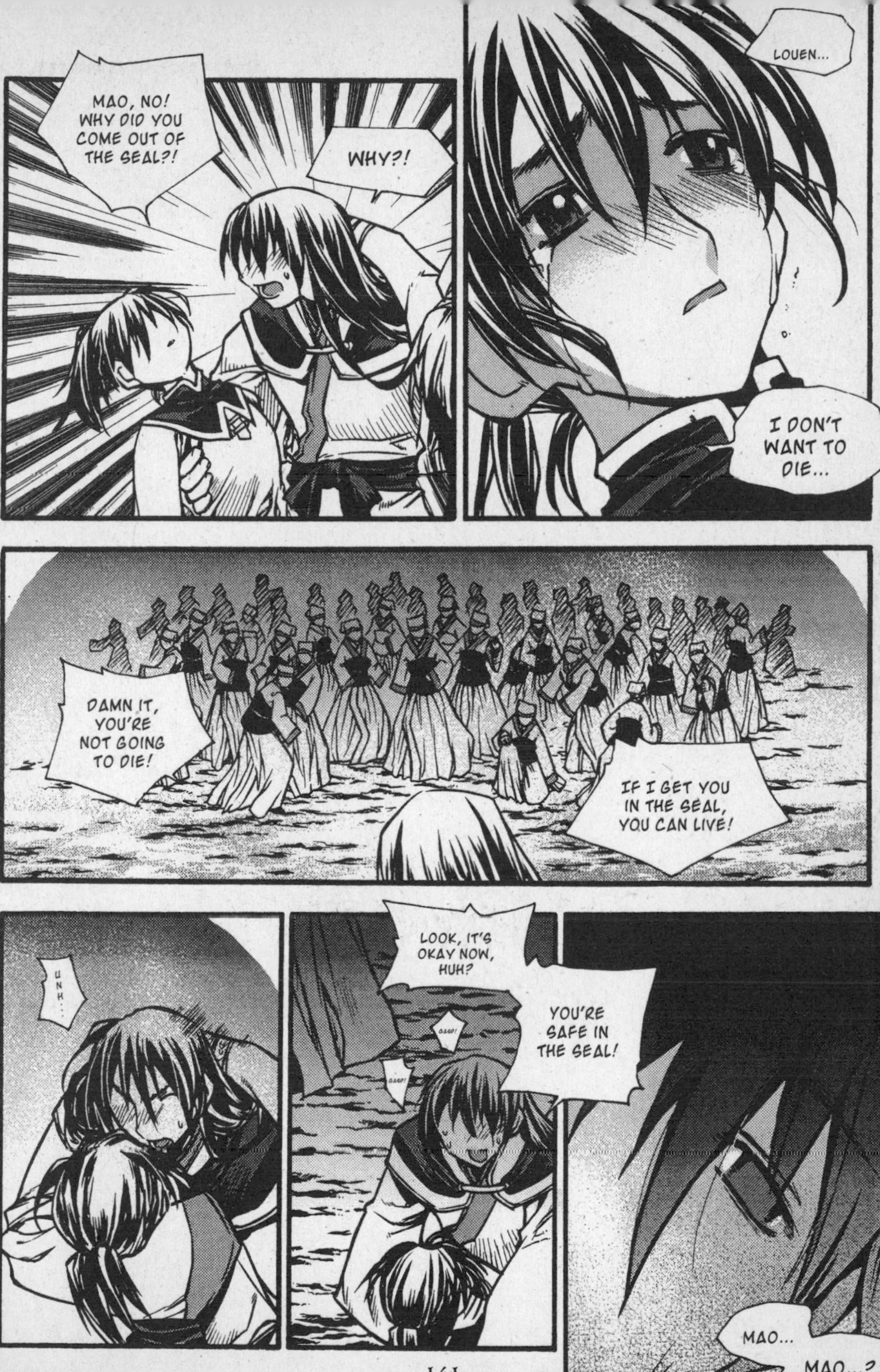

MAO, NO! WHY DID YOU COME OUT OF THE SEAL?!
WHY?!
LOUEN...
I DON'T WANT TO DIE...
DAMN IT, YOU'RE NOT GOING TO DIE!
IF I GET YOU IN THE SEAL, YOU CAN LIVE!
UNH...
LOOK, IT'S OKAY NOW, HUH?
GASP!
GASP!
YOU'RE SAFE IN THE SEAL!
MAO...
MAO...?

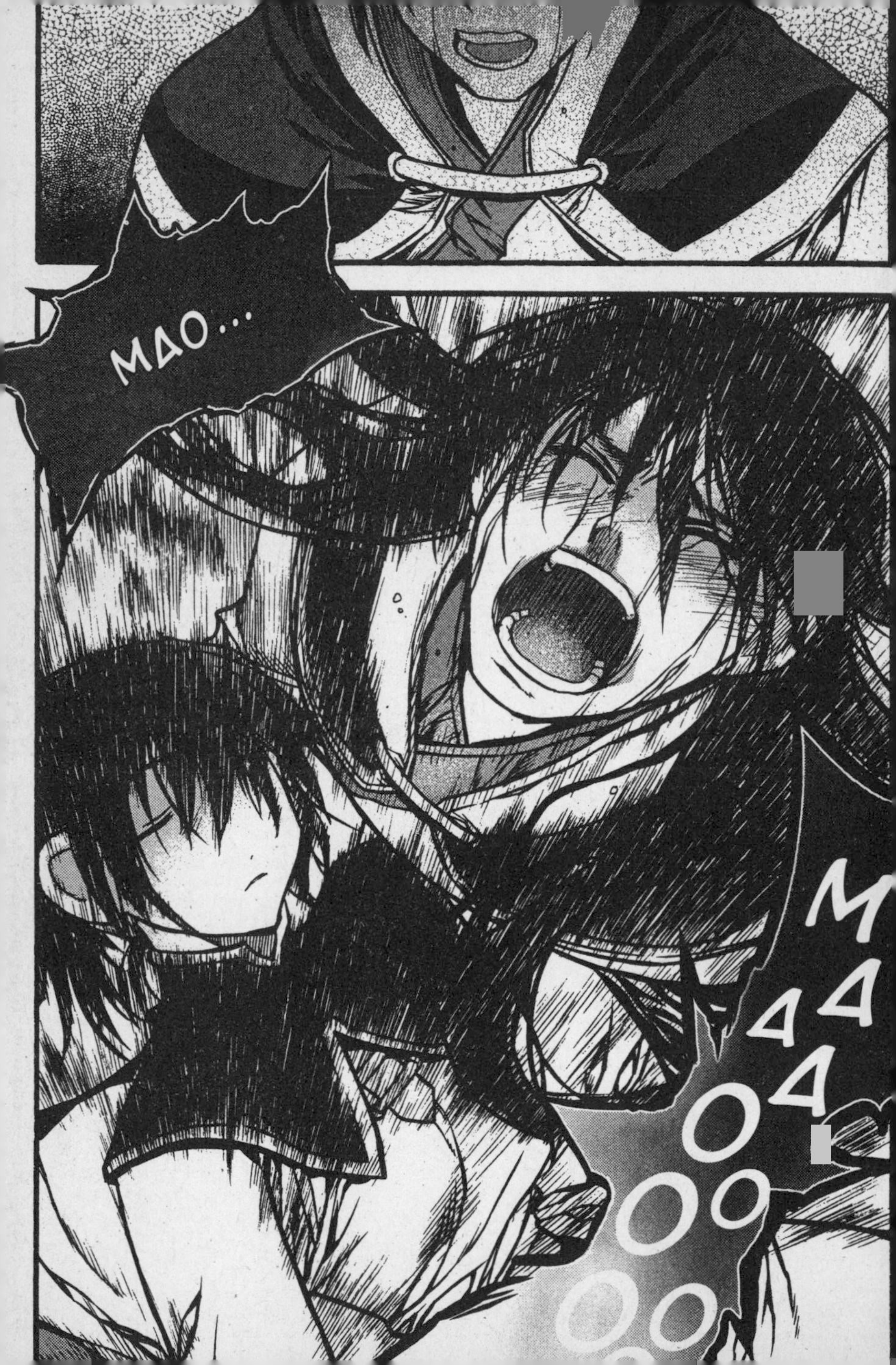
MAO...
MAAAOOOOO

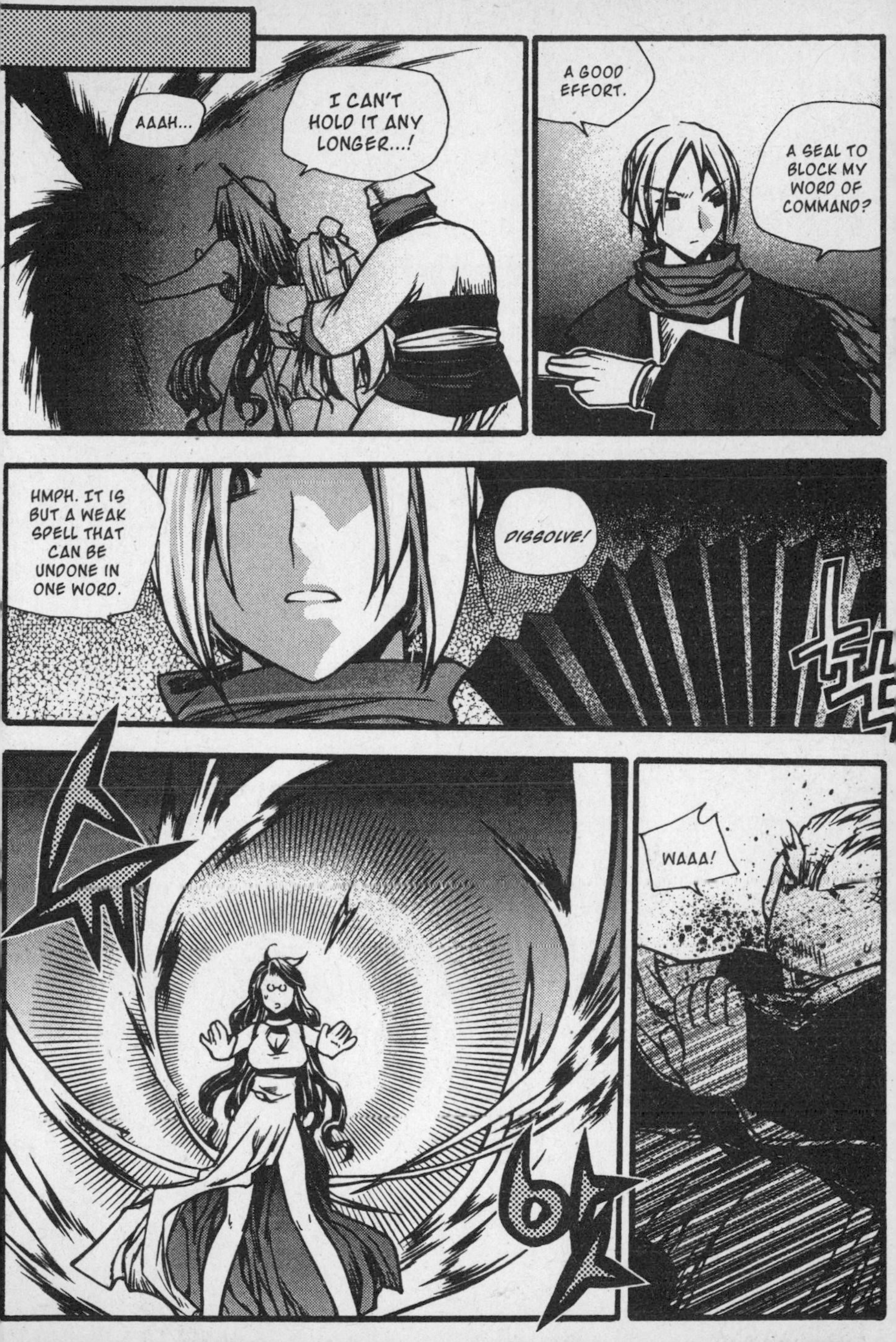
AAAH...
I CAN'T HOLD IT ANY LONGER...!
A GOOD EFFORT.
A SEAL TO BLOCK MY WORD OF COMMAND?
HMPH. IT IS BUT A WEAK SPELL THAT CAN BE UNDONE IN ONE WORD.
DISSOLVE!
WAAA!

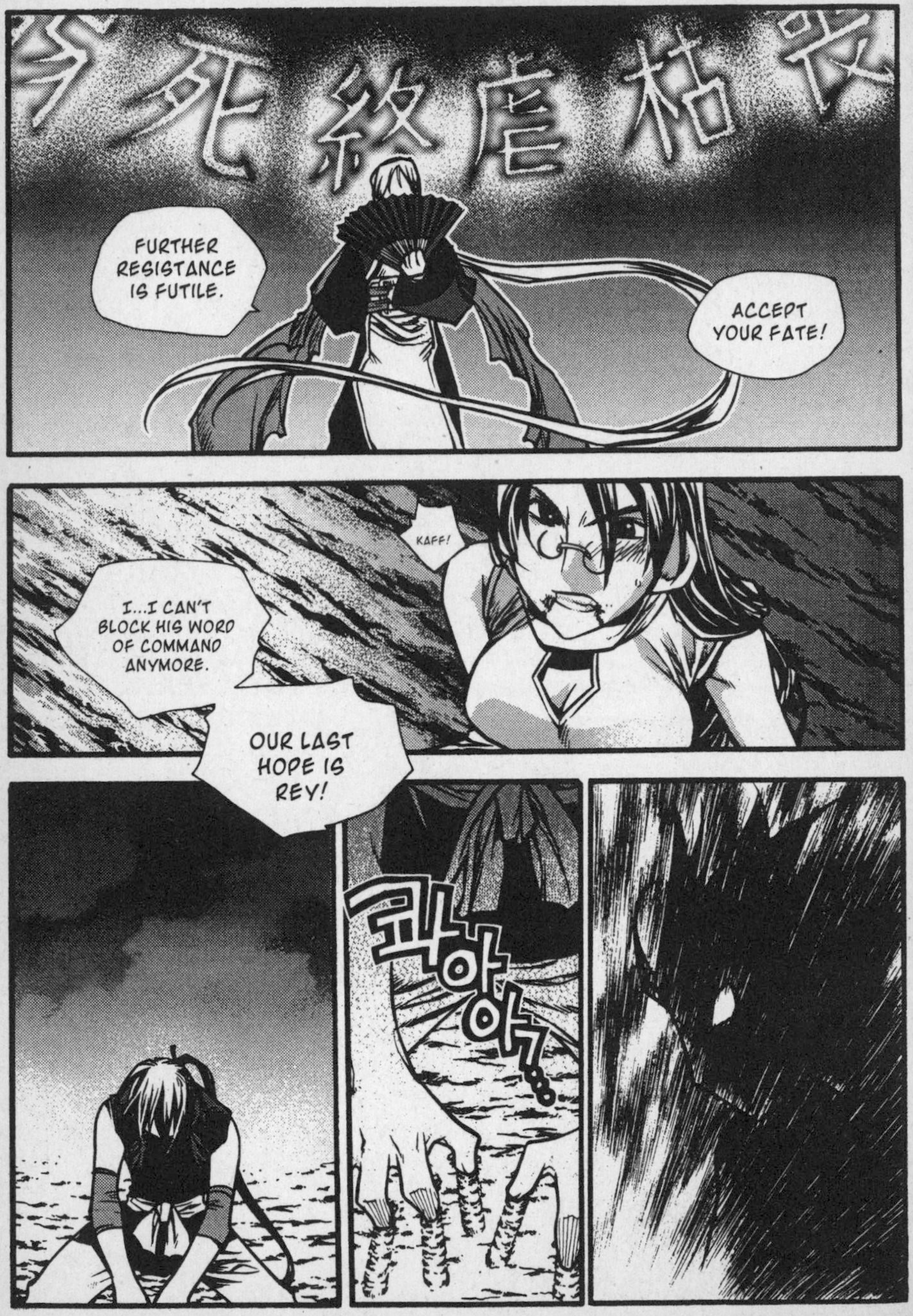
FURTHER RESISTANCE IS FUTILE.
ACCEPT YOUR FATE!
KAFF!
I...I CAN'T BLOCK HIS WORD OF COMMAND ANYMORE.
OUR LAST HOPE IS REY!
콰아아...

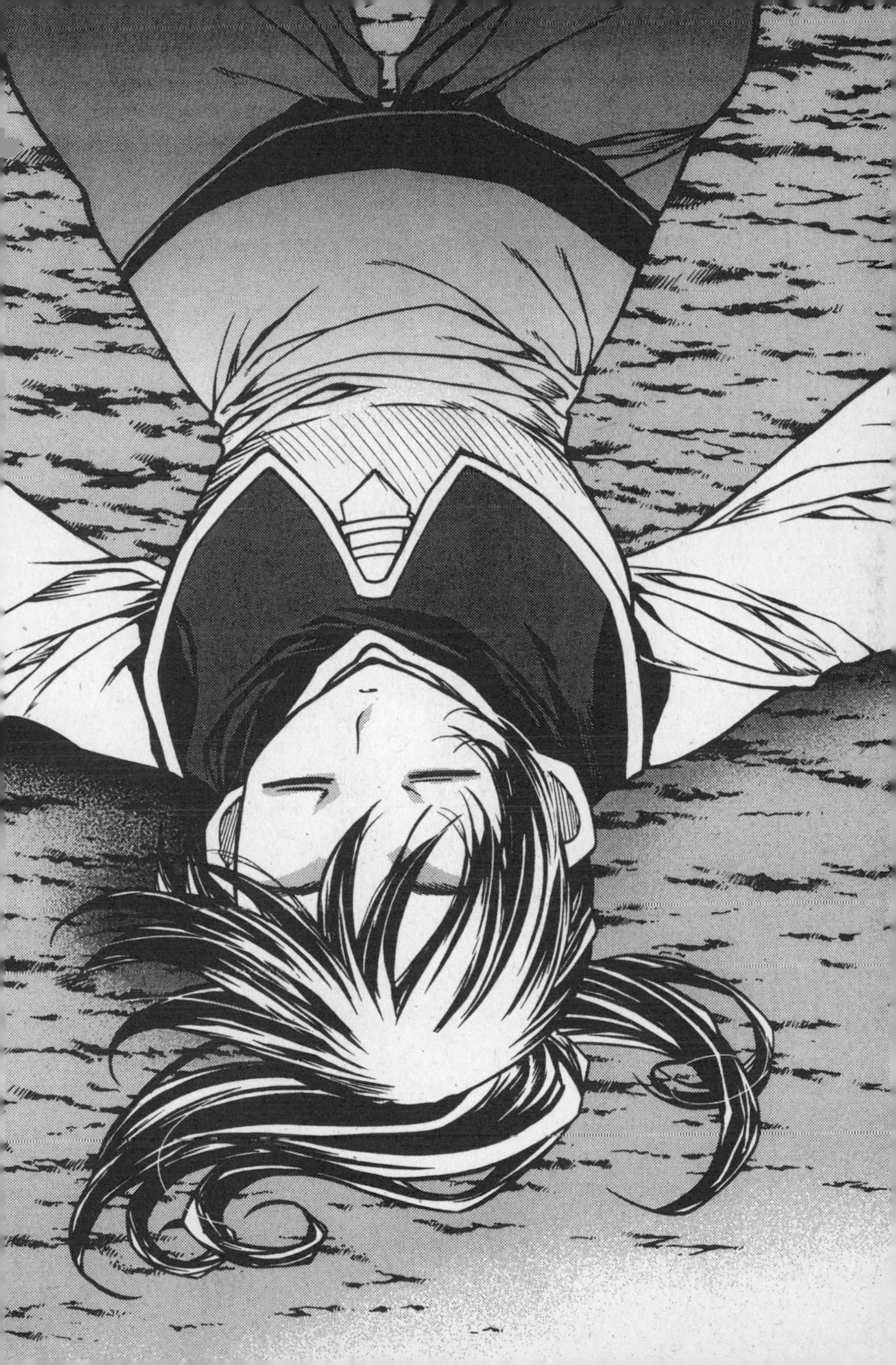

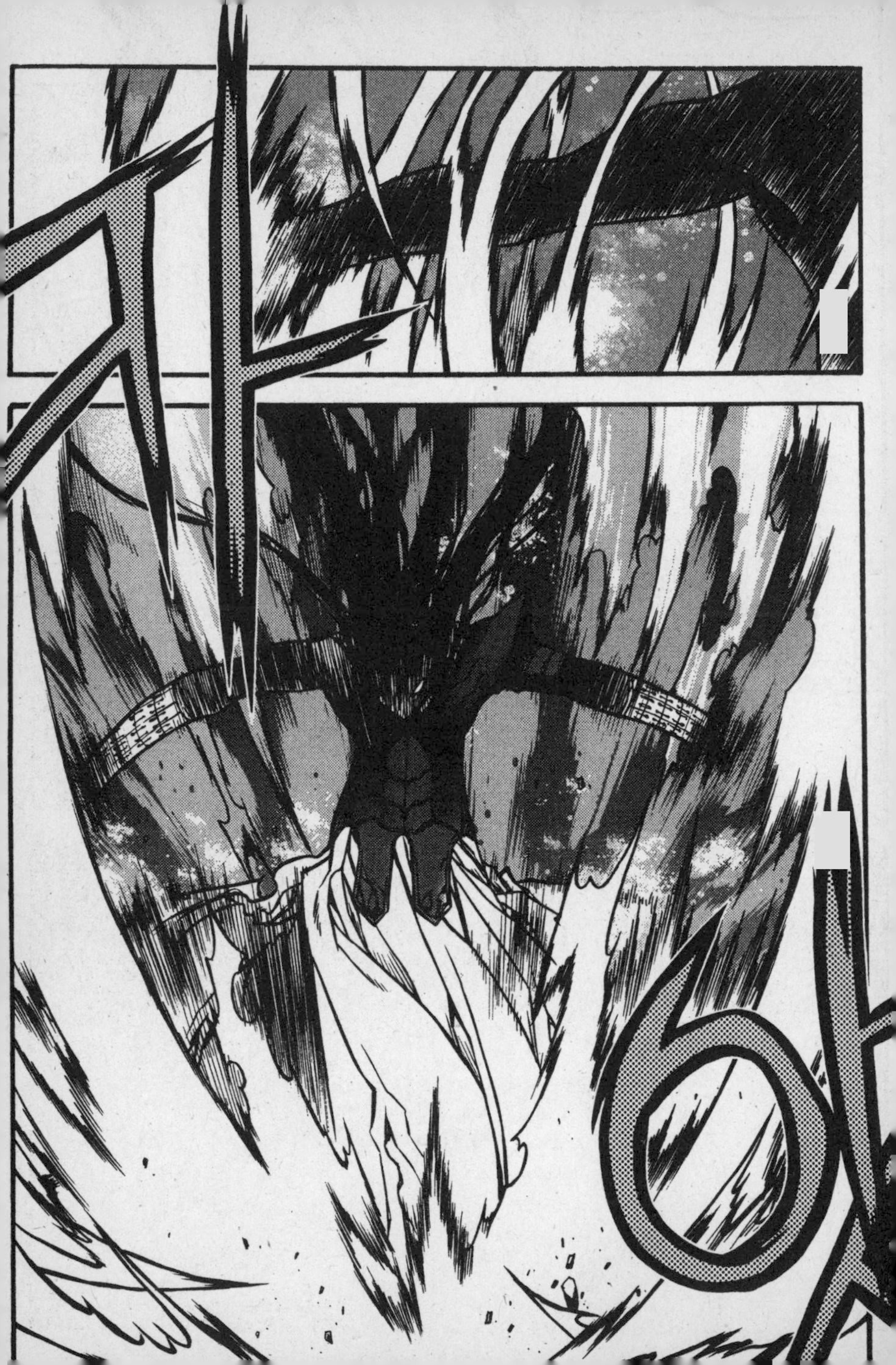

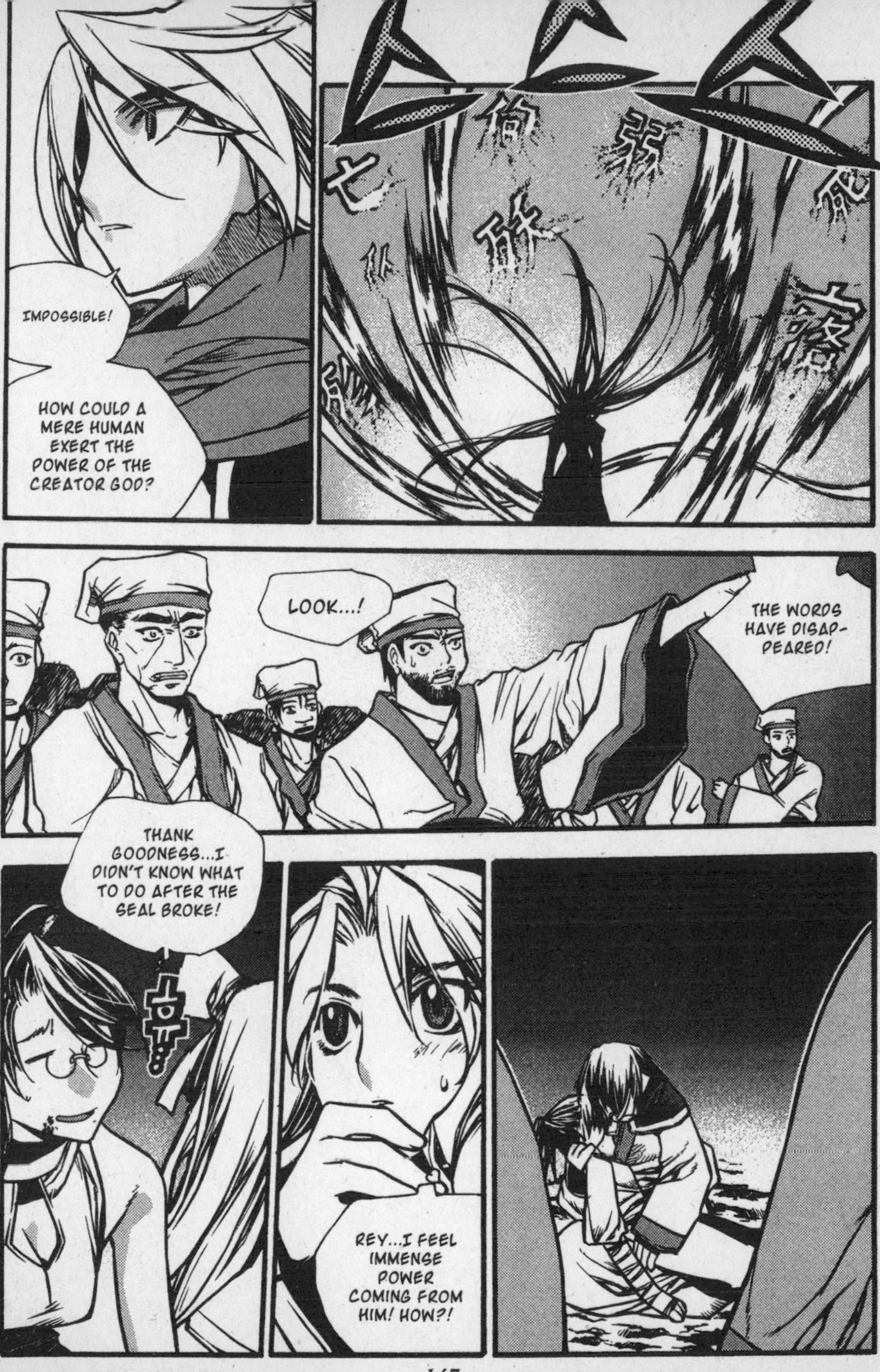
IMPOSSIBLE!
HOW COULD A MERE HUMAN EXERT THE POWER OF THE CREATOR GOD?
LOOK...!
THE WORDS HAVE DISAPPEARED!
THANK GOODNESS...I DIDN'T KNOW WHAT TO DO AFTER THE SEAL BROKE!
REY...I FEEL IMMENSE POWER COMING FROM HIM! HOW?!

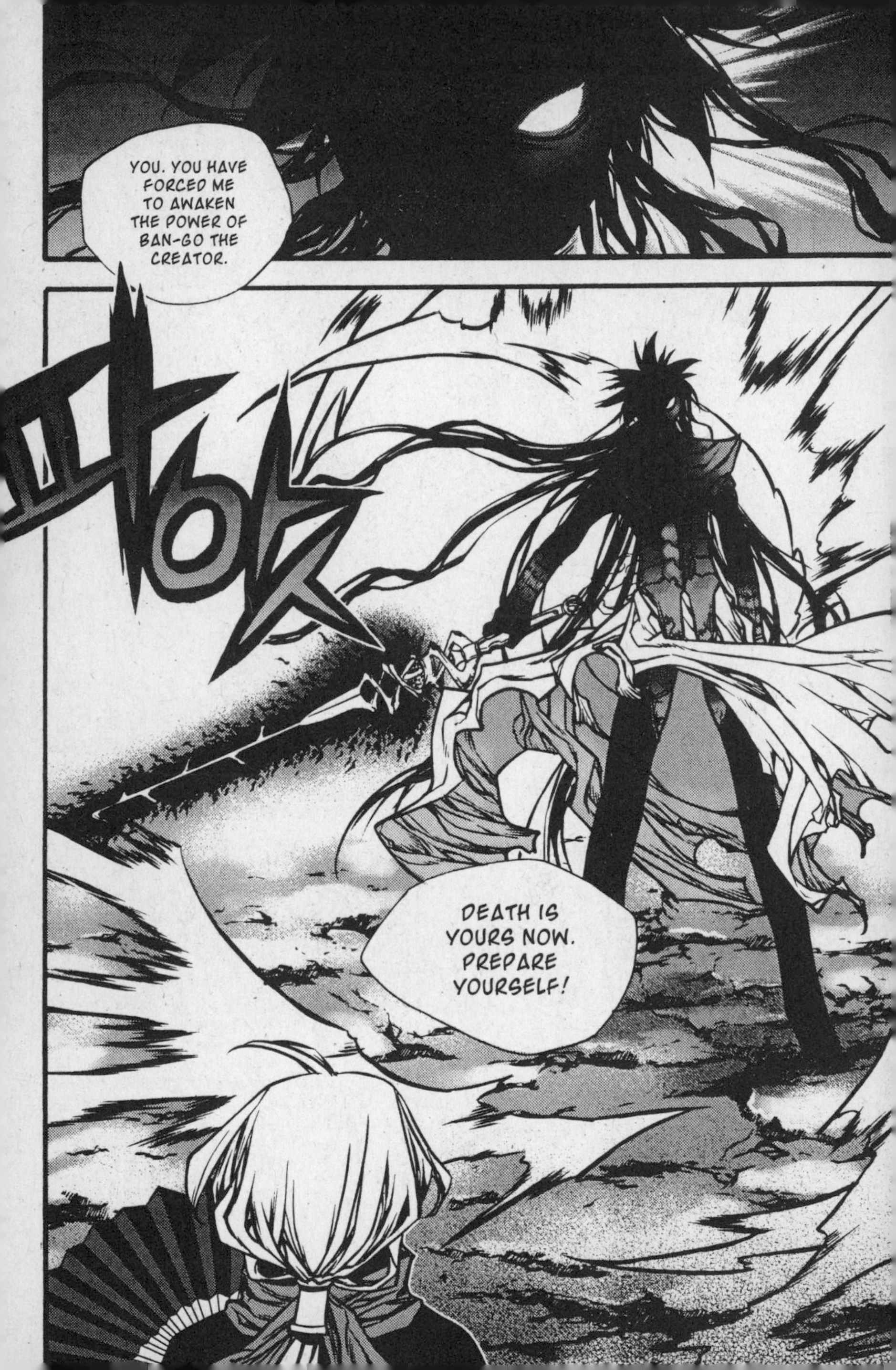
YOU. YOU HAVE FORCED ME TO AWAKEN THE POWER OF BAN-GO THE CREATOR.
DEATH IS YOURS NOW. PREPARE YOURSELF!

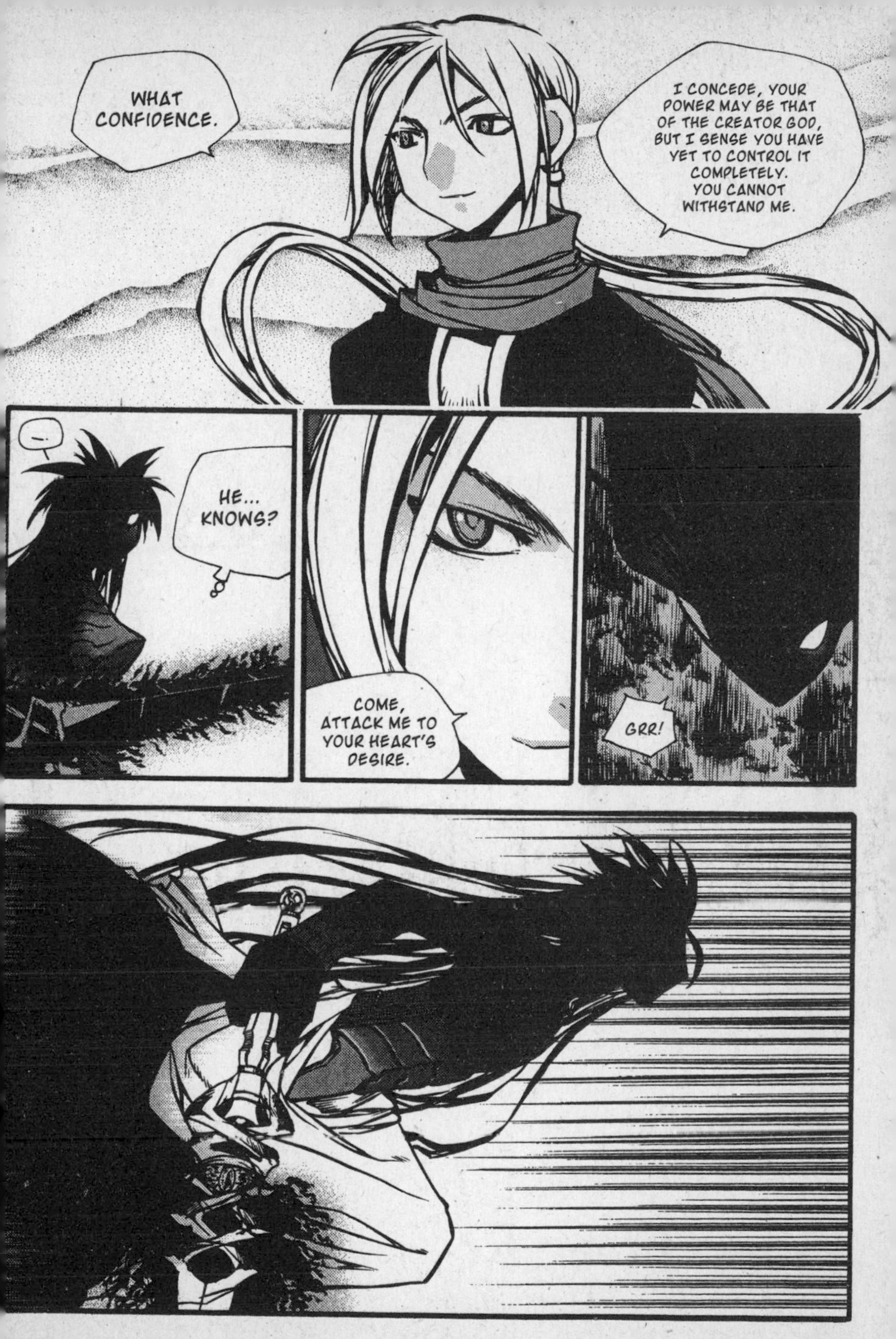
WHAT CONFIDENCE.
I CONCEDE, YOUR POWER MAY BE THAT OF THE CREATOR GOD, BUT I SENSE YOU HAVE YET TO CONTROL IT COMPLETELY. YOU CANNOT WITHSTAND ME.
HE... KNOWS?
COME, ATTACK ME TO YOUR HEART'S DESIRE.
GRR!

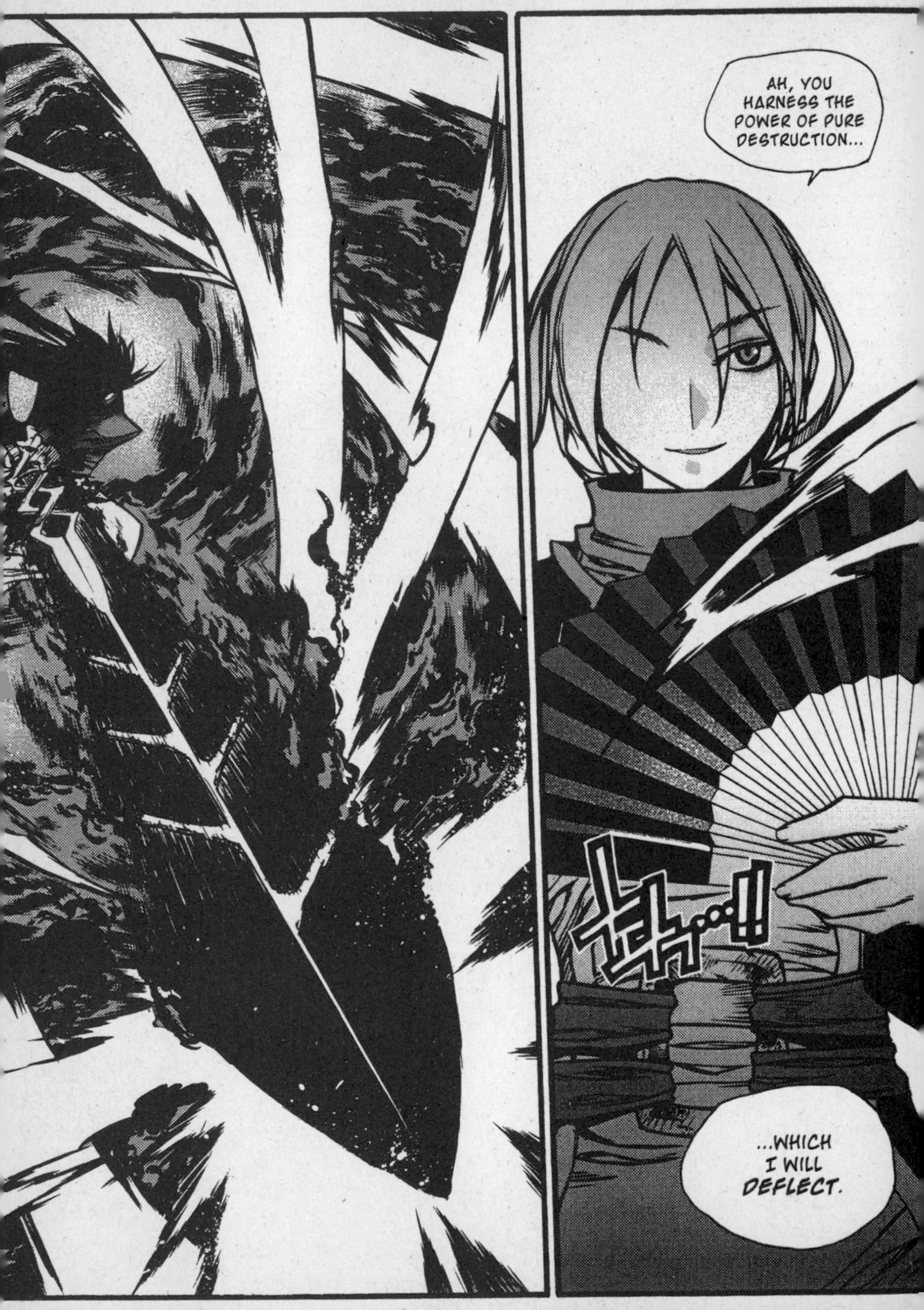
AH, YOU HARNESS THE POWER OF PURE DESTRUCTION...
...WHICH I WILL DEFLECT.

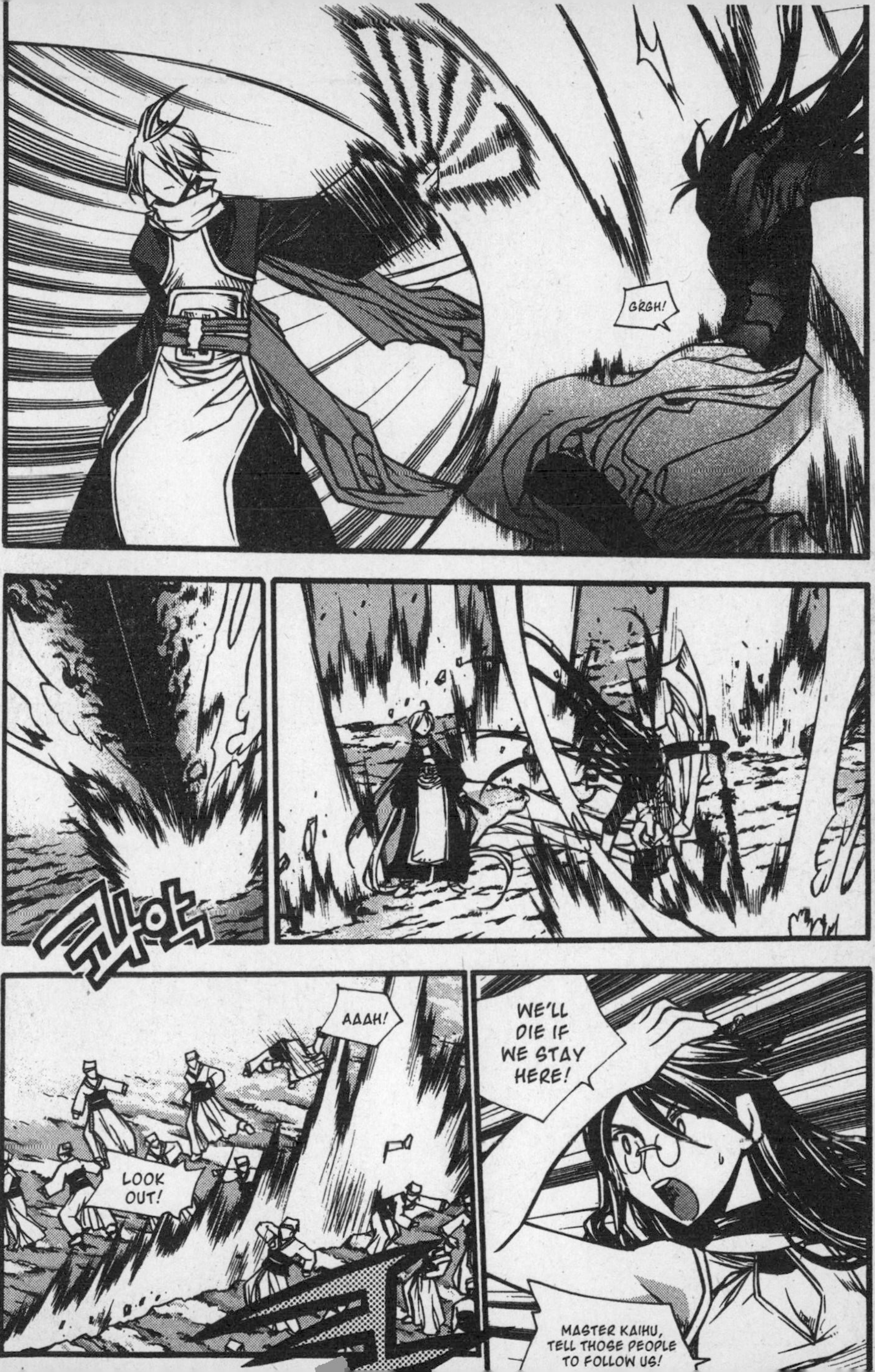
GRGH!
AAAH!
LOOK OUT!
WE'LL DIE IF WE STAY HERE!
MASTER KAIHU, TELL THOSE PEOPLE TO FOLLOW US!

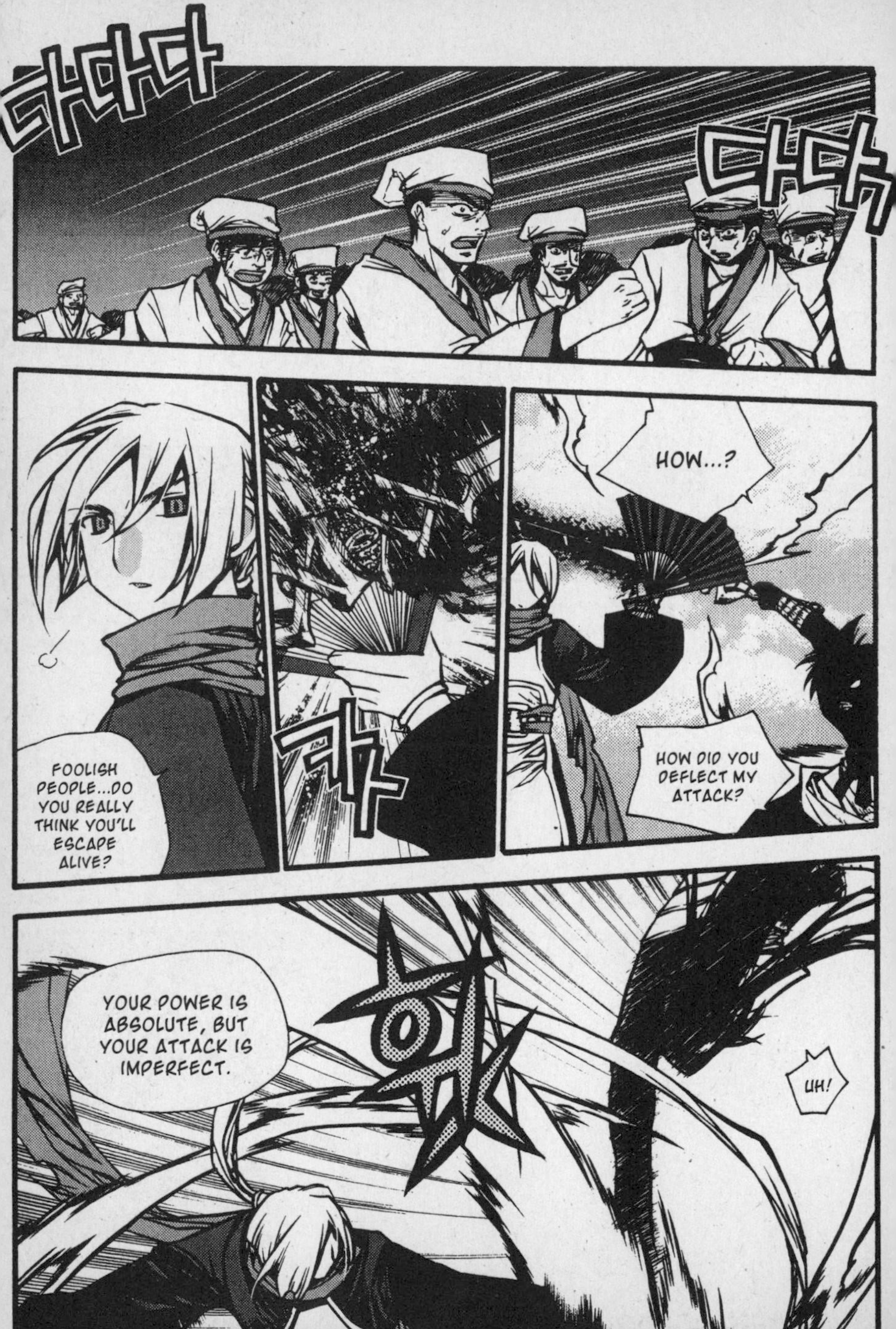
FOOLISH PEOPLE...DO YOU REALLY THINK YOU'LL ESCAPE ALIVE?
HOW...?
HOW DID YOU DEFLECT MY ATTACK?
YOUR POWER IS ABSOLUTE, BUT YOUR ATTACK IS IMPERFECT.
UH!

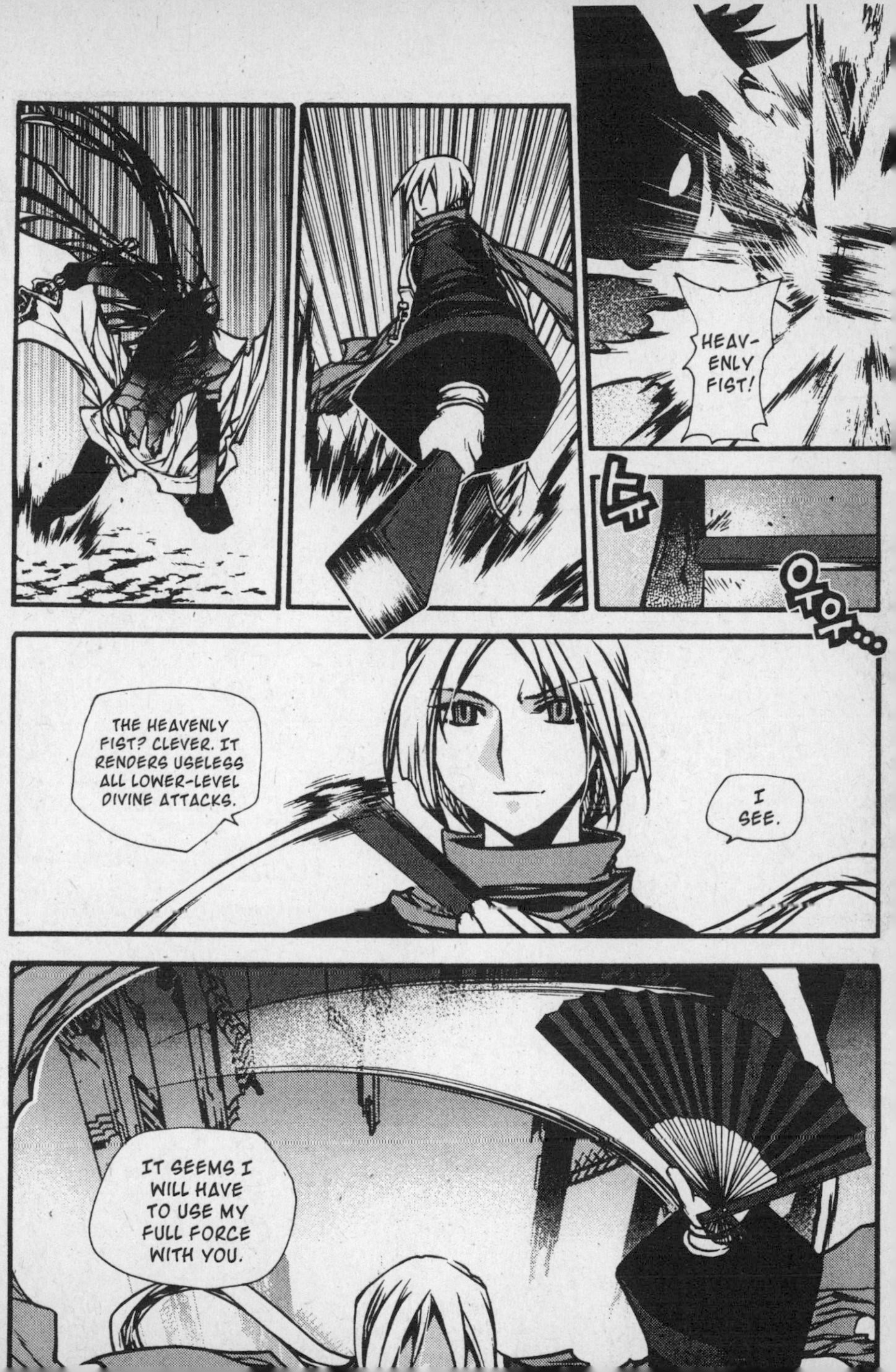
HEAV-ENLY FIST!
OTOK...
THE HEAVENLY FIST? CLEVER. IT RENDERS USELESS ALL LOWER-LEVEL DIVINE ATTACKS.
I SEE.
IT SEEMS I WILL HAVE TO USE MY FULL FORCE WITH YOU.

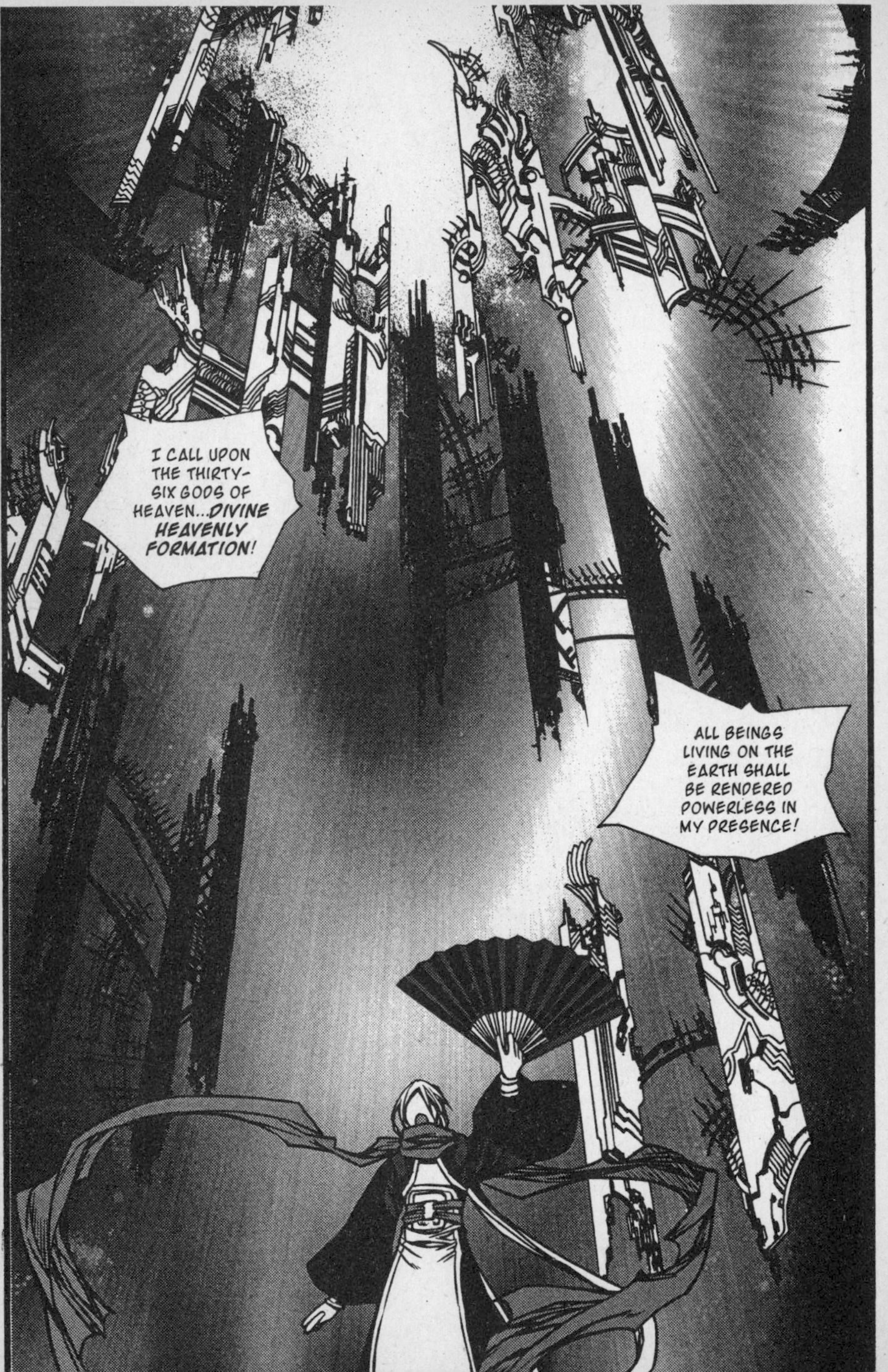
I CALL UPON THE THIRTY-SIX GODS OF HEAVEN...*DIVINE HEAVENLY FORMATION!*
ALL BEINGS LIVING ON THE EARTH SHALL BE RENDERED POWERLESS IN MY PRESENCE!

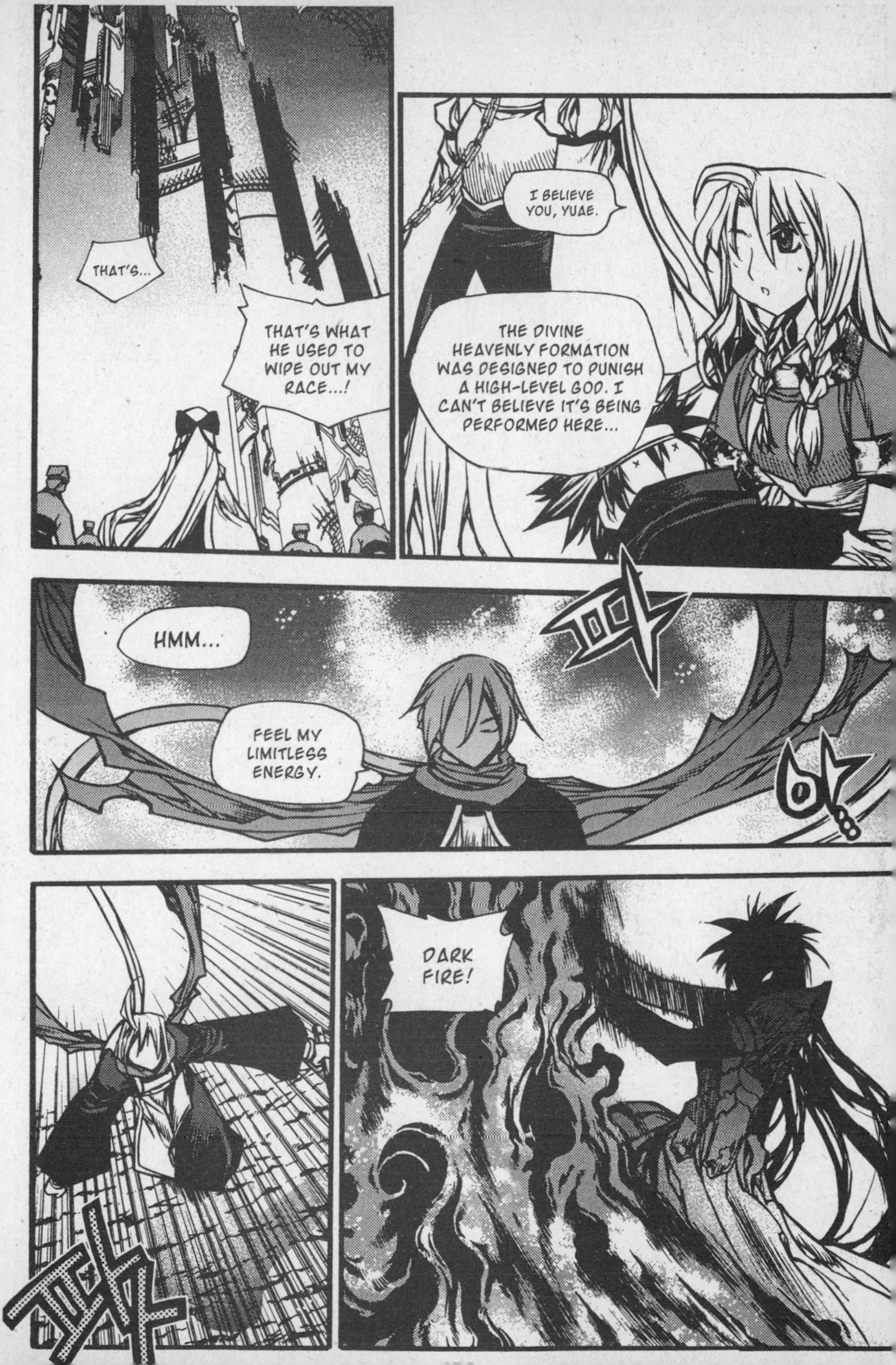
THAT'S...
THAT'S WHAT HE USED TO WIPE OUT MY RACE...!
I BELIEVE YOU, YUAE.
THE DIVINE HEAVENLY FORMATION WAS DESIGNED TO PUNISH A HIGH-LEVEL GOD. I CAN'T BELIEVE IT'S BEING PERFORMED HERE...
HMM...
FEEL MY LIMITLESS ENERGY.
DARK FIRE!

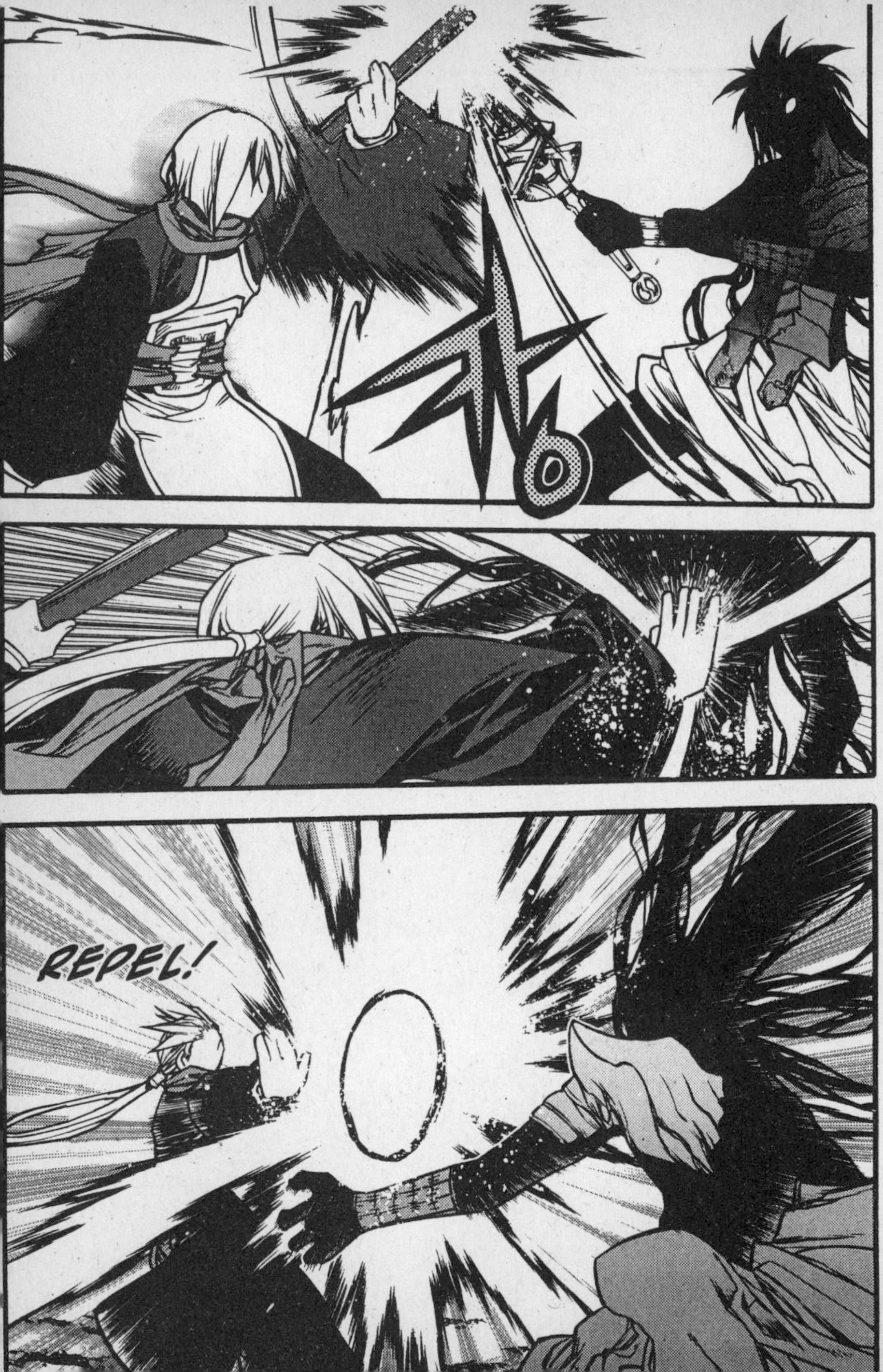
REPEL!

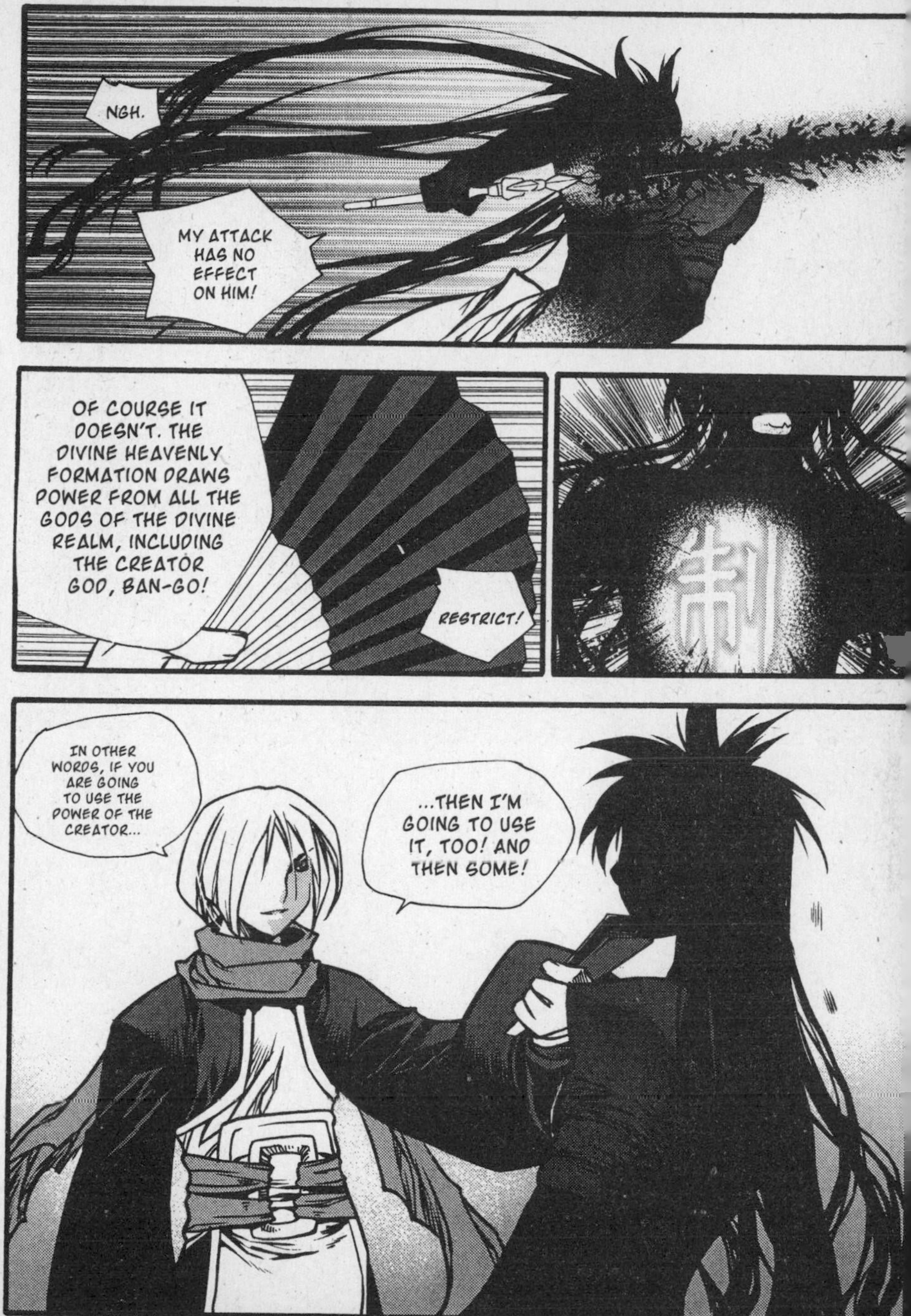
NGH.
MY ATTACK HAS NO EFFECT ON HIM!
OF COURSE IT DOESN'T. THE DIVINE HEAVENLY FORMATION DRAWS POWER FROM ALL THE GODS OF THE DIVINE REALM, INCLUDING THE CREATOR GOD, BAN-GO!
RESTRICT!
制
IN OTHER WORDS, IF YOU ARE GOING TO USE THE POWER OF THE CREATOR...
...THEN I'M GOING TO USE IT, TOO! AND THEN SOME!

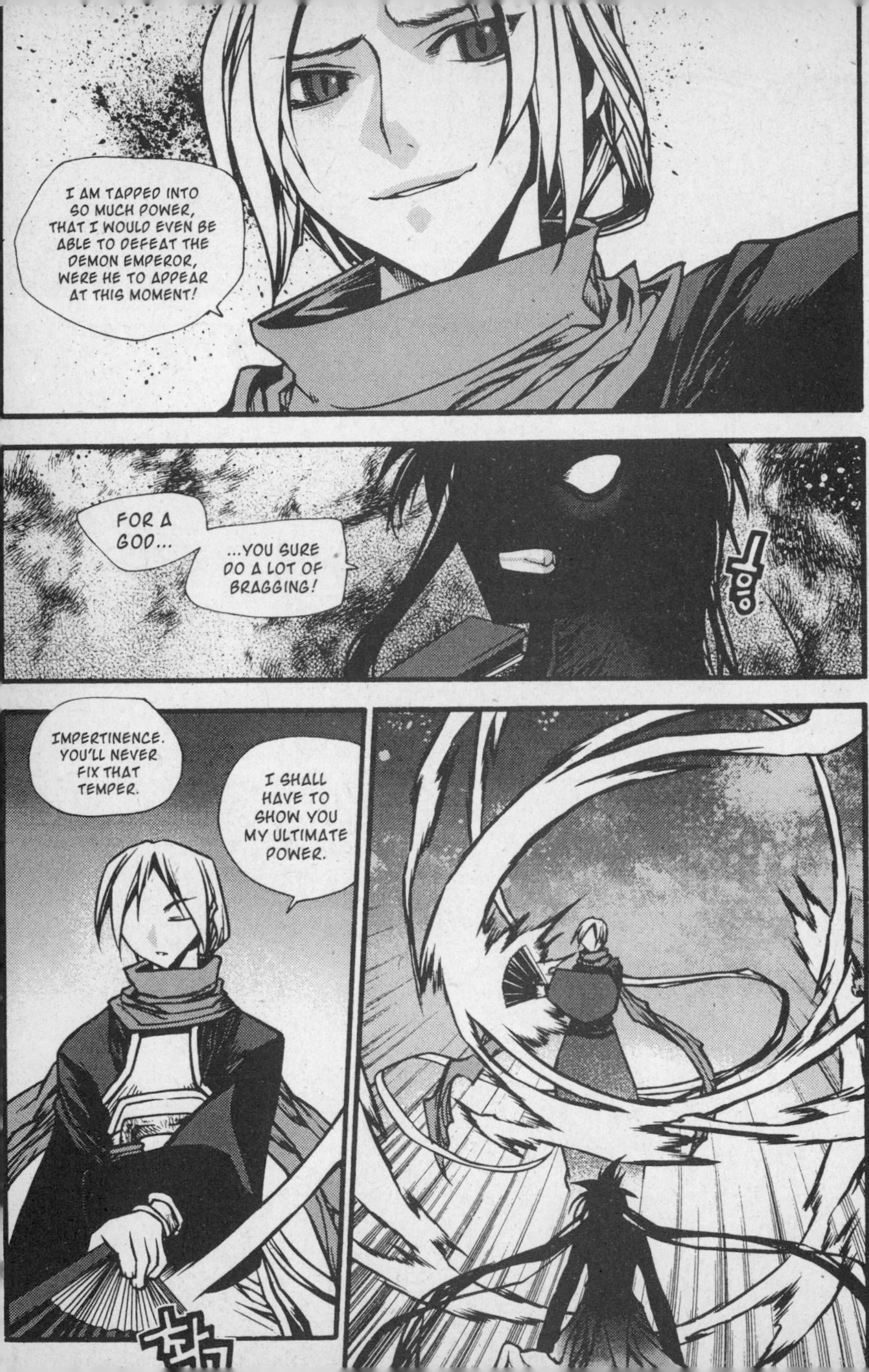

I AM TAPPED INTO SO MUCH POWER, THAT I WOULD EVEN BE ABLE TO DEFEAT THE DEMON EMPEROR, WERE HE TO APPEAR AT THIS MOMENT!
FOR A GOD...
...YOU SURE DO A LOT OF BRAGGING!
IMPERTINENCE. YOU'LL NEVER FIX THAT TEMPER.
I SHALL HAVE TO SHOW YOU MY ULTIMATE POWER.

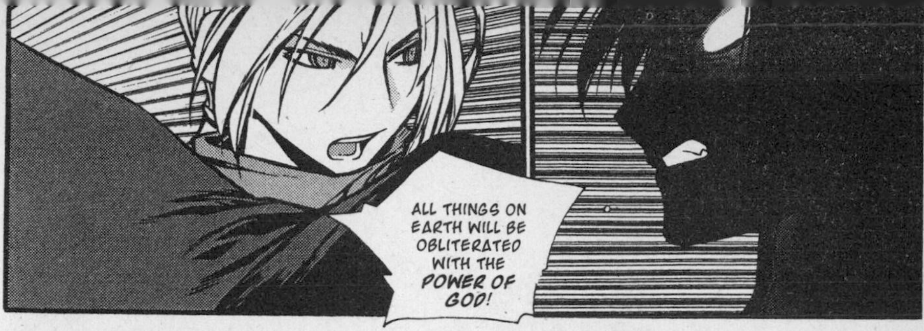
ALL THINGS ON EARTH WILL BE OBLITERATED WITH THE POWER OF GOD!

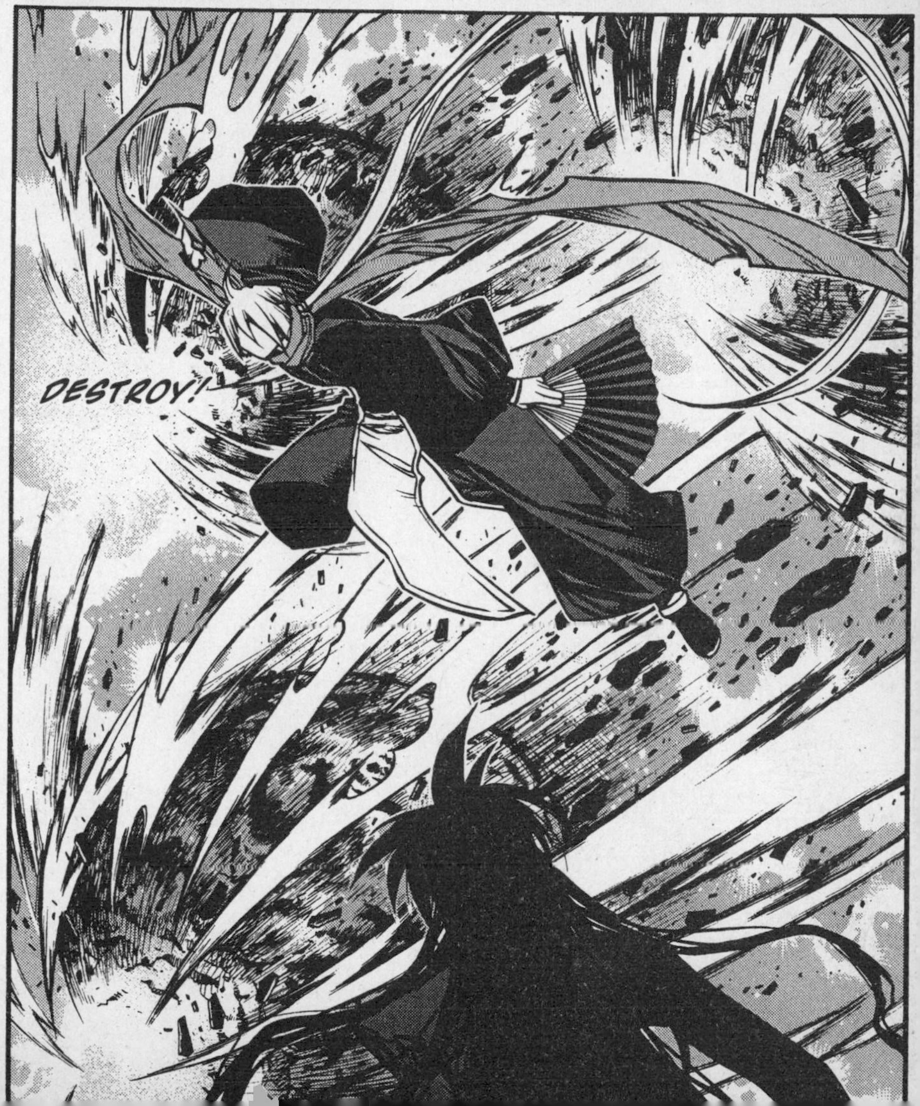
DESTROY!

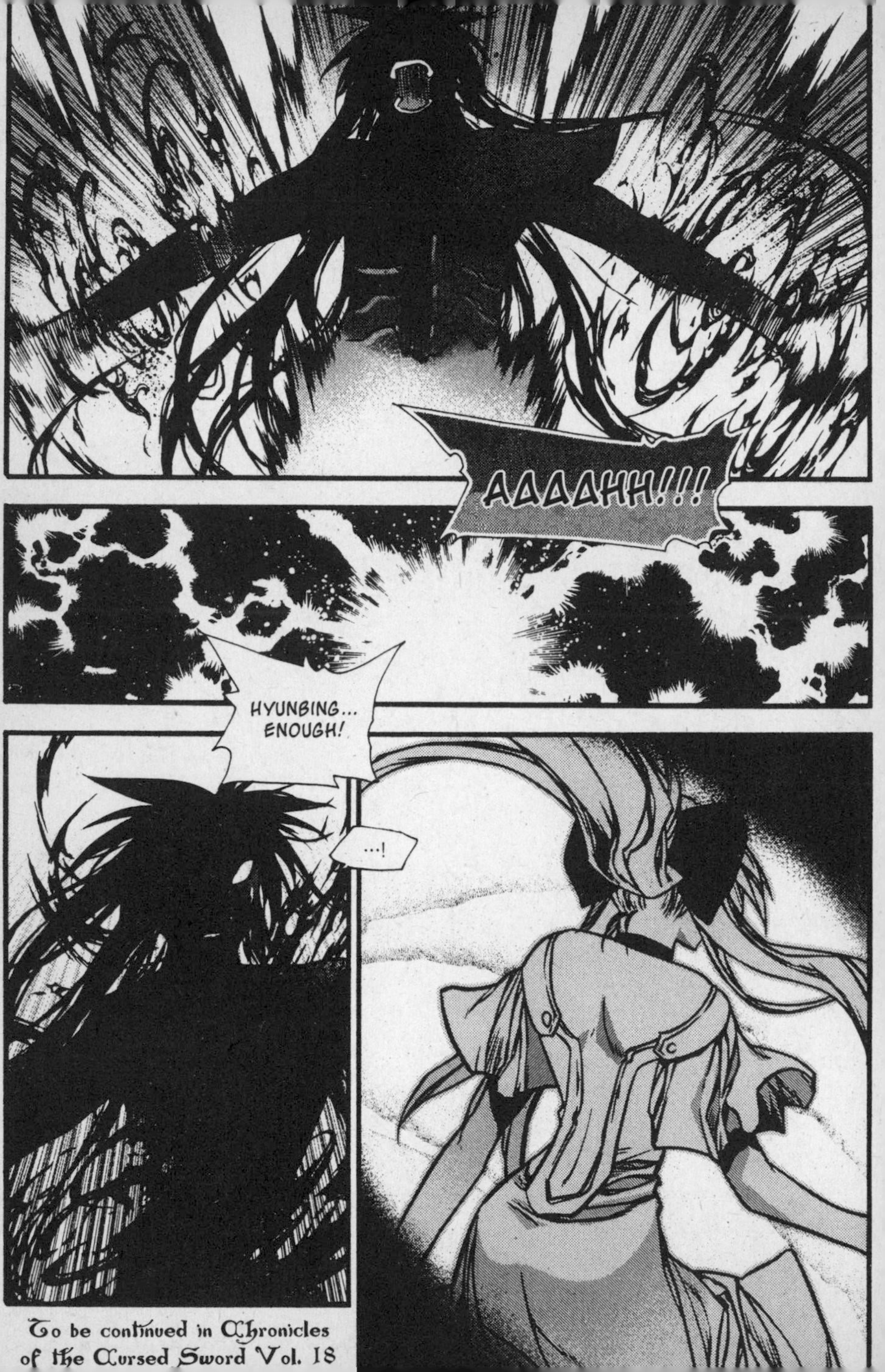
AAAAHH!!!
HYUNBING... ENOUGH!
...!

To be continued in Chronicles of the Cursed Sword Vol. 18

REY YAN, LADIES MAN!

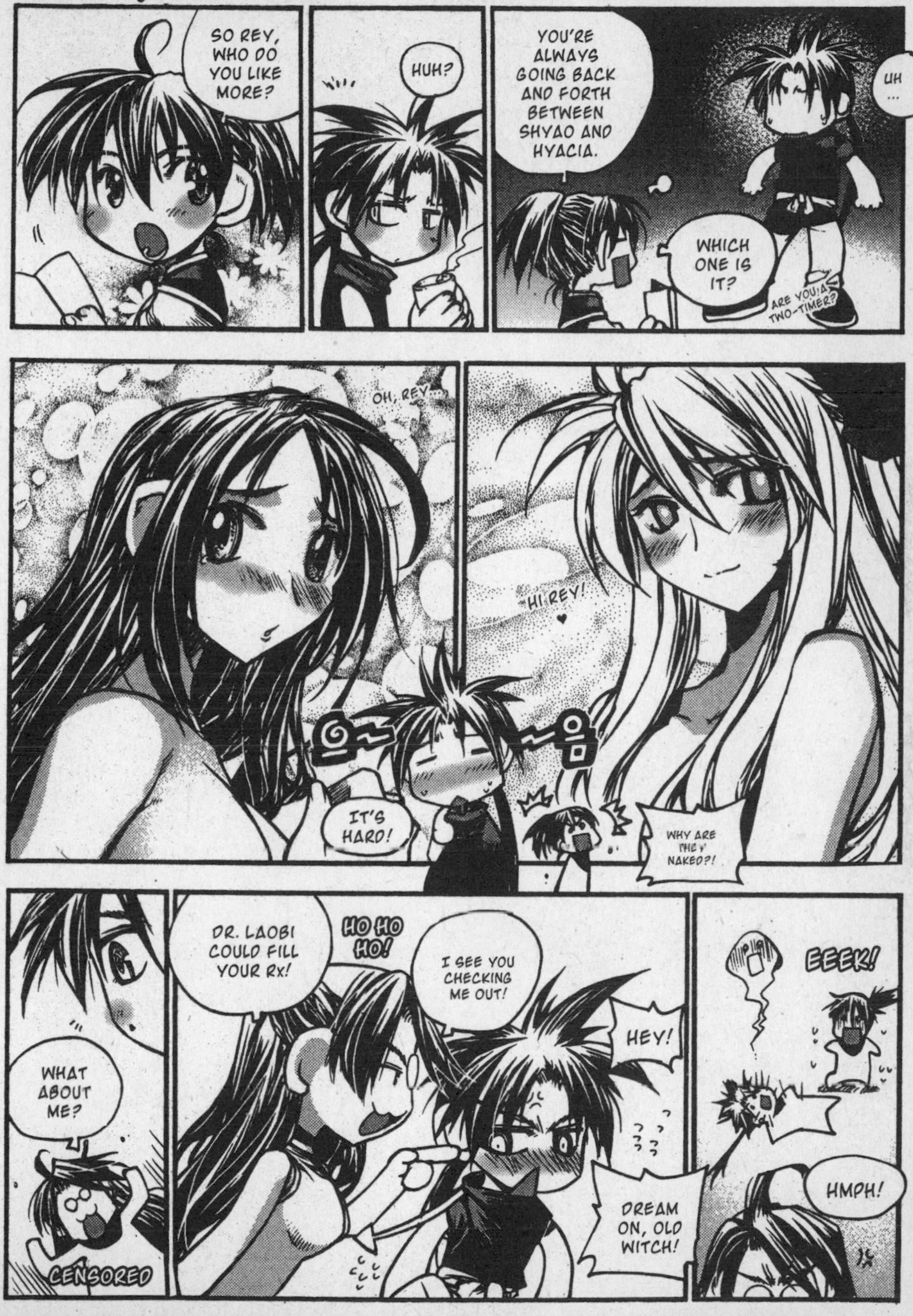
SO REY, WHO DO YOU LIKE MORE?
HUH?
YOU'RE ALWAYS GOING BACK AND FORTH BETWEEN SHYAO AND HYACIA.
WHICH ONE IS IT?
UH ...
ARE YOU A TWO-TIMER?
OH, REY...
HI REY!
IT'S HARD!
WHY ARE THEY NAKED?!
WHAT ABOUT ME?
CENSORED
DR. LAOBI COULD FILL YOUR Rx!
HO HO HO!
I SEE YOU CHECKING ME OUT!
HEY!
DREAM ON, OLD WITCH!
EEEK!
HMPH!

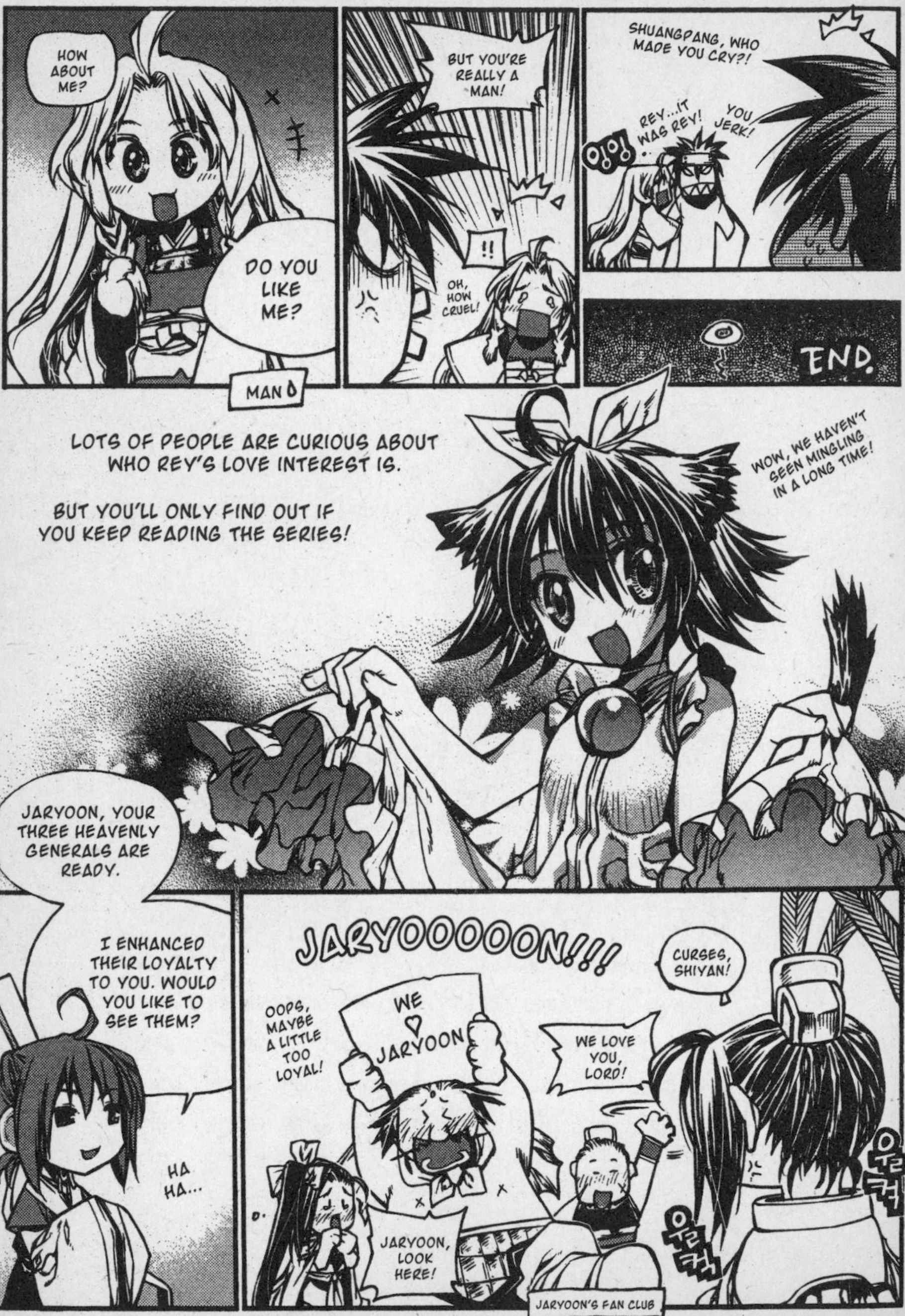
HOW ABOUT ME?
DO YOU LIKE ME?
MAN
BUT YOU'RE REALLY A MAN!
!!
OH, HOW CRUEL!
SHUANGPANG, WHO MADE YOU CRY?!
REY...IT WAS REY!
YOU JERK!
END.
LOTS OF PEOPLE ARE CURIOUS ABOUT WHO REY'S LOVE INTEREST IS.
BUT YOU'LL ONLY FIND OUT IF YOU KEEP READING THE SERIES!
WOW, WE HAVEN'T SEEN MINGLING IN A LONG TIME!
JARYOON, YOUR THREE HEAVENLY GENERALS ARE READY.
I ENHANCED THEIR LOYALTY TO YOU. WOULD YOU LIKE TO SEE THEM?
HA HA...
JARYOOOOOON!!!
CURSES, SHIYAN!
OOPS, MAYBE A LITTLE TOO LOYAL!
WE ♡ JARYOON
WE LOVE YOU, LORD!
JARYOON, LOOK HERE!
JARYOON'S FAN CLUB

NEXT VOLUME:

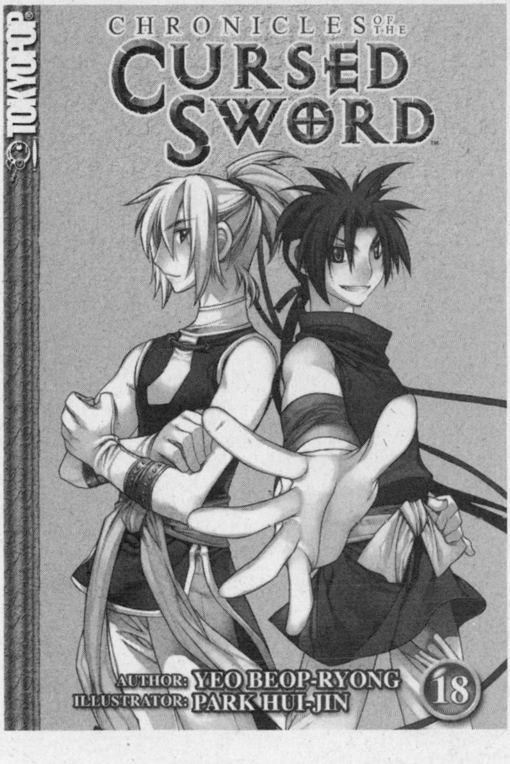
TOKYOPOP
CHRONICLES OF THE
CURSED SWORD
AUTHOR: YEO BEOP-RYONG
ILLUSTRATOR: PARK HUI-JIN
18

With the help of the godly Hyacia, Rey and company escape the wrath of the gods. As all parties tend to their wounds, the survivors find themselves to be a motley and ill-matched crew. Can demon, sage and human coexist peacefully without a common enemy?

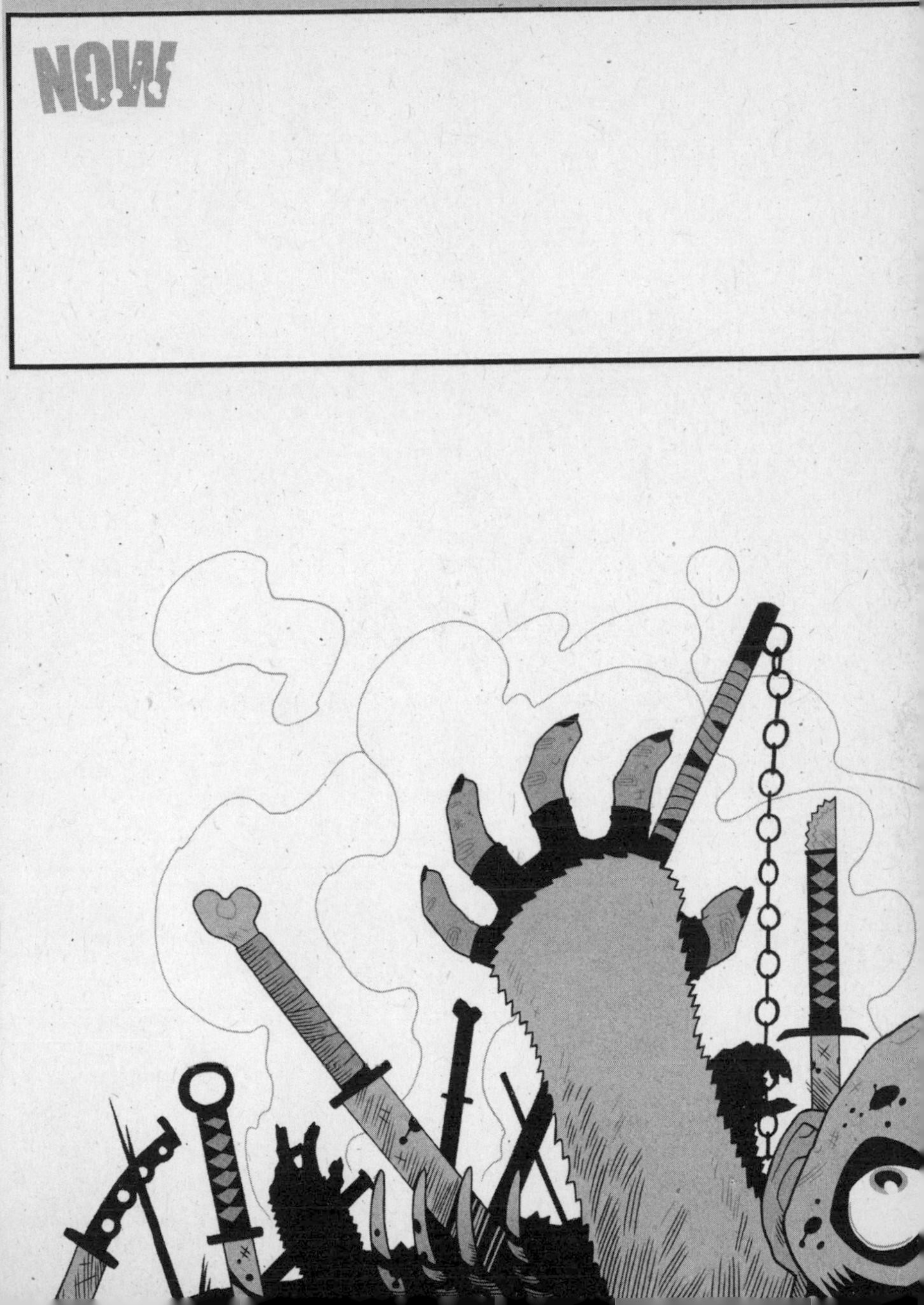
NOW!

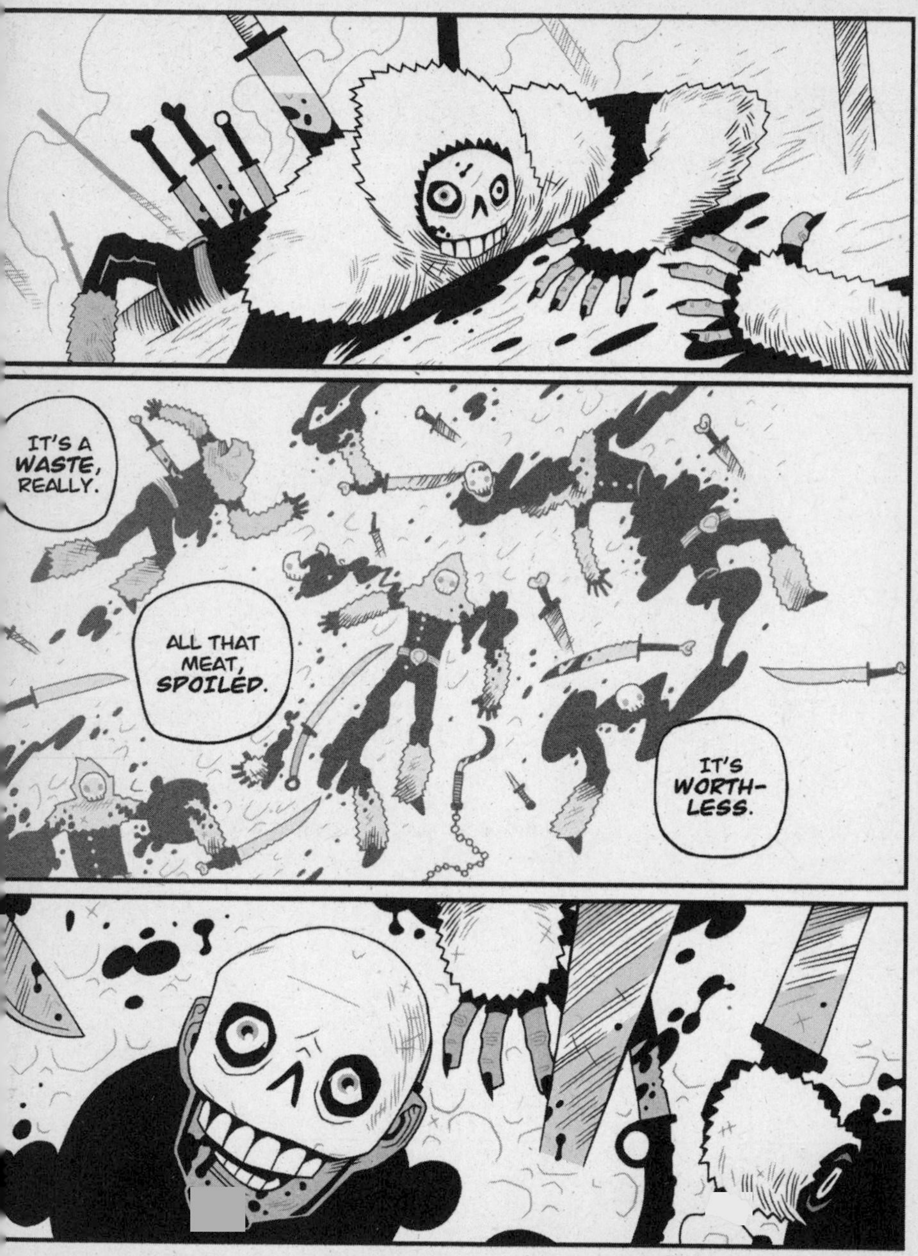
IT'S A WASTE, REALLY.
ALL THAT MEAT, SPOILED.
IT'S WORTH-LESS.

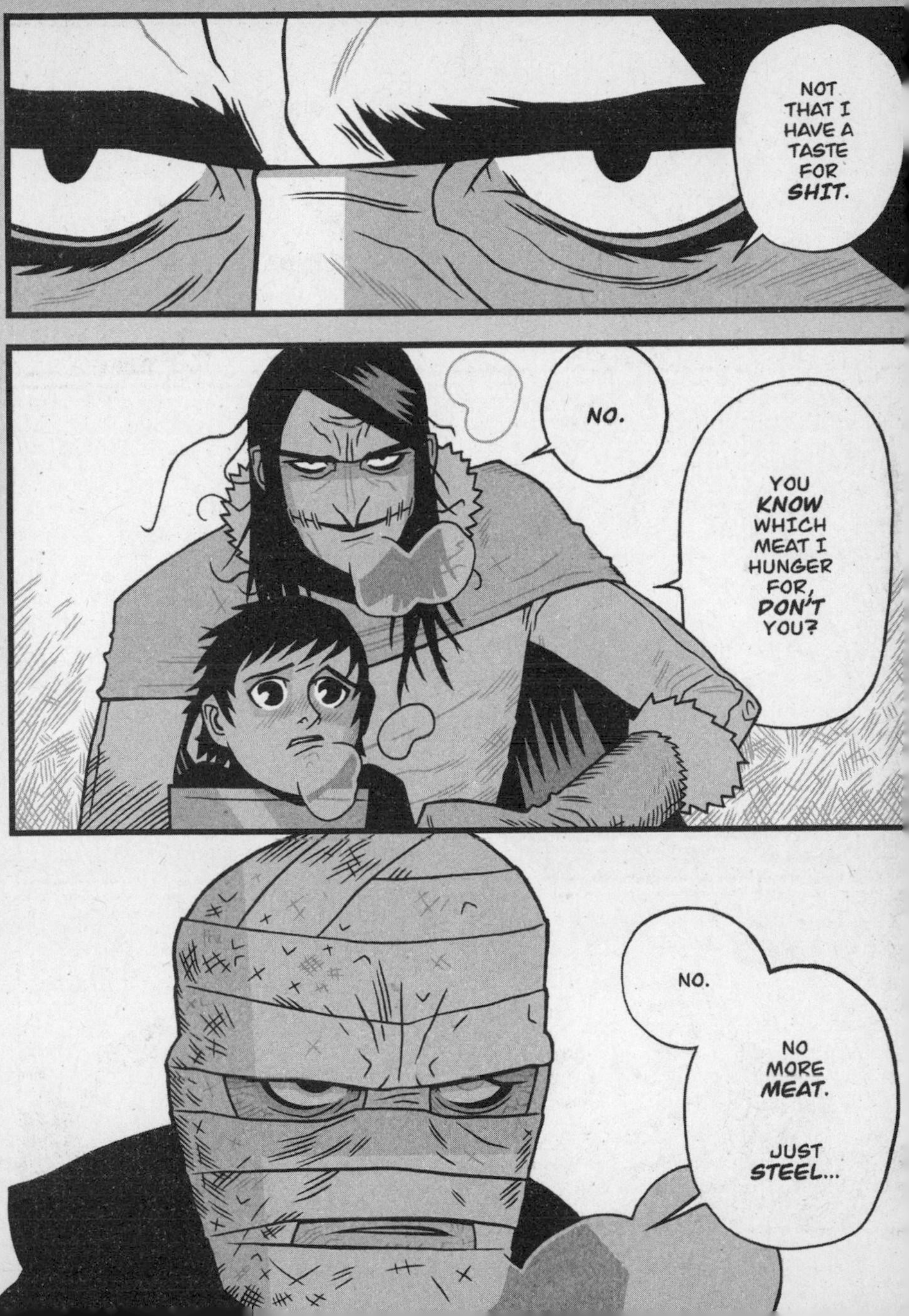
NOT THAT I HAVE A TASTE FOR **SHIT**.
NO.
YOU **KNOW** WHICH MEAT I HUNGER FOR, **DON'T** YOU?
NO.
NO MORE **MEAT**.
JUST **STEEL**...

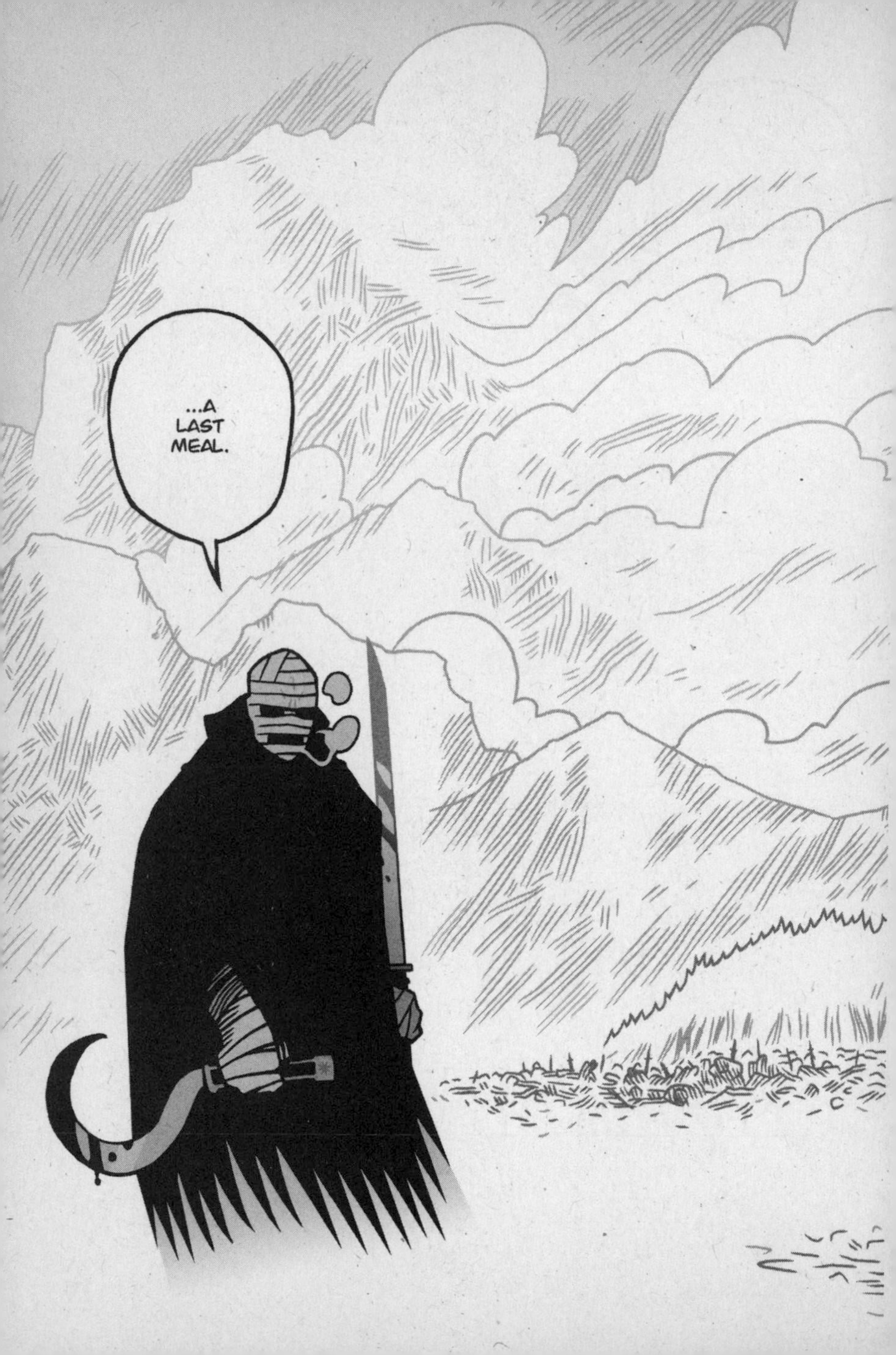
...A LAST MEAL.

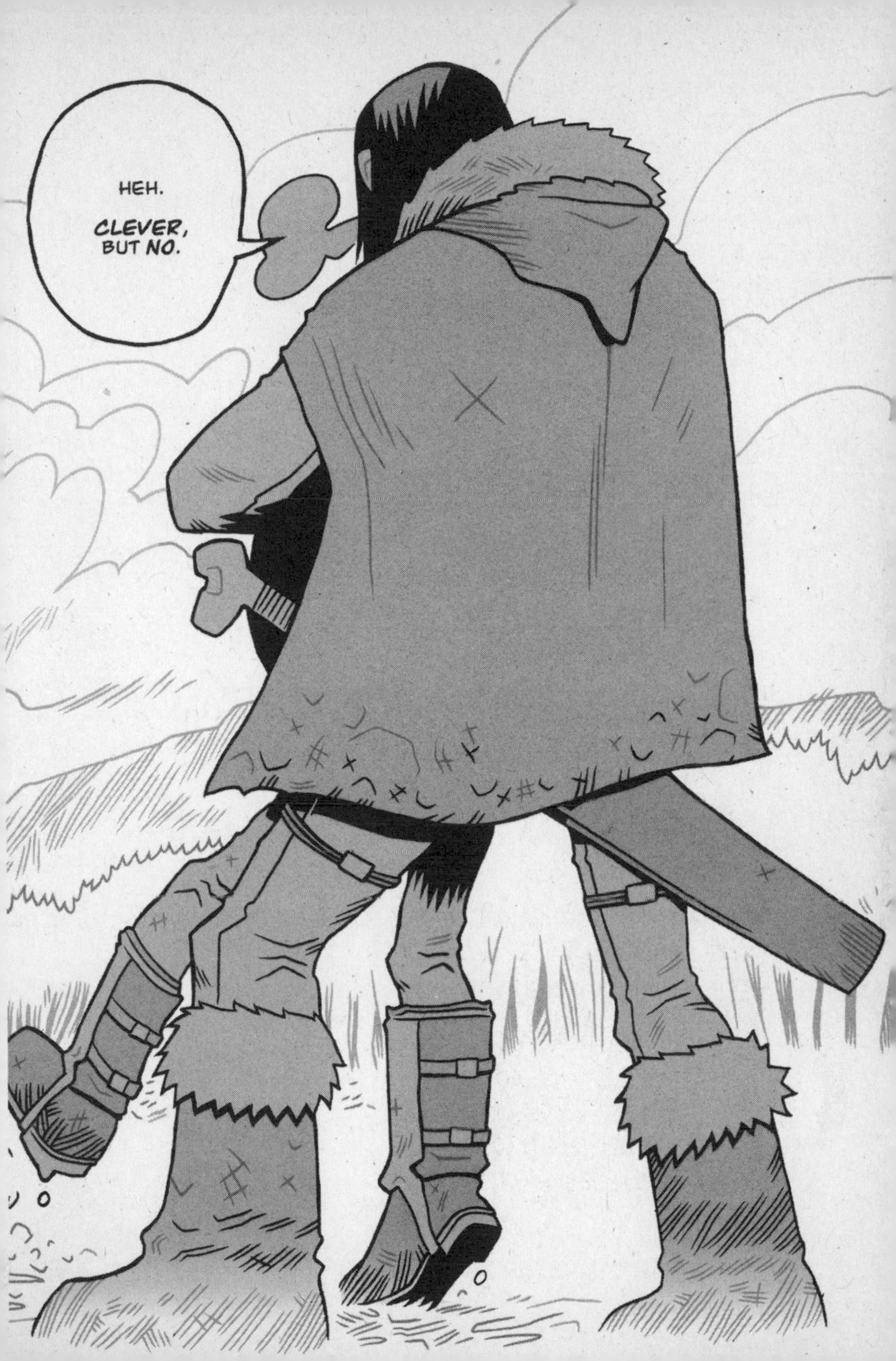
HEH.
CLEVER, BUT NO.

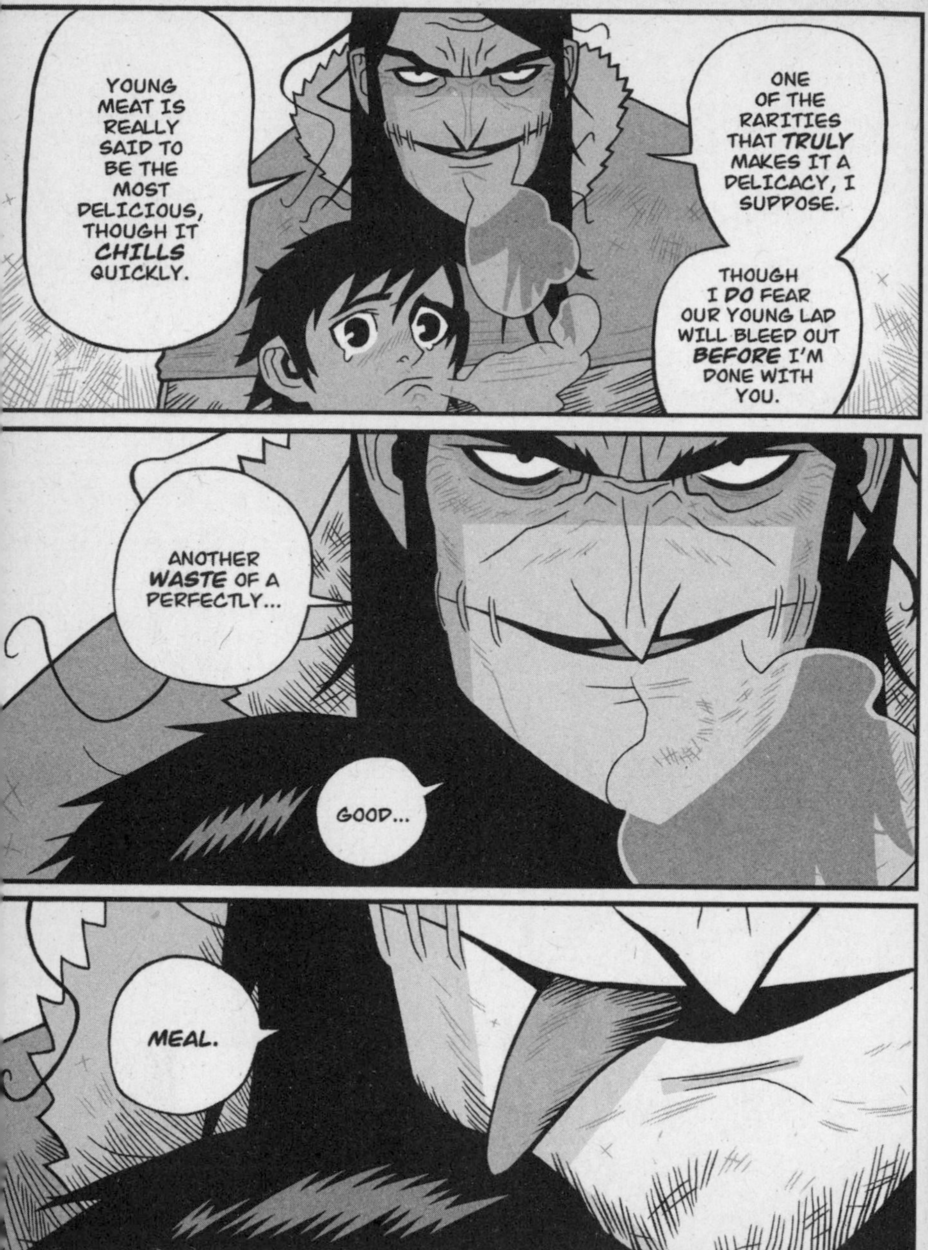
YOUNG MEAT IS REALLY SAID TO BE THE MOST DELICIOUS, THOUGH IT CHILLS QUICKLY.
ONE OF THE RARITIES THAT TRULY MAKES IT A DELICACY, I SUPPOSE.
THOUGH I DO FEAR OUR YOUNG LAD WILL BLEED OUT BEFORE I'M DONE WITH YOU.
ANOTHER WASTE OF A PERFECTLY...
GOOD...
MEAL.

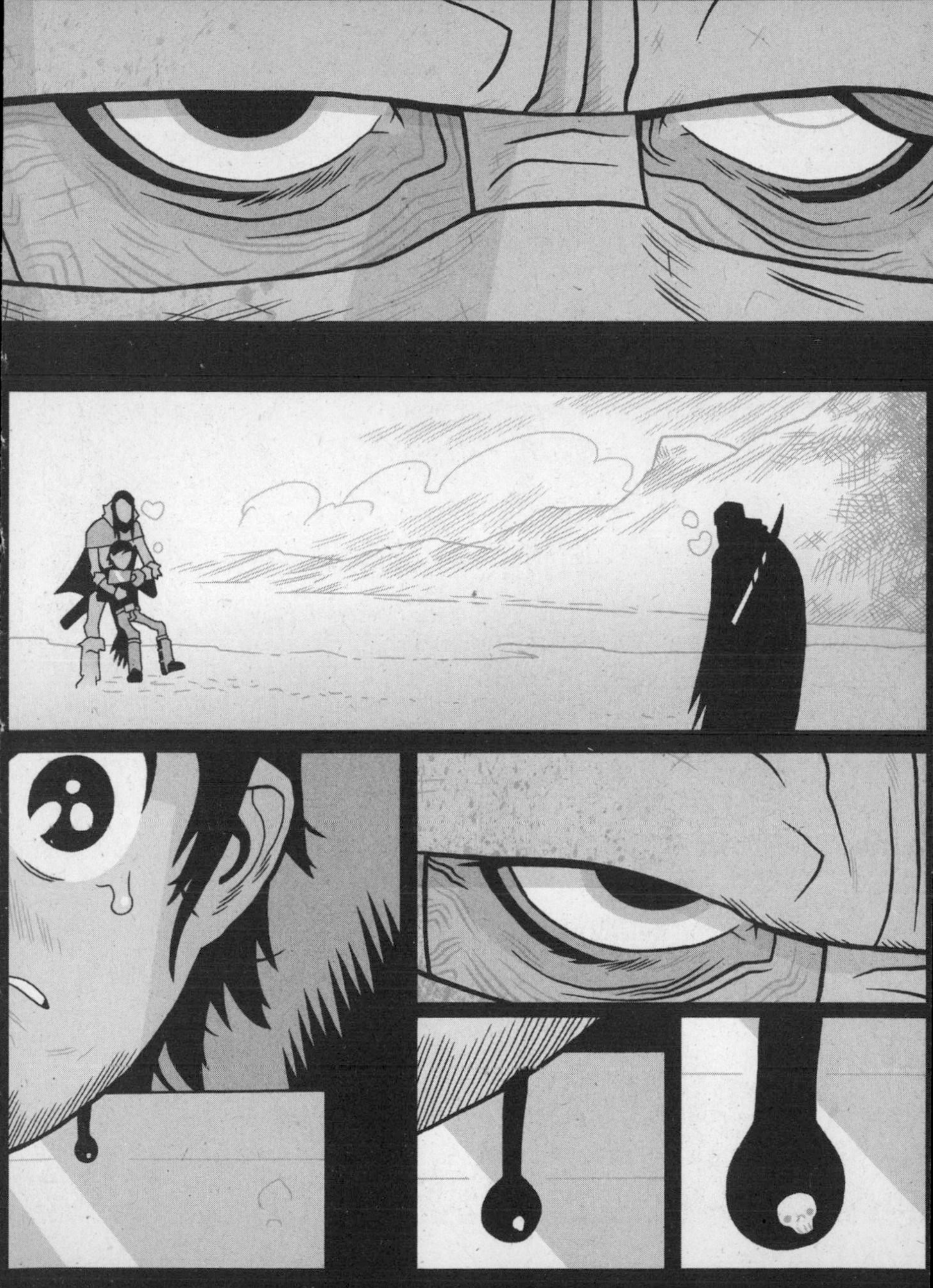

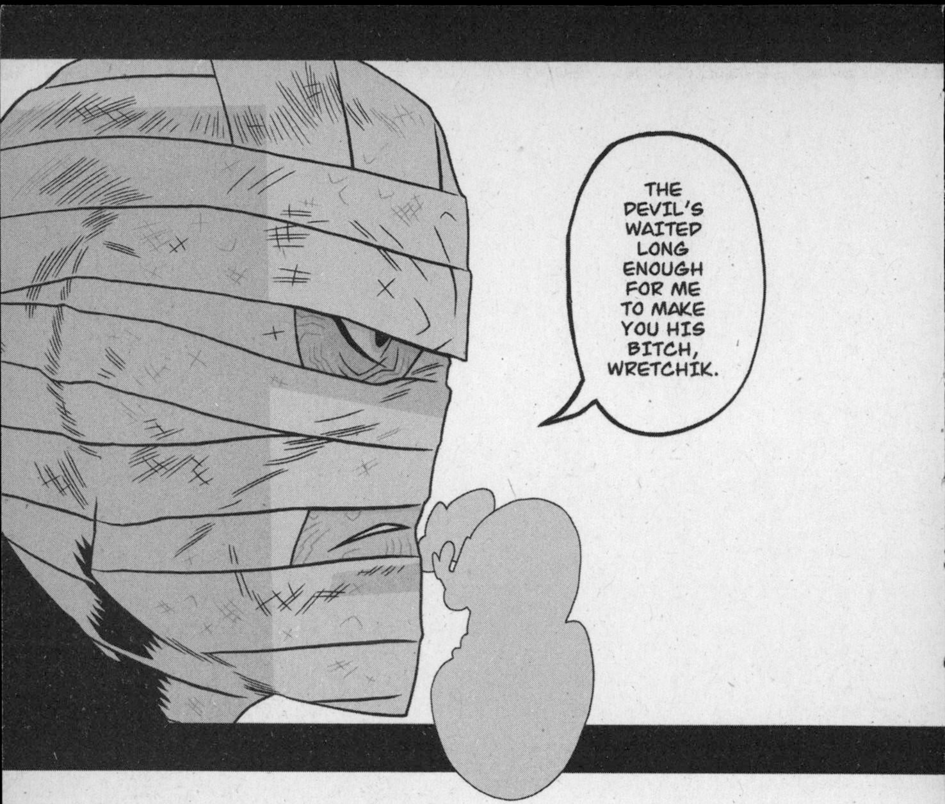
THE DEVIL'S WAITED LONG ENOUGH FOR ME TO MAKE YOU HIS BITCH, WRETCHIK.

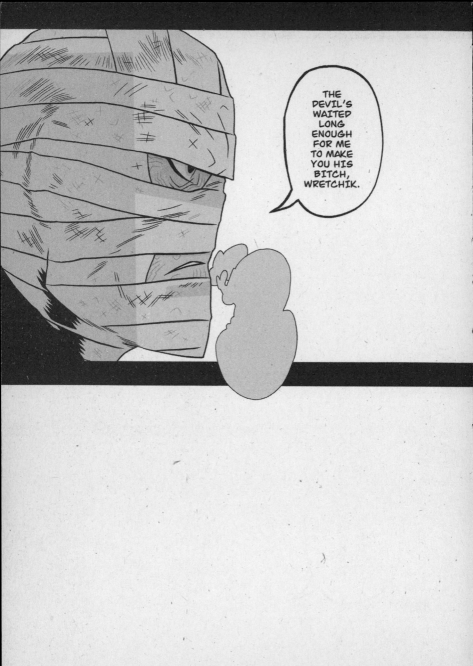

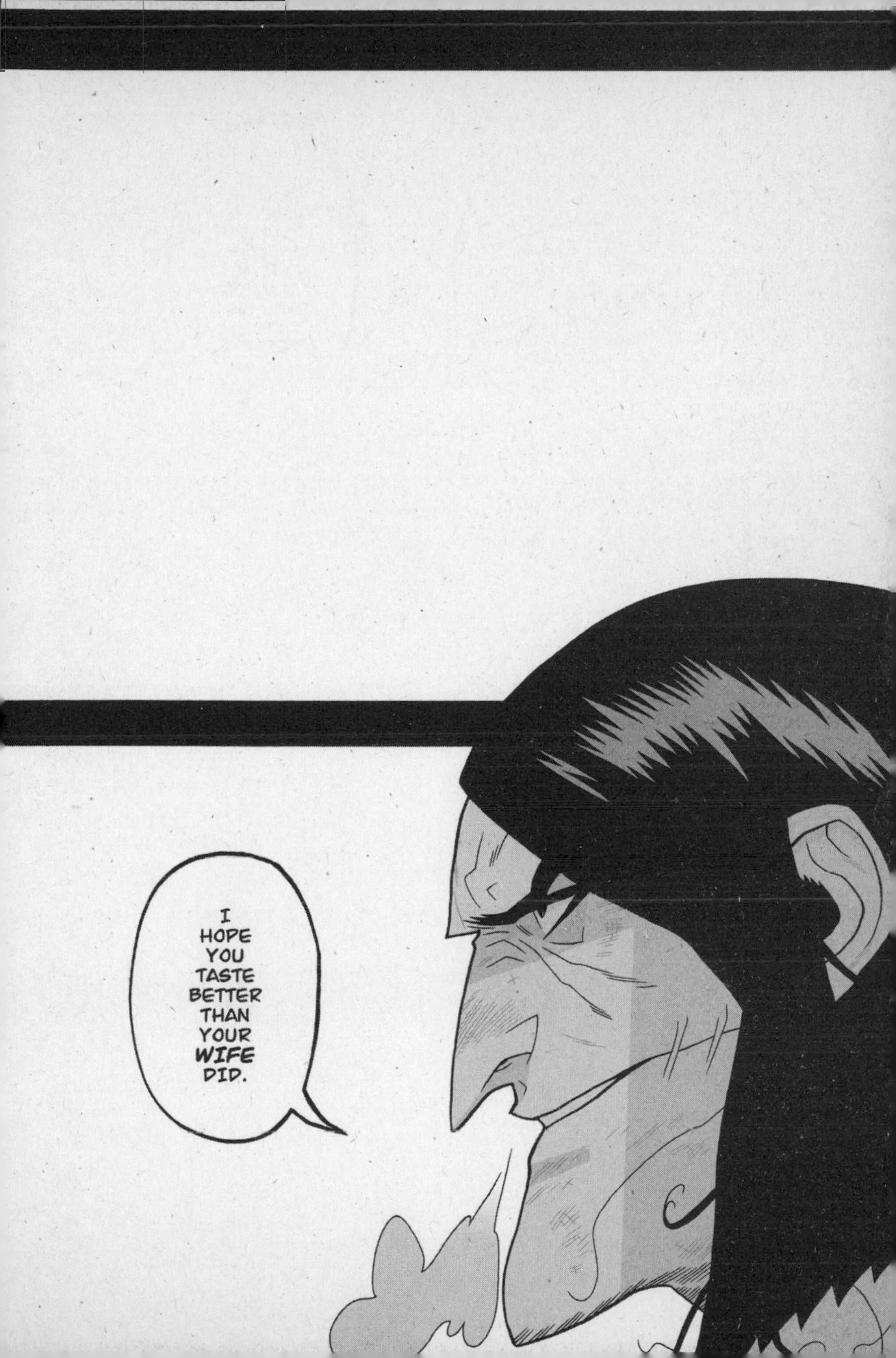
I HOPE YOU TASTE BETTER THAN YOUR WIFE DID.

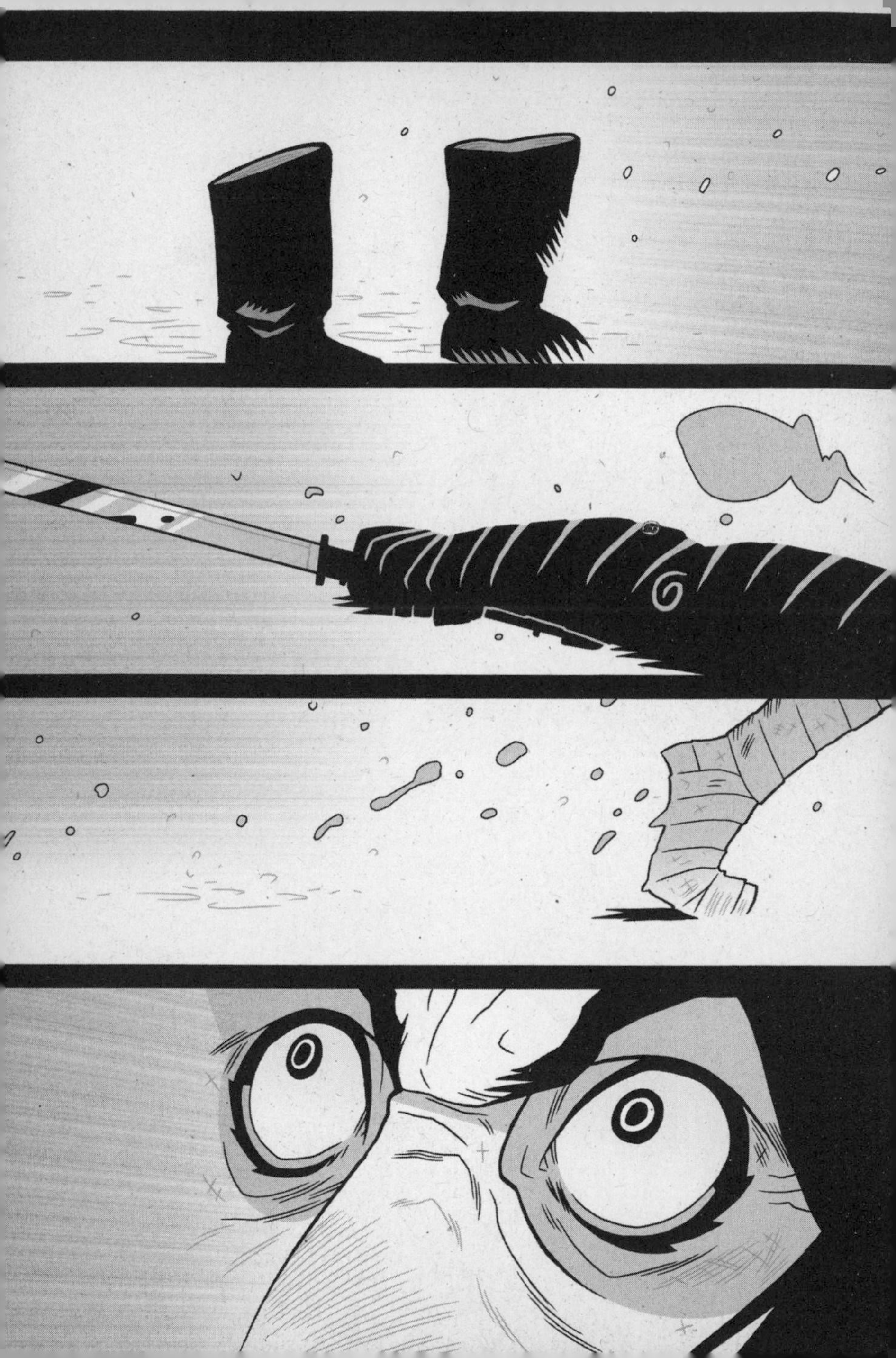

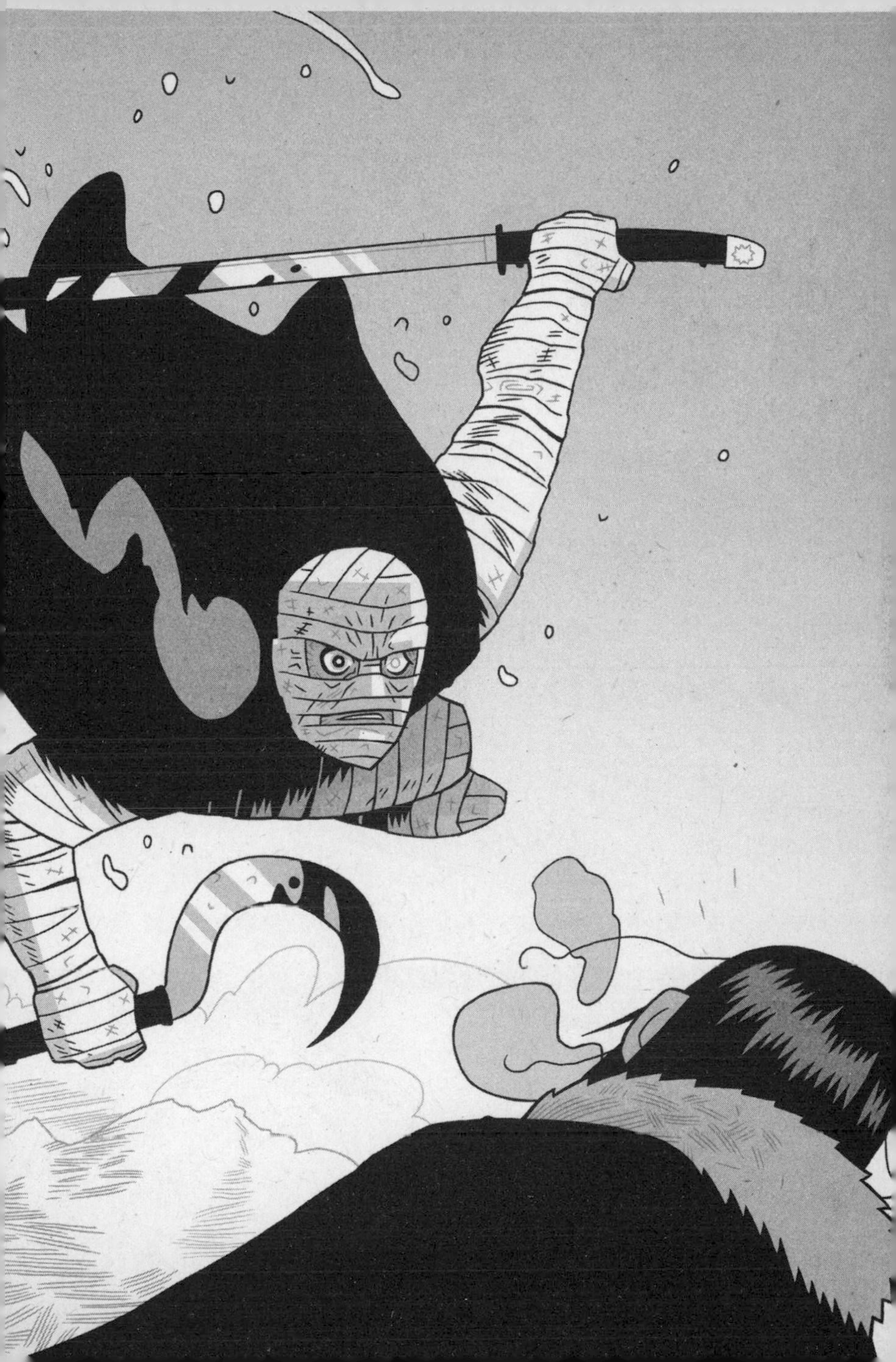

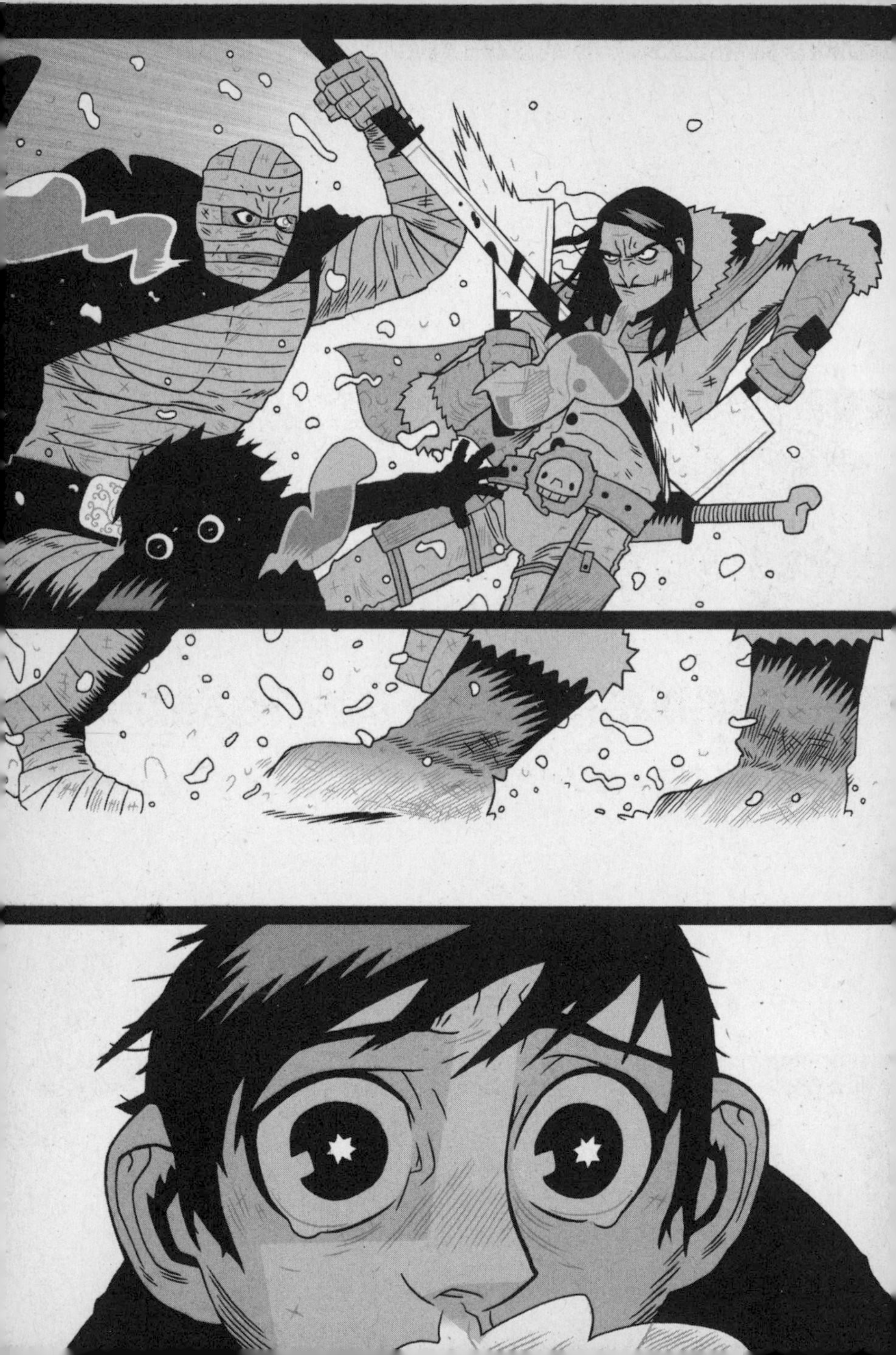

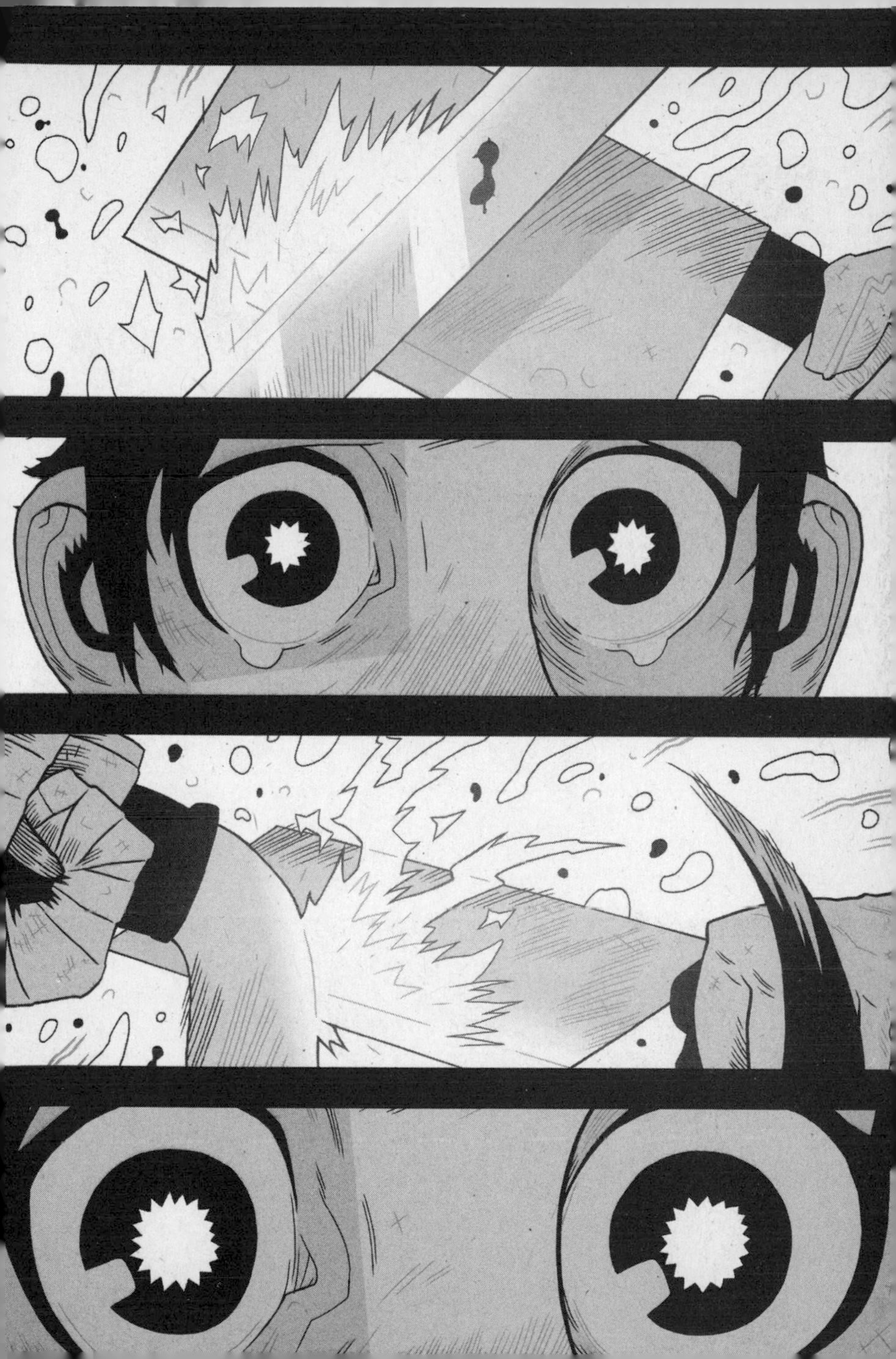

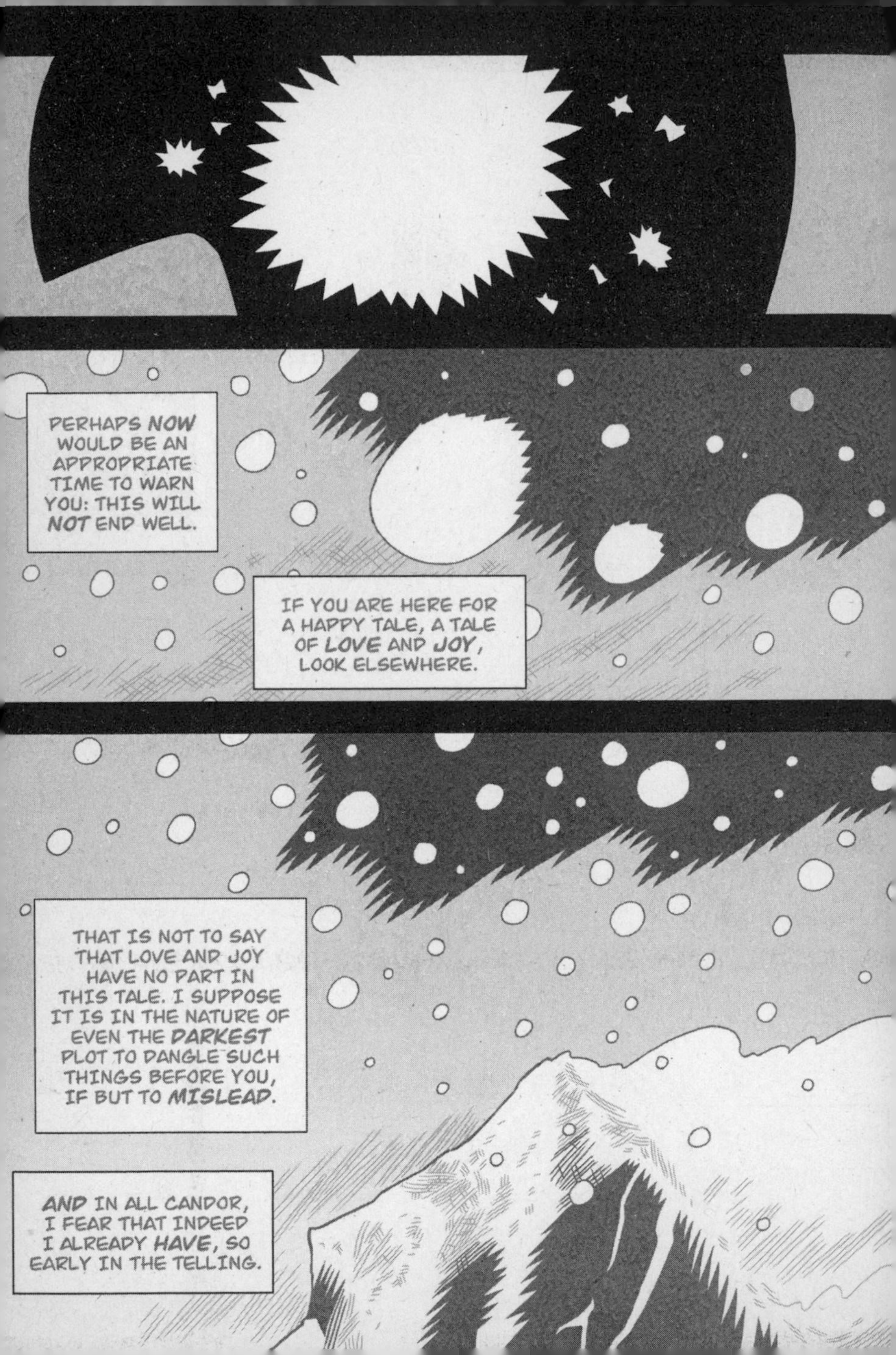
PERHAPS NOW WOULD BE AN APPROPRIATE TIME TO WARN YOU: THIS WILL NOT END WELL.
IF YOU ARE HERE FOR A HAPPY TALE, A TALE OF LOVE AND JOY, LOOK ELSEWHERE.
THAT IS NOT TO SAY THAT LOVE AND JOY HAVE NO PART IN THIS TALE. I SUPPOSE IT IS IN THE NATURE OF EVEN THE DARKEST PLOT TO DANGLE SUCH THINGS BEFORE YOU, IF BUT TO MISLEAD.
AND IN ALL CANDOR, I FEAR THAT INDEED I ALREADY HAVE, SO EARLY IN THE TELLING.

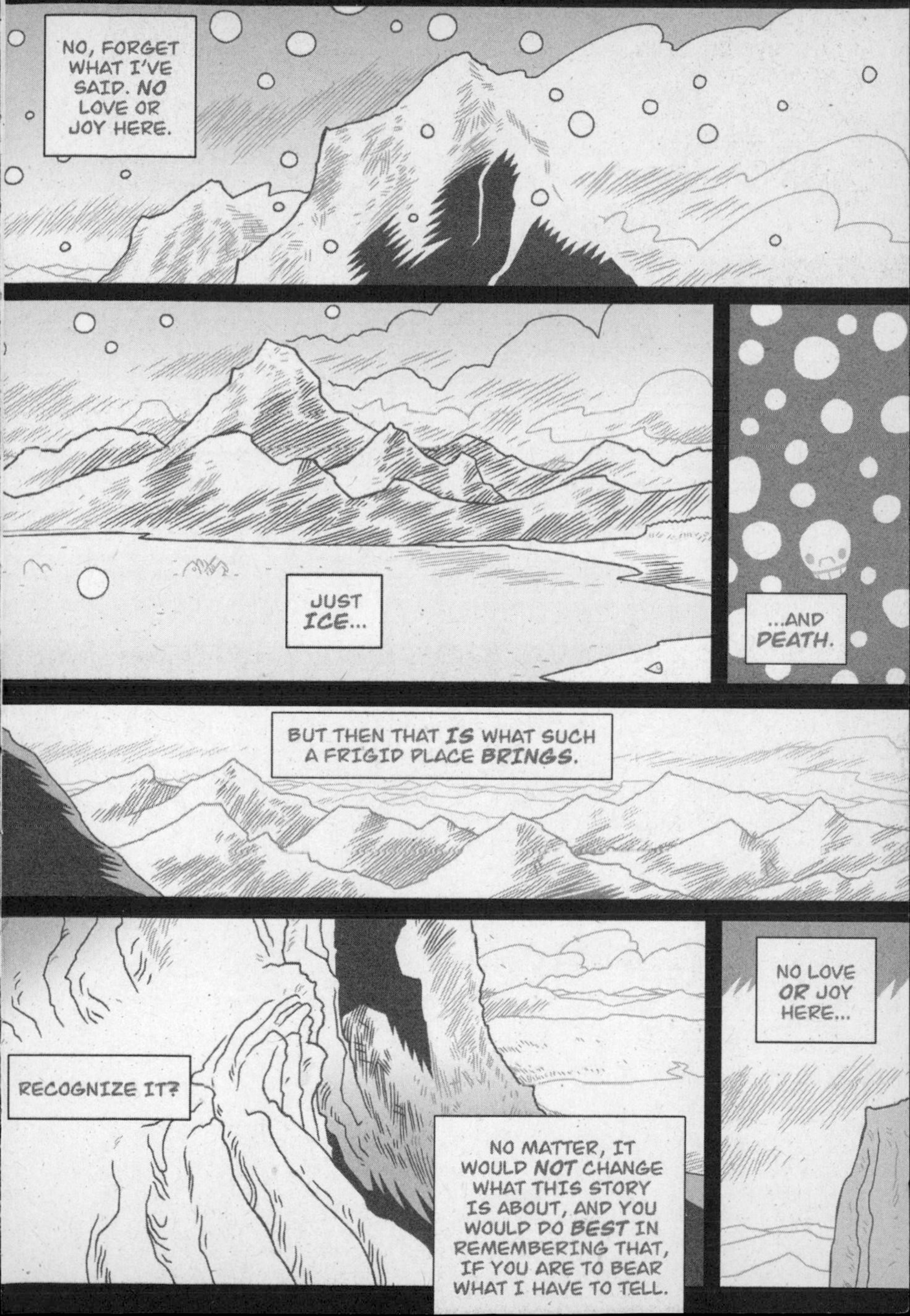
NO, FORGET WHAT I'VE SAID. NO LOVE OR JOY HERE.
JUST ICE...
...AND DEATH.
BUT THEN THAT IS WHAT SUCH A FRIGID PLACE BRINGS.
RECOGNIZE IT?
NO MATTER, IT WOULD NOT CHANGE WHAT THIS STORY IS ABOUT, AND YOU WOULD DO BEST IN REMEMBERING THAT, IF YOU ARE TO BEAR WHAT I HAVE TO TELL.
NO LOVE OR JOY HERE...

ONLY
REVENGE.

GYAKUSHU!